American-Soviet Trade
in the Cold War

PHILIP J. FUNIGIELLO

American-Soviet Trade
in the Cold War

The University of North Carolina Press

Chapel Hill and London

The paper in this book meets the guidelines
for permanence and durability of the
Committee on Production Guidelines for Book Longevity
of the Council on Library Resources.

92 91 90 89 88   5 4 3 2 1

Library of Congress Cataloging-in-Publication Data

Funigiello, Philip J.
American–Soviet trade in the Cold War.

Bibliography: p.
Includes index.
1. Economic sanctions, American—Soviet Union—
History—20th century. 2. United States—Foreign
economic relations—Soviet Union. 3. Soviet Union—
Foreign economic relations—United States. 4. East–West
trade (1945–) I. Title.
HF1413.5.F86   1988   382′.0973′047   87-35836
ISBN 0-8078-1784-8 (alk. paper)

To the late Vincent and Marina Basso

Contents

Preface

POLITICS more than economics has controlled trade relationships between the United States and the Soviet Union. This should come as no surprise to shrewd Soviet traders or to economic analysts familiar with the history of embargoes of foodstuffs, raw materials, or sophisticated technologies. Ever since the United States imposed a blockade against the new Bolshevik regime in the closing months of World War I, trade relationships have been unstable, fluctuating up and down depending not only upon American reactions to Soviet politics and policies, but also upon Soviet reactions to American politics and policies. The failure of the grain embargo in the late 1970s was simply another lesson in economic affairs. The lesson in foreign policy was more serious: it is difficult to trade an economic for a diplomatic initiative, and it is impossible to do so when the economic initiative is ineffective. Yet from the start of the Cold War, the United States and its allies have invoked economic threats and sanctions, with indifferent success, to contain or to modify Soviet behavior in the international arena.

The aim of this study is to explain why and how the United States government, beginning shortly after the close of World War II, applied economic sanctions toward the Soviet Union to achieve certain foreign policy objectives. And why, in spite of the difficulties associated with trade controls, Washington continued to resort to them as instruments of foreign policy. An examination of American–Soviet trade policy and its relation to the national security of the United States is the vehicle for answering these questions.

This is not a study of the more generalized subject of East–West trade per se, which, though important, is more complicated by virtue of the diversity of the countries involved and the accessibility or inaccessibility of the documentation. One may justify this more limited scope because the evolution of U.S. export control policy, which in the early Cold War period also encompassed the European Soviet bloc countries, had as its primary target the Soviet Union. Modifications of the prevailing policy to accommodate changing security needs or the requirements of individual satellites were made over the course of time, but they still took Moscow as their point of reference. Exceptions to trade restrictions made on behalf of Yugoslavia, Poland, or Rumania thus had as their object to loosen Russia's hold on her satellites and thereby to diminish the Soviet political and military threat to American and Western security.

Focusing upon U.S.–Soviet trade policy from the close of World War II through the Reagan administration, especially as that policy was perceived in the White House, can also illuminate the process whereby domestic politics, economic factors, and national security considerations interacted to affect cold war diplomacy. This may enable us to comprehend more fully how complex political decisions can affect the delicate balance between the executive and legislative branches of the federal government and also between Washington and the business, banking, and academic communities.

Acknowledgments

IN the course of doing the research and writing of this book I have necessarily become indebted to many people and institutions whose encouragement and information have enabled me to accomplish my task. Their suggestions and thoughtful comments have been most helpful and greatly appreciated, and I take this opportunity to record my thanks.

I wish first to acknowledge my debt—intellectual and personal—to my mentor and friend Vincent P. Carosso, Kenan Professor of History at New York University. His interest, critical judgment, and encouragement are in the finest traditions of scholarship. Burton I. Kaufman of Kansas State University subjected the entire manuscript to a critical reading. His suggestions were invaluable and helped to strengthen it throughout. Richard Lowitt of Iowa State University has shown a continuing interest in the progress of the manuscript and has been a constant source of encouragement. Cherie Luton and Connie Newman rendered yeoman's service in typing the manuscript through its numerous revisions, as did Diane LoFurno. Shirley Folkes eased my burden as graduate director to facilitate the manuscript's completion. I also wish to thank my colleagues at the College of William and Mary, particularly John E. Selby and Gilbert McArthur, who encouraged me to complete this undertaking.

Portions of the research for this study were supported by the Faculty Summer Research Program of the College of William and Mary, the National Endowment for the Humanities' Travel to Collections Program, the Harry S. Truman Library Institute, and the Lyndon Baines Johnson Foundation. Their generous assistance at a number of critical stages enabled me to devote my energies to this project. Many libraries and archives eased the work of research. I particularly want to acknowledge the assistance of the professional staffs of the Harry S. Truman Library, Independence, Missouri, and of the Lyndon B. Johnson Library, Austin, Texas, for guiding me through their extensive collections of presidential papers and agency records. The personnel of the Dwight D. Eisenhower Library, Abilene, Kansas, rendered invaluable assistance not only in identifying pertinent documents but also in shepherding me through the declassification procedure. The staff of the John F. Kennedy Library, Boston, Massachusetts, also was helpful. The archivists and record-keepers of the National Archives and the Department of Commerce, in Washington, D.C., capably guided me through their records pertaining to the subject. A special note of appreciation must go to the professional staff of the Earl Gregg Swem Library.of the College of William and Mary—particularly to Allan F. Zoellner, Sandi Peterson, Carol S. Linton, Linda F. Templeman, and Donald C. Johnson—for their uncanny ability to track down elusive government documents and periodicals.

Beyond academe, the confidence and support of my family—Joanne and Alicia—and friends helped to bring this project to fruition.

*American-Soviet Trade
in the Cold War*

CHAPTER ONE

Soviet-American Politics, Trade, and War, 1917–1946

SHORTLY after the Bolshevik Revolution of 7 November 1917, Commissar of Foreign Affairs Leon Trotsky sent a message to the diplomatic corps in Petrograd, formerly St. Petersburg, announcing the establishment of the new Soviet government and requesting its recognition. The American ambassador, David R. Francis, correctly anticipating the policy of the Wilson administration, ignored the communication. His silence initiated a sixteen-year interruption in diplomatic relations between the Union of Soviet Socialist Republics (USSR) and the United States.[1]

American officials in 1917, with the support of most businessmen, had decided that the United States should establish neither diplomatic nor economic relations with the Bolsheviks, and preferred to accord both recognition and aid to the provisional government of the March Revolution. President Wilson's policy in the critical period from 1918 to 1920 was to provide economic assistance to "democratic" Russia in the belief that economic stability would lead to the emergence of a successful democratic government. The War Trade Board of the U.S. Russian Bureau, Incorporated, designed to facilitate trade relations between the United States and non-Bolshevik Russia, was a failure. The timing was bad, and no extensive trade or aid ever developed. The Bolsheviks gained the upper hand in the civil war that raged; on the American side, bureaucratic snags, business hesitation, and an almost total failure to comprehend the obstacles to trade in war-torn and financially chaotic Russia doomed the undertaking.[2]

The policy of nationalization and the disruption of industrial production in Russia during the period of War Communism (1917–21) persuaded businessmen that the Wilson administration's nonrecognition policy and its decision to invoke certain commercial and financial restrictions against the Bolsheviks were sound. It also was well grounded ideologically. Communism challenged the American way of life, running counter to traditional notions of private property rights, individual liberty, representative government, and nationalism. Moreover, nonrecog-

nition seemed correct for the immediate future because American businessmen did not expect economic opportunities to develop more fully
under the Bolsheviks than they had under the tsars.[3]

From 1921 to 1933 the question of diplomatic recognition of the
Soviet Union was complicated by that government's repudiation of its
predecessors' foreign debts and by ideological opposition to Bolshevism
within the Republican administrations of Presidents Harding, Coolidge,
and Hoover, notably within the Departments of State and Commerce.
Concurrently, a growing number of American businessmen and firms
became attracted to the trading possibilities with the Soviet Union after
the adoption of the New Economic Policy (NEP) in 1921. In keeping
with the objectives of the NEP, Lenin had altered the earlier economic
policy of nationalization in an effort to attract American capital (and
eventually diplomatic recognition) for Soviet industrialization. In seeking
access to the Russian market, many American businessmen were becoming increasingly indifferent to the original ideological basis of nonrecognition or chose to divorce economic from political considerations.[4]

The efforts of the Soviet government and American businessmen such
as Alexander Grumberg, Armand Hammer, and W. Averell Harriman
helped American–Soviet trade to flourish in the 1920s, without the benefit of the facilities and protections usually afforded by the United States
government for trade with foreign nations.[5] Although the device of
granting concessions to Americans to operate private business enter-
prises in Russia, such as Harriman's development of the Chiatouri manganese mines, was ultimately unsuccessful, the era of the NEP did lead to
some positive gains. Trade tripled in comparison with pre–World War I
levels, and American exports reached a high point in 1930 ($111.3 mil-
lion) and 1931 ($103.4 million).[6] The development of technical assis-
tance contracts, allowing the Soviets to import American technology
despite the lack of foreign capital, proved to be the most important
medium of American economic exchange with Russia during this period
of nonrecognition. American engineers served as chief consultants on
most of the major projects of the first Five Year Plan (FYP) and, though
they did not determine the success or failure of the FYP, they did shape its
specific parameters to a significant degree.[7]

While a growing number of businessmen supported renewed commercial ties with the Soviet Union without necessarily advocating diplomatic
recognition, President Hoover and Soviet experts in the State and Commerce Departments adamantly clung to the position formulated in 1920
by President Wilson's secretary of state, Bainbridge Colby, and refused to
concede that a dichotomy had developed in the political and economic
treatment of the Soviet Union.[8] Not even the Great Depression in the

United States, which saw massive unemployment and American exports to the Soviet Union plunge to a paltry $8 million in 1933, or the growing threat of Japanese militarism to U.S. and Russian interests in the Far East, could shake the anticommunist resolve of Hoover, the State and Commerce Departments, and religious groups.[9]

Businessmen too were divided into protrade and antitrade factions and were in no position to mount a strong campaign for diplomatic recognition of the USSR. Talk of such a campaign among protrade groups surfaced in 1932 and 1933, and some advocates of trade even argued that political recognition might lead to a significant revival of commerce between the two countries and help pull the United States out of the economic doldrums. Such arguments proved illusory, simply providing a popular rationale for recognition without requiring a deeper comprehension or acceptance of communism.[10] Talk of economic opportunities for trade may also have been planted by federal officials chiefly interested in disposing of agricultural surpluses, and not by American manufacturers who had blazed the trail in trading with the Soviets.[11] In either case the publicly organized business support for recognition that did exist came belatedly in 1933, after Franklin D. Roosevelt had set his sights on recognition.

The paradox between American economic interest in the Russian market and political nonrecognition of the Soviet government persisted until Roosevelt's election as president on the Democratic ticket. He had straddled the issue of recognition during the campaign, but after his victory he worked quietly with a few trusted advisers to establish diplomatic relations. On 17 November 1933 the United States, for fundamentally political reasons, accorded diplomatic recognition to the Soviet Union.[12] The underlying disagreements between the concepts and aims of the two governments—including the war debts issue, religious freedom, legal prerogative, and propaganda—were plastered over with verbal formulas, leaving the issues unresolved. Although the act of recognition was justified in economic terms, Roosevelt also intended it as a signal to Japan to pause in its conquest of southern Manchuria.[13]

Besides granting diplomatic recognition, the president moved toward revitalizing American–Soviet trade. He removed special restrictions on the import of Soviet products imposed during the Depression, accepted for purchases gold shipped directly from the USSR, and capitalized a new Export-Import Bank with $11 million to finance trade. Disillusionment followed close upon recognition. The State Department, believing that Russia needed America as a counterweight to Japanese aggression in the Far East, subordinated the bank's lending function in the hope it could extract political concessions from Soviet officials. It invoked the debt (and indirectly the bank) as leverage to force the Soviets to abide by the principles of international economic relations with respect to property and security of contract, which it deemed vital to the expanding commercial and financial interests of the United States. The Soviets, however, persisted in refusing to make a debt settlement before the United States first granted an extended loan.[14]

The debt controversy, the inability of the two nations to cooperate in forestalling Japan's aggression in Asia, the revival of Comintern interference in American affairs, and deeply rooted State Department hostility toward the Bolsheviks contributed to the failure of recognition to exert a positive influence on either American or Soviet policy. Consequently trade with the Soviet Union remained very modest before World War II (reaching only $87 million in 1940), the promised credits were held back, the Export-Import Bank remained in desuetude, the State Department discouraged private parties from granting long-term credits or loans to the USSR, and the Johnson Debt Default Act of 1934 made it illegal for private persons or institutions to extend loans to the Soviet Union.[15]

Even if the United States had supplied the credits, it is doubtful that American–Soviet trade would have readily returned to the levels of 1930–31. Soviet Premier Joseph Stalin was suspicious of all the Western capitalistic nations, including the United States. His attitude was shaped by a combination of Marxist dogma, Russia's historical experience, and his own nature. Under Stalin a special doctrine of foreign trade developed, conditioned by the fundamental goal of national economic self-sufficiency, a principle embedded in the 1936 constitution. According to Stalinist teaching, imports had priority, because they provided scarce goods essential for building the economic plan. Exports were to be built up only to the extent necessary to pay for imports. Stalin's approach to trade harmonized with the profound antagonism toward the West epitomized in the Marxist theory of capitalist encirclement.[16]

Political differences between the two countries centered not only on economic, legal, and religious issues but also on the problem of how to build world peace. In the Far East, Roosevelt sought to preserve a balance of power to protect U.S. interests, despite strong isolationist sentiment in Congress and among the American people. He strove for a collective security agreement among the Western powers, including the Soviet Union, that would give the Japanese militarists pause. Stalin, for his part, also practiced a *realpolitik*; but he preferred a U.S.–Soviet bilateral pact to counter both Japanese and German bellicosity. Domestic and other foreign policy considerations prevented either from attaining exactly what he wanted, leaving Axis aggression unchecked.[17]

Roosevelt was far more willing to engage in balance-of-power politics than is generally supposed, but he seems never to have fully understood either the nature of Stalin's regime or Soviet foreign policy intentions in Asia or Eastern Europe, even though a number of his advisers did. The State Department and its Russian specialists were particularly suspicious of Stalin, believing that he favored a war between Japan and the United States that would weaken both nations and relieve Soviet fears of Russia's two rivals in the Pacific.[18] Instead of profiting from the advice of specialists, who wanted to link a strategy of firmness to quid pro quo tactics, the president favored compromise and generally avoided difficult negotiations with the Soviets. This habit persisted even after the outbreak of World War II. In the end, efforts to forge a common American–Soviet front against Axis aggression failed.[19]

The Nazi invasion of the Soviet Union on 22 June 1941 opened a new chapter in American–Soviet diplomatic and economic relations. The possibility that the president might invoke the Lend-Lease Act of 11 March 1941 to aid Russia was first raised as early as January, during the congressional debates on the bill. The question at that time was highly academic; the evidence strongly suggests that it was more a device of the opposition—isolationists, fiscal conservatives, anticommunists, and religious groups—to defeat the entire measure than a legitimate issue. The failure of opponents to affect passage of the act or to arouse public fears was a first milestone on the road to complete economic assistance, granted later under very different circumstances.[20]

Meantime the administration, possessing evidence of a forthcoming German attack upon the Soviet Union, attempted to keep diplomatic lines open to Moscow in order to take advantage of any situation that might offer relief to a beleaguered Britain. The American military was convinced that the Russians could not survive a German onslaught; the State Department, with the exception of Cordell Hull, wanted to do no more than to relax current trade restrictions against the Soviet Union. Roosevelt, however, was more optimistic about Russia's "staying power" and the efficacy of massive economic aid to the Soviets as a means of strengthening the democratic cause. He resorted to makeshift methods to render Russia material support, while awaiting the backing of the nation and the passage of the second lend-lease appropriation bill.[21] On 23 October 1941, without any ban on its extension to Russia, Congress passed the Second Lend-Lease Act. Secure in a majority approval of Congress, Roosevelt formally granted lend-lease aid to the USSR on 7 November 1941.[22]

The decision to aid Russia was the least dangerous and most feasible of several policy options opened to the Roosevelt administration after the Nazi invasion of the Soviet Union. The "unconditional aid" policy for lend-lease was necessary at the time because of Soviet needs and sacrifices and the importance of keeping the antifascist coalition together. Above all else, American generosity served the calculated national interest: the defeat of Germany and Japan and the preservation of American security.

Some historians have argued that Roosevelt should have extracted concessions for lend-lease while the Red Army was reeling under the Nazi onslaught. An effort to bargain might have yielded some protection against postwar Soviet domination of Eastern Europe; at the very least, a quid pro quo would have put relations with Stalin on a basis of reciprocity instead of unilateral American concessions and provided the administration with a useful gauge of Stalin's intentions and the feasibility of Soviet–American cooperation. None of this occurred. The president believed that the Soviet Union's military position was too weak and the understanding between Washington and Moscow too tenuous to risk pressing the Russians. Neither he nor his aides in 1941 were certain of their ability to deliver the promised supplies, whereas a Soviet defeat or a separate peace with Germany would have been catastrophic for the West. Instead the lend-lease program was undertaken in great haste and with little thought given to the repercussions that such a monumental unilateral effort might have on the fragile structure of international politics.[23]

The signing of the First Soviet Protocol in Moscow in October 1941 and the declaration of Russian eligibility for aid, one month later, initiated a program that began in confusion and unfulfilled expectations and ended as an extraordinary success. Roosevelt set up lend-lease for Russia as a separate program within a program, having its own organization and procedures—all under close White House scrutiny. In practice this meant that Russia's needs would receive a ready response, especially after the United States entered World War II, when the continuation of lend-lease became a test of good faith at a time when the second front was being delayed and when Roosevelt refused to consent to any of the Soviet Union's demands for territorial concessions.[24]

Lend-lease was as important to the West as it was crucial to the survival of the Soviet Union. The Western Allies could not have contemplated the invasion of Europe if the Soviets had not remained in the war to hold down the bulk of the German army in the east, nor could the invasion itself have succeeded had the Soviet Union not fulfilled its pledge of a major simultaneous offensive on the eastern front. Aid kept Russia in the war, and with Soviet help the Nazis were defeated with maximum speed and minimum cost to the United States.

Nonetheless the program mirrored the deep ideological, economic, and political differences between the United States and the Soviet Union that made their alliance not only "strange" but also continually uneasy.[25] In administering the program U.S. officials suffered indignities at the hands of Stalin and crude Russian bureaucrats, wastage occurred, Russia received preferential treatment, and Roosevelt never demanded any political concessions in return for the $11 billion ultimately loaned. The legacy of suspicion and distrust between donor and recipient was so high and the level of mutual understanding so low that aid to Russia always appeared to be extended grudgingly and received diffidently. The Soviets thought the aid was too little and too late; the American military complained it came too much, too soon.[26]

The same demands of the war that left little time for the problems of lend-lease termination also diverted the Roosevelt administration's attention from another matter that became closely intertwined with lend-lease: the problem of postwar economic reconstruction for a world whose leading industrial nations had suffered devastation so completely that the process of self-rejuvenation appeared interminable if not impossible without assistance from the United States. Most Americans, including the president, subscribed to the dictum that in economic matters what was best for America was best for the peace and security of the rest of the world. The United States' economic prosperity in turn depended on access to the world's markets.[27]

Cognizant of the immense power they possessed, American leaders in 1945 attempted to capitalize on Europe's need for economic assistance to coerce the shattered countries, including the Soviet Union, into accepting U.S. economic and political objectives. They intended to structure the postwar world around a liberal capitalism characterized by the revival of multilateral international trade, with utmost advantage to the United States. The rationale for this policy was the belief that World War II had developed from the economic nationalism of the 1920s and 1930s. Expanding international trade and breaking down trading blocs could stimulate worldwide economic development, creating the general prosperity upon which to establish a firm, durable peace.[28]

To attain this optimum state American political and business leaders were prepared to fight against restrictive or discriminatory trade practices, to champion multilateral trade agreements, and to extend preferential tariff treatment to countries that cooperated with the United States. They encouraged the revival of commerce between Eastern and Western Europe as necessary to effect the economic recovery of the entire continent. A healthy European economy would offer a market for surplus American goods to offset a depression at home. East–West trade would reduce Western Europe's need for American assistance with commodities domestically in short supply (such as coal, timber, and food) and free European currencies to purchase more American manufactured goods. Western Europe, for its part, gained from the exchange of goods with Eastern Europe by procuring the primary products it needed from a source likely to ease the strain on its dollar-short balance of payments. The Soviet Union and Eastern Europe would also obtain urgently needed capital equipment to carry out their own industrialization programs.[29]

Thus long before World War II ended, American policymakers and business leaders knew that the nation's economic well-being would depend on an activist foreign policy. Economic expansionism, an integral part of pre–Cold War history, continued to be a central feature of postwar foreign relations. The United States needed to export, not only to maintain productivity and full employment but also to pay for militarily strategic imports such as zinc, tin, and manganese. This trade was jeopardized by the economic paralysis of Europe and by discriminatory commercial practices that inhibited free trade.[30]

For domestic political reasons President Roosevelt had been very careful to make a distinction between lend-lease—a temporary wartime program—and economic assistance for postwar reconstruction. Little progress had occurred in planning for the latter by 1945, but the expectation was that the United States would materially spur European recovery to establish a durable peace based upon international economic prosperity. It was also taken for granted—at least until 1944—that the Soviet Union, as a senior member of the Grand Alliance, would be a primary beneficiary of American economic largesse following the defeat of Hitler. This was certainly the impression conveyed by American governmental and business leaders, such as Secretary of the Treasury Henry Morgenthau, Jr., Donald W. Nelson, head of the War Production Board, Ernest C. Ropes, the leading Soviet specialist in the Department of Commerce, and Clark H. Minor, president of the International General Electric Company, who participated in the Congress of the National Council of American–Soviet Friendship on 6 November 1943.[31]

Although none of these individuals was a Communist or fellow traveler, their testimonials affirmed a genuine sympathy for the Soviet Union as an ally in the common travail, and also a desire for a continuing close political, economic, and cultural relationship between the two nations.[32] General Electric's Minor reminded the audience that his firm had maintained cordial and profitable business ties with the Soviet Union since 1928, and he predicted that "because of the tremendous developments taking place in both countries, the volume of trade done fifteen years ago will seem insignificant by comparison with what will be done in the future." He further stated that "increased trade between the two countries in the future, which is inevitable, will assure a continued friendly and cooperative relationship between them."[33]

Government officials were equally effusive in their professions of friendship and linked postwar peace and domestic prosperity to American support for rebuilding the war-battered Soviet economy. Russia's potential as a market for American industrial and consumer goods—a market so large as to mitigate the effects of any downturn in the U.S. domestic economy—riveted their attention as nothing else could. Nelson's speech was indicative of the tendency of many businessmen and bureaucrats to minimize the obstacles to American–Soviet trade. He declared that "temperamentally as well as economically the Russians will make good customers for the United States and good suppliers of such raw materials as we may need from there."[34] Ropes, the spokesman from the Commerce Department, predicted that the Russians would seek out American manufacturers to rebuild the Donets Basin industrial district, which had been ravaged by the Nazis.[35]

The interdependence of the international economy, the potential impact of an American depression on the world and a global recession on the United States, and the importance of postwar assistance to the Soviet Union to America's economic well-being, was not lost on the Soviet apologists who had organized the congress. In the introduction to the published proceedings of the rally, they wrote: "When peace comes the need for cooperation between our two countries will continue, and be as vital as in war." The United States would be the chief resource for the Soviet Union to draw upon in the rebuilding of its economy; but "in its turn, American industry, facing the mammoth task of reconversion to a peacetime economy, will need this tremendous market to keep its wheels turning and its returning soldier manpower employed."[36]

These same themes carried into 1944 after the opening of the second front, when Hitler's armies, for the first time, had gone on the defensive. In December the Russian Economic Institute of New York noted the interest of American businessmen in profit-making ventures in the Soviet Union, observing that "the Soviet Union represents potentially the largest market the world ever saw; *quantitatively*, because of unceasing growth of population which does not find any comparison in the development of industrial countries of western civilization; and *qualitatively*, because of the complete urbanization of the country." These circumstances required the Soviets to engage in tremendous buying in postwar markets, which would be advantageous to the United States. To forestall competitors, the Institute advocated a bilateral commercial agreement, warning that the Soviets would purchase from the United States "only if the relationship between the two countries is . . . one of mutual understanding and trust." Lend-lease was proposed as the model for reconstruction aid to the USSR.[37]

Eric Johnston, the president of the United States Chamber of Commerce, voiced nearly identical sentiments after his visit to the Soviet Union late in the summer of 1944. Stalin had told him that the USSR looked forward to a continuing flow of American supplies for postwar replacement, reconstruction, and expansion. Mining and road-building machinery, tools, factory and railroad equipment, and hydroelectric plants were high on the list. "All of this implies that Russia will be, if not our biggest, at least our most eager customer when the war ends," Johnston declared.[38]

Implicit in the remarks of businessmen and bureaucrats who favored postwar aid to Russia was the belief that the American and Soviet economies stood in a complementary relationship. Speaking at a rally sponsored by the National Council of American–Soviet Friendship on 16 November 1944, the industrialist Henry J. Kaiser viewed the postwar world optimistically and told his audience that the two nations' future business ties were already being charted. In Kaiser's brave new world there would be no place for the theories of overproduction; wealth was something that all humankind would enjoy—not just Americans.[39] In this future global consumer society the possibility that Russia might use American aid to erect an industrial structure that would eventually crowd the United States out of the world's markets was not taken seriously. Donald Nelson declared, in 1945: "I don't expect to see Russia become what you would term a competitor for world markets for at least twenty years."[40]

Meanwhile businessmen and bureaucrats searched for clues to Soviet postwar behavior beyond the obvious need for reconstruction funds. Writing in late 1944, Ernest C. Ropes, chief of the Russian unit in the Department of Commerce, analyzed the prior history of Russia in world trade as a precedent for its future actions and concluded that the Soviets would not make any important changes in the methods that had worked well in the prewar years. Lend-lease had made them even more aware of the products available from abroad. "This greater knowledge of each other," Ropes declared, "should guarantee a continuation of close trade relations and mutual trust between the U.S.S.R. and its State-trading agencies, and the countries where foreign trade is still in the hands of private corporations."[41]

One of the primary benefits of peaceful trade relations that Ropes hoped to see develop was a better political understanding between Russia and the United States. This relationship could then become "a model for the other countries of the world," forming the basis for enhanced cultural, educational, and artistic relationships.[42] Ropes preached the themes of peace, freedom, and international trade over and over again; he even endorsed granting long-term credits to the Soviet Union for ten and possibly up to thirty years.[43] The United States would benefit as much as the Soviet economy from a generous, long-term credit policy.[44]

The argument that the United States needed to sell to Russia to avert a postwar depression was heard very frequently in 1944 and 1945.[45] Assistant Secretary of State Dean Acheson articulated the Department of State's "one world" view of economic matters before a subcommittee of the House Special Committee on Post War Economic Policy and Planning. Foreign trade was vital to postwar full employment in the United States and elsewhere, he observed, and this could be attained only by eliminating tariffs, quotas, embargoes, and other artificial impediments. Concerning the Soviet Union, Acheson observed that the United States would have to lay down "fair rules of trade, with reference to government monopolies and state trading, including trade between countries where private enterprise prevails and those where foreign trade is managed by the State."[46]

The "one world" theme was heard in other contexts as well. Addressing the American–Soviet Friendship Rally on 14 November 1945, three months after the Truman administration had turned down a Soviet request for postwar credits, Acheson reiterated the State Department's view of the need for peace and cooperation. The vital interests of the United States and Russia did not necessarily have to clash, he said; through commercial intercourse each could help the other to develop the highest standard of living for its people. Secretary of Commerce Henry A. Wallace also told the delegates: "It is fitting, proper and essential that you and all of us work for peace. Those who seek to build up suspicions of our allies and enmity between nations are the enemies of America and the advance agents of desolation."[47] Corliss Lamont, the pro-Soviet chairman of the council, argued that the new Five Year Plan was evidence of Russia's peaceful intentions and "an opportunity for American business, too, for the Soviets want very much to buy all sorts of goods from us." He further declared: "Cooperation with Soviet Russia for peace and mutual trade is the only intelligent course for America to follow and can be surely agreed upon by all political parties and all classes in our community."[48]

Peace and prosperity through trade would also advance the security and economic well-being of the United States. In an address to the New York Foreign Trade Committee on 24 May 1945 Secretary Wallace argued that foreign commerce would "make the difference between misery

and the good life for several years in many American communities."
Even though exports represented about ten percent of the nation's gross
national product, certain vital industries, such as machine tools, railroad
locomotives, steel, and farm machinery, depended upon overseas markets for a significant part of their income. President Roosevelt had made
this point to Congress just before his death, saying that "we cannot
succeed in building a peaceful world unless we build an economically
healthy world."[49]

Under Wallace's prodding, the Department of Commerce became the
foremost agency to promote foreign trade, especially with Russia, as an
antidote to a postwar depression. Both Amos E. Taylor, the new head of
the Bureau of Foreign and Domestic Commerce, and Wallace Clark, of
the National Planning Association and the Committee for Economic
Development, viewed the future as a tremendous opportunity for the
United States to rebuild a war-torn world and avoid unemployment and
depression at home. In an unabashed statement of dynamic capitalism
Clark wrote, in 1945: "Now, the penetration of our armies into practically every part of the world, has been the means of introducing still
more of this class of American goods [low-cost, high-quality] to a previously unknown market." He and Taylor indicated that American businessmen would receive more official help in promoting exports than they
had in the past.[50]

The Russian market was increasingly viewed as a godsend to American manufacturers. "If we could sell the Russians $110,000,000 worth
of goods annually, it is believed that it would go far toward keeping
up employment in this country and maintaining factory output," wrote
Robert P. Vanderpool in the *Chicago Herald American*. *Fortune* recalled
that the U.S. machine tool industry had been rescued from near collapse
in 1931 by Soviet orders and that the postwar market for U.S. capital
and consumer goods would be even more important to American prosperity. Seven hundred American companies were contributing a total of
$250,000 to advertise in the *Catalogue of American Engineering and
Industry*, a compendium being compiled by Soviet representatives in
New York for the use of purchasing agencies in Russia.[51]

Depending on the analyst or trade journal, postwar commerce with
the Soviet Union would range from a modest trade in a few luxury items
to a major market for basic American industries. Estimates of Russian
purchases also varied broadly, from $500 million annually to $5 billion.
James H. McGraw, Jr., head of McGraw-Hill Publishing Company, calculated that if political differences were resolved, $5 billion for the first
three years, leveling off to $2 billion annually, was not unreasonable.
Others put the figure closer to $1 billion or $2 billion.[52] *Iron Age* re-

ported that the Soviets were ready to purchase $10 million worth of machine tools monthly, or one-fourth of 1945 output. The American-Russian Institute observed that Russia would absorb ten percent of the United States' production of trucks in the first postwar years and more than 1.5 million tons of steel annually.[53]

Thus a consensus was evolving that Russia's material requirements, after the defeat of Hitler, would be on an enormous scale, and that this would benefit the American economy. But it also posed questions. Did American industry have the capacity, following reconversion, to produce enough of a specific type of equipment that the Soviets wanted? Would they obtain heavy equipment and sophisticated technology from Germany as reparations? Would the United States be able to keep up with foreign competitors, especially Britain and Sweden, which had the advantages of short haul distances, the metric system, sixty-cycle motors, and the like? Would the Russians demand a bilateral agreement, or should the United States insist upon a multilateral pact? Would Russia have the capacity to pay for American imports, or would she require credits? Should private credits be short-term, or long-term, commercial loans and backed by the United States government?[54]

The last two questions became the focal point of concern. Given the Soviets' trading habits, and contrary to the State Department's preference for multilateral pacts, most knowledgeable businessmen believed that a bilateral agreement was the best route to encourage American–Soviet trade. How would the Russians pay for American products, and what could the United States do to facilitate Soviet purchases? "The nub of the situation is that Russia offers an extraordinary potential market, particularly for our heavy industries which have grown so enormously during the war," declared James H. McGraw, Jr. "But if this sales outlet is to materialize, the U.S. must find a way to import from Russia . . . from ten to twenty times as much as we did before the war." The journalist William H. White told the Citizens' Conference on International Economic Union that "most of the wishful thinking on the subject of future Soviet–American trade is being done in this country and not in Moscow, where I found that a strong desire to buy American industrial products was counter-balanced with a completely realistic understanding of the difficulties in paying for them."[55]

Fortune stated the dilemma very succinctly when it asked: "How far will the United States go in favoring Russian products, how many concessions will we make in our tariff policy?" Besides gold transactions, the Soviet Union could export to the United States items such as caviar, furs, and manganese to pay her commercial obligations. But the dollar volume of Soviet exports to the United States had in the past been relatively insignificant; Russia had paid her American obligations by drawing upon surplus revenues from a favorable trade balance with Western Europe, especially Great Britain. V. P. Timoshenko, a political émigré, was dubious that this same payments procedure could continue after the war.[56] The United States would have to wait for the Western European economies to recover so that they could purchase Russian goods, giving the Soviets hard currency to pay for American products. The alternative to waiting for this triangular trade to develop was for the United States to extend credits to the USSR, "as large as they are now under the Lend-Lease agreement, or at least comparable in value."[57]

Secretary of Commerce Wallace staunchly advocated granting credit to the USSR. Loans to Great Britain and Russia were in the national interest, he told the Chicago World Trade Conference, because they would keep these markets open for American goods and avert the narrow economic nationalism that had led to World War II. "I have no hesitancy in saying that the peace would not long survive if the world is to be divided into three restrictive economic blocs—the dollar bloc, the sterling bloc and the Russian bloc."[58]

The extension of credit to the Soviets to finance imports was not without its own problems. How much credit might Russia expect to receive from the proposed World Bank, or a new Export-Import Bank? Would Congress amend the Johnson Act to permit loans to the USSR, one of the nations that had defaulted on its World War I obligations? Would private financiers be willing to extend credit to the Soviet Union? The answers to these questions were linked to the entire postwar economic and political pattern.[59]

Because the prospects for a truly bilateral trade were not encouraging due to the Soviet Union's inability to pay for American imports, some form of credit seemed necessary. Knowledgeable businessmen and government officials considered Russia a good credit risk, on the basis of her prior record. Commerce official Ropes had written: "As a credit risk the Soviet Union has traversed the distance from zero to one of the highest rated in the world and in popular esteem from the position of a distrusted disturber of world peace to that of a country without whose aid that peace will be impossible of attainment." He thought it probable that "in the near future Congress will approve an open credit of a large amount, as a loan to the Soviet Government on a long-term basis."[60]

Few doubted that the Soviets were genuinely interested in tapping America's industrial productivity and would welcome any extensions of private and governmental credit. The restoration of foreign trade with the United States and Western Europe was indispensable to economic recovery, wrote the Soviet economist Josef A. Trakhtenberg, who declared that the Soviet Union was as interested as any capitalistic state in obtaining short- and long-term credits from the Monetary Fund and the Bank for Reconstruction.[61] In July 1945 the highly respected British publication *The Statist* reported that the Soviets were seeking $6 billion to $15 billion in credit from the United States, a sign that postwar Russia would be interested in trading with the West.[62]

Private credit was yet another potential source for underwriting Soviet imports from the United States. Before American banks could act, Congress would have to modify or repeal the Johnson Act, as President Roosevelt had requested. *Fortune* reported that the American-Russian Chamber of Commerce, behind which stood the Chase National Bank, long a fiscal agent of the Soviet government, was ready to lobby for repeal. Five other large banks also were rumored to be discussing a consortium arrangement to compete with Chase. *Fortune* speculated that Russia might even prefer private to public credits despite the higher interest rates, because it would give her "a greater bargaining scope than she would have in dealing with a government agency."[63]

The questions of credit and whether the Soviets would have anything worthwhile to sell to the United States, while troublesome, did not really detract from the optimistic spirit that Russia was the new China market of the Open Door. Besides economic self-interest, many businessmen, legislators, and government officials, including President Roosevelt, earnestly believed in the slogan World Peace Through World Trade, especially with reference to the Russians. "With these people we shall have to live in peace unless we are to prepare for war," wrote the editors of *Fortune*.[64]

That the United States could not get along with the Soviet Union and would eventually have to fight her not only was wrong, but criminal, declared Louis H. Pink, chairman of the Citizens' Conference on Economic Union.[65] An economic rapprochement between the foremost exponents of the free-market and state-controlled economies would also create the conditions for international stability. This was the view of the Institute of Economic Affairs of New York University in its publications on postwar reconstruction.[66] Arthur Paul, the Commerce Department's director of the Office of International Trade, was equally explicit in advocating trade expansion to ease tensions between Russia and the United States. "*Economic blocs mean economic warfare, and peace and economic warfare are incompatible*," he asserted.[67]

Similar sentiments were being echoed on the floor of Congress and in other quarters of the federal bureaucracy. In a speech delivered before an organization to provide relief to Soviet-Jewish war orphans and reprinted in the *Congressional Record*, Democratic Senator Harley Kilgore of West Virginia declared that trade relations between the two countries would contribute to the general welfare and prosperity of both and also provide a firm basis for the United Nations as the guardian of world peace and security. He proposed that the United States lend the Soviets every possible financial assistance to accelerate their reconstruction.[68]

In June 1946 Jerry Voorhis, a liberal Democrat from California, put before the House a proposal for "an open and above-board commercial treaty" with the USSR, drafted by the economist Charles Prince, formerly of the United States Chamber of Commerce. The "web of secrecy" that shrouded relations with the Soviet Union troubled Voorhis, who insisted that "the whole future peace of the world depends primarily upon relationships between the United States and Soviet Russia." Prince's proposed treaty had evolved from conversations with the assistant secretaries of state and treasury and with Soviet officials and was consistent with the 1944 Bretton Woods Agreement. It provided for a substantial loan to the Soviets by an American banking consortium, arbitration of commercial disputes, prohibition of unfair trade practices, unimpeded access to Eastern European markets, a free exchange of information, and freedom of travel. Although nothing came of it, the treaty proposal was indicative of the belief that trade could break down the barriers of narrow nationalism and foster peace between nations.[69]

Alexander Gerschenkron, an economist with the board of governors of the Federal Reserve System, and Herbert Feis, a special consultant to the secretary of war and a former State Department adviser, also emphasized the desirability of integrating the Soviet Union into the world economy to minimize political friction. A realist in his attitude toward the USSR, Gerschenkron nonetheless thought it was not unreasonable to assume that Russia "may be willing to pursue the road of extensive international [political and economic] collaboration."[70] Feis, in 1945, declared that the trade policy of the United States should support its international political objectives: peace and stability. This required the United States to make certain economic and financial concessions to other nations. Feis was cautiously optimistic that in this integrated international economy American–Soviet commerce would expand. The Soviets might become major purchasers of American machinery, paying for such goods from their gold reserves, which Feis estimated at $2 billion to $3 billion.[71]

Despite a reservoir of goodwill for a valiant ally and a growing interest on the part of important segments of American business in trade with the Soviet Union, in 1945–46 the postwar expectations of a commercial bonanza and the foreign economic and political policies of the Truman administration were out of synchronization. Many American businessmen, perhaps misled by self-interest and Commerce Secretary Wallace's optimism, seem not to have been fully apprised of the depth and seriousness of the political difficulties that had crept into American–Soviet relations since the Moscow Conference of December 1943. Perhaps they, like many policymakers, had not wanted to believe that the wartime concert of the United Nations would not extend into the postwar world.[72]

Talk of peace and prosperity had obfuscated the more generalized fear of the Soviet Union that many Americans had shared since 1917. The editors of *Fortune* sensed this as early as January 1945, when they wrote that "Americans are now looking at Russia . . . with mingled feelings and confused perceptions. We have inchoate fears of a Soviet Russia that has found its strength and broken out of its isolation to assume an awesomely dominant military and economic position in Europe and Asia."[73]

The link between lend-lease and Soviet postwar economic aid was Ambassador W. Averell Harriman. In July 1943, while serving as the lend-lease representative in London and pondering whether to accept the ambassadorship to the Soviet Union, Harriman wrote to President Roosevelt about his own feelings concerning relations with Moscow. His views became very influential in shaping Soviet–American relations. He told the president that he was a "confirmed optimist" concerning the Soviet Union and believed that Stalin wanted a "firm understanding" with the United States after the war. In November he cabled the State Department that postwar economic aid was an integral part of U.S. diplomacy with the Soviet Union. By January 1944 he had, like many businessmen and Washington bureaucrats, tied postwar aid to Russia to the problem of unemployment dislocation in the United States.[74]

But Harriman, like others in the State Department and even President Roosevelt, also believed in the possibility of using America's economic power for political leverage with the Soviets. In March 1944 he had warned the State Department of Russia's territorial ambitions and added: "I am impressed with the consideration that economic assistance is one of the most effective weapons at our disposal to influence European political events in the direction we desire and to avoid the development of a sphere of influence of the Soviet Union over Eastern Europe and the Balkans."[75] By the fall of 1944 he had reported from Moscow of the "more than usually uncooperative" attitude of the Soviet government, and of his growing apprehension concerning Soviet policy. The anti-Western faction within the Kremlin had gained Stalin's ear, he concluded, "and the policy appears to be crystallizing to force us and the British to accept all Soviet policies backed by the strength and prestige of the Red Army"—a reference to the Soviet occupation of Poland and Eastern Europe.[76]

Disappointed but not discouraged, Harriman told President Roosevelt that "this job of getting the Soviet Government to play a decent role in international affairs is, however, going to be more difficult than we had hoped." In subsequent cables to Washington in 1944 and 1945 he called for a tough but flexible American position. He urged the new president, Harry S. Truman, to deal firmly with the Russians, who had established control over Poland and other neighboring states by force in the name of security. The United States could be tough without running serious risks, he counseled, because it was the only source of economic help for Soviet postwar reconstruction.[77]

With the war in Europe winding down, the Truman administration made four policy decisions in 1945–46 that were to affect the course of American–Soviet relations profoundly and adversely. The first decision came eleven days after Truman succeeded to the presidency. On 23 April 1945 he summoned the Russian foreign minister, V. M. Molotov, to the White House and proceeded to give him a blunt lecture, demanding Soviet adherence to the application of the Yalta agreement on Poland as it was interpreted in Washington. An astonished Molotov retorted, "I have never been talked to like that in my life." "Carry out your agreements," replied Truman, "and you won't get talked to like that."[78]

The second decision was to cut off, immediately following the surrender of Nazi Germany, all lend-lease aid to the Soviet Union. Truman, Harriman, and others appear to have seen this as both compliance with Congress's will on lend-lease and a signal to Moscow that the United States would henceforth deal with Russia (as Harriman wrote in August) only on a realistic, reciprocal basis. However, there was no prior consultation with the Soviets, and the decision may well have been implemented down the bureaucratic line more abruptly than Truman intended.[79]

The third decision concerned reparations from Germany. The United States had agreed at the Yalta Conference that the sum of $20 billion should be the "basis of discussion" for reparations and that half the sum agreed on would go to the USSR.[80] But when the reparations commission met in June 1945 to take up the matter, the Truman administration backed off from this agreement. The compromise negotiated at Potsdam at the end of July fell far short of Soviet expectations.[81]

The fourth issue concerned the Soviet application for a $6 billion loan from the United States. The matter came to a head in Washington only when the Soviet ambassador, on 30 May 1945, asked about the five-month-old application. In August the Russians were advised to apply to the Export-Import Bank, and they quickly did so, for a loan of $1 billion. Throughout the fall of 1945 negotiations on a similar loan to Great

Britain went forward, but approval for the Soviet application languished in the State Department as relations between the two governments worsened. No discussions took place, no quid pro quo was asked. The loan had become hostage to Soviet behavior.[82]

Then, after the foreign ministers' conference in December 1945, and as the British loan wended its way through Congress, the Soviets began to ask questions. On 1 March 1946 the State Department disclosed that the Soviet loan application had been "mislaid" but that negotiations might commence.[83]

The Truman administration had evidently concluded that the timing was right to use the loan application as explicit leverage to influence Soviet foreign policies. But this had no more positive effect on Moscow's behavior than had the reparations issue. The assumption that the Soviets' need for help could have pried meaningful concessions from Moscow was simply wrong. The Soviet Union put its control of Poland, and much or all of Eastern Europe, ahead of entente with the United States or economic aid.[84]

Moreover, the Soviets had their own illusions about economic aid—reinforced, no doubt, by the talk in the United States of a postwar depression. In January 1945 Stalin had predicted a severe economic crisis for the capitalistic nations of the West, caused by the wartime disruption of the international economy.[85] Through 1952 he continued to forecast that severe unemployment and acute social distress would cause Europe and Japan to fight among themselves, and also against U.S. hegemony, to secure access to markets and raw materials. To avert an economic collapse, Stalin believed, the United States needed the Soviets as customers and would provide credits on easy terms and with no strings attached.[86]

The Truman administration's rebuff of Soviet requests for assistance contributed to the widening rift between the former wartime allies. It probably convinced Stalin—if he did not already believe so—that Russia would have to go it alone economically. For the United States, the most important result of the year-long wrangling was to sensitize American opinion, both official and public, to what the Soviet Union was doing in Poland and Eastern Europe—actions that were depicted as brutal, antidemocratic, and in violation of the wartime agreements.[87]

The deterioration of political relations proceeded swiftly thereafter. Stalin asserted Soviet hegemony in Eastern Europe; he refused to join the World Bank or the International Monetary Fund, or to participate in an international conference on trade and employment. Discord persisted over the political organization of Germany and free navigation of the Danube. An American treaty to guarantee German disarmament got nowhere, and the final drafts of peace treaties for Italy, Bulgaria, Rumania, Hungary, and Finland bogged down. In 1946 the Soviets rejected a plan for the international control of atomic energy. Meanwhile, in March of that year, Winston Churchill voiced Western apprehensions that the Kremlin had lowered an "iron curtain" across Europe. Soviet expansion in the eastern Mediterranean, the Middle East, and Asia constituted a new challenge to American interests.[88]

Ben Hill Brown, a former State Department functionary, later recalled that President Truman came to believe that public and congressional opinion compelled his administration to adopt a more strident anti-Soviet policy.[89] Popular suspicion about Russian motives for a loan may well have pressured the administration to adopt a hard line. *U.S. News* reported in March 1945 that the Soviet aim was to achieve economic self-sufficiency, not a long-term trade relationship with the United States. Later it observed that Russia's behavior in the liberated nations of Eastern Europe—stripping them of industrial plants and excluding Western commercial interests—put her on a collision course with Anglo-American concern for their well-being.[90]

On 6 September 1946 American Secretary of State James F. Byrnes called for the political and economic unification of Germany, thereby implying that the United States had now become locked in a protracted struggle with its former Soviet ally for the control of Europe.[91] The optimism that the defeat of the Axis nations would usher in the "American century," a long era of peace and prosperity under the guidance of the United States, quickly dissipated. The Cold War had become a reality.

In Congress, meanwhile, opposition to any accommodation of the Soviet Union's security concerns rose to the surface, as legislators demanded that the administration use economic leverage to force the Soviets to abide by the idealistic promises of the Atlantic Charter and the Yalta Declaration. The anticommunist sentiment of the postwar period made its greatest impact in the halls of the Senate and the House, resulting in the passage of various restrictive trade measures—most notably the Export Control Act of 1949, the Battle Act of 1951, and the Jackson-Vanik amendment of 1972—that limited the White House's ability to follow a flexible foreign economic policy toward the Soviet Union. The composition of Congress helps to explain why it became extraordinarily difficult from 1945 onward for the executive to insulate aid and trade from the political disputes that divided the wartime allies.

Roosevelt had lost his magic touch with Congress long before his death.[92] In 1945 President Truman confronted a Congress that had fragmented into four discernible groups. At one end of the political spectrum were the presidential Democrats, who were liberal in domestic policy and international in foreign policy and who came from the urban areas of the Northeast, Midwest, and West. At the opposite end were the congressional Republicans, conservative in domestic policy and heirs to the prewar isolationist traditions; they came mainly from the rural areas of the North. Between the two were the presidential Republicans and the congressional Democrats. The former were more liberal and international-minded than the latter and came from the same geographical areas as the presidential Democrats, only more heavily suburban. The congressional Democrats were conservative, rooted in the South, and entrenched in important committee chairmanships because of the seniority system.[93]

These four groups were not so well distinguished by neat boundaries as this typology suggests, and generalizing about them is hazardous. But they were much more clearly defined than mere party labels—Democrat or Republican—suggested. Indeed the Democratic majorities in Congress during most of the years after 1945 proved to be only paper majorities; members crossed party lines in casting votes on specific domestic and foreign policy issues according to ideology or the perceived economic, political, social, or geographical interests of their constituents. Presidential Democrats and presidential Republicans more often than not cooperated in evolving a bipartisan approach to foreign policy, supporting such presidential initiatives as the Yalta Agreements, the United Nations Charter, aid to Greece and Turkey, the Marshall Plan, NATO, and the Korean War. Bipartisanship worked because thinking in the executive branch and in the dominant quarters of Congress (for example, Republican Senator Arthur Vandenberg, chairman of the Foreign Relations Committee)[94] ran along roughly parallel lines, and there was thorough consultation. Bipartisanship, however, rarely encompassed non-European issues and was never total.

Congressional Republicans and congressional Democrats were in the minority but often disproportionately affected the shape, size, and scope of a particular piece of legislation or program. When congressional Republicans and Southern Democrats cooperated on an issue, theirs was not simply a conservative but also a largely rural coalition. Over the years the ranks of this conservative coalition included Republicans Kenneth S. Wherry, Robert A. Taft, Styles Bridges, James P. Kem, William F. Knowland, John W. Bricker, Richard M. Nixon, Eugene Millikan, and John Taber, and Democrats Harry F. Byrd, A. Willis Robertson, Walter F. George, Millard Tydings, John Rankin, John McClellan, and Otto Passman.[95] They generally stood in arch-opposition to the domestic, foreign, and political changes that had been wrought by the New Deal, as they later would those of the Great Society. In 1945 they championed strict construction of the Constitution, fiscal sobriety, and local control. Federal budgets should be kept low and in balance, along with taxes. They were hostile to tariff protection and also to foreign economic aid.[96]

In foreign affairs this bipartisan conservative minority had opposed Roosevelt's globalism and resented the increase in secrecy in the conduct of diplomacy. They wanted for the Congress an increased share of power with the executive in foreign affairs. They blamed the wartime agreements themselves, rather than Soviet violations of them, for the Cold War. Men like Taft and Wherry did not plunge from their prewar isolationism to embrace a naive internationalism; others endorsed unilateralism—a shying away from alliances and agreements that committed the United States in advance to actions that might lead to war. They favored a strong American defense, a reassertion of congressional influence in foreign policy making, and a free hand for the United States to go it alone in pursuit of its own national interest.[97] Even when they voted for a foreign aid program, as in the case of the Marshall Plan in 1947, or for export controls in 1949 and thereafter, they showed their caution at every point, seeking a weaker commitment, a shorter duration, a lower aid figure, or more restricted presidential discretion.[98]

Fierce anticommunism was a hallmark of these congressional conservatives, who wrestled with the dilemma of how to combat communism yet remain free of political and economic entanglement. It had been relatively easy in the face of the Soviet Union's uncooperative diplomacy for them to vote to terminate lend-lease, to oppose a loan to the Soviets, and to criticize New Dealers for losing the peace and permitting the enslavement of millions. They claimed their votes coincided with the economic interest and anticommunist views of their constituents. Republican Congressman George B. Schwabe of Oklahoma had applauded the cessation of lend-lease aid but bemoaned the fact that Russia and Eastern Europe would receive 25 million pounds of meat still in the lend-lease pipeline while meat was in short supply at home. Wisconsin Republican Reid F. Murray blasted Commerce Secretary Wallace for encouraging Soviet exports of lumber, pulp, and furs in direct competition with his constituents' industries. California Congressman Bertrand W. Gearhart, a critic of federal deficits, scoffed at the notion that the Soviets could repay a $6 billion to $12 billion loan.[99]

By 1947 anticommunism would require more positive action, which also created a dilemma. Republican Senator James P. Kem of Missouri and Ohio Congressman Clarence J. Brown, coming from an isolationist legacy, wanted the United Nations to spearhead the crusade against communism, thereby keeping the United States uninvolved. Others, like Taft, A. Willis Robertson, and Karl Mundt, fretted that the Marshall Plan would erode the moral fiber, initiative, and self-sufficiency of its European recipients while draining the U.S. economy. In 1952 many of these same conservatives would focus on the disadvantages of collective security at a time when a conservative Republican president was touting its benefits and actively encouraging Europe's political and economic integration. Eisenhower, like Truman before and presidents after him, would come to rely on the presidential Democrats and presidential Republicans to retain some flexibility in foreign economic policy toward Russia and Eastern Europe.

In the early 1960s conservative Republicans and Democrats, bolstered by the military, would focus on achieving military superiority over the Russians, helping freedom fighters to retake their homelands, withdrawing recognition from the USSR, and ending trade and technological favors to the Soviets. By the late 1960s and 1970s their displeasure would be directed against the Nixon policy of détente, which they viewed as American acquiescence in the status quo in Europe, approval of Soviet foreign policy, and overgenerousness in giving the Soviets access to U.S. technology and grain while allowing them to achieve military superiority. Politics makes strange bedfellows, and the 1970s were no exception. In 1972 congressional liberals joined with conservatives in voting to deny most-favored-nation tariff treatment to the Soviet Union to protest its violations of human rights.

From Truman's administration to Reagan's, congressional conservatives would remain frustrated with America's European allies and be inclined to go it alone in foreign affairs on the theory that the allies were too fearful of communism or too cautious. They refused to understand that the Western Europeans did not share their concern over the economic and security problems raised by trade and technology transfer to the USSR and the Soviet European bloc. They did not appreciate that the Western Europeans weighed their own interests and determined that they would be best served by a trade and technology transfer policy that, though generally more liberal than that of the United States, remained within the boundaries of the strategic requirements of Western security. Their misperception became a major irritant in U.S.–European and executive–legislative relations.

In 1945, however, the immediate object of the conservatives' wrath was Secretary of Commerce Wallace. An ardent New Dealer, he was especially vulnerable because he had been the most vocal apologist for the Soviet Union within the cabinet and an advocate of close trade relations, the reconstruction loan, and recognition of a Soviet sphere of political influence in Eastern Europe as the best guarantee of peace and prosperity. His fate demonstrated how much the political climate in

Washington had changed between the presidencies of Roosevelt and Truman, and how far Truman would go to demonstrate to his congressional critics and the American people his "toughness" toward the Soviets.[100]

In the spring of 1946 Wallace asked Truman to let him head a special mission to Moscow to talk with the Russians about their economic needs and cooperation. When this request got nowhere, he wrote to the president on 15 March, asking him to instruct the new ambassador, Walter Bedell Smith, to begin negotiations as soon as possible, "along economic and trade lines."[101] Closer economic ties would foster mutual understanding, goodwill, and peace.

Wallace misjudged how much his perception of the Soviet Union and its motives differed from Truman's and his closest advisers'. Truman responded that Smith was going to Russia "with the right attitude in mind" and hoped that he would be able to put Soviet–American relations "on a better plane." The president refused, however, to comply with Wallace's request, clearly believing "little [was] to be gained from the . . . proposal."[102]

Distraught over the progressive deterioration of Soviet–American relations, Wallace renewed his efforts to persuade the president to chart a new course, again unsuccessfully. One confidential memorandum he wrote, seemingly making light of the Soviets' uncooperative diplomacy, leaked to the press and created a furor among conservative legislators, the media, and religious and ethnic groups. A second memorandum, denouncing as fatally defective the administration's proposal for the international control of atomic energy and calling for economic aid and trade with the Soviets to avoid "a disastrous atomic world war," also fell on deaf ears.[103]

Rather than moving the administration closer to an understanding with the Soviets, Wallace's various initiatives in 1945–46 had the opposite effect. They brought criticism down upon the administration from conservative legislators and the public. The secretary of commerce had become an embarrassment and a political liability to the president. His actions also were running counter to Truman's personal inclination, which was to take a hard line with the Soviets.[104]

Increasingly the president was siding with his closest advisers, who held at a discount the prospect of future cooperation with the Soviet Union. This is evident from the explosive report on American–Soviet relations written by White House special counsel Clark Clifford in September 1946.[105] In an early draft of the report Clifford had asked the State Department's Soviet expert, George F. Kennan, to comment on the economic aspects of the relationship. Kennan's observations helped to define the economic parameters within which the administration would "get tough" with the Russians. This was, he wrote, "a delicate subject" in view of the natural desire of American exporters to trade and because of the deep division within the administration over the direction of foreign policy. Kennan argued that the United States should encourage trade with the Soviets but only to the extent that it benefited the broader national interest, and not simply the interests of private businessmen. By implication, the administration should not encourage trade that did not advance the United States' national security interest.[106]

Kennan also apprised Clifford of two fundamental facts governing American–Soviet economic relationships: Moscow could not be induced to modify its political policies by "good-will gifts" such as foreign economic aid; and American economic assistance extended to the USSR or to other nations within its political orbit could not be earmarked for a specific purpose but "will go to strengthen the entire world program of the Kremlin."[107] Neither Kennan nor Clifford discounted the virtue of patience, but both, unlike Wallace, put a greater premium on firmness in persuading the Soviets to exercise restraint.

The final break between the administration and Wallace occurred soon thereafter. On 12 September 1946 Wallace delivered a speech in New York City to a predominantly left-wing, pro-Russian audience. The speech, personally cleared by the president, focused on the necessity of a political understanding with the Soviet Union and obliquely criticized Churchill's "iron curtain" address of 5 March. Reiterating familiar themes, Wallace asserted that economic issues could be separated from political ones. However, to the perceptive listener, a hint of ambiguity ran through the speech, suggesting that he did not himself really believe that the two could be kept separate. He asserted, on the one hand, that the United States could not "permit the door to be closed against our trade in Eastern Europe"; on the other hand, he stated that the Soviets *would* permit economic penetration of their sphere of influence. This ambiguity was pretty much ignored in the public outcry that ensued over Wallace's general criticism of American foreign policy.[108]

Eight days later, under pressure from many quarters but especially from Secretary of State Byrnes and Republican Senator Arthur Vandenberg, who were in Paris painfully negotiating peace treaties with the Russians, Truman ousted Wallace from the cabinet, charging with tortured exaggeration that "the Reds, phonies, and 'parlor pinks' . . . are becoming a national danger. I am afraid they are a sabotage front for Uncle Joe Stalin."[109]

THE firing of Wallace symbolized the clash of ideologies and national interests between the two remaining world powers. Unable to find a common ground after the defeat of Hitler, the United States and Soviet Russia accepted the separate ground that each already held. The Cold War became a reality, frustrating the initial American optimism that a reinvigorated Europe—West and East—would develop into a lucrative market for U.S. industry, insulate the nation from economic depression, and initiate the "American century" of peace and prosperity. At war's end the Soviet Union effectively excluded the United States from its sphere of influence, economically and politically. Russia and Eastern Europe, the new China market of the Open Door, were closed.

Of the vice-presidents who succeeded to the presidency, none entered upon his new duties under more trying circumstances than Truman. With no executive training or experience, with only the barest knowledge of his predecessor's policies and commitments, and with no intimate friends or advisers in the important executive departments, he had to assume at once all of the responsibilities involved in concluding successfully the nation's worst war, creating a new international order, and guiding the country's transition to peace. The resolution of any one of these problems would have required all of Roosevelt's knowledge, ability, and prestige. Instead Truman inherited from the deceased president a badly divided Democratic party and a coalition of legislators in Congress that was conservative and rural, hostile to New Deal reform, and critical of presidential supremacy in foreign policy.

As relations between Washington and Moscow became increasingly strained, the Truman administration came under fierce pressure from Congress and the public to adopt a tough posture against Soviet violations of the wartime agreements. Gradually American policymakers, supported by most businessmen and public opinion, concluded that the United States should utilize economic leverage to secure political concessions from the Soviet Union and to destroy, or at least to retard, the Soviets' offensive military capability. One of the primary mechanisms for accomplishing this foreign policy objective was to regulate the export of strategic materials and technologies to Russia and Eastern Europe.

CHAPTER TWO

The Politics of Export Controls:
Executive Initiatives

BY the beginning of 1947 relations with the Soviet Union had become very troubled. Stalin pronounced international peace impossible under the present capitalist development of the world economy. The USSR pursued a vituperative propaganda campaign against the United States, encouraged communist obstructionism in Western Europe, especially in France and Italy, and ruthlessly consolidated its hold upon Eastern Europe. "Patience and firmness" were the watchwords in dealing with the Soviets—the emphasis, following the recommendations of the Joint Chiefs of Staff, being primarily on the firmness.[1] In the economic sphere, the United States embarked upon an aggressive policy of export controls aimed at depriving the Soviet Union and its satellites of militarily strategic goods. American political leaders believed that economic pressure coupled with political firmness would keep the Soviet Union in a position of relative military and economic inferiority and thereby minimize Soviet flexibility in pursuing an aggressive foreign policy.

Despite nearly two years of U.S.–Soviet clashes, one could still find in 1947 an occasional plea that the United States trade and provide reconstruction assistance to the Soviet Union. Left-wing Congressman Vito Marcantonio of New York City, for example, inserted into the *Congressional Record* the text of a speech by former Commerce Secretary Henry Wallace, now editor of the liberal periodical *The New Republic*, before the Southern Conference for Human Welfare, touting the benefits of U.S.–Soviet trade to the American economy. "We need markets," Wallace told the delegates, and he predicted that the United States would experience increasing difficulty selling abroad as other nations saw their dollar reserves dwindle. A shrinking foreign market would precipitate a depression at home: "We can act now to develop trade relations with the Soviet Union and keep our plants in continuous operation or we can continue to pursue a policy of arming Russia's political enemies and reap the results in depression." Russia was both a market and a source of raw materials for the United States. He warned: "Today we have bargaining power. Tomorrow—given depression—we may not have such power."[2]

Ernest C. Ropes, who had just retired after twenty-four years as the Commerce Department's leading authority on the Soviet Union, also remained buoyantly—not to say naively—optimistic about the future commercial relations of the two countries. They were "natural" trading partners, he wrote in *Soviet Russia Today*. The United States was the industrial workshop for the USSR, which in its present rudimentary stage of development was the supplier of raw materials. The United States could be of "inestimable help" in raising Soviet living standards and thereby promote peace and prosperity. Trade expansion would stabilize economic relations and promote an exchange of knowledge and experience. "The usefulness and permanence of these relations," Ropes added, "would minimize the destructive effect of the rivalry between their two social systems, both of which possess attractions for countries to which they are adapted."[3]

Perhaps the most comprehensive brief for using trade to promote peace and prosperity came from yet another former Commerce Department official, Stella K. Margold. Her *Let's Do Business with Russia*, written in 1947 and published the following year, was both a how-to guide for the American businessman and a synthesis of all the famliar arguments of the proponents of American–Soviet trade: Russia represented a potentially enormous market because the 200 million Soviet citizens wanted to improve their standard of living; her vast natural resources guaranteed her foreign exchange earnings to pay for American imports; Soviet tariffs constituted no impediment to trade; and the government had an impeccable record for fulfilling its obligations. Further, Russia would not compete with American industry for years to come; meanwhile trade with the Soviets "can mean for the United States economic prosperity without major depression." Like Wallace and Ropes, Margold affirmed that trade "set the foundation for a lasting peace."[4]

These expressions of hope and positive thinking were misleading, however. The number of Americans who continued to view Soviet–American commerce as the talisman of domestic prosperity and international harmony had dwindled very sharply by 1947, being limited to certain Russophiles, American Communists, left-wing intellectuals, and radical politicians. A few businessmen and bankers, like Armand Hammer of Occidental Petroleum and the Cleveland financier Cyrus Eaton, still advocated doing business with the Soviets, but their pleas largely fell on deaf ears. They were out of step with the rising tide of anticommunism in the United States, and their analysis of American–Soviet relations since V-E Day was widely believed to rest on faulty premises about the USSR. *World Report*, for example, observed that the Soviets had committed a major blunder in their analysis of the capitalistic West. The economic collapse that Stalin predicted in 1945 had not occurred; nor had large loans to Russia materialized to shore up the Western economies.[5] Critics viewed Margold's book as a propaganda document and not a serious study. Its underlying premise, that the absence of American goodwill had hindered the expansion of trade, was simplistic. Trade seemed to be discussed not in the context of 1947–48 and the Soviets' refusal to sign the Bretton Woods document, but of 1918. One critic said flatly that the book offered nothing to ameliorate the very real and troublesome political and economic differences between the main antagonists.[6]

Indeed the pendulum had swung to the opposite extreme. One of the most critical assessments of Soviet actions came from the pen of J. Anthony Marcus, president of the Institute of Foreign Trade. A business executive with years of experience in the Soviet Union, Marcus had served as commercial adviser to Amtorg, the Soviet trading monopoly in the United States. His extensive background guaranteed his criticisms of Soviet behavior a serious hearing. In 1947 he published *The Real Russian Challenge*, in which he argued that the Bolshevik experiment had failed to improve the condition of the Russian people. The Soviet Union under Stalin was controlled by "the barbarian secret police," and Europe, prostrated by the war, offered "the same golden opportunity which Lenin had seen in Russia in the autumn of 1917."[7] Stalin's goal was world domination, Marcus asserted, a fact that neither Roosevelt nor Truman, nor Under Secretary of State Sumner Welles had really understood.

Marcus laid the blame for the Cold War squarely at the feet of Stalin, citing as proof of the Generalissimo's hostility to the West the decree of 10 June 1947, which forbade Soviet citizens to discuss economic matters with foreigners, and his false reports to the Russian people that the United States was suffering from an economic depression.[8] A firm believer in the interdependence of the international economy, Marcus declared that American business had much to offer a world trying to rebuild after the catastrophe of war. But there had to be some give as well as take. He accused the Soviets of denying the United States access to the raw materials and markets of Eastern Europe and concluded that the Kremlin's attempts to impose communism upon both halves of Europe and the rest of the world had made "cooperation well-nigh impossible."[9]

While accusations and counteraccusations were exchanged in print and on the lecture circuit, anticommunist legislators in both houses of Congress worked furiously to terminate what trade still existed between the two nations. On 4 March 1947 Republican Representative John P. Thomas of New Jersey, chairman of the Committee on Un-American

Activities, accused the Soviets of "legal espionage," which he defined as "the tapping of the inventive genius of America's industrial and military development for the benefit of the Soviet Government."[10] Acting through its representatives in the United States, Amtorg, and the Four Continent Book Corporation, Thomas asserted, the Soviet Union had "succeeded in obtaining practically every industrial and military patent from our Patent Office—hundreds of thousands of them—dealing with every phase of our technical development." He demanded to know why Wallace, as secretary of commerce, had countenanced this. Ten days later Republican Senator Ralph Flanders of Vermont introduced a joint resolution to prohibit all trade with the USSR until the Soviets fulfilled the obligations of the Yalta and Potsdam agreements.[11]

In June Republican Congressman Leon H. Gavin of Pennsylvania explicitly invoked the Pearl Harbor analogy to protest the continuation of oil exports to the USSR. Ten Soviet tankers were loading at that moment in the port of San Pedro, California. Gavin asked his colleagues: "Does this remind you of the days when oil and steel moved in great quantity to Japan?" Republican Congressman Alvin E. O'Konski of Wisconsin responded: "Whom the gods would destroy they first make mad," and wondered whether the United States was not already mad in shipping 1 million barrels of oil and gas to an adversary that held a reserve of 150 million barrels. The chairman of one House military subcommittee intended "to stop these shipments if it is humanly possible."[12] The Truman administration managed with difficulty to beat back conservative, chiefly Republican-sponsored bills in both houses that were ostensibly designed to curtail petroleum and gas exports to foreign countries but were in fact intended to eliminate trade with the Soviet Union entirely. Republican Senator John Sherman of Kentucky correctly observed: "I think what the proposed legislation amounts to is an embargo." If Congress wanted to put an embargo on oil, he declared, "that is a political question, not an economic one, and should not be acted upon hastily."[13]

As the level of congressional anger and frustration rose, the State Department unveiled a strategy for a general European defense "against totalitarian pressures." On 5 June 1947 Secretary of State George C. Marshall, speaking at Harvard University's commencement, disclosed that the United States would finance a massive program to rebuild the shattered economies of Europe. The Marshall Plan, officially titled the European Recovery Program (ERP), would eventually cost more than $12 billion and reintegrate Germany into European society. As initially conceived, the Marshall Plan extended aid to the countries of Europe, including the Soviet Union and its satellites in the East. The administration's objective was to achieve one of two goals: to place responsibility for the division of Europe clearly and unmistakably on the Russians if, as expected, they rejected the offer; or, in the unlikely event that they did not, to use aid as leverage to pry the European satellites away from a nearly total economic dependency upon the Soviet Union.[14]

The goals of this strategy were not immediately evident to most Americans. Some Republican legislators and disenchanted Democrats used the issues of aid and trade for partisan political purposes to attack the Truman administration both for its conduct of foreign affairs and its alleged mishandling of the domestic economy. The exchange between Democratic Senators John McClellan of Arkansas and James O. McMahon of Connecticut on 25 November was illustrative of the extent to which anticommunism and unabashed hostility to President Truman had become fused. McClellan precipitated the outburst by noting the inconsistency of continuing to trade with the Soviet Union while the American consumer was experiencing shortages at home. McMahon inquired whether his Arkansas colleague realized that in the July Paris conference held to thrash out the details of the Marshall Plan, the delegates had blatantly affirmed that the success of the recovery program depended upon resuming the traditional and normal channels of trade between Western and Eastern Europe. "I just wonder," he asked, "whether the Senator could reconcile for me the idea of cutting off export trade with Russia with the announced program that we will have of promoting trade east and west under the Marshall Plan?"[15]

The conservative isolationist Karl Mundt was furious with the administration because farmers from South Dakota were unable to send their crops to market due to a shortage of freight cars, while exporters were shipping more than two hundred such cars to the Soviet Union. At Mundt's insistence Republican Congressman Charles A. Wolverton, chairman of the Committee on Interstate and Foreign Commerce and a foe of New Deal policies, moved a privileged resolution in the House (H.R. 366) instructing the secretary of commerce to provide his committee with all data relevant to exports to the USSR. Wolverton declared that this "two-faced program didn't make sense economically or politically."[16]

Meanwhile Democratic Congressman Joseph Bryson of South Carolina told his colleagues in the House: "It does seem inconsistent that we should continue to provide funds to feed and clothe the war-torn countries of Europe with the hope of staying the hand of communism; while at the same time we trade with Russia, the mother of communism." Republican Senator William F. Knowland of California, another virulent anticommunist, also seized upon the proposed ERP to lash into the State Department for not closing down trade with the USSR. "I am unimpressed by statements made now by representatives of this Government who say there is no need at the present time to cut off these shipments to Russia," he told the Senate on 20 November. To the contrary, he insisted, "I believe that when Russia has been placing obstacles in the way of the rebuilding and rehabilitation of a war-torn world, when time after time by obstructive tactics in the United Nations, and in Germany, and elsewhere throughout the world, they have interposed obstacles in the path of economic rehabilitation of the world, it is high time for us to face realities."[17]

The Commerce Department officials who testified in the fall of 1947 before congressional committees that were weighing interim aid to Europe until the Marshall Plan went into operation were likewise subjected to merciless criticism for defending the administration's reluctance to sever all commercial ties with the Soviet Union. Republican Congressman Henry Cabot Lodge of Massachusetts, a member of the House Committee on Foreign Affairs, asked W. Averell Harriman, Wallace's successor as secretary of commerce, whether he thought that "the time has come to use the economic pistol, so to speak, in connection with Russia and her satellites with regard to export control licenses." Harriman, a proponent of firm but flexible policy, was initially evasive, and this caused Lodge to rephrase the question: "What I was really anxious to know was, do you believe the time has now arrived for us to make use of economic sanctions against Soviet Russia and her satellites?"[18]

Harriman's response was a masterpiece of obfuscation, which Lodge interpreted correctly to mean that the Truman administration did not contemplate invoking sanctions. Asked to elaborate, the secretary responded that economic sanctions should be used only as a last resort. Although the United States should continue to trade with the Soviet Union, it ought not to ship materials "which are a direct contribution to [Russia's] military strength." Then, adopting a viewpoint that afterward became identified with the State Department analyst George F. Kennan and the policy of containment, he declared that he supported the Marshall Plan because its success would "roll back behind the iron curtain" and would lead to "pressures which will force a change in [Soviet] policy."[19]

Under Secretary of Commerce William C. Foster took a similar tack in testimony before the House Committee on Interstate and Foreign Commerce. That body was conducting hearings on Mundt's resolution requesting the Commerce Department to name publicly individuals and firms that continued to do business with the Soviet Union. Foster refused, explaining that the resolution was incompatible with the public interest because the government relied upon the voluntary cooperation of American business firms for a variety of trade data. He then attempted to clarify the administration's position on trade with the Soviet Union, stating that the United States adhered to a policy of nondiscriminatory trading, in which the USSR took its place with other nations. The Soviet Union was able to purchase directly from American manufacturers, and the United States in turn benefited from the importation of certain strategic raw materials. True, trade had been "to our mutual advantage," but it also enhanced U.S. national security to foster East–West trade in order to promote the economic recovery of Europe and inoculate it against the virus of communism. Western Europe traditionally was the industrial workshop of the continent, and Eastern Europe was the breadbasket. The administration wanted this relationship to continue, in order to offset the satellites' economic reliance on the Soviet Union and to prevent a drain on commodities in short supply in the United States.[20]

A qualifying note appeared in Foster's testimony, however. By December 1947 the Soviets had decided not to participate in a project that required transmitting significant economic data to the United States, which also implied surrendering the exclusive economic controls they had instituted in Eastern Europe.[21] This led Foster to tell the committee that when the Marshall Plan went into effect, the shipment of some industrial and food items to the Soviet Union and its satellites might have to be delayed to make them available to Marshall Plan recipients, but that this should not be construed as singling out the Soviet Union for discriminatory treatment.[22]

Foster, no doubt, was sincere in his explanation. Yet even before the Soviets' announcement that Russia would not participate in the recovery program, the Truman administration began to develop a new trade policy toward the USSR and its satellites. In the spring of 1947 it had announced that it would continue in effect the comprehensive system of export controls that had complemented the military effort in World War II. Under authority of section 6 in the Act of 2 July 1940 Congress had granted the president sweeping export control powers to keep certain items of American manufacture, including military equipment, munitions, machinery, tools, and spare parts, from falling into the hands of aggressor nations.[23] Congress had retained the control system after 1945 chiefly for short supply and foreign policy objectives. The short supply controls were needed for commodities that were in great demand by the devastated countries, because Congress feared that their unrestricted export would cause severe shortages and inflationary pressures in the United States. Controls also allowed the Truman administration to treat its allies impartially, yet in accordance with Marshall Plan commitments.[24]

The extension of controls could also be used as economic leverage to modify Soviet political behavior and demonstrate to Congress that the administration was being firm with the communists. Through allocations assigned to the Marshall Plan it would become possible and plausible to deny to the Soviet Union access to American goods of potentially strategic significance that might enhance the Soviets' military capability. Export controls would become the economic equivalent of political containment, minimizing the United States' (and eventually Western Europe's) trade contacts with the Soviet bloc in order to deny Russia the major benefits of an international division of labor.[25] East–West trade was of far greater importance to the Soviet Union than to the United States. Thus it was possible to enhance U.S. national security at relatively little cost in lost income by requiring the Soviets to shift scarce resources from the military to the civilian sector. This was the theory; in practice the resort to export controls proved to be far less successful in retarding Soviet militarism and adventuristic foreign policies.

Two important observations are worth emphasizing here. First, as the testimony of Harriman and Foster indicated, the Truman administration was reluctant to cut off trade entirely with the Soviet Union. Its resort to export controls in the spring of 1947 was largely the result of congressional pressure to counter Soviet aggressiveness in a firm but careful fashion. From this perspective export controls may be seen as a delaying tactic, to quiet congressional criticism by denying to the Soviets only those American-made items of direct military value while continuing to sell them consumer goods. State and Commerce Department officials hoped that this tack would enable the United States to retain access to scarce raw materials from the Soviet Union, notably manganese. Second, neither Harriman nor State Department officials really believed in the efficacy or effectiveness of economic sanctions. Sanctions had only symbolic and nuisance value—perhaps creating a temporary bottleneck in Soviet industrial and military productivity, but of no lasting permanence. Like its American counterpart, the Soviet economy was too large and too complex to bring down with export controls, especially if the Russians were able to acquire identical or equivalent goods elsewhere. An economic embargo was destined to fail, especially if Western Europe did not support it with the same degree of rigor as did the United States.

The application of export controls to the Soviet bloc injected considerable tension into presidential–congressional relations, but the decision to take this course of action was not made abruptly. It was a logical culmination of the series of U.S.–Soviet clashes that had extended back over the previous two years and was a visible sign that the administration was doing more than simply "talking tough" to the Soviet Union. Those clashes continued: the abrupt termination of lend-lease; the "misplaced" loan request; the termination of United Nations Relief and Refugee Habilitation Administration, which deprived the Soviets of much-needed food and clothing; the decision of the American-financed Export-Import Bank to postpone a Czechoslovakian loan request after that government applauded Russian accusations that American dollars were used to promote "economic imperialism"; and Soviet "fishing" in the troubled political waters of Europe, Iran, Greece, and Turkey.

Nonetheless, slowly squeezing the Soviet bloc countries out of America's export trade marked a fundamental shift in U.S. postwar policy. As *U.S. News and World Report* observed, "The original program for postwar commerce, based upon the relations existing at the time of Germany's surrender, was for an expansion of trading all over the world." Ultimately Russia might decide that it was to her interest to deal more cooperatively with the West. "If not," the editors declared, "the United States now is prepared to fall back on Government controls to keep American products out of Communist-dominated countries."[26]

Not surprisingly, public notification that the Truman administration intended to apply the export control law to Russia and the Soviet bloc countries generated confusion and consternation among businessmen and exporters. Geraldine S. Du Puy, chief of the Commerce Department's Special Services Division, reported on 10 November 1947 that representatives from many firms had approached the agency with questions about the administration's attitude toward filling orders for industrial goods destined for the USSR. "It has been the policy of our government and continues to be the policy that we endeavor to maintain normal commercial relations with all friendly nations," she replied to an inquiry from the department's field office in Denver. She hastened to add, however, that the department was allocating virtually all commodities to its Positive List (items most in demand) according to quotas established after a country had supplied essential data to justify its need. "Up to the present time," she noted, "the Soviet Government has not seen fit to give the required data and accordingly has not received any quota of goods so allocated."[27]

The National Security Council (NSC) meanwhile was moving toward clarifying the administration's position on the cold war future of U.S.–Soviet trade. On 17 December 1947 it reaffirmed that one of the fundamental goals of U.S. foreign policy had been, and continued to be, "the revival of a working economy in the world as a necessary step toward the establishment and maintenance of world peace."[28] A free-trading, nondiscriminatory environment offered the benefits of peaceful economic competition, equal access to raw materials, and maximum efficiency through the principle of comparative advantage. An open, multilateral economic and political structure advanced the cause of peace, prosperity, and democracy.[29]

This was the ideal that Soviet political subversion—if not military aggression—of a prostrate Europe, torn apart by war, with its people hungry, its cities destroyed, its factories silent, its mines closed, and its railroads idled, threatened to undermine. Soviet refusal to participate in the Marshall Plan was simply the last straw that caused NSC to formalize the implementation of export controls. NSC justified its action by asserting that the Soviet Union, under Stalin's leadership, had become a menace to the peace and prosperity of the postwar world and, by definition, to the national interest of the United States. American security required "the immediate termination, for an indefinite period, of shipments from the United States to the U.S.S.R. and its satellites of all commodities which are critically short in the United States *or* which would contribute to the Soviet military potential." Somewhat naively in light of its assessment of the communist leadership, NSC hoped to terminate this trade "if possible without any overt act of arbitrary discrimination against the U.S.S.R. and its satellites."[30]

To implement NSC's decision the secretary of commerce solicited the advice of an interagency committee whose members included representatives of the Departments of State, Agriculture, Interior, and Commerce, the Atomic Energy Commission (AEC), and the Economic Cooperation Administration. The military and the National Security Resources Board participated as consultants. After careful deliberation the committee recommended that the Department of Commerce formulate two lists of goods that should come under export control: List 1A, goods that should be embargoed because of their direct military potential, and List 1B, items of indirect military potential that should be quantitatively controlled when their ultimate destination was the Soviet bloc. Secretary Harriman accepted this recommendation and announced that as of 1 March 1948 U.S. exporters would have to obtain from the department individually validated licenses for exports to all European destinations, a regulation carefully worded so as not to single out the Soviet Union and its satellites. Harriman cited as the authority for his action the Act of 2 July 1940 (54 Stat. 714) as amended, which was applied originally against the Axis powers.[31]

While NSC was moving to curtail American–Soviet trade, President Truman, also in December 1947, submitted his proposal for the European Recovery Program to Congress. Two months later, with the legislation tied up in a Republican Congress that was dividing its attention between slashing the budget and attacking the Democratic administration, a Soviet-engineered coup d'état in Czechoslovakia ended the last remaining coalition government in Eastern Europe. The seizure of power in Prague hastened Senate passage of the ERP on 14 March 1948. As the bill went into the House for consideration, Truman, fearful that events in Europe were moving beyond control, appeared before Congress. Somberly he declared, on 17 March 1948, that the Marshall Plan was "not enough" and asked for universal military training, the resumption of Selective Service, and quick passage of the recovery program by the House.

In a telegram to the White House on 18 March 1948 Republican Governor Harold E. Strassen of Minnesota insisted that "all shipments to Russia and her satellites, of machine tools, electrical equipment and scientific apparatus which will increase the potential power of a Communist war machine be immediately stopped" and that the Western European nations be asked to do the same "until such time as there is a definite change in Russian policy for the better and in the direction of peace." The national commander of the Catholic War Veterans, the Missouri State Council of War Dads, and the American Veterans of Essex County, Massachusetts, echoed similar sentiments.[32]

The virulence of this criticism, which was forestalling congressional action on the ERP legislation, caused Truman to rethink the initial decision not to impose economic sanctions against the USSR as his critics were demanding. At the cabinet meeting of 26 March 1948 he sought the views of both the Commerce Department and the State Department. Assessing the overall situation, Commerce Secretary Harriman pointed out that AEC already controlled exports of nuclear-grade material, State exercised jurisdiction over munitions and weapons exports, and Commerce was regulating commercial trade as best it could given Congress's niggardly funding of the Export Control Division. He reported that Commerce had been carefully screening shipments to Russia and the bloc countries and would soon seek congressional legislation to regulate both exports and imports. The latter would affect American importation of manganese, chromium, and certain other raw materials, Harriman observed, but this was consistent with the department's objective of "trying to get our trade with Russia on a *Quid Pro Quo* basis." The State Department endorsed this position but did not favor publishing a list of items that *could* be shipped to Russia and the bloc.[33]

One point was very clear. Neither Commerce nor State wished to engage in economic warfare by imposing a total embargo on American–Soviet trade as congressional critics demanded. On the other hand, the Truman administration did not want to leave the initiative in this area of foreign policy to fiercely anticommunist, partisan Republican legislators who might try to usurp presidential authority. Assistant Secretary of Commerce David K. Bruce's response to the inquiry of Congresswoman Mary T. Norton about the desirability of explicit legislation to curb trade with Russia makes this clear. Bruce said that such legislation was "unnecessary" and "undesirable," because the procedures set forth in the Export Control Act of 1940 were "adequate to protect the national interest" and to develop American–Soviet trade on a quid pro quo basis—a reference to continuing U.S. interest in acquiring strategic raw materials like Soviet manganese.[34]

With a presidential election only months away, Truman and his advisers also knew that the administration could not appear to be soft on communism. Hence the cabinet decided that the United States should maintain selective controls on specified commodities, which would be denied export licenses, while persuading European and Canadian suppliers to curtail their shipments to the Soviet bloc. The cabinet carefully hedged this decision, however. It continued to assert that East–West trade was necessary to the recovery of the Western European economies and indirectly to American prosperity. And it still sought access to Soviet strategic raw materials. "It is believed that this can be accomplished by our refusing to issue export licenses unless we are assured of the supplies which we desire," the cabinet concluded. "This would mean that we deal with the Soviets on a strictly *quid pro quo* basis with respect to the significant items of trade between the two countries."[35]

While the administration shored up its position on American–Soviet trade, the House of Representatives enacted, on 4 April 1948, the legislation establishing the ERP. From its inception the recovery program was caught up in the estrangement between Russia and the West. Section 117 (d) of the law directed the administrator for the Economic Cooperation Administration (ECA) "to refuse delivery in so far as practicable to participating countries of commodities which go into the production of any commodity for delivery to any non-participating European country which commodity would be refused export licenses to those countries by the United States in the interest of national security." As a matter of government policy the Truman administration went beyond Section 117 (d) to try to reach an understanding with the newly formed Organization for European Economic Cooperation (OEEC) governments on the desirability of adopting a parallel list of strategic goods that they would not export to the USSR and its satellites.[36]

From a security standpoint, then, the Truman administration had decided to use the recovery program to seal off the Soviet bloc from Western trade, credits, investment, and technology. The political objective was to create a Europe sufficiently coherent and cohesive to resist Soviet pressure and influence. This interpretation of Section 117 (d) conformed to the intent of the cabinet decision of 26 March 1948.[37]

The strategy of utilizing export control legislation and the ERP to retard Soviet war potential through a selective embargo, no matter how discreetly applied, aggravated the already strained relations between the two wartime allies. This was evident from Ambassador Walter B. Smith's report to Secretary of State George C. Marshall of his talks with the Russian foreign minister, V. M. Molotov. Smith had assured Molotov that the United States wished to expand its trade with the USSR and to assist Soviet economic recovery. He cited as proof of America's good intentions the wartime shipment of basic industrial plants to the Soviet Union under lend-lease, factories that could not have come into production before the war's end. The American change of attitude toward trade since then, Smith declared, "was again a direct reflection of the Soviet expansionist policies referred to in my previous conversation." Molotov had brushed aside this argument and curtly replied that the Soviets had always been grateful for lend-lease aid, "but United States policy had changed markedly in this respect—had not even fulfilled its trade agreements."[38]

Further evidence of the deterioration of American–Soviet relations came in the spring of 1948, when the Russians isolated West Berlin by blockading all highway, river, and rail traffic into the former German capital. Despite this provocation Truman reacted cautiously and fended off new congressional demands to declare economic warfare against the Soviet Union. Congressional conservatives again insisted that the United States apply export controls to nonstrategic as well as militarily important items—in effect, that it terminate all trade with the Soviets. Truman refused to be swayed by congressional pressure, continuing to believe that the United States required scarce strategic raw materials from Russia; more importantly, he feared Soviet retaliation against the Western European economies, which might sink the entire recovery program. Secretary of Defense James V. Forrestal addressed this last concern in the cabinet meeting of 25 June 1948: "The difficulty is that we have to consider dangers of an economic warfare—especially in connection with the revitalization of Western Europe and the danger of cutting off Russian exports to Europe if we cut Russia off completely."[39]

Even had the administration been willing to implement to the maximum the existing export control legislation, it probably could not have done so. It was not until 20 August 1948, eight months after NSC's decision to terminate trade in militarily strategic items, that the new secretary of commerce, Charles W. Sawyer, had in his hands List 1A of prohibited goods. Besides munitions and nuclear-related goods the list included metal-working machinery (grinding heads and spindle assemblies), chemical and petroleum equipment (for producing solid propellants and ion vacuum pumps), electrical and power-generating equipment (electric arc devices, photovoltaic cells), general industrial equipment (cable-making machinery, stenters), transportation equipment (helicopters), electronic equipment (cipher machines, pulse modulators), scientific instruments (computers, gravimeters), metals (titanium), chemicals (plastics, high-energy liquid fuels), and synthetic rubber.

The composition of that list and policy on how it should be used were the products of many experts in and out of government and by necessity amounted to something of a compromise. Thomas C. Blaisdell, a professor of political science at the University of California, Berkeley, and later assistant secretary of commerce, reflected only one viewpoint when he said that export controls should be applied in tandem with the broader objectives of American–Soviet policy and a coherent foreign economic policy. "Unless [these controls are] carried out in the full perspective of our diplomatic relationships and policy objectives, we may make more trouble than do good," he cautioned. He also advised against formulating export restrictions "in such a way as to create unfair competitive relationships between American businesses and European businesses which manufacture the same goods," a warning that was not always heeded and that proved to be the source of endless future controversy.[40]

With List 1A in hand, the Truman administration entered into negotiations with the OEEC nations that were recipients of Marshall Plan aid. The objective was to effect a multilateral rather than a unilateral approach toward export controls by persuading the Western European nations to agree to withhold from the Soviet bloc comparable items of military significance. In the judgment of American officials, voluntary cooperation rather than coercion was the key to success. Paul Hoffman, the ECA administrator and one of the point men in talks with the European governments, declared: "This is a satisfactory basis on which we can begin discussion. We think we may wind up and find that we will have suggestions for items that can be added and for some that we will ask for reconsideration."[41]

Meanwhile, on 27 August 1948 the Department of State and the ECA jointly sent a telegram to the president's special envoy to the negotiations, W. Averell Harriman, who was en route to London. The lengthy, ten-point telegram was the clearest expression thus far of the basic principles underlying the administration's policy objectives and was intended to serve as Harriman's instructions in the forthcoming talks. The communication emphasized the importance of a voluntary, multilateral approach to export controls to retard Soviet bloc war potential, with List

1A of prohibited strategic goods being identical, insofar as possible, for both the United States and Western Europe. Any differences between the two lists were to be referred back to NSC for a final determination. Further, Harriman was to accomplish this without endangering the success of the ERP, which implied a continuation of nonstrategic trade between the two halves of Europe, and without interrupting the flow of strategic raw materials from the Eastern bloc to the United States.[42]

With these guidelines in hand Harriman initiated talks with the OEEC governments. The effort to establish effective control over the sale of potentially strategic goods to the USSR and the bloc countries was marked from the outset by differences of opinion over the application of general principles and technical details. Most of the Western European countries placed primary emphasis on the principle of "net advantage," by which they meant that export controls should be administered so as not to injure free nations more than the communist bloc. The United States, on the other hand, emphasized then and later denying communist countries access to materials that might add to their military strength, often without regard to the net gain or loss to itself or its allies.

The United States could afford to take the tougher line with Russia and Eastern Europe for a very simple reason. It was one of the countries in the world that was least dependent on foreign trade. True, the foreign trade of the United States was enormous in absolute figures, but its importance may be gauged better in proportion to the size of its economy. According to this measure, as late as 1965, the United States tied for 101st place with Poland on a list of 114 countries in terms of foreign trade as a percentage of gross national product (GNP). From 1945 to 1950 U.S. foreign trade as a percentage of GNP was rather lower than it has been in most periods of this century.[43]

The OEEC nations, by contrast, had historically maintained a "workshop–breadbasket" relationship with the Soviet bloc nations. Russia was Great Britain's largest market in Europe. Sir Hartley Shawcross, president of Great Britain's Board of Trade, summed up the British—and continental—view very succinctly in 1951, on the occasion of an agreement to ship rubber to the USSR: "America has not and does not need to have any significant trade with the Soviet Union. It means little or nothing to her to discontinue the importation of furs, caviar, and crab. With us things are quite different. We obtain from the Soviet bloc essential foods and raw materials—and we believe that in these trade exchanges we get as good as we give, economically and strategically."[44]

Nonetheless, after seven months of negotiations, in which the threat of withdrawing ERP aid was an omnipresent possibility, Harriman reported considerable progress in translating agreement-in-principle into agreed-specific measures. Great Britain, the major trader with the bloc countries, consented to embargo all but 31 of the 163 items on the American List 1A and to control in part 9 other items. A handful remained in dispute because the British did not consider them to be of sufficient military significance to warrant embargo. In the case of the 31 other items Great Britain agreed only to quantitative limitations, arguing that their sale was necessary in order to secure from Eastern Europe raw materials essential to her own economic recovery.[45]

Harriman informed Washington that he believed the British modifications of List 1A were, for the time being, the version most acceptable to the other OEEC governments, especially France, Belgium, the Netherlands, and Luxembourg.[46] Greece, Turkey, Iceland, Ireland, and Portugal did not have any 1A trade with the Soviet bloc, whereas Italy, Norway, Denmark, Austria, and Bizonia (West Germany) were already prohibiting the export of 1A items. On 3 May 1949 Secretary of State Dean Acheson, Marshall's successor, recommended to NSC that the United States accept Britain's List 1A and persuade the other Western European countries to follow suit.[47]

In November seven nations—Great Britain, France, Italy, the Netherlands, Belgium, Luxembourg, and the United States—met in Paris to form the Consultative Group (CG) to develop in detail a multilateral approach for the control of strategic trade with the USSR and the European Soviet bloc. CG established in the French capital a permanent working-level Coordinating Committee (COCOM) to maintain a jointly acceptable list of goods subject to denial to the Soviet bloc. In 1952, in response to the Korean War, CG established another working committee, the China Committee (CHINCOM), to implement export controls over strategic trade with Communist China.[48]

Whether or not the Truman administration anticipated it at the time, forcing export controls upon the Western European nations for security reasons and in order to placate a hostile Congress had a profoundly disruptive effect on the future conduct of the United States' relations with its allies. Exhausted economically and weak militarily, the ERP countries had little choice except to give general consent to the American strategic embargo, modifying the details of the trade ban where they could, but reluctantly accepting it. The more arcane language of COCOM's regulations, however, allowed them some unforeseen latitude for maneuvering, and maneuver they did in response to local pressure, self-interest, and national integrity. To the dismay of anticommunist congressmen and American military and government officials, the Western allies exploited each and any loophole in the regulations to continue trading with the Soviets—even if at diminished levels.

In pressing for a multilateral enforcement of the strategic embargo, the United States had hoped to retard development of the Soviet Union's war potential and to retain its own relative military superiority over that nation. Paradoxically, the Truman administration did not believe the Soviets were ready to start a new war or to take over Western Europe. This is manifest from a Central Intelligence Agency (CIA) analysis of Soviet intentions, which concluded: "We do not believe that the events of the past six months [referring to the Berlin blockade] have made deliberate Soviet military action a probability during 1948–1949."[49]

Another aspect of the export control policy is also worth noting: the economic component of the Truman administration's containment doctrine, which George F. Kennan, a member of the State Department's Policy Planning Staff who had long experience of the Soviet Union, had so brilliantly articulated in July 1947. Writing anonymously in *Foreign Affairs*, he had argued that Soviet communism was like "a fluid stream which moves constantly, wherever it is permitted to move, toward a given goal." America's policy had to be "the firm and vigilant containment of Russian expansive tendencies." It was not to enter the Russian sphere or overthrow the Soviet regime but rather to block the Soviet effort to flow into "every nook and cranny available to it in the basin of the world." In time this would force a measure of circumspection on the Kremlin and "promote tendencies which must eventually find their outlet in either the break-up or the gradual mellowing of Soviet power."[50]

Whether economic or military means should be used to implement containment was not at all clear from Kennan's essay, but some civilian and military officials of the Truman administration perceived that economic pressure was a complement of military force to effect a modification of Soviet behavior. William S. Swingle, an official of the National Foreign Trade Committee and a member of the Commerce Department's Export Advisory Committee, told Commerce officials in January 1949 that the administration's proposed new export control law was a departure from the original purpose of the 1940 legislation, which was protection of the domestic economy. In the language of containment, he said: "You are getting away from that and you are trying to use export control now to satisfy a political situation . . . and your thinking is that you are trying to utilize export control to fight a cold war, and police the world, and using the American exporter as the medium by which you do that policing."[51]

A similar link between the application of economic pressure and containment was made by an American naval attaché assigned to the U.S. embassy in Moscow, in September 1949. Identified only as an officer who had spent most of his career analyzing the research and developmental phases of American and British industry, he wrote a lengthy report entitled "Soviet Dependence on the West, Its Nature and Implications." Prepared with the cooperation of embassy officials, the report was cast in the rhetoric of the Cold War and containment and circulated among the Departments of Commerce and State and other interested agencies. The Office of Naval Intelligence had endorsed it "as a valuable working paper serving to draw further attention to a subject that is obviously of urgent, supreme importance in United States foreign policy."[52]

Russia's aim, the author wrote, was to utilize East–West trade in order to develop her industrial economy to the point where she could underwrite world revolution. The West, unaccountably, had long underestimated Russia's dependence on this trade, a dependence that rendered her susceptible to external pressure. A strategic embargo might well cause the Soviet economy to falter and create precisely the internal strains (of which Kennan had written) that would force the Soviets to modify their aggressive behavior. Hence, though there was no real advantage to promoting trade with the USSR, there did exist a definite risk in allowing free-world trade to bail the Soviets out of their industrial problems.[53]

From this perspective Western refusal to trade with Russia constituted neither industrial sabotage nor economic warfare but simply a "failure to assist a self-appointed hostile country when it is in difficulty." A strategic embargo might cause the Soviets to develop the items being denied to them by the West, the author conceded, but they were bent on doing so anyway, under the program of autarchy. "An intelligent, increased trade blockade on the part of the West seems to be the only reasonably sure alternative to eventual war or eventual success of the Communist Revolution." It could produce as decisive a victory over the Soviets "as we could [win] by an act of war." Imposition of a blockade now might forestall an early war because the Soviets' economic deficiencies would not sustain a major conflict. On the other hand, to continue to trade and help them to reconstruct their industrial base could lead the West into an "economic Munich."[54]

As the economic dimension of containment gained currency among Washington officialdom, a new problem demanded the Truman administration's immediate attention. The 1940 statutory authority under which the president had acted to limit Soviet acquisition of strategic technology was due to expire on 28 February 1949. In an attempt to head off more drastic legislation, such as a total ban on trade with the Soviet Union, the executive petitioned Congress to extend the law. The Eighty-first Congress, as had its three immediate predecessors, approved the request after brief hearings, until 30 June 1951.[55]

The House and Senate Banking and Currency Committees both held open hearings on H.R. 1661, the extension bill. There was little business or public opposition to continuing the program, and the bill, enacted into law on 26 February 1949, did not differ substantially in scope from the original legislation. The same discretionary authority was given to the executive to approve or reject proposed exports of "any articles, materials, or supplies, including technical data." However, the objectives of export controls were now restated in the context of the deteriorating relations between the United States and Russia. The new law stated that in addition to safeguarding against a drain of scarce materials from the domestic economy, restrictions were required "to exercise the necessary vigilance over exports from the standpoint of their significance to the national security."[56]

The United States would thus exercise controls on the export of strategic materials and equipment in a manner that would limit the growth of the war potential of the Soviet bloc. It would not interfere with trade in goods that had little or no strategic significance. Acting Assistant Secretary of Commerce Thomas C. Blaisdell affirmed this interpretation of the proposed law in testimony before the House committee. "In the light of the growing concern of democratic nations over the policies of the Eastern European nations, it is quite clear that our national security requires the exercise of such controls to complement export controls over arms, ammunition, and implements of war which are administered in the State Department," he observed. He added that it was hoped this could be done without interrupting East–West trade or disrupting the flow of raw materials from Russia to the United States.[57]

In complying with the Export Control Act of 1949, the Department of Commerce regulated exports to Soviet bloc nations by means of two types of licenses: the validated license, a formal document issued to the exporter, which authorized shipment to the bloc country of the commodities and amounts specified therein; and the general license, a blanket authority that authorized the exporter to ship a specific list of commodities, adjudged to be of little strategic value, without filing applications for individual licenses. If an item proposed for shipment appeared on List 1A, the Commerce Department routinely denied the request for an export license.[58]

Subsequent enforcement of the 1949 law was severely criticized because of loopholes large enough for an American exporter or friendly Western nation to drive a Mack truck through to the Soviet Union. The CIA, for example, reported on 31 May 1949 that the intent, if not the letter, of the law was being systematically disregarded.[59] Some Western European countries were not cooperating with the strategic embargo policy, and as a result ball bearings, which were on List 1A, were still being shipped from Sweden and Switzerland to the USSR. The entrepôt trade and transshipment of strategic commodities of American origin behind the Iron Curtain were proceeding largely unchecked through third parties (Belgium and the Netherlands).[60] Russia, moreover, was successfully using clandestine and indirect attempts (for instance, dummy corporations established in Vienna) to obtain strategic items from the West. Other nations' resale of U.S. Army surplus equipment (such as crawler tractors powered by diesel engines of the type included in List 1A) also allowed the Soviet bloc to acquire strategic goods.[61]

One classic example of the early confusion in enforcing the law involved a shipment of molybdenum from the United States to a private purchaser in Great Britain, and its subsequent resale to the Soviet Union. A metallic chemical element used in alloys and windings for electrical resistance furnaces, molybdenum was on List 1A and therefore could not be exported behind the Iron Curtain. At the request of Commerce officials who became suspicious about the cargo's final destination, the State Department telegraphed its embassy in London to ascertain whether the metal would be used in Great Britain. For some unknown reason U.S. officials in London delayed their investigation. When at last they came up with specific information, the molybdenum was on the high seas bound for Russia. Secretary of State Dean Acheson, irate and embarrassed, demanded to know why embassy officials had procrastinated and had not taken steps immediately to recover the shipment while it was still in Great Britain. The damage already done, Acheson was reduced to asking sarcastically whether the British government had put molybdenum on its List 1A before, or after, the transshipment.[62]

Unlike other federal agencies, especially the military, the Department of State had little confidence in the efficacy of the strategic embargo to exploit Soviet weaknesses or to wring concessions for the West. Export controls might have an important qualitative impact on the Soviet economy, by intensifying bottleneck conditions in the manufacture of ball bearings, precision instruments, electrical equipment, or spare parts, but they had not prevented the Russians from fulfilling their Five Year Plan. Nor had the strategic embargo seriously affected the functioning of the Soviet economy thus far.[63]

In the fall of 1949, with Nationalist China collapsing before the Communists—which touched off a sharp political debate in the United States —the Department of State was unable to persuade the American people and other government agencies of the essential futility of export controls. Congressional and public opinion focused instead on why the Western European ERP countries were dragging their heels and refusing to take action parallel to the United States'. Secretary of Commerce Sawyer, for example, complained to James S. Lay, Jr., the executive secretary of NSC, on 25 April 1950: "For many months we have urged the need for bringing Western European countries into line with our embargo and restrictions. This has not been accomplished." The Soviets and European manufacturers, particularly the British, had benefited from leaks in the system; the real sufferers were "American manufacturers and anti-Communist activity." The next day Sawyer elaborated on his complaint in a report to NSC marked "Top Secret," asserting that the United States had reached "a critical point in the use of export control powers in the interests of national security, as a consequence of our inability to persuade the nations of Western Europe to adopt a standard of control as strict as that applied by the United States."[64]

If the current gap in enforcement of the export control system persisted, Western Europe not only would be abetting the Soviet war machine but also would become economically dependent upon Soviet and Eastern European markets. American manufacturers, who had willingly excluded themselves from the same markets, would suffer because of their patriotism. "To continue a differential standard of control," warned Sawyer, ". . . would unduly encourage the selective expansion of strategic industries in Western Europe and would also discriminate unjustifiably against U.S. producers of export goods."[65] The threat to Western security, economic dependence on the communist enemy, and the loss of potential markets by American businessmen were arguments that the Truman administration could ill afford to ignore while Congress was snapping at its heels. On 4 May 1950 NSC instructed Secretary of State Acheson to use the upcoming meeting of the foreign ministers of Great Britain, France, the United States, and the NATO council to impress upon the European allies the importance the United States attached to parallel action in the sphere of security export controls.[66] Despite the preponderance of American power, this course of action would prove hazardous and fraught with difficulties for Western unity.

With few exceptions, American officials never fully appreciated the overwhelming importance that Western Europeans attached to trade with the East for their economic recovery and prosperity. Their seemingly laissez-faire attitude drove American congressmen and bureaucrats to distraction, because it meant the strategic embargo could not be made ironclad. A CIA memorandum written in the fall of 1950 provided some insight into this problem: "The reluctance of Western European governments to restrict exports of security items to the Soviet orbit . . . stems in part from their concern with maintaining and developing export markets in areas capable of supplying in return 'dollar-saving' food and raw materials. The importance of 'East–West' trade in contributing to the solution of Western Europe's balance of payments problem has been taken as axiomatic."[67] The assumption of a "natural complementarity" of the industrial and agricultural/raw-material producers of Europe had led to a widespread belief that the United States was interfering with Western Europe's lifeline by trying to curtail East–West trade. The Western countries clearly wanted that trade to rise to the high levels of the prewar period. "Furthermore," the CIA reported, "in Western Europe [*sic*] capitals the pressures of private sellers may have produced an exaggerated estimate of national economic interest in uninterrupted trade with the Soviet orbit."[68]

W I T H the onset of the Cold War, politics more than economics became the determining factor in American–Soviet trade relationships. The Truman administration was under intense pressure from congressional conservatives and right-wing groups to eliminate every commercial as well as political, social, and cultural contact with the Soviet Union and its Eastern European satellites. Trade controls became the economic equivalent of political containment. A trade embargo, coordinated with political firmness, would presumably keep the USSR in a position of relative military and economic inferiority to the United States—possibly even lead to a collapse of the Soviet regime—and thereby minimize Soviet opportunities for aggression in foreign policy.

However, in the interest of promoting European economic recovery, preventing a drain on scarce U.S. goods, keeping Eastern Europe from becoming economically dependent on the Soviet Union, and retaining access to certain strategic raw materials, the Truman administration initially resisted domestic pressures for a Western trade embargo of the socialist countries. It did not truly believe that economic sanctions could topple the Soviet regime or compel the Stalinist government to modify its behavior. However, as anticommunist sentiment in Congress became more vocal and public opinion turned against the Soviet Union, the pressures to "get tough" became real enough to compel the administration toward a stronger anti-Soviet policy.

To quiet criticism but also to avert a rupture of American–Soviet diplomatic relations, the administration had to walk a fine line. It accepted congressional legislation that ostensibly continued wartime prohibitions on the export of items in short supply in the United States but that actually was intended to curtail exports of commodities that might contribute to the military potential of the Soviet regime. In 1948 the Department of Commerce placed most exports to the Soviet bloc under mandatory licensing controls (it extended the same requirement to Communist

China in 1949). The capstone of this initial effort to deny militarily strategic commodities to the USSR was the Export Control Act of 1949, which Truman accepted only because it left the executive some leeway in implementing the law.

Harassed by congressional critics, the Truman administration also gave institutional expression to the demand that the Western Europeans adopt parallel controls. In 1949 the British and French formulated a list of strategic commodities that was minimally acceptable to American officials. At the United States' behest the multinational COCOM and its senior body, the Consultative Group, were established in 1949 and 1950 as informal agencies to coordinate the system of Western restrictions on the sale of strategic goods to communist countries.

COCOM was based on the recognition that an effective embargo required European and Japanese cooperation. But from the outset these nations reacted to the United States' more stringent unilateral embargo and to the multilateral export control system with much hesitation and indecision. Besides political differences, economic factors made the functioning of COCOM much less than smooth. In 1948–50 Western European nations viewed trade with Russia and Soviet Eastern Europe as indispensable to economic recovery from the war. Such trade would alleviate the dollar gap to the extent that it would become possible for Western Europe to import raw materials from nondollar areas rather than from dollar areas. Further, nurturing East–West trade might also strengthen the prices of certain commodities, chiefly staple goods, produced by the Western European economies.

For these reasons many Europeans considered Americans to be insensitive to the importance and benefits of their trade with the Soviet bloc. And despite the preponderance of American power, enforcement of the multilateral export control system was fraught with difficulties for Western unity. Differing political and economic imperatives portended that the Truman administration—and its successors—would be preoccupied by the need to bring into line the trade of many industrialized nations whose interests were numerous and divergent. Trade statistics reflected this. U.S. exports to the Soviet Union dropped from $236 million to $10 million between 1946 and 1950, and American exports to the entire Soviet bloc were a mere $2 million in 1953. The reverse was true for its Western European partners. Noncommunist European trade to Russia and Soviet Eastern Europe actually increased from $622.8 million in 1948 to $626.1 million in 1951, despite the Western embargo. With the definition of strategic exports as elastic as it was, there also flourished a considerable illicit trade between Western and Eastern Europe, to the further consternation of critics of the Truman administration.[69]

CHAPTER THREE

The Politics of Export Controls:
Legislative Responses

THE entire question of trade sanctions took on a new urgency with the outbreak of the Korean War. On the morning of 25 June 1950 some 75,000 troops of the Democratic People's Republic of Korea bolted across the thirty-eighth parallel, the boundary drawn after World War II by the United States and Russia that had sliced Korea into North and South. The Korean conflict was the catalyst for a hardening of American attitudes toward the Soviet Union and for a reassessment of the Export Control Act of 1949. The war also exacerbated the growing differences of opinion between Congress and the executive over the nature, extent, and effectiveness of the strategic embargo and brought more clearly into focus fissures within the highest levels of the executive branch on the appropriate application of export controls in the cold—now hot—war with the Russians.

Congressional response to the Korean War was swift and furious. Legislators, especially Republicans and conservative Democrats, blamed the Soviet Union for the conflict; the United States' ungrateful allies who had received ERP aid, for supplying the communists with the tools to fight the war; and the Truman administration, for being the dupe of an international conspiracy. Republican Congressman John Phillips of California declared on 27 July 1950: "It is sophistry to me . . . to say that we are not paying for the aid sent by the Soviet Union [to North Korea] because the materials shipped are manufactured in a Marshall Plan country if, at the same time, we are contributing in money or goods to the sustaining economy of that country." Congressman James T. Patterson of Connecticut observed, in September 1950, that "[the] continuing practice of ECA [Economic Cooperation Administration] countries supplying Russia with materials necessary to the prosecution of a war demonstrates a shameful disregard for the lives of our forces in Korea."[1]

In the wave of anticommunist hysteria that swept the United States the onus of the blame for the loss of American lives was attributed to Russian machinations and the greed of the Western European allies, but several legislators argued that the United States was also at fault.[2] Congressman Russell V. Mach of Washington noted that his country had purchased nearly $3.5 million in goods from Russia, mostly the luxuries of furs and canned crab. "We must stop this unholy trade with the enemy and insist that all nations allied with us do likewise." Mach singled out the State Department, which he alleged was riddled with subversives, as the offender, and insisted that the agency needed "an immediate and thorough house cleaning." Congressman H. Alexander Smith of Wisconsin, a member of the House Foreign Affairs Committee, resurrected memories of Pearl Harbor to insist that the United States and all Marshall Plan aid recipients cut off trade and diplomatic relations with Russia and her satellites. Outside Congress, William Green, president of the American Federation of Labor, advocated a complete boycott of trade with the Soviet Union.[3]

Besides criticizing leaks in the West's embargo policy, Republicans maintained a drumfire of accusations that the Democrats had not done enough to deter Soviet aggression. Often resorting to McCarthy-like demagoguery, they implied that the Truman administration was itself being subverted by communists and fellow travelers and betrayed by its erstwhile allies in Europe. Retired Brigadier General Frank L. Lowley, formerly the commandant of the American sector of Berlin, accused State Department officials—"our wax mustached boys"—of appeasing the Russians. Former Republican Governor Alf M. Landon of Kansas denounced the president's foreign policy for being "confused, faltering and invariably late, without a clear cut positive objective." It should have sought the destruction of Russian communist power not necessarily by force but by economic warfare. Melchior Polyi, an Eastern European émigré, took the Western European nations to task not simply for their trade but for giving the Soviet Union access to American technology. "The East–West trade of Europe and Hong Kong, which our allies use even for such unethical purposes as to divert ECA materials, also permits drawing upon our [the United States'] store of technology."[4]

A common theme running through the words of critics of the administration's handling of export controls was the importance of *effective* economic coercion to modify the Soviets' aggressive behavior. Former President Herbert Hoover, addressing the American Newspaper Association in April 1950, declared: "If the free nations join together they have many potent moral, spiritual *and even economic* weapons at their disposal." Retired Army General Lucius D. Clay explicitly connected the Cold War to the economic component of containment. The Cold War, he told delegates to the National Foreign Trade Convention in October 1950, was as much an economic war as it was a political conflict. Russia's huge rearmament program made it "desirable to stop certain types of goods immediately helpful to her war effort being sent behind the Iron Curtain."[5]

Impassioned partisan rhetoric aside, congressional anger manifested itself in a flurry of resolutions and bills to punish the Soviet Union for instigating the Korean War, and the United States' NATO allies for abetting the communist war machine by evading the strategic embargo. Prodded by the Truman administration, Democratic leaders in the House of Representatives successfully and quietly interred these expressions of protest in the Rules Committee.[6] The one notable exception was the attempt of Senate conservatives to cut off economic and financial assistance to any country that exported strategic items to the USSR in violation of the Export Control Act of 1949. This was the Wherry amendment to the Supplemental Appropriations Bill for 1951. Sponsored by Republican Senator Kenneth Wherry of Nebraska, the amendment was targeted against the Western European nations that were the recipients of ERP funds.[7] Its co-sponsors in the Senate were influential conservatives from both parties, including the Republicans James P. Kem of Missouri (an implacable foe of Secretary of State Dean Acheson) and George W. Malone of Nevada and Virginia Democrat Harry F. Byrd. In the House the powerful Mississippi Democrat John D. Rankin strongly supported the intent of the amendment.

The likelihood of the amendment's being enacted so alarmed administration officials, who feared its effect on Western unity, that the president himself was forced to intercede to engineer its defeat. At the cabinet meeting of 15 September 1950 Averell Harriman voiced this concern, warning that the amendment was likely to disrupt the United States' delicate relations with its NATO allies, whom it was trying to persuade to accelerate their rearmament.[8] Truman responded that he would try to persuade the Democratic leadership to "knock it out" in conference. Five days later he wrote to the chairman of the House Appropriations Committee, Clarence Cannon of Missouri, a long letter urging the conferees to drop the amendment from the final bill in the interest of national security. He hinted that he would veto the legislation otherwise.[9]

Truman's letter voiced the administration's fear that the Wherry amendment would play hob with diplomatic efforts in progress to persuade America's NATO allies to rearm and to support the Export Control Act of 1949 more vigorously. "This amendment," he explained, "is of such grave importance, and is fraught with such danger to the United States and to world peace, that I feel I must make a special request to Congress to eliminate it in completing action upon this bill." He conceded that he had no quarrel with its spirit; but the effect of the amendment, because of its indiscriminate ban, would be to weaken the free world more than the Soviet bloc. The amendment would precipitate a total embargo on East–West trade, including commerce in peaceful goods, which was contrary to U.S. security interests and might push the underdeveloped countries of Asia and Africa into the Soviet orbit. By contrast, Truman wrote, quiet diplomacy among the United States' allies and friends was "far superior to the arbitrary blanket approach prescribed in the amendment now in question."[10]

The president's personal intercession was for the moment successful. The House and Senate conferees endorsed, and Congress passed, the Supplemental Appropriations Bill without the Wherry amendment. Instead, after stormy debate in which new evidence surfaced that the Western European nations were violating the intent of the export control law, a majority of irate legislators enacted, on 27 September 1950, the Cannon amendment to the Foreign Assistance Act of 1948. This amendment, which applied during any period in which American forces were engaged in combat at the behest of the United Nations Security Council, gave the president restricted discretionary power to cut off all U.S. economic and financial aid to a country whose trade with the Soviets was contrary to the national interest as determined by the National Security Council (NSC). Congress also extended the restrictions on credit and financial transactions with debt-defaulting nations, as specified in the Johnson Act of 1934, to include the Soviet Union. The Department of Justice interpreted the loan prohibition to apply to credit beyond 180 days, thereby rendering it impossible for American exporters to grant long-term loans to finance trade with Russia and Soviet bloc nations. The law was theoretically intended to cripple the Soviet economy, which required credit of several years' duration when placing orders for large shipments of Western manufactured equipment. The denial of long-term credits (like most-favored-nation trading status) by the United States turned out to have more symbolic than substantive support, even though as a matter of self-esteem the Russians strove in the future to have the Johnson Act prohibitions lifted.[11]

Contrary to congressional intent, invoking the Johnson Act adversely affected American manufacturers, for it operated as a practical competitive handicap upon businessmen who wanted to sell their goods in the Soviet and East European markets. The chief beneficiaries of the ban turned out to be exporters in the major Western trading countries who were not subject to similar limitations. Indeed, in planning for economic recovery in the late 1940s, the Western European nations had deliberately relied on trade with Eastern Europe, their traditional market. Besides this direct government interest in keeping open Western Europe's foreign trade channel with the East, there also existed large vested interests. Important segments of industry and labor in the West were directly or indirectly linked to the eastern trade and feared that an embargo of railway equipment, generators, heavy machinery, and oil machinery would only promote more intense competition in already crowded markets, or domestic unemployment. One British Labour party leader in 1952, commenting on American pressures to conform to the U.S. embargo policy, asked: "Against whom is the cold war being conducted—Britain or the Soviet Union?"[12]

This observation was widespread among Western Europeans and symptomatic of the embargo's adverse effect on European–American relations in the 1950s. Western Europeans utterly detested America's high-handed actions such as the Battle Act and the Cannon amendment, which violated two fundamental principles, one guiding the behavior inside an alliance like NATO, in which solutions to conflicts must be resolved through compromise, and the other being a cardinal tenet of international law and behavior, in which contracts negotiated between sovereign entities are to be kept. The Battle Act had provided no exception whatsoever for the fact that many contracts between Western exporters and Eastern importers had been entered into before the law's enactment.

Despite Western Europe's reluctance to follow the American lead, Congress directed the president in June 1951 to take steps, as soon as possible, to withdraw tariff concessions that had been extended in the 1930s to the USSR and the countries of Eastern Europe. This was embodied in the Trade Agreement Extension Act. To comply with this directive Truman served notice to the affected countries (the USSR on 23 June and the bloc nations on 1 August 1951) that the United States was initiating the legal machinery to abrogate its commercial treaties with them. This action effectively denied most-favored-nation status to imports from the Soviet bloc (except Yugoslavia, which had broken with Moscow in 1948). The higher duties went into effect in January 1952, after expiration of the notice required under treaty provisions. Russian manganese ore, which the administration had previously considered to be essential to U.S. security, was now to be taxed at the rate of one cent per pound of metal content, as compared with the previous duty of one-fourth cent per pound.[13] Section 11 of the 1951 law further authorized the president to prohibit imports from Russia of seven types of furs and skins, which accounted for thirty percent of all American imports of Russian undressed furs.[14]

Congressional conservatives also attempted to gut the economic recovery program. In the late summer of 1950, while the administration fought a rearguard action to prevent these legislators from reducing or eliminating altogether allocations to Marshall Plan recipient countries,

NSC began a comprehensive reexamination of its export control policy. Affirming that no executive department or agency was at that time advocating all-out economic warfare against the Soviet Union, which would mean terminating Western trade in peaceful goods, NSC groped toward a policy that balanced national security with European economic recovery; identified which commodities were to be restricted, and how tightly; determined whether neutral Austria and Sweden should be subject to different licensing procedures; and resolved differences between the European and American embargo lists.[15]

On the first of these issues the battle lines were reasonably clearly drawn, with the State Department and Economic Cooperation Administration (ECA) contending that the problem was not merely a matter of military security versus European recovery, but considerably more complex. The State Department's position rested on the assumptions that a general war in the early future was not certain; that Eastern bloc trade still was important to the economic strength of Western Europe; that the political repercussions in Europe, if that trade were lost, might be serious; and that American pressure to curtail that trade, if applied heavy-handedly, could "impair the growing sense of political solidarity among North Atlantic Treaty countries."[16] This last point was particularly relevant to State Department officials because the Truman administration had been eager to get the Western European countries to rearm, using foreign aid as an inducement. In one form or another, the issue of maintaining Western solidarity would become an overriding consideration in virtually every future effort to revise, modify, or soften the basic export control policy of the United States and the COCOM nations.[17]

The Departments of Defense and Commerce and the National Security Resources Board (NSRB) placed military security ahead of economic recovery and used as their justification NSC Paper no. 68, of April 1950, which had emphasized the importance of retarding the development of Soviet war potential. The position of the Department of Defense was understandable given its mission; Commerce's reasoning was more controversial. It argued that Western European dependence upon trade with the East for economic recovery had not been a valid argument since March 1948, the date of the Marshall Plan.[18]

The lineup was not nearly as predictable on the second issue: the range of commodities and the extent of restriction. The Department of State took the position, essentially concurred in by ECA and the Department of Commerce, that the United States should update its own control list in light of the Korean War experience, adding newer militarily strategic items and dropping older, less strategic commodities, doing so regardless of whether its allies followed suit. However, State Department officials decided that the presumption "should be against major additions to the U.S. proposals" at the forthcoming COCOM negotiations in Paris. Motivating this cautious approach was a concern that a "full speed ahead" attitude by the United States could result in a greater disparity between the American and European control lists, or that the United States would be demanding that its allies make a greater economic sacrifice than itself. By contrast, the Department of Defense and NSRB contended that the United States should maintain severely restrictive export controls, automatically denying export licenses for all commodities, old and new, that had significant war potential. The Defense Department's rationale for opposing any cuts in the Positive List was that Russian economic dependence on the West was so great that it afforded the West "a powerful tool" for obtaining major concessions from the Soviets.[19]

On the third issue, how to handle Austria and neutral Sweden, the division was again evident. The Department of State and ECA preferred to treat both countries in accordance with policy for the other OEEC nations in the hope that Sweden, especially, could be aligned with NATO in the event of war. The Department of Defense and NSRB, fearing that the industrious Swedes and Austrians would continue to act as conduits for the shipment of strategic machinery and advanced technology to the Soviet Union, wanted to enforce the List 1A (absolute prohibition) and List 1B (quantitative limits) controls against both countries. The Department of Commerce stood somewhere between the two: it wanted to deny the Austrians all strategic items except where political considerations dictated otherwise; and instead of cutting off Sweden, it preferred to allow export license applications for that country to accumulate—which then could be used as a negotiating chip with the Swedes.[20]

The lengths to which the United States should go to persuade the OEEC countries to impose parallel (that is, identical) export controls engendered the sharpest disagreement. The Department of State, ECA, and NSRB firmly believed, in light of the Korean war effort, that the United States should not threaten to invoke sanctions against its allies; rather the administration should give American negotiators in COCOM room to maneuver by allowing them to relax controls on some items in return for agreement to include others of greater military significance. This was consistent with the Truman administration's multilateral approach to export controls. NSRB argued cogently that by impeding European rearmament and morale, sanctions posed a greater threat to U.S. security. The threat of sanctions would be recognized as a bluff, and backfire. "The prime necessity," NSRB declared, "is to speedily break the present stalemate, achieve joint agreement with our allies on consistent, if not identical policies, and achieve consistency within our own government." Only the Department of Defense insisted that the amount, nature, and timing of economic aid to Western Europe be made conditional on the OEEC countries' enforcing export controls identical to those of the United States.[21]

The Commerce Department's response was in some respects the most interesting, because it illuminated the dilemmas inherent in formulating a coherent and effective policy when individual national interests were so diverse. It also indicated that even within a department there could be far from unanimity on how best to proceed. To cite one example: the Commerce Department's stance before NSC was that Western Europe had, thanks to the ERP, completely recovered from the wartime devastation and was now functioning as the largest supplier of strategic material to Russia and Eastern Europe. The Truman administration should therefore employ every stratagem at its disposal to negotiate an ironclad agreement on parallel controls.[22] Yet within the department Assistant Secretary Thomas C. Blaisdell, sensitive to the tension that had developed within the Western alliance under the existing policy, argued that the United States ought to consider the relative requirements of the different countries rather than insist upon parallel controls.[23]

Blaisdell's concerns were overruled as the department reacted to past criticisms of its enforcement of the Battle Act. Furthermore, the department warned that a rebellion was brewing within the OEEC, under British leadership, against the very principle of export controls. "Unless the attitude of the countries of Western Europe can be changed at a high level, with the result that the U.S. export control program is accepted," it advised, "the United States cannot exercise a wholly effective control of strategic goods to the Soviet bloc." Once this dissension was quelled, the Commerce Department advised NSC to announce a moratorium on additional controls, in order to allay allied fears of even more stringent controls.[24]

At last, on 24 August 1950, NSC issued Action no. 347, which attempted to accommodate the divergent views. This directive stated that the government of the United States should continue to negotiate with the OEEC countries for agreement on a common export control policy, but that it also should deny strategic items to any Western nation that persisted in shipping identical items or equivalent amounts to Russia and her satellites. To comply with this, on 18 September the Department of Commerce issued Program Determination Order no. 381, which tried to reclassify export items more closely in accordance with the terms "strategic," "identical," and "equivalent amount."[25] Unfortunately, rather than clarifying which goods fit into the List 1A and List 1B categories, the order caused a rush of applications for export licenses. Nearly 22,000 requests ran afoul of the Commerce Department's red tape, of which 1,500 were for the shipment of essential items to ECA countries. This bottleneck greatly distressed State Department officials, but it was not until the end of October that Secretary Acheson finally persuaded Commerce Secretary Sawyer to break the logjam and get the urgently needed goods moving again to ECA recipients. Even then Sawyer, a cautious man, would not act until he had President Truman's approval.[26]

When that was forthcoming, Sawyer agreed to use as the criteria for determining security-strategic items the guidelines that were in force prior to September 1950. Then, on 24 November, after three months of discussion and revision, President Truman approved NSC's revised statement of export and control policy. The new document declared that after formal notification any disputed List 1A items that the United States deemed sufficiently strategic to warrant continued embargo would be denied to any Consultative Group (CG) country, unless it gave assurances that identical items would be totally denied to Russia and her satellites.[27] The same principle applied to items on List 1B, unless each CG country gave assurances that the quantities exported to Eastern Europe were consistent with America's security interest. This was true also of the export of capital equipment capable of producing 1A and 1B items, especially in cases where evidence of transshipments to the Soviet bloc existed. NSC also empowered the Department of Commerce to review all items in dispute with the OEEC governments and to determine whether they should remain on the United States' embargo list, reserving to itself jurisdiction over classification disputes between the Department of Commerce and any other federal agency.[28]

This new statement of policy, which was directed toward placating Congress as much as it was to show the ERP countries that the United States was serious, was to become effective at the conclusion of the current COCOM negotiations; in any event, not later than 8 January 1951. The significance of the changes that had occurred in the objectives and implementation of the Export Control Act for America's relations with the USSR, its European allies, and its domestic political economy was not lost upon officials of the Truman administration. Charles A. Frank of the Commerce Department, for example, had noted in April 1949 that the shift in emphasis of export controls, from short supply at home to security considerations, had directed attention toward the growing importance of foreign policy rather than domestic economic factors. Sixteen months later, Assistant Secretary of Commerce Thomas C. Blaisdell described the implications of the Export Control Act and the Cannon amendment more succinctly when he stated: "The development of our security licensing policy toward the Soviet Union and other Communist states has introduced into our international commerce policy the dominant note of national interest as contrasted with our former policy of freedom of private trade."[29]

The best example of this adjustment in policy was the Truman administration's reaction to the breach between Yugoslavia and Russia, which had developed in 1948 and became final two years later. Thanks to the presence of extremely competent embassy personnel in Belgrade, Washington became convinced that the split between Tito and Stalin was real, that it was in the interest of the United States to see that rift continue, and that steps should be taken toward that end.[30]

Despite Yugoslavia's communism and lack of freedom Tito's independent stand against Moscow was the first important setback for Soviet postwar imperialism, and therefore a significant symbol in the Cold War. If that war were at any time to become a hot war (and Korea demonstrated how this could happen), Tito's thirty-three divisions constituted the largest fighting force in Europe outside the Soviet Union. The strategic advantage of a truly independent Yugoslavia was undeniable: giving aid to Tito to maintain his army at a high level of preparedness was viewed within the administration as the cheapest way of defending Western Europe against possible Soviet aggression. Of future import, U.S. aid to Yugoslavia might encourage anti-Soviet elements within other communist nations.[31]

The first concrete embodiment of this reorientation in policy was an administrative decision to change export licensing procedures so that American goods could be exported to Yugoslavia without running into the obstacles put in the way of deliveries to other communist countries. Other executive-inspired actions soon followed, including Export-Import Bank loans to Yugoslavia in 1948–49, the transfer of Marshall Plan flour, stored in Germany and Italy, to Yugoslavia in 1949, and creative interpretation of existing aid laws (such as the 1950 Mutual Defense Assistance Act) to provide food for Tito's armed forces.[32]

The precise nature of these actions was less important than the fact that the Truman administration had deliberately chosen to assist a communist country to maintain its independence. This decision was not made without initial hesitation and was given less than wholehearted support even within the executive branch. Secretary of Defense Louis Johnson, for example, had delayed the export of a steel mill that Yugoslavia had purchased until the president personally ordered him to cease his obstructive tactics. Likewise a segment of public opinion, especially the Roman Catholic hierarchy, joined with some members of Congress in opposing, on religious or ideological grounds, aid to Yugoslavia and friendly relations with Tito's regime.[33]

The argument ran that this was a communist government that had taken power by force, persecuted religion, and denied human rights to its own people; that it wanted American aid for its own ends, which were basically hostile to the United States; that in a showdown it would be with the Soviets against the West; and that the United States was not acting morally or in its own interest in aiding any communist regime, whatever its difference with others. Some critics even contended that the whole Yugoslavia–Soviet controversy was a gigantic fraud.[34]

Successive crop failures in 1948, 1949, and 1950 had meanwhile brought the Yugoslav economy to the point of collapse. Fearing that if weakened, Tito's regime might fall prey to a Korean pattern of aggression, in which the Soviets would engineer the use of satellite forces to squelch Yugoslav independence, the Truman administration recognized that stopgap measures would no longer suffice and went directly to Congress for assistance. On 29 November 1950 President Truman sent a letter to Congress supporting a Yugoslav Emergency Relief Act that authorized $50 million in food supplies. "The continued independence of Yugoslavia is of great importance to the security of the United States. We can help preserve the independence of a nation which is defying the savage threats of the Soviet imperialists and keeping Soviet power out of Europe's most strategic areas. This is clearly in our national interest," he wrote—a statement that remained the basic rationale of U.S.–Yugoslav policy through the next decade of cold war.[35]

Although Truman's request did not go unchallenged, fortunately for the administration self-interest and good sense prevailed over ideological fervor.[36] Key members of both the House and the Senate were persuaded by the president's reasoning, especially the strategic argument. Hence some normally conservative, anticommunist, or anti–foreign aid Republican legislators, such as Knowland, Taft, Bridges, McCarthy, and Nixon, who might have been expected to vote against the bill, supported the president. The final vote, in December 1950, suggests that with the exception of certain anticommunist diehards of both political parties who repeated the by now familiar admonitions, the relief bill passed easily with bipartisan support: it was approved 60 to 21 in the Senate, and 225 to 142 in the House.[37] Among the Senate Republicans who voted against it were conservatives with isolationist credentials: Bricker, Capehart, Jenner, Kem, Malone, Mundt, and Wherry. Democratic opponents were Senators Byrd, McCarron, Johnston, McClellan, and O'Connor. Thereafter the administration went ahead with the inclusion of Yugoslavia in the regular appropriations of the ECA. In October 1951 President Truman would determine that Yugoslavia was vital to American security and eligible for military assistance.[38]

Having made an exception of Yugoslavia, the Truman administration devoted the fall and winter of 1950 to a new round of talks with the OEEC countries to effect stricter compliance with COCOM's export controls to the rest of the Soviet bloc. The discussions progressed smoothly in the opinion of government officials, who hoped that announcement of the allies' compliance with the strategic embargo would mute congressional criticism. On 16 February 1951 Philip C. Jessup, the ambassador-at-large, wrote to James S. Lay, Jr., of NSC that "the outcome of negotiations over the last four months, in summary, is that all of the important manufacturing and trading companies of Western Europe, except Switzerland and Sweden, have now voluntarily reached agreement on a very substantial expansion in their export controls on strategic shipments to the Soviet Bloc." He revealed that he had approached Britain and France jointly to have them persuade the two neutrals to enforce, insofar as possible, the same export controls as the other Western European nations.[39]

While Jessup was in Paris negotiating with the COCOM nations, the effectiveness of the Export Control Law again came under congressional scrutiny. At the same time, a consensus was emerging within the executive branch that the present level of the strategic embargo was having little or no impact on Soviet war potential. The CIA reported on 19 February 1951 that in the current international climate U.S. policy was being eroded by the failure of the Western Europeans to adopt parallel controls.[40] The development of more or less covert trade channels had enabled the Soviet Union to obtain items on Lists 1A and 1B. ECA corroborated these findings in its own report to NSC.[41] And, like the Departments of State and Defense, it concluded that "economic warfare cannot be a decisive weapon in dealing either with the Soviet bloc in Europe or with China."[42]

Beyond this, the consensus broke down. No federal agency recommended forgoing controls altogether on the grounds that technology, once perfected, would inevitably be acquired legally or illicitly by any nation wanting it. Advancing that proposition would have been political suicide in the wave of anticommunist hysteria that accompanied McCarthyism. Instead the question was whether to unleash total economic warfare against the USSR and her satellites, to tighten the present sieve-like system of controls, or to try some combination of the two. The CIA presented the options confronting the policymakers when it observed: "This gap in enforcement could be closed to a significant extent through the cooperation of the non-Soviet countries and the application of instruments of economic warfare not widely employed at present or not employed at all." The tactics alluded to included preclusive buying, blacklisting, foreign funds controls, and denial of shipping facilities. Even then the CIA doubted that a total embargo of strategic and nonstrategic trade with the USSR could be effective.[43]

The secretary of defense alone, representing the views of General Omar N. Bradley and the Joint Chiefs of Staff, advocated a total ban on trade, arguing that the United States should deny all items of strategic importance that furthered Soviet war potential directly or indirectly, as well as any items in short supply. Given the state of the Soviet consumer economy, the last reference could have applied to almost any item of trade. To implement this policy of economic warfare the Joint Chiefs of Staff preferred to have Commerce Department officials issue a presumptive denial of export licenses to goods that were not even specifically included in Lists 1A and 1B and to have the administration centralize all facets of economic warfare in a wholly new and distinct agency.[44]

The push being made in Congress and among the military to transform export controls from an essentially defensive to an aggressive policy incurred opposition from both ECA and the State Department. More sensitive to the international ramifications of economic warfare, both argued against a total embargo of trade with Russia and the bloc countries. ECA, with the concurrence of the State Department, contended that the cost to the free world of an assault on the basic economic strength of the Soviet bloc would be very great; that it would lead to short supply controls at home in order to compensate the allies for loss of imports from the USSR (feed grains in the case of Great Britain); that it would disrupt Western Europe's economic recovery while making the satellites more economically dependent on Moscow; and that it would intensify communist pressure on Asia to gain access to raw materials.[45]

Further, an aggressive policy of economic warfare would provoke dissension within the Western alliance and disrupt sensitive rearmament negotiations, a major White House objective after the establishment of NATO and the Soviet detonation of a nuclear device in 1949. Acting within the framework of the administration's policy, in 1950 American military authorities had begun to move in earnest toward building a large conventional European army to resist Soviet expansionism. The proposed army included German military units despite deep-seated fears of a revived German militarism within NATO and concern that costly arms expenditures would impede Europe's economic recovery. The rearmament talks were stalled over these issues. If the most powerful nation within the alliance now attempted to resolve differences over the embargo policy by laying down dictates, contrary to the will of its partners, ECA and the State Department feared, this would initiate a process of doubts and disintegration of the alliance itself.[46]

Total economic warfare was justifiable only if the Truman administration believed a military conflict was inevitable in 1952. Neither the State Department nor ECA adjudged this to be the case, and both advocated continuing the policy of selective controls, but with modifications to strengthen the existing policy. They recommended plugging leaks in the present system, forming agreements on international allocation of raw materials to prevent Soviet stockpiling, preclusive buying, neutralizing Russia's use of gold in international markets, tightening security in American firms that were developing high technology, and persuading the OEEC countries that there was no future in trade with the East, because Russia was seeking autarchy.[47]

They also advised flexibility, assuring friendly countries of the United States' support while recognizing, in the words of the State Department, that "political, economic and military considerations may make it impossible for them to parallel U.S. controls precisely." Talk about economic defense, not economic warfare, said State Department analysts, who adverted to Kennan's earlier advice that the United States develop new techniques to exploit Russia's political and economic weaknesses, "as well as to increase strain on political and economic relationships within the Soviet bloc."[48]

Upon careful examination of the alternatives NSC advised against unbridled economic warfare directed against the USSR and its European satellites. It recommended instead that the administration close the loopholes in the existing system, as outlined by the State Department and ECA, and renew its efforts to persuade the OEEC countries to do the same. President Truman approved the recommendations toward the close of February 1951 and once more instructed Commerce Secretary Sawyer to oversee their implementation.[49]

Despite the administration's efforts to avoid a new confrontation, congressional criticism of the export control policy had become more intense and focused upon an economic embargo of all trade, including peaceful goods, with the Iron Curtain countries. This was apparent when the first session of the Republican-dominated Eighty-second Congress convened in January 1951. Democratic Congressman William C. Lantaff of Florida told his colleagues that he, like many Americans, was shocked to learn that several Western European nations were conducting business as usual with the Russians. "If we expect the American public to fully support the effort of adequately preparing ourselves, and of helping other freedom-loving people resist Communism, then we must put a stop to this unscrupulous trade." Republican Congressman Horace Seely-Brown, Jr., of Connecticut concurred and said outright that the free world should "unite in a complete embargo of the Communist world."[50]

The Korean War had intensified the hawkish attitude of many legislators toward trade with the Soviet Union. They acted as though trade itself were the enemy, to be extirpated regardless of cost. "As usual," Secretary of State Acheson later wrote, "Congress saw the issue in moralistic terms of black and white." The problem was not that simple, because trade with the East was far more vital to the economic well-being of the OEEC countries than it ever was—or would be—to the United States. "To interrupt this [trade], except in the case of strategic materials," warned Acheson, "could have grave political and military, as well as economic results." This was a reference to the parallel U.S. diplomatic initiatives to persuade the European democracies to rearm themselves to ward off potential Soviet military threats.[51]

European military budgets had in fact doubled since the Korean War, and industrial production, including military, had risen twenty percent. This had necessitated a sharp rise in high-cost imports, prices, and the cost of living. In the case of Great Britain the trade deficit had widened by 1 billion dollars, and national reserves had plummeted. To Acheson the withdrawal of aid in order to punish the OEEC nations for refusing to adopt an identical set of controls, thereby injuring their economies and retarding progress toward rearmament, hardly seemed a logical course. Hence the State Department had consistently maintained that a voluntary, multilateral approach to export controls was preferable to coercing Western Europe into enforcing a list identical to the United States'. Departmental analysts argued that congressional threats to cut off assistance would not necessarily inhibit the flow of Western European goods to the Soviet Union; rather, such strong-arm tactics would cost the United States COCOM support in negotiations with neutral Sweden and Switzerland.[52]

Acheson's strong reservations and appraisal of the Cannon amendment as an intolerable encroachment upon presidential authority in foreign policy explains why Truman never applied the sanctions of the 1950 law to any OEEC country that blatantly traded with the USSR and its satellites. With the support of NSC Truman exploited the executive's discretionary authority to define "the national interest" in this case as requiring blanket exceptions to the law's stringent penalties. He also conducted quiet diplomacy to persuade the Western European nations that it was in their interest to tighten trade controls.[53]

However judicious the president's restraint in the interests of preserving Western unity, his action returned to haunt him. Partisan Republican legislators and antiadministration Democrats once again seized on the ineffectiveness of the Cannon amendment to attempt to eliminate all aid to any country accused of selling any of a broad category of goods to the USSR and its satellites. Acheson's concern was about to be realized when, on 9 March 1951, an angry Senator Kem wrote to the president that he and Mrs. Kem had just returned from visiting wounded GIs at Walter Reed Hospital, "and, as always, we came away with heavy hearts at the sight of boys, some of them from Missouri, whose bodies and lives have been mangled in Korea."[54]

The greater part of Kem's letter, which subsequently was published in the *Washington Star*, consisted of a diatribe against the United States' allies: the British, for selling $329,000 worth of machine tools to the Russians; the Belgians and the French, for selling the USSR iron and steel; the Italians, for shipping $1.6 million worth of electric cranes and thermal power stations from Genoa to Moscow. NSC should have invoked the Cannon amendment and terminated ERP assistance to these nations, Kem lectured the president. "For my part," he declared, "I am against sending so much as a thimble or a hair pin as a gift from the American people to any country which persists in sending war materials to the Reds now slaughtering our boys in Korea."[55]

Kem's admonition and demands were not taken lightly. He was among Secretary Acheson's most carping and suspicious critics. In 1949 he had sought unsuccessfully to deny aid to any country that nationalized privately owned industries and had voted against the NATO pact. The following year he voted against aid for Yugoslavia when the Truman administration was seeking to exploit the rift between Tito and Stalin. He had also spearheaded a Republican drive to force Acheson's resignation.[56] No wonder his letter to the president had the administration in a frenzy throughout the spring and summer of 1951, fearing that it would precipitate a new round of congressional legislation to punish the Western European allies for trading with the European Soviet bloc. Loring K. Macy, acting head of the Office of International Trade of the Department of Commerce, was not exaggerating when he wrote to Thomas C. Blaisdell on 4 June that Kem's activities had "all of Government in a muddle."[57]

Kem's letter, which probably reflected the sentiments of many other Americans, was politically explosive and needed to be answered very carefully. Truman requested NSC to draft for his signature a thoughtfully worded response—one that reaffirmed the administration's essential position without making light of the problem. The result was a letter that couched East–West trade in the context of preventing future Koreas through "the building of greater defensive strength in the free world relative to that of the Soviet Union and its satellites." Kem was asked to examine this trade in relation to overall Western security rather than to focus on specific shipments. The letter reminded him that Western Europe also purchased goods from the bloc countries that were important to its economic defense and that the United States and the OEEC countries had agreed to the export control policy to meet mutual security objectives. The present task was "to close the remaining gaps and make the controls more effective."[58]

Not unexpectedly, this reply failed to satisfy Truman's fellow Missourian, who counterattacked with a new resolution to replace the Cannon amendment with a tougher law. Kem's proposed amendment of 9 May 1951 plugged the loophole in the Cannon amendment by removing the president's discretionary authority and was to take effect automatically, within fifteen days after Congress approved it. To fend off Democratic attempts to kill the new amendment Kem shrewdly attached it as a rider (section 1302) to the Third Supplemental Appropriation Bill for 1951, which the Senate was then considering.[59]

Had the amendment been enacted in its original form, a major piece of legislation affecting the foreign policy of the United States would have gone into effect without ever being considered by either foreign relations committee of Congress. Fortunately for the administration, when the appropriations bill went into conference Democratic leaders, thanks largely to the lobbying efforts of ECA administrator Paul Hoffman, successfully modified section 1302 to authorize presidential exceptions from its requirements in the interest of national security. Truman continued to believe the rider was seriously defective, but he signed the bill on 2 June 1951 because of the government's need for money and the last-minute exception to section 1302. He made clear at the time his intention to grant exceptions "on a broad scale" until Congress had an opportunity to reconsider the Kem amendment and to ask for new legislation that would not cut off trade and aid blindly but only where such action enhanced American security.[60]

Within a matter of days NSC took under advisement the potential implications of section 1302, concluding that a blanket termination of economic and financial aid to every free-world nation trading with the USSR and its satellites would call into question the integrity and sovereignty of the OEEC countries and ultimately jeopardize the national security of the United States. To do nothing, however, would convey the impression that Washington was satisfied with their behavior, which was untrue. "Points of weakness" persisted in OEEC's control of strategic trade with Eastern Europe. Rather than plunge headlong into action that could irreparably damage relations with the United States' NATO partners, NSC advised the president, it would be better to issue a general interim exception from section 1302 until NSC had examined each country's case for trade on its own merits. This approach upheld the principle of multilateralism, avoided the stigma of coercion, and would not drive friendly nations into an ironclad neutrality.[61]

What appeared to be a cavalier attitude toward the Kem amendment by the administration infuriated conservative Republicans and Democrats in both houses of Congress and generated a new outburst of criticism. The provision of an exception, argued Senator Wherry, who had been one of the original conferees, was intended to cover certain commodities and was not to be construed as giving the executive branch carte blanche to evade the law. He accused both Truman and NSC of a "willful and premeditated nullification of the law, and the constitutional responsibilities of the President to administer the laws which are passed by Congress." NSC had assumed "an authority which does not exist in the law"; section 1302 vested the authority to terminate foreign assistance in the ECA administrator—*not* NSC, which Wherry denounced as "a closed corporation of administration thinking." Angered, he threatened to block future economic and military foreign aid bills until Truman carried out the law.[62]

Passage of the Kem amendment and the bitter dispute it had engendered between congressional conservatives and the Truman administration were widely and correctly interpreted as a rebuff of the president's more flexible handling of the East–West trade problem and relations with the United States' European partners. Nonetheless, while Congress was enacting this rider to the Supplemental Appropriations Bill, the administration had been active elsewhere to nullify its potential for damage. The House Committee on Foreign Affairs, similarly distressed by persistent reports that American, British, and Italian factories were shipping strategic goods to Communist China and the USSR, was considered more amenable to rational arguments. While the Kem amendment was going forth in the Senate, the chairman of the Foreign Affairs Committee of the House appointed a subcommittee to investigate two bills dealing with the export control system. H.R. 1621 and H.R. 1939, like the Kem amendment, mandated that the United States not provide economic or financial aid to any country that shipped strategic goods behind the Iron Curtain.[63]

Chaired by Democratic Congressman Laurie C. Battle of Alabama, the subcommittee held executive hearings beginning on 5 March 1951. It too concluded that the strategic embargo had not denied war material to the Soviet bloc, and it blamed the Truman administration for not clarifying its policy on East–West trade, noting that "the precise statement of this policy is and always has been kept secret even from the committee."

The subcommittee also faulted the administration for not assigning the responsibility for conducting "the economic cold war against Russia and the satellites" to any one agency, department, or bureau.[64]

Despite its negative evaluation the subcommittee concluded that a total economic embargo of Western trade would defeat the objective of encouraging the satellite countries to break away from Russian domination and would injure relations with the United States' allies.[65] Administration officials argued forcefully that H.R. 1621 and H.R. 1939 were contrary to the national security interest. Loring K. Macy of the Office of International Trade in the Department of Commerce testified that the government already had adequate statutory authority to regulate the shipment of strategic goods to the Soviet Union and bloc countries and cited statistics demonstrating that trade had fallen precipitately since 1948. A policy of retaliation might well undermine the Western alliance and lead to withdrawing financial aid from Latin American countries that traditionally had been friendly to the United States. In conclusion, Macy voiced the subcommittee's own concern that these bills would discourage other "Yugoslavias" and impede Western economic recovery.[66]

After intense lobbying by administration officials the subcommittee recommended a substitute bill, the Mutual Defense Assistance Control Act (H.R. 4550), drafted by Congressman Battle. The Battle bill was a compromise between the much more far-reaching demands of conservative Republicans and Democrats to punish the allies, as exemplified by the Kem amendment, and the wishes of the more moderate defenders of the administration in Congress. It prohibited exports to the Soviet bloc of arms, ammunition, implements of war, and other strategic items but retained the president's discretionary authority to terminate assistance to any country making such shipments.[67] Section 103 (b) prohibited economic or financial assistance to the bloc. The full committee assented to the compromise on the grounds that it offered "a comprehensive and constructive procedure which takes into account the complexity of the problems involved while firmly and clearly defining the United States' policy in this field and providing for its effective administration."[68]

The Truman administration accepted the substitute bill, which passed in the House on 2 August 1951, with misgivings, but as the best one that could be obtained from an angry Congress. Republicans and many Democrats, for partisan political and ideological reasons, had grown increasingly hostile to the very principle of trading with the enemy and, as the Kem amendment showed, vindictive toward the United States' European allies. That anger peaked in the summer of 1951. On 7 July Congress jointly approved the McMahon-Ribicoff Resolution, a cynical expression of friendship for the Russian people that drew a distinction between the Russian people and the Soviet government. This action precipitated a sharp response from Nikolai Shvernik, president of the Presidium, that further exacerbated relations between the two countries.[69]

On 6 August Shvernik addressed a long letter to President Truman that listed eleven "measures of a discriminatory character" that the United States had adopted against the Soviet Union. He specified five that erected "artificial barriers" to American–Soviet trade: the March 1951 order of the Department of Commerce that had annulled the license to export scientific and technical literature to the USSR; renunciation of the 1937 Trade Agreement on 23 June 1951; the Kem amendment; the list of banned export items of 7 June 1951; and the Battle bill. He welcomed the resolution but added sarcastically that Congress's words should have been matched by peaceful actions.[70]

While American–Soviet relations deteriorated and a political revolt brewed in Congress, the Truman administration endorsed the Battle bill. On 16 October Assistant Secretary of State Jack K. McFall wrote to Budget Director Frederick J. Lawton that "while State had some serious questions upon which H.R. 4550 is based," the bill was more workable than any existing legislation—a reference to the Kem amendment. The State Department preferred not to give the Battle bill too much publicity: "Many countries, particularly our NATO associates in Western Europe, view legislation such as the Kem amendment and H.R. 4550 as instruments by which this country seeks to impose a policy of economic warfare upon them." These nations were willing to cooperate in a multilateral program of export controls, "but they do not feel that it is in the security interests of the free world to undertake outright economic warfare." They especially wanted policy questions to be decided through negotiations rather than dictation by one country. "They have made their views on this subject," McFall observed, "particularly clear since the passage of the Kem amendment in June."[71]

Senate conservatives were not oblivious to the reasons why the administration was endorsing the Battle bill, and even as H.R. 4550 made its way through the legislative process they began erecting obstacles. On 9 August Kem, with the encouragement of Senators Wherry, Byrd, and Malone, attempted to short-circuit House action with a new amendment that would close the exception provision of section 1302 and also deny *military* aid to a country that sold strategic goods to the USSR. He coupled this with a stinging denunciation of the president, NSC, and the Battle bill.[72] On 14 September he again took the president to task, blaming Truman for a speech given by British Foreign Secretary Herbert Morrison to the National Press Club, in which Morrison had defended

Britain's trade with Russia as essential to her economic well-being, and her recognition of the Communist government of China as a "practical matter." In an emotional outburst Kem declared that Congress's abdication of its responsibilities had been blueprinted by Acheson, engineered by the majority leadership in both houses, and launched with the aid of "high-pressure bull-dozing."[73]

Kem's criticism of the Battle bill was echoed beyond the circle of Senate conservatives and virulent anticommunists, but from a rather different perspective. *Fortune* observed that the Battle bill "might improve Mr. Truman's relations with Congress but it would not get at the root of the East–West trade problem"—which was that the allies had to temporize with the Soviets as long as they depended upon supplies from the East. Like the Kem amendment, the Battle bill represented a half-policy: "the other half is to help the Western Europeans discover new sources of imports and realign their trade pattern." The implication of *Fortune*'s remarks was that the United States would have to lower its tariff barriers in order to wean the OEEC countries away from Eastern European markets.[74]

While *Fortune* was extolling the merits of freer trade, Kem's maneuver to shore up section 1302 had run into a roadblock. His carping criticism ran counter to the Truman administration's bipartisan foreign policy, supported by the majority of Democrats and Republicans, of rearming the NATO European allies as swiftly as possible. On August 28 the Senate passed the Battle bill to supersede the Kem amendment. President Truman, heeding the advice of the State Department and the Budget Office, delayed signing the Mutual Defense Assistance Control Act (Battle Act) into law until 26 October, the last possible moment. The reasons for the delay were tactical: to minimize opposition to the new law abroad, and to give the new Mutual Security Director, W. Averell Harriman, the full thirty days to publish a new list of prohibited goods as required by law.[75]

The Battle Act quickly became the focal point in the continuing conflict between congressional conservatives, whose ultimate objective was to eliminate all free-world trade with the Soviet bloc countries, and the proponents, represented by the Truman administration, of a more pragmatic and more flexible policy that served the broader national security interest. The latter believed that if trade policy was to be used to curb aggressive behavior from the Soviets, this needed to be done multilaterally to be effective. The use of export controls had to be attuned to the economic and political requirements of the OEEC countries.[76]

The stage was thus set for a new clash when the Eighty-second Congress reconvened in January 1952. President Truman, exercising his discretionary authority, refused to cut off aid to OEEC countries that were selling strategic goods to the Soviet bloc. Conservative, anticommunist legislators of both parties mounted a new drive to eliminate the escape clause of the Battle Act. On 16 January Kem introduced yet another resolution (S. Res. 250) seeking a broad investigation of the State Department for pursuing policies that "may be endangering the safety and security of this nation." His immediate target was Secretary of State Acheson, whom he accused of secretly urging Japan to sign a trade agreement with Communist China. If, as the *New York Times* speculated, his real purpose was to launch "a sustained campaign among Republicans, particularly those generally considered to be isolationists, to force another 'great debate' on foreign policy in this election year," the gambit failed. The Rules Committee consigned Kem's resolution to the Foreign Relations Comittee, where the Democratic majority buried it.[77]

Shortly thereafter, on 3 April, an economic conference convened in Moscow, attended by 471 manufacturers, traders, economists, and trade unionists from forty-nine nations, including Great Britain, France, Belgium, Italy, and the United States.[78] The formal agenda was to discuss the economic consequences of rearmament and to facilitate revival of East–West trade. Officials of the Truman administration, however, and Western reporters such as the executive director of the *Commercial and Financial Chronicle*, viewed the proceedings as a propaganda event intended to split the Western alliance by winning over Western businessmen and unemployed workers with promises of large purchases and also to wean third world countries away from dependence on Western technologies.[79]

Coming so soon after the congressional fight over the Battle Act, the implications of the Moscow conference for both international and domestic politics were not lost on American policymakers. Secretary of State Acheson moved swiftly to belittle the importance of the meeting, declaring: "The whole thing seems directed toward raising doubts as to whether the defense of the West is an urgent matter, and should be carried forward with the zeal that we all believe is necessary."[80] Harry Schwartz, the Soviet expert of the *New York Times*, saw the conference as "an open admission that the Western embargo on strategic goods is pinching the Communist economies and pinching hard." A Soviet offer to purchase $1 billion to $1.4 billion in goods from the United States and to buy surplus consumer items from the OEEC countries, such as British textiles, in exchange for badly needed machinery, tools, and industrial raw materials was, he declared, "a supreme Communist effort to create pressure for lifting of the crippling restrictions on Western exports of strategic goods to the Soviet Union and its satellites."[81]

Politically and economically the Moscow conference had to be a disappointment to the Soviets. Not only had the Western governments boycotted the meeting, thereby denying it the legitimacy the Stalinist regime was striving for, but the prospect of purchasing Western machinery, tools, and technology in exchange for grain, timber, coal, furs, and raw materials did not occur on the scale the regime had envisioned. Nonetheless, that Western businessmen (including some Americans) attended the conference and even negotiated bilateral agreements for nonstrategic goods afterwards stirred up resentment in the United States among legislators and the fervently anticommunist head of the National Institute of Foreign Trade, J. Anthony Marcus. Missouri Congressman O. K. Armstrong told his colleagues in the House that the purpose of the conference was "to confuse foreign traders in order to break down the American embargo on shipments of strategic materials to the Soviet countries."[82]

As Acheson had feared, the significance of the Moscow meeting was blown entirely out of proportion by conservatives and led to a new assault on the Battle Act and the Democratic administration. Senator Kem again spearheaded the attack, using as his weapon a proposed amendment to the pending Mutual Security Act of 1952. On 28 May he took the floor of the Senate to denounce the agreements signed in Moscow by representatives of the depressed British and French cotton and wool textile industries, and also President Truman for granting an exception to permit the Dutch to supply drilling equipment to Poland. His amendment would eliminate the president's discretionary authority to invoke sanctions against non-U.S. violators of the Battle Act. The Senate accepted the amendment, 40 to 32, with 24 not voting.[83]

The administration was saved from an embarrassing defeat only by the action of the House, and after the most intense lobbying. When the Mutual Security Bill went into conference, House conferees strongly objected to Kem's rider, arguing that its adoption "might well result in throwing some of our friends in Western Europe into Communist arms." Perhaps the more persuasive argument in the decision of the joint conference to strike out Kem's amendment were confidential statistics provided by the Department of Commerce, which showed that shipments of strategic items to the Soviet bloc had decreased from $7.5 million in 1951 to less than $400,000 in the first half of 1952. As Democratic Senator Tom Connally of Texas, chairman of the Foreign Relations Committee and an opponent of the amendment, observed, the conferees felt they were moving in the same direction as Kem, but "without rushing headlong without guidance."[84]

With bulldog-like determination Kem fought to revive his amendment on the Senate floor, a maneuver that brought down upon him the wrath of the Democrats. His patience exhausted, Senator Connally lashed out at his Republican colleague: "He wants to bring it out of its tomb, wants to pull off its shroud, and bring it back and make it appear that it is something that has blood in its veins and arteries and breath in its lungs. But it is dead, and it ought to stay dead." The majority of senators agreed; on a vote of 59 to 11, with 26 not voting, they accepted the joint conference report without Kem's rider.[85]

With the Mutual Defense Assistance Control Act (Battle Act) of 1951 the essential legal framework for the policy of export controls was in place. The rationale for that policy—which many officials of the executive branch considered fallacious—was that the national security of the United States could be protected by denying potential war material to the USSR and its satellites. However, the Truman administration had won only a round and not a final victory in its protracted struggle with Congress to determine where export controls fit into the overall foreign policy of the United States, who should be responsible for administering the policy, and how the policy should be implemented.

This much was clear from a conversation between Secretary of State Acheson and the Italian ambassador, Alberto Tarchiani, on 16 June 1952. Acheson asked Tarchiani to convey to his government "our great concern" that Italy held contracts to ship $1 million worth of ball bearings and rolling mill equipment behind the Iron Curtain, and he explained that the Senate's vote should not be misconstrued. Acheson deemed it vital that "our friends abroad should not be lulled into a sense of security as a result of this action," and he told Tarchiani that had this issue of the Kem amendment alone come before the Senate apart from the Mutual Security Bill, "it was highly probable that the Administration would have been defeated and the amendment adopted."[86]

THE outbreak of the Korean War in 1950 marked a significant turning point in the evolution of the multilateral system of export controls. The conflict was the catalyst for a hardening of American, particularly congressional, sentiment against the Soviet Union as an aggressor nation. Congress generally applauded President Truman's commitment of American ground forces to the defense of South Korea, but it was less happy with his refusal to sever all economic ties with Russia and its satellites. Indeed the Korean War exacerbated a growing divergence between the legislative and executive branches over the efficacy of economic sanctions and the reluctance of Western Europe to enforce an embargo against the Soviets that was identical to the United States' list of prohibited goods.

Congress reacted to the Korean conflict by reassessing the Export Control Act of 1949, to determine how the Soviet Union had been able to build up its own and its client's military strength to wage aggressive war. The net result of its analysis was to shore up the 1949 legislation by withdrawing most-favored-nation status from the USSR and Soviet Eastern Europe in 1951, by cutting off financial credits and abrogating commercial treaties, and by prohibiting the importation of seven types of furs from Russia. Only Yugoslavia, which had broken with Moscow in 1948, retained (after spirited congressional debate) nondiscriminatory trade treatment. In making a distinction among socialist states, Washington wanted to encourage polycentric and nationalistic tendencies among Eastern Europeans and offer others the hope of reducing their economic dependence on the Soviet Union.

Congress also had identified the Western European allies as a source of weakness that was compromising the whole embargo system. The allies had indirectly facilitated the North Koreans' attack upon the south by illicitly supplying the Soviets with the precision tools, machinery, and technical knowledge to manufacture the weapons of war that were killing U.S. soldiers. Ignoring the different but legitimate economic and political concerns of the Western Europeans, including their strong disbelief that economic sanctions could moderate Soviet foreign policy objectives, Congress complemented its hostility toward Russia with a policy of economic warfare against Western Europe. The Battle Act of 1951 threatened to eliminate economic, financial, and military assistance to any ally that traded with the Soviets, even though its members had no legal obligation to abide by COCOM's directives.

The Truman administration was caught between congressional indignation and the economic priorities of the United States' allies at a time when the Western European economies were recovering from wartime devastation and American political and economic leverage was becoming less potent. Compounding its problems was evidence from U.S. intelligence sources that indicated that the Western European assessment of the embargo was more nearly accurate: trade sanctions were having little adverse effect on the Soviet Union's military capabilities, and none on its repressive political system or international behavior. Nonetheless Truman went along with the policy of sanctions, to assuage legislative and right-wing critics who felt that he had not been tough enough on communism, and also because it might enhance U.S. national security at relatively little cost.

One year into the Korean War, Congress passed and the president reluctantly signed into law the Battle Act. In accepting the legislation, Truman could respond to his critics quite plausibly that he was acting vigorously against communist aggression. Meanwhile, because the law invested the executive with discretionary authority to suspend or hold in abeyance its most severe penalties in the national interest, Truman also could maintain that he had preserved presidential prerogative in foreign affairs without any diminution of power. So despite the Battle Act the president retained the ability to negotiate quietly with the allies through diplomatic channels in order to persuade them to be more circumspect in their trade with the Soviets, and even to deny them access to strategic materials if they persisted in shipping the same or equivalent amounts to the USSR. When the Western Europeans balked at even these mild initiatives toward calming an outraged Congress, President Truman put the unity of the Western alliance above national differences and generally acquiesced in violations of the strategic embargo. This established a precedent that every future president followed whenever the issue of economic sanctions threatened to disrupt Western unity.

Holding the Middle Ground: The Eisenhower Administration and Trading with the Communists

ON 12 and 13 January 1953, shortly before he took office as the nation's thirty-fourth president, Dwight D. Eisenhower, the former World War II commander of Allied forces in Europe, held an unusual pre-inauguration meeting at the Hotel Commodore in New York City. The purpose of the gathering was to brief prospective cabinet appointees on formal operating procedures, solicit advice on the inaugural address, and build rapport and cohesion among the members of the team. After Eisenhower read a draft of his inaugural address, Defense Secretary-designate Charles Wilson was troubled at the implication that the United States might begin trade in nonstrategic goods with the USSR and Iron Curtain countries. He complained that he had never liked the idea of "selling firearms to the Indians." "Remember this," Eisenhower replied:

> You are trying to set up out of Moscow what you might call a series of centrifugal forces. The last thing you can do is to begin to do things that force all these peripheral countries—the Baltic states, Poland, Czechoslovakia and the rest of them—to depend on Moscow for the rest of their lives. How are you going to keep them interested in you? If you trade with them, Charlie, you have got something pulling their interest your way. . . . You just can't preach abstraction to a man who has to turn for his daily living in some other direction.[1]

Wilson was not convinced, but Eisenhower said: "Charlie, I am talking common sense."

Pragmatic by nature, Eisenhower was committed to keeping the Cold War manageable, reducing American–Soviet tensions, and preventing large-scale nuclear warfare. The clash with the Russians was a problem to be managed, not an all-consuming crusade against the forces of evil. As the exchange with Secretary Wilson revealed, Eisenhower was to shape foreign policy far more than contemporary historians, political scientists, and journalists suspected, making full use of his considerable leadership abilities to preserve the peace and to resist communist encroachments around the world. More so than his predecessor or his successors, he respected the authority of the executive departments by resisting the tendency to centralize and isolate policymaking in the White House. Management of export control policy through the machinery of the executive branch was a significant area in which he skillfully employed his leadership talents and management style to persuade a reluctant Congress to accept liberalization of East–West trade to preserve allied unity and thus the nation's security.[2]

The circumstances that prompted the Eisenhower administration to address East–West trade policy were the death of Stalin in March 1953, which brought in its wake a number of new foreign policy initiatives by the Soviet Union, and the enhanced allied interest in reopening trade with their traditional markets in Eastern Europe. The post-Stalin leadership proposed to counter the power of the United States by the policy of "peaceful coexistence," which Georgi Malenkov, chairman of the Council of Ministers, enunciated on 15 March, in the Great Hall of the Kremlin. Malenkov had declared that there was no existing dispute that "cannot be decided by peaceful means, on the basis of mutual understanding by interested countries." He repeated this speech on 20 August, and it was extended by Nikita Khrushchev in the seminal "Secret Speech" of 25 February 1956. Instead of emphasizing the inevitability of military confrontation with the West, the Soviet leaders' rhetoric was one of peaceful economic cooperation and competition. As part of this new policy they sought to reopen old and establish new channels of East–West trade, even as the USSR competed with the capitalist countries in the third world.[3]

Evidence of this dramatic shift in policy soon followed. On 27 July 1953 the armistice was signed ending the Korean conflict. In the United Nations, Russia agreed to make its first contribution to fund multilateral technical aid to less developed countries. Soviet commercial agents appeared in several Western European capitals to negotiate new bilateral trade agreements. The Ministry of Foreign Trade encouraged Western salesmen to travel to the Soviet Union and to submit specific offers for goods of interest to it. At the trade transaction level, Soviet purchasing agents placed sizable orders for various types of ships to be constructed in Western Europe and also concluded deals calling for Soviet purchase of electric power equipment, machine tools, construction equipment, and machinery for timber and paper products. A delegation of British businessmen returned from the USSR with the general impression that the chief interest of Soviet trade agencies was in procuring all the latest production equipment they could obtain from the West.[4]

Even before the Soviets' new emphasis on peaceful coexistence, Western business communities were beginning to press their governments to reduce the scope of strategic export controls to permit the expansion of East–West trade. From the time East–West trade was made the subject of congressional scrutiny and action in 1951, U.S. policy had exasperated responsible and influential segments of opinion in nearly every Western European nation and many countries outside Europe. What irritated Europeans most was that Congress seemed to believe that they were less interested than Congress in keeping down the Soviet war potential (even though they were constantly in the shadow of the Red Army) and that even if their instincts were sound, the OEEC countries were incompetent to decide upon the balance of advantages in their trade with the communists.[5] In August 1951 the influential *Economist* of London remarked: "The Battle Bill implies that America's allies are disloyal or that they are incapable of deciding for themselves what is the balance of gain and loss in their exchanges with the Communist countries—in short, that they are either fools or rascals."[6]

By openly threatening to cut off aid to countries that did not conform to U.S. control standards, Congress seemed to be making a favorite Soviet propaganda theme come true: that aid was only a device to impose U.S. hegemony on Western Europe. The revolt against American restrictions, then, occurred even before the thaw in the Cold War. The post-Stalin leadership capitalized on the growing discontent in the West with the existing high level of trade restrictions.

While the Bonn Government of Chancellor Konrad Adenauer was cooperating with the COCOM controls, West German businessmen were forming organizations and enacting resolutions demanding complete freedom to negotiate sales in Soviet Eastern Europe. In May 1952 the Bundestag voted unanimously to recommend to the Allied High Commission the resumption of "normal" trade relations with the Soviet bloc. Paris's *Le Monde* issued a blistering criticism of U.S. policy and asserted: "Must Mr. Battle still dictate France's response to the commercial proposals of the East?" In August 1953 Rome's *Il Sole*, which mirrored business opinion, demanded revision of the Battle Act on the ground that it curtailed Italian exports of perfectly harmless goods to the East.[7]

The United States' response to the dramatic shift in Soviet policy was a mixture of cautious optimism and unrelenting suspicion and distrust. Having attuned itself to psychological warfare, the administration could not appear insensitive to the new Soviet attitude. Four days after Malenkov's speech in March 1953 President Eisenhower told a press conference that any Soviet peace proposal was "just as welcome as it was sincere," and that his administration would seek peace by every honorable and decent means. He reiterated this pledge on 16 April, at a meeting of the American Society of Newspaper Editors in Washington, D.C.[8]

There was an element of calculation in the president's declaration. Public and private discussion across the Atlantic since 1951 had shown very clearly that the United States could not arbitrarily impose its trade views on other members of the Western alliance. To attempt to do so would rupture the multilateral control system and force the United States to pursue a unilateral embargo, which Eisenhower, like Truman before him, considered unworkable and destructive of Western unity. Ultimately a consensus would evolve within the Western community that the safety of the free world would best be served by preserving multilateral controls over strategic trade with the communist world. The disagreement during Eisenhower's presidency focused around the definition of "strategic" and how much control was desirable.

Having taken the propaganda initiative away from the Soviet leadership, Eisenhower nevertheless still acted cautiously. Accepting the peaceful Russian overtures at face value could place the president in the untenable position of opposing reduced spending for foreign aid and military programs while simultaneously having to convince the militant anticommunists that coexistence with the Soviets was possible and even desirable. The president would also have had to discard the entire character of the Republican party's foreign policy platform and campaign vows.

The public's negative view of Russia and communism, combined with the potent influence of the Republican right wing, made any substantive concessions by the administration to foreign opinion politically hazardous.[9] The Senate already had sent the executive branch a warning signal. On 6 May 1953 it passed legislation extending for one more year the United States' export controls. In the course of debate on the bill conservative legislators not only had rejected efforts at peaceful coexistence but also had accused the administration of subverting the intent of the Battle Act by permitting strategic goods to enter the USSR through third countries. Conservative Republican Senators Knowland, Styles Bridges, and Eugene Millikan coupled their demand for a trade embargo of the Soviet Union with insistence on punishment of OEEC countries, like Britain, France, and Italy, that were trading with communists.[10]

The stage seemed set for a replay of the Truman administration's battles with Congress, only with the Republican Eisenhower substituting for the Democratic Truman. Fortunately Eisenhower did not lose his composure. Responding to conservative demands to invoke the sanctions of the

Battle Act against the United States' European allies, he reiterated Truman's admonition that terminating economic and military assistance to Western Europe would put American security at risk, and forcing the allies to relinquish a profitable trade in peaceful goods with Eastern Europe would injure their economies and render the satellite countries even more dependent on the Soviet Union. Carefully sidestepping an open confrontation with Congress and alienation of his Republican colleagues, the president wisely replied to reporters' questions that his administration had not yet formulated a fixed position on East–West trade. Trade controls, he observed, like foreign economic policy in general, were under review.[11]

The president was not being purposely evasive. Several considerations had prompted the administration to initiate a comprehensive review of the nation's economic defense policies soon after taking office. Admiral Walter S. DeLany, deputy director for the Mutual Defense Assistance Control (MDAC) division of the Foreign Operations Administration (FOA), testified in 1954 that these included the growing realization that the Cold War was likely to be a protracted period of tension short of actual combat; the necessity, in this situation, of reexamining Soviet strategy and techniques in world trade; and the emerging international economy resulting from improved economic conditions in Western Europe and the shift from a seller's to a buyer's market.[12] With respect to East–West trade, DeLany indicated that the main thrust of the review was to streamline and tighten the enforcement of strategic export controls. This was consistent with Dulles's early policy of opposing any American–Soviet agreement or reduction in East–West tensions that might cause the free world to let down its guard.[13]

One of the criticisms of the Truman administration had been its failure to integrate its separate programs into a coherent foreign economic policy. In August 1951 *Fortune* had trumpeted the strength of America's industrial capitalism and business enterprise, noting that the United States' economic behavior affected the future course of history whether it was intended to or not. "This being so, it might be thought that the United States would mold this great asset into an economic policy, coordinated with our military policy and subordinate to our political aims, in order to make our leadership as effective as possible in the rest of the world."[14] Nothing was further from the truth. Instead of a coherent foreign economic policy, *Fortune* asserted, the United States had a collection of ad hoc programs and concepts, like the Point Four economic aid program for the underdeveloped countries of the world, rearmament, and economic nationalism. It had not fit Western Europe into a consistent and expanding pattern of world trade with the United States at the center. Europe was viewed as a "problem" in the world struggle with communism, instead of a tremendous asset. Although *Fortune* did not say so specifically, the editors would undoubtedly have included the United States' clashes over strategic controls with its European allies among the symptoms of the absence of a foreign economic policy.

President Eisenhower sought to reverse this drift by laying down important new directions for the conduct of U.S. foreign policy. He attempted, not altogether successfully, to reorient the mutual security program away from military aid and toward a new emphasis on economic assistance; to shift foreign aid to less developed countries; to drag a reluctant Republican party into accepting a reciprocal trade program; and to promote economic growth.[15] On 7 August 1953 he established a commission to study the entire question of foreign economic policy. One aspect of the work undertaken by the Commission on Foreign Economic Policy (CFEP) was to examine the problem of strategic export controls from the perspective of national security and foreign economic policy. At the urging of the secretaries of commerce and the treasury, Sinclair Weeks and George Humphrey, Eisenhower named Clarence B. Randall, head of the giant Inland Steel Company, as chairman.[16]

A lawyer by training, Randall had become familiar with European economic problems as a consultant to Averell Harriman on the administration of the European Recovery Program. His belief in freer trade was in harmony with most large industrialists' and financiers' as well as the administration's own views. In *A Creed for Free Enterprise*, published in 1952, he had written of businessmen and foreign policy that "once we adopt the hypothesis that American aid to Europe is justified for no other purpose than to advance American security, much that has been confused in our thinking can be cleared up." The steel industry, he observed, had benefited from Russian manganese and chrome, and alternative sources had not been easy to find.[17]

While CFEP was organizing its agenda, the *Economist* of London reported on 24 September that the Eisenhower administration would shortly issue its first official statement on East–West trade, in the form of a report to Congress by Harold E. Stassen, the administrator of the Battle Act. It predicted, with considerable accuracy, that Stassen's report would hold fast to the total embargo on trade with China and North Korea, as aggressor nations, but would recommend a switch of emphasis elsewhere, mainly by placing maximum emphasis on strict enforcement of existing regulations and moving some items into the quantitative column. This would occur because of business pressures within the country, the tapering off of military spending, and the diminishing defense orders in the West after the Korean armistice.[18]

In this climate of foreign and domestic pressures CFEP conducted its inquiry. It had to address the economic need of the Western European nations and Japan to broaden their trade opportunities with the United States or else to turn eastward, selling strategic and nonmilitary commodities to the Soviet Union and its satellites. The problem, Randall wrote in January 1954, with considerable understatement, was "not free from difficulty." A gray area existed that presented a dilemma for American policymakers: the trade "between the East and West in Europe in commodities which do not strengthen the forces of military aggression." He advised the commission's members to be flexible and realistic. Given his own preference for freer trade and evidence of the mounting illicit Western trade with Soviet bloc countries, Randall not surprisingly endorsed the commission's preliminary recommendation that "so far as it can be done without jeopardizing military security, the United States encourage the resumption of normal trade in peaceful goods between Western Europe and the Soviet bloc."[19]

The commission presented its report to the president and Congress on 23 January 1954. Adopted by a 12 to 5 vote, the document became the basic foundation for the Eisenhower administration's economic policy. To open up the American market to European producers, it recommended a three-year extension of the Reciprocal Trade Agreements Act and the grant of authority to the executive to reduce current tariffs and lower to 50 percent of the value of the commodity all rates in excess of that figure. The commission also recommended increasing nonstrategic trade with the European Soviet bloc, much along the lines proposed by Stassen as Battle Act administrator, while retaining the existing controls on strategic items. The commission's staff had been greatly influenced on this point by the strain that maintaining the present level of controls was putting on the political ties of the free-world countries, by the contribution to the balance of payments problem greater East–West trade could make, and by its contribution to relieving unemployment at home and abroad.[20]

Despite the majority's endorsement of the principle of peaceful trade, the commission's decision was far from unanimous. Labor leader David J. McDonald, president of the United Steel Workers, argued forcefully that his colleagues' recommendation contravened the thrust of the United States' export control policy, though he admitted that he favored lowering tariff barriers "to keep Western Europe from turning to the Soviet Union." Two Republican congressmen on the commission, Daniel A. Reed of New York and Richard M. Simpson of Pennsylvania, maintained that American–Soviet trade had national security implications best left to Congress.[21] Within the administration the Department of

Defense took a dim view of any trade whatsoever between the United States (and its NATO allies) and the Soviet bloc, arguing that it was difficult to distinguish between militarily strategic and nonstrategic goods and that "any reliance upon the Bloc as a market, even for non-strategic goods, weakens the bargaining power of a free country, and makes it susceptible to Bloc attempts to extract strategic goods from the free country, thereby contributing to the Bloc's industrial and military potential."[22] Labor Secretary Martin P. Durkin protested that the commission's recommendation raised "a number of difficult questions, one of which relates to the possible expansion of trade in commodities which are the product of forced labor."[23]

Despite these objections President Eisenhower formally embraced the commission's report as the foreign economic policy of his administration in a special message to Congress on 30 March 1954. He thus supported an expansion of East–West trade in nonstrategic goods, as long as such commercial intercourse did not jeopardize national security or include trade with Communist China and North Korea, which the administration viewed as aggressor nations. In defense of this decision Eisenhower pointed to escalating demands in and out of Congress to curtail the number and amounts of aid programs to the OEEC countries. Withdrawal of American assistance combined with the industrial recovery of the European economies, he asserted, had created intense pressures to allow Western Europe to resume its historic patterns of trade with the countries of Eastern Europe.[24]

Implicit in the president's statement was an admission that his administration would take a realistic attitude toward East–West trade, despite congressional objections, in order to preserve the system of multilateral controls. It would also resist pressures to discard the controls altogether. Despite this last assurance Eisenhower's message met with a mixed reception in Congress. Republicans generally were eager to go along with the passages that related to free enterprise and the curtailment of government interference, but they were ominously silent on the matter of East–West trade. Archconservative Republican Senator William F. Knowland of California, the powerful leader of the China lobby, thought the section on East–West trade needed "careful consideration"; as a matter of principle he believed that any trade with the bloc countries benefited the Soviet war machine. His noncommittal statement, when coupled with that of fellow Republicans who did not wish to embarrass a highly popular Republican president and Democrats who now saw East–West trade as a partisan political issue, was a signal to the administration that here was a minefield fraught with booby traps and snipers, and that the president had best proceed cautiously.[25]

In this political atmosphere Eisenhower used his enormous personal prestige to advantage to orchestrate the shift away from the decline in East–West trade that had occurred at the height of the Cold War under Truman. Eisenhower intended to act before the Western European nations could torpedo the whole voluntary system of controls. As early as 13 January he had told reporters that the question of nonstrategic trade was under continuous examination. In February Stassen as Battle Act administrator endorsed the CFEP report's proposal for increased peaceful trade with the bloc countries. On 26 February State Department officials and Democratic Senators Wiley, Fulbright, and Gore voiced support for easing export control regulations, on the grounds that American businessmen were losing the nonstrategic trade to their European competitors. Then, on 5 March 1954, President Eisenhower informed Congress that Western European nations, including Great Britain, had shipped strategic goods to the Soviet bloc. For reasons of national security, he added, he would not invoke the sanctions of the Battle Act.[26]

Immediately thereafter the administration began a new dialogue with the Consultative Group (CG) countries, which were pressing for a general relaxation of the international control lists. The United States was represented in these negotiations by Stassen, who was operating under guidelines formulated by an interdepartmental group representing the Departments of State, Commerce, and Defense and FOA's Advisory Committee on Export Policy, which had been reappraising the security importance of commodities under export control.[27] From the outset Stassen took the position that international controls must be maintained on all exports that contributed "directly and significantly to the Soviet bloc's military capabilities." If these controls were adhered to, it would then be possible to relax restrictions on other items and permit expansion of civilian trade. A preliminary exchange of views in London on 9–10 March, and more extensive talks in Paris in April, disclosed that all the Western European countries, and especially Great Britain, wanted to go further than the United States in easing trade restrictions and broadening the scope of East–West trade. While voicing general agreement with the American position, they also made it clear that they intended to define strategic goods more narrowly than the United States, and nonstrategic goods more broadly.[28]

The Europeans' position rested on the premise that the danger of a general war had receded with the Korean armistice agreement and that it now was necessary for the free world to achieve a position of economic preponderance that would endure over a long period of tension and competition with the communists.[29] While accepting this analysis, the

United States nonetheless insisted that the controls were necessary to retard potential Soviet military aggression. To avert an impasse the task of evaluating items on the international control lists was turned over to COCOM, which met in Paris from 27 April to 17 June 1954. The members of COCOM ultimately reached an agreement on all but 70 of the nearly 475 under scrutiny. They agreed that the 70 items that the United States regarded as strategic to the Soviet military would remain on the embargo list until their status could be resolved at the ministerial level.[30] Once the task of reviewing the commodities was completed, COCOM submitted its recommendations to the fifteen participating countries.[31]

While the negotiations were going on, the Joint Chiefs of Staff took the strongest exception to COCOM's tampering with the international controls list. The military hoped that whatever the outcome of the Paris meetings, the United States would unilaterally impose more severe restrictions upon its trade with the Soviet bloc than its allies were willing to accept for themselves. Observing that the USSR viewed East–West trade as a political weapon to further its cold war objectives, General Nathan F. Twining, chairman of the Joint Chiefs of Staff, outlined the military's opposition in a memorandum to the Secretary of Defense on 15 June. Besides their obvious interest in denying the Soviets access to strategic materials that would enhance their military potential, the Joint Chiefs of Staff interpreted Russia's desire for trade with the West as a sign of internal economic weaknesses. Rather than permitting their amelioration by relaxing trade controls, they insisted, *"measures should be taken to foster and aggravate these economic stresses and strains."*[32] If, for political reasons, controls had to be relaxed, they believed that this should occur only after the Geneva Conference of Foreign Ministers (planned for October 1955), or else the Soviets would interpret advance concessions as a sign of Western weakness.

The military's concerns found a sympathetic ear in Congress, especially among conservative Republicans. Senator H. Alexander Smith of New Jersey, a member of the influential Foreign Relations Committee, voiced criticism of any step-up in shipments to the Soviet Union of what Stassen had described as "peaceful goods." Smith declared that by giving the Soviets some of the necessities of life, "we will only enable them to give more attention to the development of their military position." Republican Senator Herman Welker of Idaho warned that if the limitations of the Battle Act were not strictly adhered to, "the American people will be heard from."[33]

Although there were misgivings about the breadth and depth of COCOM's assault on the strategic list, the National Security Council

(NSC) accepted its recommendations while reserving for the United States the option to maintain its own, stricter set of controls. The revised agreement, announced by Stassen on 25 August, was described by him as "a move in the best interests of the United States." It would, he declared, "result in a net advantage to the free world of expanded peaceful trade and more effective control of the war potential items."[34] He gave reporters a gross breakdown of the revisions agreed upon but did not specify individual commodities, following COCOM's usual practice. The number of items on the embargo list was reduced from 260 to 170, exclusive of the arms, ammunitions, and atomic materials category, which was not changed. Products deleted from the list or downgraded included certain types of chemical, petroleum, electric power, industrial, and transportation equipment; machine tools and precision instruments; scarce metals; and rubber and rubber products. The number of items on the quantitative controls list was reduced from 90 to 20, and those on the "watch" list were reduced from 100 to 60. COCOM had made no alterations in the China list.

Stassen concluded that the process of revision had gone further than the United States had desired, but he asserted that the "arithmetic of controls" and the downgrading of specific items did not tell the entire story. Some items, he explained, had been redefined to increase the effectiveness of the controls; others that were downgraded included only certain types and sizes considered to be of minor strategic importance. The net effect was not to prejudice U.S. security but to strengthen the economies of other free-world nations.[35] What Stassen left unsaid was that the American negotiators, reflecting the view of the administration, had assigned a higher priority to maintaining overall cooperation with Great Britain, France, and the other NATO countries than to the strategic importance of the commodities that were in dispute. In any event, the Department of Commerce announced on 29 August 1954 that it was reducing its own list of banned items from 1,450 to 787.[36]

The Eisenhower administration's decision to adhere to what in essence was the Truman attitude toward export controls was motivated primarily by political and diplomatic rather than economic or military considerations. It was an attempt to preserve Anglo-American harmony and strengthen the NATO alliance by being responsive to the perceived needs of other friendly countries in order to ward off a total collapse of the export control system. That, in turn, might well unleash congressional wrath against military and foreign aid programs. As one Commerce Department official put it: "The United States doesn't need Russian trade the way other countries do. We can get along without it." Like Truman's before it, the Eisenhower administration also had come to the belief that effective controls required voluntary, multilateral cooperation. More cynically, support for nonstrategic trade could be used to expose Soviet propaganda. As one deputy assistant secretary of state said, on 19 October, the United States was giving Russia the opportunity to prove that she really wanted to expand East–West trade.[37] In fact United States officials believed that the Russian trade offensive was little more than a device to split the Western alliance; and even if the intention were serious, the Argentine and Greek experiences convinced these same officials that the USSR would be unable to meet its contractual commitments.[38]

There was one other result of the COCOM meeting. It prompted the administration to conduct a cabinet-level review of the entire question of East–West trade. On 28 November 1954 the *New York Times* reported that a number of high government officials, unnamed, were disturbed that the Soviet Union had purchased $600 million worth of capital goods from Western Europe since the start of the year. The bulk of these purchases were of machinery and equipment that had previously been on the international control list and embargoed by the United States for security reasons. These officials attributed the spurt in Soviet purchases to American concessions made in the COCOM meetings and wanted to take another look at the results of the decisions made in Paris. However, as the *Times* pointed out, any attempt to rein in the volume and kind of trade that had developed after the Paris negotiations would run into fierce opposition, because the OEEC countries "desperately need the business to keep their economies going."[39]

That review got under way early in January 1955, when the CIA briefed Secretary of State Dulles and members of CFEP on the current status of East–West trade and the techniques of economic warfare. On 20 January NSC established a task force to reassess economic defense policy; a week later CFEP set up its own steering committee.[40] In the interim the administration received an early indication of what congressional sentiment was likely to be. Secretary of Defense Charles E. Wilson testified on 18 January before the Ways and Means Committee of the House, which was considering legislation to extend the Trade Agreements Act scheduled to expire on 12 June. Wilson's remarks in favor of expanding nonstrategic trade with the USSR contradicted his opposition to such trade in a memorandum of 29 March 1953 to Senator Joseph McCarthy, and were indicative of just how far the administration had gone to accommodate the NATO partners. Conservative Republican Congressman William E. Jenner of Indiana accused the State Department and FOA of advocating the trade and using the secretary of defense as "window dressing to impress Congress." Burned by the criticism within his own party, President Eisenhower disavowed Wilson's testimony as a "casual statement" that did *not* have his "considered approval."[41]

Still another complication arose from the unexpectedly abrupt change in Soviet leadership in early February 1955, which caused some American officials to have second thoughts about the wisdom of relaxing export controls. The emergence of Nikita S. Khrushchev as the number one man in the Kremlin hierarchy and the sudden departure of Anastas I. Mikoyan as minister of foreign trade pointed to a major redirection of Soviet economic policy, away from expansion of the consumer goods sector in order to raise Soviet living standards. On 7 February Joseph M. Dodge, the conservative successor to Randall as chairman of CFEP, informed Robert Amory, Jr., deputy director of the CIA, that the Soviets' 1955 budget, which sharply increased appropriations for the military and heavy industry, with "its inevitable relation to war production," had serious implications for East–West trade policy. Dodge expected the Russians to use Western imports to bolster their sagging consumer sector, which would free domestic resources for military purposes. "Doesn't this combination of circumstances suggest," he warned, "that any contribution through trade to improved living standards, no matter what its nature, becomes a direct contribution to military power and the industrialization that supports it?"[42]

Amory agreed with Dodge's assessment. "The new administration is quite clearly telling its people that heavy, war-supporting industry takes clear precedence and that the people must in effect as patriots be willing to tighten their belts," he replied on 10 February. Khrushchev's buildup of the military and heavy industry, however, might give American policymakers the leverage they needed in talks with the Western European governments. "I have reason to hope that it may make our COCOM friends more receptive to the U.S. position," Amory told Dodge, and asserted that he would even be willing to loosen the China trade controls in return for "a substantial tightening of COCOM controls," which he described as "an excellent bargain from our point of view."[43]

Against the background of congressional suspicions and some reservations within the government, the administration pushed ahead with its review of export controls in the context of economic defense policy. On 23 March 1955 CFEP's steering committee presented to NSC some interim recommendations for endorsement and transmission. These in many respects paralleled the thinking and procedures that culminated in the final statement of policy. For the immediate moment, the steering committee recommended no substantive change in the status quo. This meant maintaining the China embargo in order to discourage aggressive behavior and induce in the regime the kinds of stresses that "can ultimately lead to disintegration." With respect to the European Soviet bloc, the steering committee again recommended no change in the status quo: the recently revised controls seemed to have satisfied the basic objections of the United States' allies, even though they fell short of what the United States preferred. Freed from external pressure, the administration now had breathing space in which to review the rationale and mechanism of the controls system and work toward securing "a larger measure of fundamental agreement between cooperating countries."[44]

CFEP adopted the steering committee's recommendation on 5 April and established a new task force to undertake the more comprehensive, long-term review of economic defense policy. Thorsten V. Kalijarvi of the State Department headed this new group, which periodically presented progress reports to CFEP. Within a space of three months the group prepared eighteen intelligence papers and staff studies covering the full spectrum of economic defense policy. Typical of the studies were "Evaluation of objectives and criteria for selective controls" (by the Department of State and CIA), "Flexible application of controls to promote Soviet bloc disunity" (State), "U.S. controls vis-à-vis multilateral controls" (Commerce and MDAC), "U.S. attitudes toward non-strategic trade, including Free World economic entanglements" (State), and "Use of U.S. sanctions or inducements" (Commerce).[45]

Once the studies were completed, the task force submitted them to a special Drafting Group for discussion and revision in order to square their contents with the provisions of a revised policy statement. The Drafting Group met its deadline of 30 June and put its draft report and recommendations back into Kalijarvi's hands. Despite the Drafting Group's best efforts the proposed policy revision of 8 July 1955 contained two unresolved points, one relating to the implementation of the United States' antifrustration policy to shipments to friendly European countries and the other relating to the timing and procedure for altering U.S. controls after a finding that Communist China should no longer be regarded as an actual, rather than a potential, aggressor. Unable to reconcile interagency differences on these two points, Kalijarvi decided nonetheless to forward the entire document to CFEP.[46]

On 20 July Chairman Dodge briefed the other members of CFEP on the report and proposed policy statement, which would replace wholly or in part previous pronouncements on economic defense. A consensus developed not to take any action for the time being, for fear that knowledge of any change in the present policy "might prejudice the U.S. negotiating position at the October meeting of the Foreign Ministers." Instead CFEP requested the task force to prepare new position papers on East–

West trade, particularly on subjects that might prove useful to American negotiators at the foreign ministers' conference, which was scheduled for 27 October in Geneva.[47]

Pursuant to its instructions, the task force came forth with its recommendations on 4 October. With respect to controls over strategic items, the task force concurred in the present policy, endorsed by the COCOM-participating countries, that linked any adjustment in the scope of such controls to substantive Soviet concessions in the arena of international security: "The justification for U.S. actions to reduce or remove barriers to peaceful East–West trade need not be looked for in the trade field alone, but may be found in the wider field of cultural or technical exchange, or in the fields of security and East–West political relations."[48]

As to nonstrategic items, the task force advised that the negotiators be prepared to facilitate this commerce within the existing legal and policy framework. Specifically, Washington should send a clear signal to the business community that it welcomed peaceful trade and participation in Soviet trade fairs; the Department of Commerce should reverse its usual practice of denying export licenses in borderline cases; and the department should gradually phase out the onerous requirement of special individual export licenses. Beyond this, the United States should encourage the barter of agricultural surpluses for strategic materials such as chrome, amending P.L. 480 to facilitate this and accepting European Soviet bloc currencies if need be;[49] and it should enter into commercial, licensing, and copyright agreements with Russia and the satellite countries. Although the task force refrained from asking for specific concessions from the Russians, it hoped they would give a sign of good-faith willingness to participate in peaceful trade.[50]

As for any significant departure from the existing legal and policy framework at Geneva—this was a reference to the possible restoration of most-favored-nation status to Russia and the bloc countries—the task force advised the secretary of state to withhold that privilege until a later stage in the negotiations, "until the Soviets themselves have made sufficient accommodation toward reducing the barriers to East–West economic and cultural exchanges."[51]

These fairly liberal views represented the thinking of the majority of the task force, who were sensitive to the domestic pressures that were mounting for increased trade in peaceful goods. For example, the emphasis on selling agricultural surpluses behind the Iron Curtain was a direct result of pressure from the farm lobby.[52] But there also existed a minority dissent that went forward in the group's recommendations to CFEP. Representatives from the Department of Commerce and the Treasury opposed amending P.L. 480 to allow the barter of agricultural surpluses. And although the task force endorsed the retention of strategic controls, it warned CFEP to be skeptical about the present level of multilateral controls, because of confidential information that Great Britain intended to propose a further reduction of the Positive List regardless of the outcome of the foreign ministers' meeting.[53]

On 11 October Dr. Gabriel Hauge, a White House aide, acting in the absence of Dodge, presented the task force's position paper to the members of CFEP.[54] After brief discussion they endorsed the document, but with certain revisions. They asked the task force to tone down language that stated that the United States "actively favors" the conduct of peaceful trade and other promotional activities (such as trade fairs) with the Soviet bloc. And, because they could not agree on whether to accept bloc currency, they suggested deleting any reference to local currencies and apprising Secretary of State Dulles of their disagreement. Once the revisions were made, CFEP's position paper was forwarded to Dulles, on 17 October.[55]

On the major issues confronting the Big Four—disarmament, German reunification, and elections in South Vietnam—the Geneva Conference of Foreign Ministers that opened on 27 October 1955 led to no real mitigation of cold war tensions. In terms of U.S. foreign economic policy, the conference encouraged the movement for relaxation of controls on East–West trade. Secretary of State Dulles indicated that the United States would proceed with its plan to ease some restrictions governing the export of nonstrategic items to the Soviet Union and the European Soviet bloc (China and North Korea being excepted). This announcement was consistent with the president's objective of opening channels of peaceful trade and communication with the communist bloc or, in the words of Secretary of Commerce Weeks, of creating "conditions which will encourage nations to increase the exchange of peaceful goods throughout the world."[56]

The administration's decision to relax some East–West trade restrictions was more propagandistic and symbolic than substantive and probably had more to do with pressures from the Western European governments than to the so-called spirit of Geneva. This is evident from the letters of Under Secretary of State Herbert Hoover, Jr., to Secretary Weeks and Joseph Dodge, on 3 December. The talks had afforded the United States an opportunity to demonstrate its sincerity and constructiveness on the issue. "On the other hand," Hoover added, "they demonstrated the fact that blame should be accorded to the Soviets for preventing progress toward this objective." The State Department's position was to continue for the moment "our flexible and reasonable treatment of trade control questions," to emphasize the record of good faith that the United States had established earlier at conferences in Geneva, and "to allow the attitude and actions adopted in furtherance of the President's policies to have the fullest opportunity for gradual and cumulative effect."[57]

President Eisenhower had not been lulled into believing that the United States could slacken its efforts to contain the communist threat or that the Soviets had suddenly embraced the concepts of honor, decency, and integrity, on which international law and order rested.[58] American businessmen, meanwhile, were quick to point out that easing restrictions would have little impact on the total volume of trade between Russia and the United States, primarily because the Soviets had little to offer except timber, furs, and caviar. The most concrete effect of the president's decisions would be to relieve American exporters of the burdensome chore of applying for a license each time they had a shipment to export to the USSR.[59]

Although the original intent was to ease the restrictions in January of the new year, the Department of Commerce did not promulgate a more liberal set of regulations until 26 April 1956. The delay was due in part to technical and bureaucratic snags but also, and unhappily for the proponents of "peace through trade" on both sides of the Atlantic, to Soviet cold war economic, political, and military activities that rendered obsolete CFEP's policy revision of 8 July 1955 and the promises of the foreign ministers' conference. Increasing evidence came to light in late 1955 and early 1956 of the Soviet bloc's progress in important military and industrial fields, as exemplified by new operational military aircraft and production and research advances in atomic energy.[60]

Moreover, as part of a shift in policy after the death of Stalin, from the inevitability of a military confrontation with the West to one of global peaceful economic competition, the Soviet Union accelerated its courtship of third world countries. Soviet leaders wooed underdeveloped nations, visiting India, Burma, Afghanistan, Indonesia, Egypt, and Syria, where they proffered generous offers of economic assistance. In the United Nations, Soviet delegates supported expanded programs of economic aid to the third world.[61]

The Eisenhower administration and Congress were greatly perturbed by this "economic offensive," which peaked under Khrushchev's leadership. They interpreted the Kremlin's tactics as threatening to align third world nations closely with the communist bloc. And given the spread of neutralism and nonalignment among the underdeveloped countries of Asia, Africa, and the Middle East, which Secretary of State Dulles publicly branded as immoral, the Soviet challenge raised fundamental questions about the purpose and effectiveness of the United States' mutual security legislation, export controls, and foreign aid programs.[62]

The globalization of the Cold War proceeded apace after the Geneva conference. Despite this challenge to Western interests, several COCOM-participating countries and other cooperating Western nations showed a marked unwillingness to continue even the much-reduced multilateral system of controls on trade with Russia or China. Great Britain was the most serious offender. On 25 November 1955 Commerce Secretary Weeks complained to Under Secretary of State Hoover about the large quantities of copper being exported from the West to the European Soviet bloc—amounts that rendered the embargo on copper a sham. Hoover conceded that the problem existed but said that the British Cabinet had been very insistent that copper *wire* not be restored to the international controls list.[63] Equally serious, the British were openly criticizing the rationale for retaining the system and were flagrantly abusing the exceptions procedure to ship embargoed items to Communist China.[64] Diplomatic initiatives to persuade the COCOM countries that the strategic controls system was integral to their national security had not gotten anywhere.

CFEP Chairman Dodge perceived a direct correlation between Britain's insistence that trade restrictions be further eased and the Soviet Union's economic offensive in the third world. On 13 January 1956 he wrote to Hoover that because of the totalitarian nature of the Soviet government Russia could arbitrarily extract from her gross national product a percentage in various categories of production for sale abroad, regardless of domestic consumer needs. This posed an "aggressive threat" to the West and the third world. "The substantial reduction already made in the level of the COCOM controls, coupled with some degree of evasion and weakness in its implementation, undoubtedly has contributed to the Soviet ability to undertake this offensive without too much penalty on its domestic economy," Dodge declared. To ease curbs on trade now would further alleviate strains on the Russians' domestic economy and heighten the threat to the West's economic and political stake in the underdeveloped countries. Further, it would facilitate the Soviets' obligation to help China industrialize. For these reasons, Dodge concluded, the commercial and political interests of the free world in the underdeveloped nations might be "better protected by *increasing* the level of controls and *strengthening* their implementation."[65]

Hoover concurred in this analysis, for he wrote to Dodge on 16 January: "In my opinion, you have presented a strong argument for not having a substantial reduction in CHINCOM or COCOM controls." He also circulated Dodge's memorandum to State Department officers assigned to the problem of East–West trade and those—especially Secretary Dulles—who viewed the neutrality of the third world countries as a step toward communism.[66]

In contrast to the foreign pressures for relaxing the existing level of controls were the domestic pressures on the Eisenhower administration to retain and improve them, as evidenced by the continuing critical attention of Congress to the 1954 revisions. By mid-1956 the administration found itself on the horns of a dilemma. If the United States did not acquiesce in some further substantial relaxation of the controls system as the Western Europeans demanded, it might jeopardize the principle of voluntary, cooperative multilateral control. On the other hand, if it did acquiesce in any substantial relaxation, such action might provoke opposition at home, particularly in Congress, which could affect the strategic controls program and jeopardize other military and foreign economic aid programs that contributed to the mutual defense effort. In July CFEP's task force again recommended that the present level of controls remain in place. Predictably, it also advised further study of the relationship between economic defense policy and the system of multilateral controls.[67]

The problem for the remainder of Eisenhower's first term as president was not so much the inability of the administration to chart a bold new direction in its handling of the multilateral controls system, one that was more sensitive to the economic needs and desires of the COCOM countries but that did not sacrifice the security interests of the West, as it was to maintain even the very slight crack in the door to a more liberalized East–West trade that was developing in the wake of the 1955 Geneva Conference of Foreign Ministers. Even this prospect was extinguished in the fall of 1956, when Russian tanks brutally crushed the popular uprising in Hungary. Having earlier ruled out U.S. military intervention in communist Eastern Europe as a viable policy, despite the rhetoric of liberation in the 1952 Republican party platform, and now preoccupied with the Suez crisis in the Middle East, which reached its height at about this time, the Eisenhower administration had few arenas other than East–West trade for making known its displeasure with Soviet actions. In November 1956 the United States once again suspended all trade contacts with the Soviet Union.[68]

DURING Eisenhower's first administration U.S. economic defense policy underwent a sweeping reexamination in the light of changing economic and political circumstances, both in the Soviet bloc and in the free world. Policymakers reviewed Soviet strategy and techniques in the trade field and considered new conditions in Western Europe brought about by an improving economic situation and a shift from a seller's market to a buyer's market. Russia was changing its economic tactics with the West by emphasizing trade instead of autarchy and challenging the West for influence in the third world. Conversely, economic interests within the free world were becoming more receptive to trade with the Soviet Union and Eastern Europe, especially in the wake of the Korean armistice in 1953. This review did not change the basic policy or objectives of the export control program, but it did result in a new direction and a change of emphasis to meet the changing circumstances and conditions of the world.

The courses of action decided upon were made in the framework of Eisenhower's directive that the program not increase the risk of war, but rather keep open the path to a sounder peace. The policy review resulted in an affirmation of the practice that U.S. interference in trade between the Western allies and the Soviet bloc (excluding China and North Korea) should occur only where there was a clear security advantage to the West in doing so. This was based on the realization that over the long term, even if trade controls might withhold a contribution to the overall Soviet bloc economy, they would not seriously impair it. In the short term and in selected areas only, the growth of Soviet war potential might at best be delayed.

Over congressional and conservative protests, the administration's policy was to achieve its security objectives while respecting the sovereignty of the allies. The White House believed that expanding the number of items on the strategic controls list no longer served a useful purpose; instead it chose to concentrate on more effective multilateral control of a smaller number of items that, if shipped, would make a significant contribution to Soviet war potential. This was the background of the liberalization of Western trade controls in 1954.

In reviewing its policy, the Eisenhower administration did not neglect the fact that even nonstrategic trade had a bearing on the policies and actions of other countries. It foresaw two potential risks if the West became excessively dependent on Soviet markets for nonstrategic commodities and on Soviet sources of supply for raw materials. Excessive dependence might put the Soviets in a stronger position to insist on inclusion of strategic commodities as a condition for continuing or enhancing a profitable trade in civilian goods; or they might use trade leverage to influence the political policy or disrupt the economies of the free world. Washington officials believed that to avert these potential threats to U.S. and Western security, the United States and its allies should develop markets and sources of raw materials other than those in the Soviet Union and Eastern Europe. Implementation of this practice proved to be politically difficult, for Congress was reluctant to lower U.S. tariff barriers.

By the close of Eisenhower's first term of office, the administration was pursuing several policy objectives simultaneously. It was attempting to control selective exports of commodities and services from the free world that contributed significantly to Soviet war potential; to obtain maximum security advantage for the free world in the trade that did occur; to reduce Western reliance on trade with the Soviet bloc, recognizing that this was an international cooperative effort, though the United States had independent responsibilities in this regard as well; and to be certain that the United States' actions tended always to increase the political and economic unity of the free world. Attaining these objectives was not always easy, as President Eisenhower discovered when he had to balance the legitimate economic interests of the Western allies with the equally legitimate security concerns of Congress and the American public.

CHAPTER FIVE

China, Russia, and East-West Trade

IN the 1950s Americans perceived communism as a hard, monolithic bloc that had no crevices or cracks within it. The Soviet threat was fundamentally ideological, indivisible, and posed a danger everywhere in the world. As late as 1956 the Eisenhower administration shared this view of a bipolar world, of the international arena as a struggle between the two competing power blocs: the communist world and the free world. From this perspective problems in Europe and in Asia were linked, as Joseph Dodge had linked Russia and China in his memorandum to Herbert Hoover, Jr. This made it possible for the Eisenhower administration to talk about Russian communism and Chinese communism as though they were identical. After repeated attempts to use economic sanctions as leverage against "International Communism" the administration soon learned that the Soviet Union was not China, and that foreign economic policy toward the one could not necessarily be directed toward the other.[1]

At the outbreak of the Korean War the United States and its NATO partners had imposed an economic quarantine on mainland China and North Korea. The armistice of 1953 unraveled allied support for that policy.[2] Having successfully questioned the need for a trade embargo of the Soviet Union after Stalin's death, the Western European governments, responding to their own domestic pressures, logically and inevitably voiced doubts about the need for an economic blockade of China. Whether and how best to preserve the more rigorous multilateral system of export controls on trade with Communist China became an urgent matter in U.S. foreign policy in December 1955, when Secretary of State Dulles advised the president that "our efforts to maintain the current differential export control toward Communist China have passed the state of being divisive; they present us with the prospect of total disintegration."[3] The British, in particular, were pressing to have CHINCOM controls scaled down to conform to those that applied toward the USSR. Dulles requested presidential authorization to initiate talks with the Western allies in order to preserve the multilateral system. Any discussion of the China trade issue was bound to affect the United States' position on trade with the Soviet Union.

Eisenhower recognized this and instructed Dulles to urge the British government to defer unilateral action until he could speak directly with Prime Minister Anthony Eden, at their meeting scheduled for 31 January 1956. While Dulles was conveying the president's wishes to London, the National Security Council (NSC) issued a directive to the Council on Foreign Economic Policy (CFEP) to formulate a position paper for the president to use in his negotiations with Eden.[4]

A subcommittee of CFEP, headed by Herbert V. Prochnow, deputy under secretary of state, recommended on 11 January 1956 that the president advise the British that the United States did not intend to modify its embargo on trade toward Communist China, which it branded an aggressor nation.[5] Mindful of the adverse effect that such action would have on public and congressional opinion (a reference to the Battle Act), the subcommittee argued that the free-world nations should stiffen rather than soften controls against mainland China. However, if concessions had to be made to preserve the principle of multilateralism, the subcommittee proposed a minimum reduction of controls, limited to nineteen items selected from exceptions recently requested by Japan. In return for this concession, the Eden government should pledge to tighten controls against the Soviet Union, especially to restore controls over copper wire exports. Should the British reject this quid pro quo, the president was to make "no further concessions," unless the entire multilateral control structure was endangered. In that event the United States would have to review its position.[6] After some discussion, CFEP endorsed the recommendations of its subcommittee and forwarded them to NSC.

The issue of China trade controls led President Eisenhower to question in general the validity of using economic sanctions to influence Soviet behavior. Thus when NSC staff convened on 25 January to review the CFEP subcommittee's document, they also had before them a presidential request for an analysis of the dollar gains or losses to the United States and its allies if virtually all controls were removed from trade with Russia and the bloc countries. On short notice the CIA and the Department of Commerce drafted reports for the president's inspection before his meeting with the British prime minister.[7]

The CIA's analysis was cleared with the Departments of State, Defense, and Commerce and the International Cooperation Administration (ICA) of the Foreign Operations Administration (FOA); although there was some disagreement on emphasis, there was consensus on the major conclusion: the elimination of controls on all goods, except arms and atomic energy, would result in a very small (about fifteen percent) increase in trade relative to the free world and, because of the Soviet Union's policy of autarchy, would have little effect upon the European Soviet bloc.[8] The aggregate level of East–West trade, the report concluded, was much more a function of Soviet economic policies than of Western trade controls. "Thus there is a strong presumption that Western trade controls do not greatly restrict the total level of trade and that total East–West trade would not undergo a spectacular increase if Western controls were abolished."[9]

In other words, pressures to ease curbs on trade were fundamentally political in nature rather than economic. Armed with this information and the recommendations of CFEP's subcommittee, Eisenhower met with Prime Minister Eden. During the talks Eden put forth a list of items that Britain proposed to have removed from the multilateral embargo of Communist China. If necessary, Britain was prepared to act alone, which would undermine the multilateral approach to controls that was the cornerstone of U.S. policy. The paltry nineteen items that CFEP had reluctantly approved for decontrol clearly were not going to satisfy the British, so Eisenhower told Eden that he would ask his experts to examine the British list. Until then, the two leaders agreed, any adjustment of the China trade controls "should be effectuated in such manner as to avoid any public misapprehension that changes had been made in basic policies or attitudes." This was a British concession to the president in order to allay the fears of congressional conservatives and the public that the United States was easing up on communism.[10]

That same afternoon the president asked CFEP to review the CHINCOM control list and to make recommendations on whether further adjustments could be made without jeopardizing the security of the free world. CFEP chairman Joseph M. Dodge transmitted the request and the British list to the Economic Defense Advisory Committee (EDAC) to determine which Western items would most enhance China's military potential, which Chinese exports would benefit free-world countries other than Japan and the United States, and which would benefit principally Japan. EDAC reported back to Dodge on 2 March 1956, listing 34 items out of 297, in ascending order of importance, as being of least advantage to the economic and military potential of China.[11]

EDAC could not come to a consensus on the American position concerning the second and third questions. The Department of State, ICA, and the Mutual Defense Advisory Committee (MDAC) advised that, if necessary, the United States should agree to a decontrol of eighty items on the CHINCOM list without requiring a quid pro quo from the British. The Treasury and the Department of Defense, however, tied concessions on the China trade to the European Soviet bloc. They proposed that the United States agree to decontrol List 1A plus natural rubber, but to go no further unless Britain supported the American position for a unified export control program that was substantially broader in scope than the present COCOM list. The Department of Commerce endorsed this position, arguing that the small commercial and economic benefits that would accrue to the free world from a relaxation of CHINCOM controls did not justify the pressures of friendly governments for such action. These pressures were political in origin and should be treated on that level. Hence, the Commerce Department advised, the president should not agree to decontrol any items beyond the nineteen that CFEP had recommended on 26 January. Other items could be traded for political concessions, such as a satisfactory conclusion of the Geneva talks on the release of American prisoners of war and Chinese guarantees for the safety of Taiwan.[12]

The Eisenhower administration was caught between the proverbial rock and a hard place. On the one side, pressure was intensifying from the British, the Japanese, and other free-world countries to relax the CHINCOM controls on nonstrategic items. If the United States did not demonstrate flexibility, the entire multilateral control system might well unravel, in Asia and in Europe. On the other side, a Republican administration that had come into office on the charge that Truman and the Democrats had been "soft" on communism could ill afford to arouse right-wing suspicions of appeasement. On 27 February 1956 Dodge had written to Herbert V. Prochnow that "a general attitude of resistance to further decontrols has been apparent in the press, . . . on the part of certain commentators, and from publicity about an investigation of the subject by a Congressional Committee." He further declared that "our friends abroad," especially Great Britain, "should be made fully aware of the negative domestic attitudes."[13]

Secretary of State Dulles disclosed his own concerns in a personal and confidential letter to the British foreign secretary, Selwyn Lloyd, dated 19 April.[14] The administration's political position was precarious, he wrote, because Senator McClellan's investigating committee had taken "a very active and aggressive interest" in East–West trade. Congressional conservatives might use a further relaxation of trade controls as an excuse to truncate the foreign aid program or to attach conditions "which would seek to penalize heavily any trade with the Soviet or Chinese Communist bloc in whatever Congress might define as strategic goods."[15] The danger was not imaginary. To defuse conservative hostility, Dulles sought a quid pro quo that would enable the administration to give the appearance of taking a firm stance against international communism while accommodating the needs of the allies: "I feel that under all the circumstances the best we could contemplate would be a package which would (a) put copper wire back on the COCOM list and tighten up somewhat the entire control system and (b) take rubber and a number of miscellaneous items, perhaps 30 or 40, off the CHINCOM list." The Department of Defense and the Joint Chiefs of Staff, he noted, felt "most strongly" about denying copper and copper wire to the Soviet military.[16]

Although both Britain and France believed that the COCOM/ CHINCOM differential should be eliminated altogether, they were willing to dismantle the controls over a protracted period, if that would help the administration on the domestic political front, where the specific problem of China trade controls was melding into another general debate over East–West trade.[17] As Dulles had feared, the Senate Investigations Subcommittee, chaired by Democrat John McClellan of Arkansas, threatened to investigate the administration's decision to drop nearly two hundred items from the strategic list, the most sweeping revision since 1954. Speaking to a White House news conference on 7 March, President Eisenhower defended the decision, explaining that the increase in Western Europe's production of civilian goods and the inability of the American market to absorb the surplus, along with Congress's reluctance to continue financial grants to OEEC countries, had made it necessary for the Western Europeans to reestablish their traditional commercial links with Eastern Europe. But he also was cautious in responding to newsmen's questions about further reductions, saying that "they would have to be studied on a day-to-day basis as to security."[18]

Continued partisan attacks by the Democratic majority of the McClellan subcommittee underscored the explosive political nature of adjusting domestic and foreign commercial needs to the requirements of free-world security. On 18 July 1956 McClellan filed the subcommittee's majority report, signed by Democrats Henry "Scoop" Jackson, Stuart Symington, and Sam Ervin, with the Government Operations Committee. It accused the Eisenhower administration of secretly agreeing to a dangerous liberalization of export controls to the Soviet bloc in 1954 and of withholding "the fact that foreign nations receiving aid from the American taxpayers are in turn helping the Communists to arm themselves against the United States and the free world." The report also denounced the administration for having disregarded "the clear intent of Congress" in downgrading nearly two hundred items that had formerly been classified "strategic" and that experts asserted "could be of tremendous help to the Soviet war economy."[19]

Echoing a refrain from the Republican side of the aisle during the Truman years, the report also noted the frequent complaints from Congress that the executive branch had withheld vital information relating to the Battle Act lists and to revision of international controls. McClellan insisted that the subcommittee not only had a right to examine all relevant records and working papers but also a duty to make such information public in order to inform the American people. The administration's insistence on secrecy, he intimated, stemmed from pledges given to France and Italy, which feared that publicity for the control lists would stir up the large Communist parties in those countries.[20]

McClellan's innuendo precipitated a fight over executive privilege, with various cabinet officials volunteering to testify in closed sessions of the subcommittee but refusing to supply relevant documents on an unclassified basis. Acting Secretary of State Herbert Hoover, Jr., had explained the administration's position to McClellan on 20 February. Voluntary cooperation was the sole means of achieving effective international control of strategic material. "The system of controls depends for its very existence on the good faith of the participating nations," he wrote. "Any of those nations is free to take unilateral action at any time if for any reason it does not wish to abide by the suggested control list." The administration had promised the OEEC governments that the details of their negotiations would remain secret. Public exposure, Hoover asserted, would jeopardize the principle of multilateralism upon which export controls rested and "would endanger our national security."[21]

Neither the offers to testify in executive session nor Hoover's explanation satisfied the Democratic members of the subcommittee. Ironically, two of the most conservative Republicans, Senators Karl Mundt of South Dakota and George Bender of Ohio, found themselves coming to the defense of the administration's actions. The Mundt-Bender minority report castigated the Democratic majority for distortions, unsupported findings, oversimplifications, and giving "a wholly erroneous picture." It asked Congress to put the recent revisions in the context of the trade controls' primary objectives: to increase the strength of the United States and its NATO partners, and to impede a Soviet military buildup. The administration's policy had succeeded on both counts. And, though Mundt and Bender voiced regret that the OEEC countries were not as hard-nosed as the United States in implementing export controls, they praised the Eisenhower administration for its competent leadership, persistence, and continued application of the export control laws.[22]

East–West trade was threatening to become a partisan political issue in the fall presidential election, especially after McClellan threatened to hold hostage the administration's $4 billion foreign aid bill if Eisenhower did not cut off financial, economic, and military assistance to the OEEC countries that were trading with the Soviets. Fortunately, cooler heads prevailed. After intense lobbying, the Senate Foreign Relations Committee and the House Committee on Foreign Affairs both deleted amendments that would have required the executive to invoke the sanctions of the Battle Act against the Western European allies.[23]

Badly frightened, the administration continued to pursue the middle ground between European pressure to wipe out the "China trade differential" and congressional pressure to enforce the Battle Act blindly. President Eisenhower wrote to Prime Minister Eden on 27 April, again urging his government to restore copper wire to the strategic list. He hinted that the United States would acquiesce in "Britain's liberal use of the exception procedure" for rubber and a number of other items on the CHINCOM list. Eden's response was not encouraging.[24]

Again the China controls became the focal point of discussions within the administration. In July CFEP asked EDAC to develop definitive policy recommendations by the end of October. Meanwhile it requested the State Department to draft temporary guidelines for a new round of negotiations with the Western European governments before the CHINCOM meetings in September. Under Secretary for Economic Affairs Prochnow once more coordinated the interim recommendations, which Dulles approved and forwarded to Dodge's successor as CFEP chairman, Clarence B. Randall.[25]

Prochnow reported that the administration's inability to advance some negotiable terms on the China trade issue had resulted in the United States' temporary loss of leadership within CHINCOM to Great Britain and was having a corrosive effect upon multilateral cooperation. Unless the United States devised a realistic agenda for negotiations, the damage might spread to the European COCOM system. Prochnow proposed that the administration develop a new list of items that could be liberally excepted from the CHINCOM controls and, to minimize the dispute's effect on COCOM, advised the White House to agree to quantitative control of copper wire exports to the Soviets rather than the embargo that had been mentioned to the British. Meanwhile negotiations should proceed toward a permanent solution.[26]

Although CFEP accepted the interim recommendations of the State Department, not everyone within the government was pleased with how they actually were operating. Gordon Gray, the assistant secretary of defense, complained to Randall in October of "both the volume and flagrant use of exceptions" by the CHINCOM-participating countries and feared that their liberalizing tendencies would have a detrimental effect on curbs of Russian trade. "This rate of exceptions by CHINCOM members is rapidly vitiating the security significance of the China differential and, in my opinion, will also have a corrosive effect on the Coordinating Committee (COCOM) list as well," he warned. "Under these circumstances the COCOM/CHINCOM forum will cease to represent the security interest of the free world and instead will soon have only a political and commercial basis."[27]

Like Dulles earlier, Gray worried that congressional hostility to the slightest relaxation of the China trade controls might jeopardize the future of all foreign aid programs, including the military ones. If the trend toward liberalizing the CHINCOM/COCOM controls persisted, he warned Randall, "it would be difficult for this Department to support a position which attaches any particular strategic value to the level of controls to which we are apparently heading." Gray's views found support from Commerce Department officials, who also saw a "basic conflict" between the provisions of the Battle Act and how the Positive List of controlled commodities was being implemented.[28]

Despite these concerns the Eisenhower administration conceded the futility of attempting to maintain an ironclad embargo against mainland China in face of countervailing pressures from the Western allies. Washington policymakers recognized, too, that the issue was bound to surface in future meetings of COCOM, CHINCOM, and the Western foreign ministers. So, in the summer and fall of 1956 EDAC began to draft a new policy proposal for NSC to forward to the president for use in discussions with Western leaders. This proposal, adopted with slight modification in the winter of 1956, accepted the fact that the allies would continue to ease controls on exports to China, however much the United States disapproved. The real problem was to prevent the same thing occurring in Soviet Eastern Europe.[29]

To preserve the multilateral system from total disintegration, not only as applied to China but to Eastern Europe as well, the United States would reluctantly tolerate this breach of solidarity. EDAC recommended that in return for this concession the Eisenhower administration should lobby the allies for tighter restrictions on Western trade with the Soviet Union and Eastern Europe, especially British exports of copper wire. In any event, whether or not the allies cooperated, the United States would not risk a rupture of the Western alliance but would unilaterally enforce stricter export, import, and financial controls on both China and Soviet Europe. A partial exception to this policy was to be permitted in the case of Poland and Yugoslavia; they would be allowed to trade and obtain financial credits from the United States in keeping with the administration's intention of utilizing trade to encourage national self-determination and independence.

It was not until the spring of 1957 that the CHINCOM-participating countries embarked on a new round of discussions of the "China trade differential." On 7 May the French representative proposed a sweeping liberalization of the export controls. Following NSC directive no. 5704/1, the U.S. representative, seeking to retain a significant differential in the level and the severity of controls applied to China as compared with the Soviet Union, countered with a more modest proposal to open up the China trade. After listening to arguments on both sides, twelve of the fifteen countries endorsed the French plan. Isolated, the United States had to give ground in order to obtain an agreement and, indeed, did make a number of concessions. Although these concessions did not win substantial support, they markedly changed the atmosphere of the talks. Four nations, led by West Germany, offered a compromise that maintained the China differential and retained quantitative controls on only twenty-five items that could be sold to the Soviet Union. To maintain the facade of multilateral cooperation the U.S. delegate reluctantly agreed to the German plan.[30]

Before the American delegate acquiesced, Secretary of State Dulles had instructed the U.S. ambassadors to Paris, London, and Tokyo to impress upon the heads of those governments the importance that the president attached to their accepting the German plan. If they remained intransigent and the negotiations collapsed, "public reaction in U.S. will be strongly adverse to governments which force such result, and will also affect position other PCs [participating countries] in eyes U.S.," he telegraphed. "U.S. believes maintenance significant differential is important element in restraining military potential and aggressive intentions Chinese Communists. In view of fact that U.S. bears primary responsibility for defense of free world in Far Eastern area, U.S. would find it extremely difficult explain to American public refusal leading allies cooperate in reaching reasonable compromise."[31]

Despite Dulles's clear warning the effort to maintain the China differential came apart when Britain and France both refused to accept the German compromise and announced that they would trade with China.[32] Such action, of course, would pressure the other participating countries to follow suit and thereby nullify the principle of multilateralism, which was the keystone of U.S. export control policy. The best Washington could hope for was that the same controls applicable to Eastern Europe would be extended to China.[33] The administration strongly suspected that Britain and France had acted in collusion, but C. Douglas Dillon, the U.S. representative at the negotiations and deputy under secretary of state for foreign affairs, put the best possible interpretation on what was patently a diplomatic defeat for the United States. On 11 June he wrote: "While we were unsuccessful in obtaining unanimous acceptance of a differential, our negotiations succeeded in aligning a majority with us, proved that we were flexible and cooperative, and created, by their reasonableness, substantial goodwill among all the other negotiating countries."[34]

In a slightly modified but undated memorandum to the State Department Dillon was more candid about the setback for the American position. "If we had been able to accept something like the proposed compromise about six months or a year ago, we might have been able to retain a significant differential," he admitted. "Our failure to consider a modified position at an earlier date apparently led the British to conclude that our concessions would never be enough to suit them, and consequently to promise their domestic pressure groups, before negotiations began, that they would not agree to the maintenance of any differential at all." Although the British recognized that the U.S. administration had gone a long way to accommodate them, they were evidently so firmly committed that they could not consider the compromise on its merits.[35]

Uppermost in the mind of CFEP Chairman Randall was the domestic political and economic repercussion of the diplomatic defeat in Paris. On 6 June he wrote to Commerce Secretary Sinclair Weeks, a hard-liner, that the British decision would cause the other CHINCOM countries to abandon the China differential. With the cornerstone of the multilateral policy gone, "it would seem reasonable to expect that competitive pressures will build up that will be prejudicial to American businessmen." Washington would be pressured into reconsidering its unilateral treatment of Communist China. Since Eisenhower had spoken publicly and privately in favor of liberalizing trade with mainland China for purely diplomatic reasons, Randall observed, "it might be well for us to re-examine the whole question of United States trade policy toward Communist China before events force us to take that direction."[36]

The military viewed the collapse of the China differential with by far the greatest alarm and deduced that this was the prelude to a new assault on the Soviet COCOM restrictions. Vice Admiral Arthur Radford, chairman of the Joint Chiefs of Staff, wrote to Secretary of Defense Donald A. Quarles on 13 June that the CHINCOM negotiations had demonstrated "clearly a trend on the part of most participating countries to subordinate national and collective security aspects of the trade control question to purely commercial and political considerations. . . . In the wake of Western failure to preserve a united front in maintaining the China differential, there are indications that relaxation or elimination of controls on trade with the U.S.S.R. and her European satellites may be next on the calendar of policy modifications by one or more of our allies."[37]

These developments spurred the Joint Chiefs of Staff to reassess both the CHINCOM and COCOM controls as they affected the national security. The recent split over the China differential was likely to enhance Beijing's image abroad at the expense of the United States, open China to increased Western trade, and accelerate her industrial and military buildup. How did the China dispute influence relations with the USSR? The Joint Chiefs of Staff contended that Russia also employed free trade as a weapon of cold war and would attempt to undermine COCOM controls. "Through it they achieve political and economic penetration of countries in which they wish to promote the aspirations of international Communism," wrote Admiral Radford. He cited as evidence the "shopping lists" of Soviet leaders during their visit to Great Britain in the spring of 1956 and Khrushchev's plea on British television for greater trade and business contacts with the West. Russia was seeking to obtain selected strategic and technologically advanced commodities in order to accelerate its industrial and military growth without major commitment of resources to research and development. The Joint Chiefs of Staff concluded gloomily that "relaxation of COCOM controls will, therefore, work to the direct benefit of Soviet cold war apparatus."[38]

This analysis led inevitably to the conclusion that the United States' national and collective security interests could be protected only by undiluted enforcement of both the CHINCOM and the COCOM controls.[39] The Joint Chiefs of Staff further recommended that NSC, in concert with congressional leaders, again review the economic defense policy with the purpose of enforcing sanctions against the OEEC countries that unilaterally traded with China or violated the strategic controls system.[40] They believed that COCOM approached the problem from a narrowly commercial rather than a strategic security perspective; hence they advocated transferring the enforcement or export controls to NATO "to insure that the strategic and security aspects of this vital Western cold war instrument are accorded proper emphasis vis-à-vis economic and commercial considerations." The military adhered to this position for the remainder of Eisenhower's presidency.[41]

Meanwhile, in Congress, on 4 June an influential group in the Senate, led by Lyndon Johnson of Texas and composed mostly of Democrats, had made a cautious move toward creating a new atmosphere more conducive to relaxing the embargo against Communist China, should President Eisenhower be inclined to emulate the British action. These advocates of a "new look" at China trade policy were themselves responding to pressures from local agricultural and business interests eager to compete with Britain for control of the China market and to deflect cheaper Japanese textiles away from American shores. They were offering the president a unique opportunity to reassess the current policy and to lay the groundwork for modifying the embargo. Eisenhower preferred not to take the initiative but to await the report from NSC, which had been reexamining the American position in the wake of the Paris CHINCOM meeting.[42]

NSC's review, completed on 16 September 1957, suggested that liberals and businessmen who were hoping for a major redirection of American political and foreign economic policy toward mainland China would be disappointed. The report summarized in one place the Eisenhower administration's past and future approach to the prickly issue of East–West trade. The rationale behind the document was revealing in its embrace of a number of prevailing and often contradictory strategies: containment, rollback, unilateralism, and multilateralism, with all the shades of flexibility and rigidity inherent in them. In the end, the report was an accurate reflection of the divisions within the government on the importance and effectiveness of export controls in retarding communist war potential.[43]

As a general policy the NSC report stated that the economic defense of the United States should be framed and administered with full recognition of the fact that the nation was part of the larger system of free-world military and political alliances and depended upon the cooperative efforts of the free nations to enforce the export controls system. As such, the United States had to be flexible and sensitive to the domestic political and economic problems that controls might create for its allies. Flexibility in keeping the embargo list current was also emphasized. "Extensions or reductions of the multilateral controls should be proposed or supported, whenever justified by new technology, new intelligence or altered evaluation of the significance of particular imports to the Sino-Soviet bloc."[44]

Elsewhere the document spoke directly to the United States' role, and it was here that contradictions reflecting differences of opinion within the administration became most apparent. It articulated a course of action that was considerably less flexible, more restrictive, and ultimately at odds with the principle of multilateralism. It declared that the United States should maintain such "unilateral controls as will have a significant effect on the growth of the war potential of the bloc or will effectively support other U.S. policies or fulfill U.S. legislative requirements"—a reference to the Battle Act. The United States, and by implication other free-world countries, should avoid excessive dependence upon the Sino-Soviet bloc as market or source of supply; institute more severe controls against China and North Korea; and use trade controls to encourage the

Soviet European satellites to gain national self-determination and independence (hardly a high priority of the OEEC countries).[45]

The NSC report was most explicit on the implementation of this policy. The United States, alone and in concert with other nations, should maintain the existing control apparatus, modifying it to reflect vulnerabilities of the Soviet bloc and to close loopholes in enforcement; manipulate the list in the case of the satellite countries "to encourage and support progress toward national self-determination and independence"; encourage free-world nations to resist Sino-Soviet economic penetration and undue dependence on trade in that direction by fostering alternative markets and sources of supply; and retain the present level of controls toward China.[46]

The report really did not provide the unambiguous guidelines the president was seeking, as the next challenge to the CHINCOM/COCOM control system—the first since the May meeting in Paris—demonstrated.[47] On 31 January 1958 CFEP chairman Randall wrote to the president's chief of the executive staff, Sherman Adams, that Great Britain was expected shortly to propose a substantial easing of controls on trade with the Sino-Soviet bloc. The British rationale was that controls should be limited only to items that had a direct bearing on Soviet military capabilities in a thermonuclear attack, and not directed against its industrial base. Randall hoped to counter the British proposal by having the State Department and CFEP examine its implications "just as promptly as possible." However, Under Secretary Douglas Dillon informed Randall that Dulles, who was en route to Washington from Ankara, wanted to alert the president to the problem himself. Although this short-circuited the normal procedure for examining East–West trade problems, Randall acquiesced.[48]

After Dulles spoke with the president, NSC asked CFEP to prepare a new position paper responding to the British petition to cut the existing controls drastically. On 6 February Randall appointed an ad hoc committee, chaired by Dillon and consisting of Mansfield Sprague of the Department of Defense and Walter Williams of the Department of Commerce, to draft recommendations. Two days later General Robert H. Cutler, national security adviser to the president, informed Dillon that he needed CFEP's recommendations no later than 14 February, if he was to review them in time for the 27 February meeting of NSC. This timetable would also enable the military to make their views known.[49]

In the interim Randall had also written to Dulles, voicing his concern that the British proposal could rupture the Western alliance, a situation that had to be avoided at all cost. "I hold the strong conviction that this matter must not be allowed to disrupt NATO unity," he declared. The

United States must negotiate the best deal it could with the British and hold out for the maximum degree of control that hard bargaining could produce; "but," Randall added, "I would be prepared to go the whole distance to meet their viewpoint rather than risk the serious consequences of an open rupture." He reminded Dulles of just how deeply divided the government was on the issue of East–West trade: "It is one of the most difficult problems I have had to handle since I have been here." Like Randall, Dulles believed that in the final analysis Western unity was paramount.[50]

Randall's observations accurately reflected the division between the United States and its allies, and within the government as a whole, on the question of security controls. In a memorandum to CFEP on 13 February Dillon confirmed that the divergence between Washington and its principal NATO allies and Japan had "in recent months tended to isolate the United States in COCOM discussions and threatens to disrupt the international control machinery." Dillon's committee was similarly split. The Departments of State and Commerce wanted the administration to restore the community of design and purpose essential to the effective functioning of the multilateral control system. This meant seeking from the COCOM countries the maximum possible agreement with the United States' version of criteria, lists, and administrative and exceptions procedures, but being flexible even to the point of scaling down the scope and severity of controls for the sake of unity. The Department of Defense, by contrast, did not think any change in current policy was required and wanted the administration to press the COCOM countries bilaterally and through the Consultative Group (CG) to accept the U.S. standard of controls.[51]

As General Cutler requested, CFEP convened on 14 February to consider the Dillon Committee's recommendations. After extensive discussion the members recorded their opposition to the British petition to pare down the strategic controls list. Paul H. Cullen spelled out CFEP's reasoning in a memo to Cutler: "The United States agrees with the assumption that strength in being is the primary deterrent in a global thermonuclear war but stresses the importance of *effective* trade controls directed at the industrial-military capability for fighting such a thermonuclear war." The United States also believed that "trade controls should have, as a secondary objective, limiting mobilization capability after the initial exchange of blows in a general thermonuclear war."[52]

To deflect British and allied pressure, Cullen continued, the administration should agree to a symbolic reduction in controls at the forthcoming meeting of COCOM-participating countries, but impress upon the British the security as opposed to the commercial aspects of control.

This might cause a rift within COCOM; if so, the issue then would be "whether to be more influenced by the objective of maintaining what the U.S. considers to be an effective multilateral control system or achieving a unified Allied position with respect to the level of multilateral controls." CFEP asked NSC to address this issue at its meeting on 27 February, with the intention of obtaining guidance from the president. Finally CFEP agreed to study and report by 15 March on whether the criteria for multilateral controls should cover items necessary to limit Soviet mobilization capabilities after an initial nuclear exchange and whether controls should be limited only to items required by the Soviets for fighting limited wars or extended to materials for conducting economic subversion.[53]

After its meeting of 27 February NSC issued a directive adopting the CFEP's recommendation to liberalize export controls slightly in order to preserve harmony with the OEEC countries, and to facilitate an agreement at the forthcoming negotiations of COCOM. Specifically, the United States would reduce the number of militarily strategic items prohibited from export to the Soviet bloc from 181 to 31 and would agree to eliminate quantitative controls over nonstrategic goods. Certain items that the United States had maintained on a surveillance list would also be removed.[54] By July the fifteen participating countries of COCOM were at work in Paris slashing the strategic trade list by thirty to fifty percent, paving the way for the USSR to purchase certain machine tools, equipment, ball bearings, and raw materials hitherto prohibited. They would retain a selective ban on items of high technology or advanced design and critically scarce raw materials. A final list would be drawn in August after a review of items in disagreement.[55]

While the American representatives at the COCOM meeting fought to keep the reductions to a minimum, they had to give ground in face of widespread pressure from the other participating countries.[56] On 16 July Sir David Eccles, president of the British Board of Trade and a critic of the embargo lists, asserted that "the free world should not hesitate to increase its trade with the Communists, for it is through trade and growing rich together that we have the best chance of making them prefer a quiet life."[57] Although it did not endorse the idea that a prosperous communist is a content communist, CFEP advised President Eisenhower to approve the new level of controls negotiated at the Paris meeting, but noted the Defense Department's objection that overall coverage of the present controls list was being reduced by seventy to eighty percent.[58]

In mid-August 1958 COCOM announced the long-anticipated easing of controls. The revised list contained only 155 items considered strategic, as compared to 282 after the last major revision, in 1954. The separate American list was still stricter than the international controls list, but it too made concessions that would take effect in October. Following standard procedure, neither COCOM nor the United States specified individual items, but it is reasonable to assume that they encompassed several types of commodities: metalworking machinery; chemical and petroleum equipment; electrical and power-generating equipment; general industrial equipment; transportation equipment; electronic and precision instruments; metals, minerals, and their manufactures; chemicals and metalloids; petroleum products; and rubber and rubber products. COCOM's decision had domestic political ramifications for the Eisenhower administration: how long American businessmen and exporters would tolerate the stricter American controls, especially when their European competitors were turning a handsome profit from the Soviet bloc, was uncertain. As the *New York Times* observed, "The main significance of a potential increase in East–West trade abroad is that it could lead to a substantial reduction in U.S. export controls."[59]

Judging from the administration's actions in the weeks that followed, the *Times*'s assessment was unduly optimistic. On 28 August Secretary of Commerce Weeks issued a new directive outlining the criteria for reviewing the classification of items on the American control list. Using national security, foreign policy objectives, and congressional intent as his guidelines, Weeks declared that the Department of Commerce would maintain appropriate levels of control over items that had direct military importance to the USSR, or incorporated advanced technology; items that only the United States could supply to advance Soviet military industrial progress; and items whose acquisition from the United States would enable the Russians to divert similar resources to military production. More ominously for relations with the United States' Western partners, the department would enforce appropriate levels of control against countries *outside* the Soviet orbit whose trading practices undermined the American control system.[60]

Because Weeks was the pivotal figure in implementing the export control program, his views were influential and offered insight into the thinking of the administration. Whatever action other countries took, the United States was not ready to open up trade with the European Soviet bloc beyond a token amount; the decision was political rather than economic. This was clear from the discussion that undergirded President Eisenhower's response to a letter from Khrushchev of 2 June 1958. In his letter the Russian leader had called for a massive expansion of U.S.–Soviet trade in nonstrategic items. The USSR, he wrote, was not interested in purchasing military hardware, but rather in synthetic materials, like plastics, and finished goods. He suggested that Soviet purchases might be financed by exports of raw materials, adding that Russia would be willing to buy even larger quantities from American businesses if long-term (U.S. government) credit were made available.[61]

Khrushchev's offer was likewise couched in political as well as economic terms. He broached the trade issue in the context of recently concluded agreements on exchanges in the cultural, technical, and educational fields as evidence that relations between the two atomic powers could improve. Rather cleverly, he reminded Eisenhower of the words of Cordell Hull, President Roosevelt's secretary of state, that "commerce and association may be the antidote for war," observing that the world, as never before, needed such an antidote. Moreover, Khrushchev declared, "a positive solution of the question of Soviet–American trade would also be an important step toward a rapprochement between our two countries."[62]

The timing of this letter, while the United States and the COCOM countries were reexamining the question of controls, put pressure on the Eisenhower administration not only to ease restrictions but to demonstrate to its European allies that the United States was interested in easing cold war tensions. Khrushchev's letter provoked considerable discussion at the highest levels. On 23 June CFEP received a copy of the State Department's memorandum summarizing the implications of his offer.[63] "The major considerations in our response . . . are political," observed the State Department. "The economic consequences of an affirmative reply would be relatively small." Accepting Khrushchev's offer would be viewed abroad as tangible evidence of American interest in easing East–West tensions, desire for a rapprochement with the Soviet government, and goodwill toward the Russian people. On a practical level, if the United States refused to sell nonstrategic goods to the Russians, they would most likely purchase them elsewhere, from Great Britain or Germany.[64]

On the negative side, strong anticommunist sentiment in the United States and the noncommittal attitude of business toward legal trade with the Soviet Union were inhibiting factors. But the State Department noted other, more fundamental reasons for discouraging Khrushchev's overture. An attitude suggesting rapprochement might weaken the solidarity of the anticommunist coalition, especially NATO, and discourage anti-Soviet elements in the satellite countries, thus undermining the policy of self-determination. A positive response might also accelerate the trend, in Africa and Asia, of primary producing countries' expanding their trade with communist countries and entering into long-term purchase and sales agreements. Moreover, an expanded volume of imports from

Russia would come at the expense of free-world trading partners, particularly the primary producers of the third world, and undercut American influence in those countries.[65]

Geopolitical, economic, and ideological reasons thus argued against accepting Khrushchev's offer. Despite this, State Department officials believed that the letter was not entirely a propaganda gambit but was consistent with his speech of 6 May, in which he had announced plans for the rapid expansion of Russia's chemical industry and for boosting the production of consumer goods. Increased trade would contribute to the economies of both countries to a limited extent, but it would not become a large proportion of the trade of either, or directly affect their military strength.[66]

The State Department also noted that the USSR could expand its trade without any change in policy, whereas American exporters were impeded by a variety of legal, extralegal, and administrative obstacles.[67] The Trade Agreements Extension Act of 1951 prohibited extending most-favored-nation status to the Soviet Union; the Tariff Act of 1930 blocked the importation of products (such as canned crabmeat) made by forced labor; the Johnson Act of 1934 prohibited private American loans to any debt-defaulting nation that was not a member of the International Bank or Monetary Fund; the Battle Act could be read as preventing the United States from granting economic aid to the USSR; the Export Control Act of 1949 empowered the president to curtail strategic exports to Iron Curtain countries. Of all this legislation, the State Department thought that the executive could alter only the last through administrative action. It did not consider the Soviet request for credit legally or politically feasible and thought Russia should pay for goods from its vast gold reserves.[68]

Eisenhower replied to Khrushchev on 14 July 1958, observing that at the Geneva Conference and in his own letter to President Nikolai Bulganin in January, the United States had endorsed expansion of peaceful trade with the Soviet Union. Since American commerce was conducted by private firms, the government did not enter into the picture. In fact Soviet organizations were even now free to pursue peaceful trade opportunities in the United States. Long-term governmental credits raised "complex legal and political questions," but private commercial credit to underwrite trade expansion was already available. Eisenhower closed his letter by saying that he had instructed the State Department to examine Khrushchev's specific proposals and to communicate further with him.[69]

State Department officials did not follow up the president's directive until mid-1959. The delay, Under Secretary Dillon explained to the Senate Foreign Relations Committee, was occasioned by hostile Soviet actions in the summer and fall of 1958 that had heightened tensions between the two superpowers, and also by an anticipated visit of Soviet Deputy Premier Anastas Mikoyan to the United States. Dillon's reference was to Khrushchev's support of the Chinese Communist shelling of Quemoy in the Formosa Strait in August 1958, followed in rapid succession by a new Russian threat to Berlin and Soviet ventures in the troubled Middle East, most notably in Jordan and Lebanon. "In the circumstances," Dillon testified, "it seemed that a reply to the Soviets couched in constructive and conciliatory terms might be misunderstood."[70]

State Department strategists, moreover, thought it was more prudent to discuss Khrushchev's offer directly with Mikoyan, who had been minister for trade, than to proceed through impersonal correspondence.[71] The subject was discussed fully and frankly in a private meeting between Dillon and Mikoyan on 18 January 1959. Dillon later observed that Mikoyan had adopted a deliberately distorted view of the system of export controls as allowing American businesses to sell to the Russians only "chewing gum, firewood and laxatives," ignoring exports of agricultural and textile machinery, scientific instruments, stainless steel pipe, and numerous other items. Dillon had told Mikoyan that if they were serious about expanding peaceful trade, the Soviets would have to earn the confidence of American businessmen. He specifically mentioned settling the lend-lease debt, allowing private American firms to have greater access to more producer and consumer units in the USSR, guaranteeing protection of foreign patents and copyrights, and divorcing business from politics. Dillon further observed that current legislation prohibited the executive from extending most-favored-nation status or long-term credits to the USSR. Nor would the administration ask Congress to alter the laws without a significant improvement in political relations. In what later became known as the "policy of linkage," trade concessions were tied directly to political concessions.[72]

Dillon afterward told the Senate Foreign Relations Committee that Mikoyan had emerged from the meeting with a clearer perception of the impediments to American–Soviet trade. If so, this was not evident in the deputy premier's statement to American reporters that "the cold war is still making itself felt in the State Department." Upon his return to Moscow Mikoyan continued to display an air of exasperated resignation about the prospects of any immediate expansion of Soviet–American trade, telling a press conference on 24 January that the Soviet Union needed only to bide its time, "since anachronistic U.S. restrictions and export controls must inevitably be swept away by the pressure of modern times." Soviet Minister of Trade N. S. Patolichev took a similar line in *Pravda* on 17 February, accusing the State Department of obstructing normal trade relations by injecting political issues into economic affairs. However, he left the door ajar for future discussion, observing that "the considerations set forth by the two sides . . . should be studied . . . so as to find a mutually acceptable basis for the development of Soviet–American trade."[73]

There the matter rested through the spring of 1959. When reporters at a White House press conference on 4 March asked the president whether an increase in Anglo-Russian trade, resulting from British Prime Minister Macmillan's recent visit to the Soviet Union, would have any impact on U.S. export control policy, Eisenhower was pessimistic: "I do not believe that at this moment we are ready for any radical change in policy with respect to trade."[74] The president's assessment was ultimately correct, but events in the spring and summer of 1959 appeared to create a thaw in U.S.–Soviet relations that might lead to a new initiative in trade talks. Khrushchev relented on his demand that West Berlin be demilitarized and made a free city under international control; in March, thanks to Macmillan, the West agreed to a new summit meeting; in May Dulles died of cancer and was replaced as secretary of state by Christian A. Herter, a less strident anticommunist; and on 24 July Vice-President Nixon paid a visit to Russia and Poland, and Mikoyan again toured the United States. While opening an American trade exhibit in Moscow, Nixon and Khrushchev became engaged in a vociferous debate in the kitchen of a model home, on the merits of washing machines, capitalism, the free exchange of ideas, summit meetings, rockets, and ultimatums.

These exchanges paved the way for the extraordinary visit to the United States by Prime Minister Khrushchev in September 1959. American officials carefully described the visit as largely a social one. Nonetheless, in a speech to the Economic Club of New York on 18 September, the Soviet premier put in a strong bid for opening a new era of economic relations and trade between the two superpowers. His offer was predicated on the United States' removing restrictions on trade, which he said were ineffective, a nuisance, and had only spurred the Soviet Union to develop its economy independently of the West. Marked by a series of picturesque incidents, Khrushchev's tour reached its climax in private discussions between the premier and the president at Camp David, in Maryland.[75]

In preparation for the Camp David meeting, CFEP Chairman Randall had drafted a memorandum that outlined the position the president should take when Khrushchev raised the issue of U.S.–Soviet trade.[76] Randall suggested that at an appropriate point in the discussions Eisenhower should refer to the Soviet leader's letter of 2 June 1958, and the president's reply of 14 July 1958. That response had indicated that although the United States favored expansion of peaceful trade with the Soviet Union, trade, like peace, needed to be based upon clearly defined principles that dispelled any doubts among business and labor leaders about the Soviets' intentions. Such trade would be conducted by private enterprise; modification of export controls would be contingent upon "action toward progressive betterment of our relations." Randall recommended that the president instruct Secretary Weeks to expedite the licensing process as an initial gesture of goodwill.[77]

Despite talk of the "spirit of Camp David" the Eisenhower administration made settlement of the World War II lend-lease debt a precondition for requesting Congress to ease trade restrictions.[78] The debt question arose when Khrushchev complained about the discriminatory trade restrictions. According to Under Secretary Dillon, Eisenhower then informed the Soviet leader that any change in the existing legislation required congressional action and, inevitably, was contingent upon the state of American–Soviet relations and the public perception of the USSR. A satisfactory resolution of the debt dispute would create a more favorable atmosphere in which the president might approach Congress and would also free private American companies from the credit constraints of the Johnson Act. Khrushchev was willing to discuss the debt question, but in the end nothing came of it and the lend-lease issue remained a symbolic but potent political obstacle to expanded trade for future presidents.[79]

Hopes for a marked expansion in American–Soviet trade and a lessening of cold war tensions received a final setback in the last year of Eisenhower's presidency. On 27 January 1960 the State Department announced that it had broken off lend-lease debt talks with the Russians, accusing them of attempting once more to link settlement of the debt to the granting of most-favored-nation status and the extension of long-term U.S. government credits. Washington continued to insist that the two issues were separate. Former Ambassador Charles E. Bohlen, the American representative at the trade talks and special adviser to Secretary of State Herter, informed the Russians that the settlement of lend-lease was "an essential prerequisite before the Executive branch could take up with Congress the possibility of removing some of the restrictions which have an effect on U.S.–Soviet trade."[80]

Notwithstanding repeated Soviet attempts to reopen trade talks, lend-lease remained an insurmountable obstacle. But even without the debt controversy, which had become an emotional and symbolic issue, the prospects for advancing U.S.–Soviet trade were bleak. Russian intransigence over Berlin in April 1960 and Khrushchev's announcement, on 5 May, that the Soviets had shot down an American U-2 spy plane,

torpedoed the Geneva summit meeting scheduled to open shortly thereafter. In November Eisenhower himself became a lame-duck president.[81]
Protectionists and professional anticommunists, and conservative legislators who feared that more liberal trade policies would aid international
communism, together effectively prevented the administration from real-
izing important commercial and fiscal objectives that would use East–
West trade to rectify the nation's growing imbalance of payments.

In April 1960 William G. Sullivan, the chief of research of the FBI's
domestic intelligence unit, told businessmen attending the Sixth Military-Industrial Conference, in Chicago, that in order to avoid becoming
pawns of the communist conspiracy, they must abandon the thought of a
profitable trade with the Soviet Union. CFEP Chairman Randall read a
news account of the speech and was so furious that he dashed off an
angry letter to FBI Director J. Edgar Hoover. Sullivan's speech, Randall
declared, was a blatant attempt to appeal to American business leaders
over the heads of government officials. The policy of increasing American exports to alleviate the balance of payments deficit would benefit
from an orderly trade in peaceful goods with the Russians. "The reasons
why our exports to Russia do not increase," he explained, "is the psychological barrier existing in the minds of businessmen that to engage in
such trade is unpatriotic." But the damage was already done. Randall
feared—and rightly so—that such a view, coming from the FBI, would be
taken as "complete gospel."[82]

IN 1949, when Mao Ze-Dong's revolutionary movement overturned the
government of Chiang Kai-shek, the United States withheld diplomatic
recognition of Communist China, choosing to regard the exiled regime
on Taiwan as the legitimate government of China. In the following year
the Truman administration extended its trade embargo policy to include
the People's Republic of China in consequence of the Korean War. As a
matter of politics and an expression of moral indignation, the Eisenhower administration continued the policies of diplomatic nonrecognition and commercial nonintercourse on the grounds that the Beijing
regime persisted in actions that had led the United Nations to condemn it
as an aggressor.

Refusing to deal with Mao either by war or by diplomacy, the Eisenhower administration, like its predecessor, was reduced to the pretension
that his power was only temporary. This approach became difficult to
sustain, because in the wake of the Korean armistice the Western allies
and Japan, which had maintained diplomatic ties with the People's Republic in spite of severe provocations, moved to bring their trade policies
toward that country into line with those followed for the USSR and

Soviet Eastern Europe. The Western industrialized nations' and Japan's insistence on the end of the "China differential" called into question the Eisenhower administration's policies of nonrecognition and economic embargo, especially after 1954, when, to maintain Western unity, the United States reluctantly consented to a liberalization of controls in Europe. From 1955 until the end of Eisenhower's presidency the "China differential" dominated discussions among the United States and its allies concerning the system that defined the limits of East–West trade.

The Eisenhower administration viewed communism as essentially global in scope and monolithic in its goal of destroying democratic capitalism. Any relaxation of trade restrictions either by COCOM in Europe or CHINCOM in Asia would lead to pressures against the other and eventually precipitate a total disintegration of the system of multilateral controls. COCOM's united Western front was formally breached in 1954 with the drastic reduction of the number of items on the strategic embargo list. As the administration correctly feared, this led to allied pressures to eliminate the "China differential." The administration's difficulty in responding to these pressures was compounded by its own inability to work out a more flexible China trade policy than the simple, ironclad embargo.

Debate over the "China differential" brought to the surface deep divisions within the government concerning the utility of export controls in general. The Department of State and ICA favored some easing of trade restrictions by the allies, in order to preserve the unity of the Western alliance; the Departments of Commerce and Defense and the Treasury consistently opposed relaxation of controls, whether in Europe or in Asia. In Congress the issue was mired in partisan politics. Now the Democrats used the trade issue to lambast the Republicans for being "soft on communism" and the Eisenhower administration for not enforcing the Battle Act.

Given the absence of a clearly defined U.S. policy on the "China differential," the initiative passed to the Western allies and Japan. Great Britain, especially, utilized the exceptions procedure in meetings of CHINCOM to bring about de facto liberalization of the China trade controls. The Eisenhower administration's initial response was to hold the line as firmly as possible against the China trade; then, bowing to the inevitable, to use the "China differential" as a bargaining chip with the allies, with the object of restoring tighter trade controls against the USSR, notably in the export of copper wire. When this stratagem failed, in order to maintain the unity of the anticommunist coalition Washington tacitly acquiesced in the British and allied insistence upon opening normal commercial ties with China. Once the Western industrialized nations resumed nonstrategic trade with both the Soviets and the Chinese, some U.S. businessmen, academics, and political figures reopened the question of American participation in East–West trade.

For the immediate future the Eisenhower administration indicated that it would unilaterally adhere to a more stringent export control policy than the Western allies'. Several considerations prompted this steadfastness: domestic political pressures and the administration's own anticommunist rhetoric, its view of the People's Republic of China as an aggressor state, its fear of discouraging anti-Soviet and anticommunist elements behind the Iron and Bamboo Curtains, and its belief that any sign of American weakness would lead to closer economic ties between Russia and the less-developed countries. These concerns also helped to rationalize the administration's decision in 1959 to make settlement of the lend-lease debt a precondition for easing export controls on U.S.–Soviet trade, which helped to erode the "spirit of Camp David." The decision disappointed the United States' allies, who had interpreted the curtailment of American pressures as a possible harbinger of a change in the policy of the United States itself.

CHAPTER SIX

A New Look: Kennedy, Détente, and Trade Policy

THE United States Constitution is cryptic and ambiguous in its alloca-tion of powers affecting foreign policy, and this uncertainty historically has had the effect of rendering executive–legislative relationships often negative and adversarial.[1] At the root of the conflict is the doctrine of separation of powers that is so basic to the governmental structure of the United States. Either branch can frustrate the other, but it is very difficult for either to control the other. A good deal of the executive–legislative relationship in foreign affairs, consequently, has revolved around maneu-vering on the part of the president and Congress to avoid the potential for impasse or delay built into their respective constitutional powers. When John F. Kennedy entered the Oval Office in 1961, he was no more immune ·to the Founding Fathers' masterful ambiguity than were his predecessors.

The president's power in foreign affairs underwent a qualitative trans-formation during and immediately after World War II, reaching a pinna-cle in the 1960s. The pressures of a global conflict resulted finally in almost total domination of foreign affairs by the executive. As the cold war replaced the hot, Congress, under the strain of repeated crises, de-ferred more and more to the executive branch. From 1946 to 1960 Congress remained reasonably well in step with the executive branch in its attitude toward the Soviet Union. Indeed a national, bipartisan con-sensus had evolved in support of the containment of aggressive Soviet power.[2]

Even in the 1960s the net thrust of congressional action paralleled that of the executive branch—toward closer, cautious cooperation with the Soviets. This was most noticeable with respect to arms control and disar-mament, especially control of nuclear weapons. By the same token, an uneasiness had often characterized the cooperative spirit between the executive and legislative branches in formulating and managing interna-tional policy. Congress was much more reluctant than the executive to approve economic measures that might increase trade with Russia and

Soviet bloc countries, arguing that any trade was a form of aid that eventually would help the Kremlin in its avowed design to "bury" the United States.[3]

The kernel of the dispute, when Kennedy took office, was whether the forces of change in the USSR after Stalin's death were real or only apparent, whether efforts to encourage them represented a reasonable hope or a delusion, and whether one viewed the Cold War as an ideological struggle to the death or primarily a conflict of national interests that could be adjusted peacefully over a period of time. A majority of legislators, especially in the House of Representatives, took the more pessimistic view. Indeed throughout the 1960s congressional initiatives in the trade field were usually in the direction of making U.S. economic policy toward the socialist countries more restrictive.

Utilizing its oversight functions and appropriations power, Congress tied up presidential initiatives with all manner of prescriptions, rigid stipulations, and detailed specifications, against the desire of the executive. The congressional effort to shape East–West trade policy through these tactics frustrated the Kennedy administration and indicated that Congress was not ready to surrender its role in the formulation and management of international economic policy.[4]

Kennedy's concept of a dynamic presidency and his views on the future of U.S.–Soviet relations made a clash with Congress for control of the foreign-policy-making process unavoidable. Like Franklin D. Roosevelt, Kennedy believed that the presidency required "a vigorous proponent of the national interest," that the White House should be "the vital center of action," and that the president "must be prepared to exercise the fullest powers of his office—all that are specified and some that are not." Although he fully subscribed to the containment policy, Kennedy also realized that the key to world peace was improved relations with the Soviet Union. He sought to relax East–West tensions by abandoning the old clichés of the Cold War and persuading a dubious Congress that honest trade helped one side as much as the other. Development of commercial contacts offered an important means of breaking down the Soviet Union's isolation and encouraging the forces of constructive change in the communist world.[5]

Like Eisenhower before him, Kennedy was very sensitive to the importance of foreign economic policy to the nation's political and economic well-being. Influence and power in foreign relations had increasingly become functions of economic capabilities. A strong domestic economic base was a critical prerequisite if the United States was to maintain its status as a superpower and deal with the Soviet Union from a position of strength. The period when the U.S. economy was invulnerable to import competition, a veritable colossus, and the dollar was the linchpin of the international monetary system, was rapidly drawing to a close. Increased trade with Russia and Eastern Europe not only served political ends but might also contribute to reducing the trade deficit, which was becoming chronic, and bolster the dollar abroad.[6]

The debate over whether the United States should modify its trade policy toward communist nations was already nearly two years old when Kennedy entered the White House. The elaborately constructed system of export controls had been the focus of numerous congressional hearings, studies, and reports, which had varied in extent and intensity with the cold war cycles of crisis and relaxation.[7] The 1958–59 Berlin crisis, the erection of the Berlin wall in 1961, the Soviet military buildup in Cuba, the mounting volume of exports from Western Europe to the Soviet bloc, and the demand for a "new look" at United States policy generated documents from fifteen congressional committees and subcommittees between 1959 and 1963. This was an indication of the broad and uncoordinated interest in the subject in Congress. On 25 May 1962 the House Select Committee on Export Controls had taken the unusual step of recommending—without success—the creation of a permanent joint committee to provide more effective legislative oversight of congressional interest in East–West trade.[8]

During this period debate in Congress concerned whether the United States, Western Europe, and other noncommunist nations should adopt a unified trade strategy, or whether each would act unilaterally.[9] In 1962 the Joint Economic Committee complained that the United States had been "virtually 'going it alone'" in restricting trade to the European Soviet bloc and concluded that closer U.S.–Common Market cooperation was unlikely.[10] The next year a Special Study Mission to Europe of the House Foreign Affairs Committee also found that "the industrialized nations ... lack a coordinated policy which would marshal the economic resources of the West for strategic economic defense and initiative in the cold war."[11] From 1960 to 1962 congressional delegates to the NATO Parliamentarians Conference in Paris urged a coordinated policy within NATO. The Economic Committee of the 1963 conference went further still in stressing that member governments should adopt a uniform embargo list of strategic materials.[12]

The hearings, study papers, and reports reflected important policy differences on the international level between the United States and its allies, and domestically between Congress and the executive branch. Although there were varying shades of opinion with respect both to the basic issues and to the range of solutions and possible alternative strategies, the prevailing opinion in Congress, to the extent that it can clearly

be gauged, consistently favored stricter controls and the United States'
taking the initiative in persuading its allies to do likewise.[13] Both those
who advocated a relaxation of U.S. controls, to conform more nearly to
the policies of the Western European nations, and those who favored
stricter allied controls agreed that a *unified* policy, however oriented,
would be more realistic and more effective than the existing disparity,
which penalized American businessmen without comparably constrain-
ing their competitors or the Soviets.[14]

Regardless of Congress's views the executive branch, whether Republican or Democratic, tended to favor more flexible controls and acceptance of the "double standard" in the interests of Western unity. This
view was manifested in testimony before congressional committees, in
the media, and before business organizations, such as the World Trade
Advisory Committee Task Force. In 1959, 1960, and thereafter, former
State Department official Will Clayton wrote and testified that the
United States should ease its restrictive policy on nonstrategic trade in
the interest of Western unity. The economist Robert Loving Allen told
the Joint Economic Committee in 1960 that strategic controls were
"probably doomed" because open societies were, in the long run, unable
to deprive potential enemies of technology and goods. Allen, Willard
Thorpe, and others argued that within the limits of national security the
Soviet Union should be allowed to buy whatever it wanted from the
United States.[15]

Journals as diverse as *Business Abroad, Congressional Digest, U.S.
News,* and the *Harvard Business Review* were candidly discussing, debat-
ing, and, in some instances, advocating a more liberal trade policy toward Russia and Eastern Europe.[16] Whatever consensus existed at the
height of the Cold War that strategic trade should be embargoed was
gradually being replaced by another argument: that, with the exception
of military goods, the United States should trade equally with communist
and noncommunist countries. As American businessmen saw an increasing volume of commerce fall into the eagerly outstretched arms of their
Western European colleagues, and as Washington officialdom projected
a balance of payments deficit of $2 billion or $3 billion, even the definition of a militarily "strategic" item was subjected to closer scrutiny and
construed more narrowly.[17]

Two tendencies are worth noting about the transitional mood of the
nation between 1959 and 1963 with respect to East–West trade policy.
For the first time since the beginning of the Cold War and McCarthy's
exploitation of the public's fears, government officials, businessmen, academic experts, and the average American were freely discussing the merits and deficiencies of and alternatives to the existing policy. The process

of reexamination, born of widespread dissatisfaction with the present system of controls, a growing perception that communism was not monolithic, and a trade account moving from the black into the red, afforded the executive branch greater latitude to pursue diplomatic and trade options that previously had been closed.

President Kennedy moved immediately to take advantage of this opportunity even though the Cold War seemed to be at its worst and most dangerous point since the death of Stalin. In the wake of the U-2 fiasco Khrushchev was at his most belligerent and truculent; the Soviet threat hung over Cuba, Laos, and Berlin. Despite this Kennedy believed that the world had changed since 1950: the conflict between Russia and China was real, the military threat to Western Europe had receded, the third world was the new battleground, and military measures had to be supplemented with vigorous political and economic programs.[18]

A changing world demanded flexibility and initiative. Diplomatically, Kennedy hoped to achieve détente—a standstill agreement—with the Soviet Union and to make progress toward a general disarmament. Though they did not occupy center stage during the Kennedy administration, U.S. export control policy, and East–West trade generally, were nonetheless important instruments in the pursuit of détente and sometimes a political barometer of American–Soviet relations. To unfreeze American–Soviet commerce and use trade to liberalize the Eastern European regimes and wean them from their Soviet dependence were aims clearly articulated during the election campaign and were, in fact, consistent with Kennedy's senatorial interest. As the junior senator from Massachusetts, he had proposed (unsuccessfully) in 1957 a bill to amend the Battle Act to permit granting aid to communist nations that showed polycentric tendencies. On 2 October 1960, as the election campaign was entering its last phase, he had reminded voters of this action and said: "In the Eighty-seventh Congress, under new Presidential leadership, it must become law."[19]

In the interval between his election and inauguration president-elect Kennedy established several task forces, one of which investigated the trade aspects of U.S. foreign economic policy. Headed by the future under secretary of state for economic affairs, George W. Ball, and composed of prominent economics experts from academe and government, this task force completed its work shortly before Kennedy took the oath of office.[20] The Ball Report constituted the basic rationale for the liberalized trade program that Kennedy was planning to ask Congress to enact to replace the soon-to-expire Trade Agreements Act of 1951.

The Ball Report marked a fundamental change in tone and thinking about economic defense policy at the highest level of the executive

branch. It asserted that since 1949 "our approach has reflected the negative proposition that commerce with Communist countries is immoral,
dangerous, and of doubtful economic benefit." Of course U.S. trade with
the Soviet bloc was of only marginal interest, but other Western countries had found such trade to be advantageous and hence had refused to
follow American export control policy "docilely." The COCOM machinery had "all but broken down." State monopoly of trade in communist
bloc nations threatened to undermine the open and multilateral patterns
of international commerce that had been laboriously constructed by the
United States since 1945. Although Russian trade with the economically
stronger nations had thus far been dictated "by commercial rather than
political considerations," the reverse was true with less-developed countries. In the third world, commerce had generally taken a back seat to
politics.[21]

To blunt the dangers and exploit the opportunities inherent in the
bloc's expanding economic commitments, the Ball Report concluded, the
United States and its allies and friends had to act in concert. The United
States needed to persuade the others that "we are genuinely prepared
to recognize the potential economic advantages of expanded East–West
trade." Only then would it be in a position "to assert positive leadership
in the formulation and enforcement of safeguards."[22]

On the basis of this analysis the task force recommended that the
Kennedy administration seek a common strategy with regard to Soviet
bloc trade within the framework of the Organization for Economic Cooperation and Development (OECD); invite the USSR to trade with free-
world countries after agreeing to a code of fair practices; amend the
Trade Agreements Act, authorizing temporarily relaxed import restrictions for any country under communist economic pressure; amend the
Battle Act to extend its policy aim beyond the control of strategic exports
(thus giving the executive greater flexibility "to cope with the politically
and economically disruptive activities of Communist state trading"); establish "a constructive policy image" by restricting Export Control Act
prohibitions "to exceptional products likely to contribute to the Soviet
military potential in an important, direct and immediate way"; and
amend the Trade Agreements Act to give the president discretionary
authority to suspend provisions that would embargo imports of certain
furs from the Soviet bloc or would withhold most-favored-nation status
from communist-dominated countries. "This discretion should be used,"
the task force suggested, "as a bargaining chip in future bilateral or
multilateral negotiations with the Soviet Union."[23]

The Kennedy administration never made the Ball Report officially
public, despite chiding by congressional conservatives, and for that very

reason it became controversial by implication. The president was reluctant to risk congressional rejection of his trade program at the outset of his administration and so did not formally submit the report's recommendations as a legislative package for Congress to vote on.[24]

Nonetheless President Kennedy used the task force's rationale as the basis of his actions to liberalize East–West trade. He broached the topic in his State of the Union Message for 1961 and followed up on 8 February, in a memorandum fired off to Secretary of State Dean Rusk. "In our State of the Union address we committed ourselves to changing the Battle Act. This is a matter which I worked on when I was in the Senate. George Aiken [Republican, Vermont] co-sponsored the bill with me." He asked Rusk to arrange for Aiken to co-sponsor a new bill—"if we can get a Democrat interested in it"—with Senator Mike Mansfield, the Democratic whip. A week later Kennedy dashed off another memorandum, this one to his national security assistant, McGeorge Bundy, who had taken charge of the administration's foreign economic policy: "What means are we taking to proceed with the Battle Act? Are we sending a message to Congress on it?" Then, responding to Khrushchev's dropping of the U-2 incident and release of the RB–47 fliers, the president permitted the import of Soviet crabmeat, banned for a decade because it had once been produced by forced labor.[25]

In March 1961 the president was on the verge of easing restraints on nonstrategic trade when an administrative snafu caused him to shrink back.[26] The case involved forty-five pieces of ball-bearing machinery destined originally for the Soviet Union. The Department of Commerce had licensed the export, but the Department of Defense opposed its issuance. At the hearings of the Senate subcommittee on internal security, officials of Miniature Precision Bearing, Incorporated, said that the machines were of the greatest strategic significance in the manufacture of miniaturized ball bearings and that it would be "a tragic mistake" to permit their exportation. Under pressure from Democratic Senator Thomas J. Dodd of Connecticut, who was vice-chairman of the subcommittee, Commerce Secretary Luther Hodges revoked the license, on 2 March. He acted not on security grounds but on the alleged need of the Department of Defense for all the machines![27]

This was a classic example of the fumbling and bureaucratic infighting characteristic of the previous administrative history of export control policy, from which the Kennedy administration itself was not immune. The two departments most closely identified with formulating and implementing the policy could not even agree on the definition of a strategic item. Embarrassed, Kennedy told reporters that the confusion was unfortunate, though he hoped that in the future "we can set up better procedures so that a better judgment can be made."[28] He also informed the press of his interest in liberalizing what he considered an overly restrictive policy. Observing that other Western nations were conducting a vigorous commerce with the Soviets, he declared that "we are anxious to permit some degree of trade which does not weaken our security or increase our danger to be carried on with communist countries." On 12 March Commerce Secretary Hodges picked up this theme in a radio and television interview during which he urged an increase in trade with Soviet bloc countries as long as there was no threat to U.S. security interests.[29]

The administration's efforts to clarify its bureaucratic procedures were interrupted in mid-April by the Bay of Pigs fiasco, but on 28 April Attorney General Robert F. Kennedy transmitted to the White House a proposed executive order drafted by the Commerce Department that would establish an Export Control Review Board (ECRB). Composed of the secretaries of commerce, state, and defense and vesting in the secretary of commerce the power of successive redelegation, ECRB would act as the final authority in licensing matters. President Kennedy signed the executive order on 24 May, and copies were distributed to the heads of the departments concerned, including the Department of Agriculture, the Treasury, and the Office of Civil Defense Mobilization.[30]

Having clarified administrative procedures, at least on paper, President Kennedy continued to pursue his major policy objective of liberalizing trade with the European Soviet bloc. During the first part of May 1961, officials from the Departments of Commerce, State, and Defense and from the White House met to ascertain whether a review of the current criteria for export controls was needed. "We agreed that the existing definition of 'strategic goods' approved by the NSC was an appropriate one, but that some of the specific items now placed under 'presumption for denial' are no longer clearly in line with the definition of 'strategic,'" Assistant Secretary for International Affairs Rowland Burnstan informed Secretary Hodges on 18 May. The interagency operating committee had scheduled a meeting with the Advisory Committee on Export Policy Procedures to reassess the classification of the items on the denial list. The intent was to move from the List of Presumption for Denial to the Presumption for Approval List any items that were no longer strategic as a result of the changing needs for material for military purposes. Redefinition through the use of the executive's discretionary authority was the route to ease export restrictions. "In this way," Burnstan concluded, "I think we can develop a more satisfactory and expeditious export control procedure."[31]

The State Department, influenced by Under Secretary George Ball and Walt Rostow, head of the Policy Planning Staff, was even more sanguine in defining the new administration's agenda. On 25 May it produced a lengthy document that surveyed the United States' economic relations with Russia and the European Soviet bloc countries. The ideological assumptions that underpinned the report and the general statement of U.S. economic defense policies were largely a recasting of ideas contained in the unpublished Ball Report, but it was far more specific in making recommendations for policy changes and actions. Not only did it seek to integrate foreign and domestic economic defense policy into a coherent whole and to achieve greater executive flexibility in the implementation of policy, but—more so than in any previous administration—it hoped to encourage tendencies toward national self-determination within the Soviet European bloc. Unlike its predecessor, the Kennedy administration attempted to capitalize on the inclination of countries like Poland, Yugoslavia, Rumania, and Bulgaria to respond to national concerns and to pursue national policies.[32]

The State Department recommended that the United States' embargo list be made to conform to COCOM's and that in nonstrategic trade, including technical literature, the United States operate under the general rule of approval. These two recommendations, if adopted and implemented, would mark a sharp departure from the practices of the previous decade. It further advised the administration to seek amendments to the 1951 Trade Agreements Extension Act and the "friendly nation" requirement of P.L. 480 (the food-for-peace measure), in order to grant the president authority to restore most-favored-nation status to bloc countries, allow the importation of previously banned furs from Russia, and permit the sale of surplus agricultural commodities whenever he determined that it was in the national interest. The State Department further recommended that to encourage polycentrism the administration should endorse H.R. 1130, a bill before Congress that would authorize the executive, in the national interest, to grant economic or financial assistance to any nation except the USSR, North Korea, and Vietnam. Lastly, it advised the administration to lobby to eliminate riders in the 1961 appropriations acts that would forbid the Departments of Labor and Health, Education and Welfare to purchase equipment (especially educational) from communist nations, a restriction that was "an unnecessary pin-prick in our relations with the Soviet bloc," and to modify the 1934 Johnson Act, which served "no national purpose" in U.S. relations with the satellite countries.[33]

With respect to the Soviet Union itself, the State Department moved cautiously to encourage trade by seeking an agreement in advance with the Russians on fair business practices and copyright and patent protection. Lend-lease still persisted as a problem. U.S. policy under Eisenhower had made a settlement a prerequisite for asking Congress to remove legislative restrictions on American–Soviet trade. Nonetheless progress on other aspects of trade might still be possible, even in the absence of a resolution of the debt controversy.[34]

The precise volume and dollar amount of the trade that might develop from these actions was uncertain. With an eye on the trade deficit, State Department experts estimated that if the United States were to remove the barriers to closer economic relations and restrict its export controls to narrowly defined strategic items, the Russians might increase their annual purchases of American goods from the present low of $38 million to nearly $200 million by 1963. The maximum would be $300 million. They anticipated that Soviet purchases would be concentrated on the most sophisticated machinery and technologies, in which the USSR lagged behind the West.[35]

Fortified with reports and statistics, the Kennedy administration sought to amend the Battle Act to render it more flexible and compatible with a policy of encouraging national self-determination in Eastern Europe. The proposed amendment would allow financial and economic aid to any Eastern European country (except Russia and communist-held areas in the Far East), even if it was shipping arms and strategic goods to other areas of the Soviet bloc, upon executive determination that the aid was important to the national security of the United States and the recipient country was told the aid emanated from the United States. Supporters of the amendment argued that it would facilitate the sending of aid to an Eastern European country in the event of an uprising such as the 1956 riots in Posnan.[36]

Unfortunately for the Kennedy trade initiative, the president's encounter with Soviet Premier Khrushchev in Vienna on 3–4 June 1961 was a disaster. Perhaps misled by the Bay of Pigs into seeing the youthful president as a man of irresolution, Khrushchev adopted an intransigent, bullying attitude. He threatened to make a peace treaty with East Germany before the end of the year, to extinguish Western rights of access to West Berlin, and to transform West Berlin into a neutralized city. Kennedy responded by making it clear that the United States had a vital interest in the freedom of the people of West Berlin and access to the city; upon returning to the United States, he ordered an increase in American armed strength.[37]

The Berlin crisis torpedoed whatever hope Kennedy had, early in his administration, of persuading Congress to ease restrictions on East–West trade. For example, on 22 June 1961 the Commerce Department announced that it would lift its ban against exports of subsidized surplus agricultural products to Soviet bloc countries, notably Poland, and sell them for American dollars or for currency convertible to dollars. In high dudgeon over this most recent threat to Berlin, Congress reacted negatively by adding to the Agricultural Act of 1961 an amendment prohibiting the sale of such commodities to unfriendly nations. During the debate on the amendment, its sponsor, Republican Congressman Delbert L. Latta of Ohio, argued that selling any subsidized foods to the Soviet bloc would give those countries the benefit of subsidies paid by the Commodity Credit Corporation to American producers and exporters. Because that agency was authorized to sell for export at less than the domestic price, Latta argued, "the American taxpayer will now be picking up the difference between the world price and the domestic price."[38] After enactment of the Latta amendment, the Department of Commerce suspended its plans.

The Battle Act amendment, which had passed in the Senate, never emerged from the foreign affairs committee of the House. Although overwhelmingly Democratic, Congress remained in the grip of a conservative coalition that intended to block any liberal initiatives on East–West trade and firmly retain control of foreign economic policy in its own hands. On 19 July Assistant Secretary of Commerce Jack N. Behrman wrote to Secretary Hodges expressing his concern about the mood of Congress and suggested that Hodges bring this to the attention of the White House. His office had received a flood of inquiries from legislators "adamant against feeding the Russians or easing any agricultural difficulties in the Bloc." Worse, Virginia Democrat Howard Smith, the conservative chairman of the House Rules Committee, indicated that he would release Res. 170, introduced by California Republican Glennard P. Lipscomb. The resolution, which called for an extensive investigation of export control procedures, had been languishing in the Rules Committee since April.[39]

To complicate matters further, ECRB had decided not to change the export control criteria, despite the Berlin crisis. The Department of Commerce would proceed to license for export a variety of precision tools for the automobile industry in Russia, including Transfermatic machines that Congress already was eyeing suspiciously. Behrman expected the $40 million deal to raise congressional hackles. "In view of these developments," he warned Hodges, "we may need the highest policy guidance as to actions to be taken and the source of explanations to those who object, i.e., the White House or Commerce."[40]

Behrman's prediction quickly came true, as the Republican Policy

Committee of the House of Representatives adopted a declaration of concern about the level of trade with the Soviet Union and talked of yet another investigation of export control policy. Meanwhile the State Department disclosed that it was studying, but for the moment had decided to hold in abeyance, proposals to curtail trade in retaliation for the threat to Berlin. The State Department was no doubt influenced by divisions within the Western alliance: the British adamantly opposed a trade embargo; Adenauer favored it. Nine days later the Russians erected the Berlin Wall, severing movement between East and West. This precipitated another anxious moment for the administration, for on 18 August the Senate narrowly voted down, 45 to 43, New Hampshire Republican Styles Bridges's amendment to the Foreign Assistance Act of 1951, which would have eliminated aid to Western and third world countries that shipped strategic materials to the Soviet bloc. Badly scared, the administration quietly curbed exports to the bloc, deferring the approval of licenses but denying that the move constituted "sanctions."[41]

By rejuvenating conservative opposition in Congress, the Berlin crisis threw a monkey wrench into the administration's plans to move early and decisively toward easing restrictions on nonstrategic trade. In response to congressional criticism that American exports to Iron Curtain countries had increased sharply in the three weeks immediately following President Kennedy's July address to the nation on Berlin, Commerce Secretary Hodges admitted that his department was being doubly cautious in processing export licenses. He played down the significance of the sudden spurt in the dollar volume of the licenses sought in the wake of the president's speech, saying it was the department's policy to give businessmen applying for licenses a quick response.[42]

That explanation did not satisfy congressional conservatives. On 17 September the House of Representatives approved a resolution to establish a five-man committee (the Select Committee on Export Control) to investigate U.S. exports to Russia.[43] This parry caused the administration to be very careful not to further antagonize conservative Democrats and Republicans who were hot to legislate a total ban on trade with the Soviet bloc. The committee's inquiry, which occupied the remainder of Kennedy's first year in office, effectively hamstrung the administration's hope to capitalize on nationalistic differences within the communist world. Instead representatives of the administration spent an inordinate amount of time explaining its policy objectives and educating the committee to the realities of Soviet power and the limitations of economic warfare.

At a closed meeting of the committee on 25 October Secretary of State Rusk told the panel that an embargo on all trade was not in the United

States' interest. An embargo would not hurt the bloc in any permanent sense, and it might injure the United States by undermining its relations with its allies. Like his predecessors, Rusk attempted to enlighten the legislators. "While our policy of control is a selective one and while we cannot expect to cripple Soviet bloc economic or military power through an export control system, we can accomplish something useful if we recognize that our objective must be a limited one," he testified. "That objective is to delay the development of Soviet military capability in selected areas where a coordinated denial policy by Western suppliers may have an impact. We cannot hope to erect an absolute barrier to Soviet advancements in military production; we can make it more difficult or more time consuming for the Soviets to make certain kinds of progress."[44]

From this perspective the trade control system and the use of trade policy to exploit nationalistic tendencies within the Soviet bloc was compatible with the basic objective of U.S. national defense policies, namely to preserve and, if possible, widen the lead time of America's military capabilities. "It is this margin in ultimate military power which is the hope of the West in the near term," observed Rusk, "and whatever contribution the trade control system has made to its maintenance is valuable."[45]

While Congress debated the wisdom of the president's use of trade to achieve certain foreign policy objectives, in the winter of 1961–62 presidential control of foreign economic policy toward nations on both sides of the Iron Curtain came under increasing scrutiny and criticism. On 15 February 1962 Senator Jacob Javits, a liberal Republican from New York, introduced S. 2840 as an alternative to the administration's Battle Act amendment, expressing the "sense of the Congress" that the president should use his discretionary authority to negotiate a treaty with the United States' NATO allies and Japan that would present a unified trade policy toward the Soviet bloc.[46] The treaty should effectively control shipments of strategic goods and extensions of credits to communist countries and compensate Western nations that would be injured by opening up alternative markets in the United States. Although supporters of the Kennedy administration's trade expansion bill did not object to a "sense of the Congress" amendment, they fought against anything more binding, on the grounds that it would seriously hamper U.S. negotiations with the European Common Market.[47]

In a nationally syndicated column that appeared late in February 1962, former Vice-President Richard M. Nixon lent his support to Javits's bill. He wrote that the Kennedy administration should adopt as "a top priority target" the development of a solid Western trade front in all dealings with the communist bloc, and take the initiative in persuading its Western allies that "the fight against Communism is not a spare-time hobby to be fought after the profitable deal is made." Future reciprocal trade negotiations, Nixon wrote, "could well afford an opportunity for exerting such leadership."[48]

One of the most vocal legislative critics of trade with the European Soviet bloc was Republican Congressman Thomas M. Pelly of Washington. In frequent speeches before the House, Pelly scored the "laxness" of policy toward the bloc and implied that the administration was conspiring to dismantle export controls. He was especially irked by the proposals to ship food to Eastern bloc countries and sought to amend the Export Control Act such that it would bar any shipment, whether subsidized or unsubsidized, of agricultural goods behind the Iron Curtain, unless the president certified that the recipient was not controlled by international communism. This amendment, if enacted, would have effectively terminated the Kennedy administration's use of foodstuffs as a tool of diplomacy.[49]

Increasingly, congressional hostility focused on the Export Control Act, which was scheduled to expire on 30 June 1962. On 9 April the Kennedy administration requested Congress for a permanent extension of the law, in the hope of mollifying some of the criticism. It justified its request by arguing that the act was needed for the foreseeable future, and so there was little point in going through the renewal process every two years. As a practical matter, it was difficult to get high-caliber personnel to administer the law when it might run out in two years, or who would have to confront, explain, and justify their implementation of it every two years. The two-year duration also interjected a note of uncertainty into COCOM negotiations in Paris. This was particularly burdensome because it placed the United States on the defensive when trying to convince the allies to be more restrictive in their own shipments to the Soviet bloc.[50]

Congress, of course, as the administration must have known, had held to the two-year renewals precisely because that limit afforded legislators a convenient opportunity to review the efficacy of the act and, in the case of conservatives, to put pressure on the executive.[51] In June the House and Senate passed a three-year extension of the Export Control Act, and, even though it did not quite give him what he had wanted, President Kennedy signed the new law on 1 July 1962.[52]

Although the prevailing opinion in Congress was in favor of strict controls and of persuading the United States' allies to adopt similar restrictions, interagency differences continued to dog the administration.

This too rendered real progress toward liberalizing East–West trade a chimera during most of Kennedy's second year in office.

The spring of 1962 was consumed in sub rosa bickering over which executive department should assume the burden of enforcing the export control regulations. Commerce Department officials, who over the years had unfairly borne the brunt of congressional criticism, had the primary legal responsibility but saw in the more fluid political situation of the moment an opportunity to jettison this very unpopular chore. On 19 March 1962 Commerce Secretary Hodges forwarded to the president the draft of a proposed executive order that would transfer from his office to the secretary of the treasury the function of administering the Export Control Act.[53] In his cover letter Hodges explained that Treasury already had broad jurisdiction in international economic matters; the Customs Bureau already was enforcing the export control laws; and trade restriction was fundamentally incompatible with the Commerce Department's mission to promote, develop, and expand trade.[54]

When Treasury Secretary Douglas Dillon read the draft, he moved swiftly to quash it. On 3 April he sent a memorandum to the president, saying: "I am reluctant to accept this responsibility essentially because I do not believe that the formulation of policy with regard to our export trade is an appropriate function of the Treasury Department." He then proceeded to rebut point by point each argument Hodges had advanced in support of the transfer, concluding that "a Secretary of the Treasury would be particularly vulnerable to attacks from critical Members of the Congress and the public if he attempted to assume responsibility for determining or recommending to the president policy in the field of export commodities, a field which bears no reasonable relation to his fundamental responsibilities."[55]

Like Hodges, Dillon recognized that enforcing the Export Control Act was a thankless task and would subject the Treasury Department to relentless criticism from Congress, businessmen, the public, and professional anticommunists. He wanted no part of Hodges's scheme.[56] The next day, White House Assistant Myer Feldman sent the draft executive order, with Dillon's commentary, to Kenneth Hansen, assistant director of the Bureau of the Budget (BOB), and asked him to canvass the reactions of knowledgeable people, especially Carl Kaysen, who was on the staff of the National Security Council (NSC).[57]

On 10 April Hansen responded informally to Feldman, telling him that BOB was against the proposed transfer. "I think it is fair to say . . . that a possible motivation behind the move to transfer the administration of this program to the Treasury Department may arise from the fact that Commerce does not wish to 'bite the bullet' for the Administration on this controversial area of trade policy."[58] Hansen then got into specific objections, pointing out, like Dillon, that the proposal was administratively duplicative, inefficient, and wrong politically. The Treasury Department did not have the Commerce Department's staff, expertise, or ties to the business community; and Hodges's argument of existing "organizational schizophrenia" lacked merit. "It is doubtful that establishing a different lightning rod for the Congress will improve the situation in any event and such a change would probably result in less effective administration (as Secretary Dillon suggests) and merely add to the difficulties of the Administration vis-à-vis the Congress," Hansen concluded.[59]

Carl Kaysen wrote separately to Feldman on 17 April that the proposed transfer was undesirable from both the technical and the policy points of view. Logic might actually dictate putting export controls in the hands of the State Department, but Kaysen considered that to be unwise. The Department of Commerce, he wrote, "because it represents the domestic interests of business, is much more able politically to take the criticisms that inevitably arise from the administration of the function than State would be." Feldman concurred and ultimately vetoed the proposal. On 30 April he wrote to Hodges that in view of the strong position Dillon had taken against the transfer, it was better not to pursue the matter. "For the time being," he advised, "we have no alternative but to continue Export Control activity as at present."[60]

Unable to jettison responsibility for export controls, the Department of Commerce determined to shore up its position with its congressional critics by taking a tough stance on license applications for shipments to Iron Curtain countries. This touched off a new clash with the State Department, which supported the president's strategy of easing trade restrictions in order to foster diversity within the communist world. On 10 July Secretary of State Rusk informed NSC that the pending applications and total trade with the European Soviet bloc were quantitatively unimportant, but a fundamental principle was at issue. Total sales to Eastern Europe in 1961 had amounted to only $133 million, $42.6 million of which was to the USSR. The value of the pending applications was only $2.4 million. Nevertheless, he explained, "Trade is an instrument of our over-all policy toward the bloc and export licensing should be consistent with that policy." The items in question and the technology were nonstrategic by the United States' definition, available from Western Europe and Japan, and would not enhance Soviet military strength.[61]

Rusk pursued the policy issue. "There is another and I think a decisive point involved. Denial of those applications would work at cross purposes with our attempt to establish sober communications with the

USSR and the Eastern European bloc. The underlying premise for our export control policy has been, of course, that trade is one of the few means for influencing the peoples of the Soviet Union toward a national attitude that will tend to make the USSR a more reasonable and peaceful member of the international community."[62] He restated this argument in a follow-up memorandum to NSC, and added: "We can make it more difficult or more time consuming for the Soviets to make certain kinds of progress. From this standpoint, the trade control operation is closely akin to the basic objective of our national defense policies—namely, the preservation and if possible the widening of our margin of military advantage."[63]

Rusk had developed this argument in testimony before the House Select Committee on Export Control earlier, in October 1961. He now elaborated on the State Department's position in his memorandum to NSC. The State Department wanted to maintain and strengthen the multilateral control system, adjusting it to reflect changes in the Soviet bloc's vulnerability and the needs of the United States' allies; extend bilateral agreements with non–Consultative Group (CG) countries to support the system; continue unilateral controls over only those few items whose export would be detrimental to the national security; show flexibility toward Soviet bloc countries "in line with the objectives of encouraging and assisting these countries to achieve increased self-determination and greater pursuit of their own national interests"; improve enforcement procedures; and maintain the current level of controls against China, North Korea, and North Vietnam.[64]

Rusk's endorsement of freer trade rested on the belief that the Russians attached a psychological importance to American trade policy that was totally disproportionate to the small amount involved. However incomprehensible this might seem, the Soviets interpreted trade as an indicator of the United States' general attitude toward them. "At a time when we are engaged in a series of diplomatic discussions with the Soviets about Berlin and other matters," he explained, "nothing is to be gained by giving the Russians a misleading impression of our point of view about the kind of relationship we hope ultimately to have with them. On the contrary, so long as the Soviets are in a mood for rational conversation, it is important that we avoid actions in trade control policy or elsewhere which seem to the Soviets to belie our expressed readiness to maintain normal contacts with the USSR as long as these are possible."[65]

This was doubly important, Rusk observed, because in the judgment of Ambassador Llewellyn Thompson, "Soviet policy may now be at a crossroads, that it can move either toward détente or toward increased pressure against the West, and . . . our export policy may well have a bearing upon the Soviet choice." Although the United States should not sacrifice any vital interest, and might not be able to affect the Soviets' decision, Thompson had felt (and Rusk agreed) that the United States "should not risk tipping the balance by actions in matters that are not otherwise of genuine strategic significance." Moreover, the United States' friends and allies abroad were "entirely opposed" to increasing the severity of controls, and the United States should have "no illusions that restrictions by us would be effective in preventing such trade between the Soviet bloc and the rest of the free world."[66]

The recent congressional debate before voting to extend the Export Control Act for another three years was, in Rusk's judgment, "on the whole more helpful than otherwise." After strenuous lobbying by the administration, House and Senate conferees rejected Congressman Alvin Kitchen's amendment to establish a presumption of denial of all export license applications. Thus, in the judgment of State Department analysts, presidential flexibility was maintained. Rusk concurred, for he told NSC that the final bill represented "a Congressional affirmation that the Executive Branch should be allowed to proceed on the long-standing premise that trade with the Soviet bloc is consistent with the national interest."[67]

The Commerce Department's reading of the legislative debate was, not surprisingly, quite different. Hodges had been far more impressed by the strong concerns of the House and Senate committees over the ineffectiveness of the multilateral control system. On 10 July 1962 he wrote to President Kennedy that "the recent passage of the Export Control Act calls for a reassessment of the use of export controls to achieve U.S. national security and foreign policy objectives." He summoned the president's attention to two major changes in the law: the first, that the United States must assume the leadership in bringing about the coordination of the trade policies of the major free-world industrial nations and the creation of an organization to implement a unified control policy; the second, that the control system should take into account not solely the military but the "economic significance" of exports to the communist bloc. The first provision, Hodges declared, could imply use of the entire gamut of American political, military, and economic leverage to achieve maximum controls, and the second could lead to a virtual embargo of all trade with Russia and Eastern Europe.[68]

The crucial questions were whether and how the system of export controls could contribute to our national security. The answers, Hodges pointed out, depended on how one perceived the Soviet threat. If the danger was military, then a control system that denied Russia militarily strategic items was certainly necessary and the United States should use its economic and political leverage to persuade its allies to adopt parallel controls. If, on the other hand, unilateral American controls that went beyond the COCOM list had no appreciable adverse affect on the communist bloc, the United States should abandon them and bring its prohibited list in line with COCOM's. The implication of this decision was that the United States, in competition with its Western European allies, would engage in nonstrategic trade with the European Soviet bloc.[69]

The first approach would satisfy Congress but create difficult problems with Western Europe, which not only refused to tighten restrictions but was positively eager to expand trade with Russia and the bloc. If the administration went this route, the United States would need "considerably better intelligence than we have to determine the type and weight of tactics needed to persuade our Allies to become more restrictive." Once the data were gathered, "we could determine more accurately the cost in other economic and political relationships with our Allies of pressing for tighter controls." Hodges was also sensitive to the domestic political consequences: "only after a strong attempt in this direction, could we convincingly demonstrate to Congress that the failure to expand controls did not rest on the shoulders of the Administration."[70]

Pursuing the second approach—relaxing controls—would be more compatible with the wishes of the United States' allies, but they would also find the United States more competitive. Congress, however, and the general public "would be ill-satisfied with an unexplained adoption of a policy which apparently does not coincide with the intention expressed in the Export Control Act." The president would have to persuade Congress that the goods in question did not contribute militarily to the communist bloc but would lead gradually to a mellowing of Soviet aggressiveness.[71]

Whichever the course of action ultimately decided upon, there was no denying that the existing policy was ineffective, mainly because it attempted, unsuccessfully, to wed the contradictory principles of multilateralism and unilateralism. The result satisfied no one: not Congress, not the public, not American businessmen, and definitely not the United States' European allies. "It therefore seems to me," wrote Hodges, "that we have chosen the least potentially successful policy—that of seeking neither maximum adverse impact on the Soviet economy nor the maximum economic trading contacts with the Bloc for commercial and political advantage." Hodges believed that if the administration could decide on one of the two approaches he had outlined, a series of pending cases and procedural questions would be resolved.[72]

In a memorandum to NSC Hodges continued to rebut the State Department's and Rusk's position, arguing very forcefully that the United States should do nothing to give the Soviet economy a qualitative boost or to ease trade restrictions simply because the United States' European allies refused to follow its lead. The administration had to demonstrate to Congress that its efforts were unsuccessful in persuading the Western Europeans to adopt a more stringent trade policy. His assessment of Congress's mood differed sharply from Rusk's. "I cannot agree with the distinguished Secretary of State that the recent Congressional discussion on the Export Control Act was helpful to the Administration," he wrote, and predicted that Congress would react negatively to any easing of trade restrictions by amending the law to further constrict executive discretion, or by "prejudicing other legislative programs of the Administration."[73]

Finally, Hodges outlined his own recommendations for NSC. The United States should negotiate bilateral commercial pacts with Russia and the European satellites to allow the export of specified nonstrategic items in return for a Soviet settlement of outstanding debts, an agreement on patents and copyrights, and a promise not to dump surplus commodities (such as oil) on the international market. He also advocated an aggressive American program of promoting exports and establishing a strong commercial presence in Eastern Europe. Until then, Hodges advised, the adminstration should maintain the present level of controls. And pending a resolution of policy differences, the Department of Commerce would defer action on export license applications valued at $48 million.[74]

Hodges's comments had their intended effect. On 16 July Secretary Rusk informed NSC that the State Department had temporarily decided to support the Commerce Department's position that a clause providing for unilateral controls should be inserted into any statement of economic defense policy, to cover those special cases where the United States had a "moral" obligation not to sell to the Soviet bloc regardless of what other free-world countries decided.[75]

While the bureaucratic infighting raged, the Kennedy administration was giving the highest priority to a bill that would give the executive sweeping authority to negotiate freer trade with foreign nations. The proposed Trade Expansion Act of 1962, linking expanded trade to domestic economic growth and an economically united Atlantic community, became the centerpiece of the administration's legislative efforts in the second session of the Eighty-seventh Congress. The president's message that accompanied the bill also asked for continued latitude for the executive to grant most-favored-nation status to socialist countries as provided in the Trade Agreements Extension Act of 1951. Poland and

Yugoslavia were the two socialist countries uppermost in the minds of Washington officials, but there also was a recognition that trade policy could be useful in the larger quest for détente with the Soviet Union.[76]

In spite of President Kennedy's request, more restrictive language emerged in the substitute bill that finally went to the floor of Congress. The president was empowered to negotiate tariff reductions of up to fifty percent for the European Common Market. However, subsection 231 (a) of the Trade Expansion Act, which Kennedy signed into law on 11 October 1962, removed the executive's discretion and required him to deny most-favored-nation status to "products whether imported directly or indirectly, of any country or areas dominated or controlled by communism." The object of 231 (a), whose insertion coincided with a right-wing campaign against the purchase of consumer goods from Eastern Europe, was to deny preferential tariff treatment to Poland and Yugoslavia, and thus it reflected conservative congressional feeling that all socialist countries should be denied access to U.S. foreign exchange.[77]

Congress's action was a rebuff of the administration's policy of encouraging polycentrism or diversity within the communist world. Despite the provision that presidential action was to be effected "as soon as practicable," Kennedy delayed rescinding the most-favored-nation status accorded to Poland and Yugoslavia as late as October 1963. At that time, when Congress was considering a new foreign aid bill, he asked the body to reconsider its earlier action. After lengthy debate, congressional supporters of the administration's position affixed section 402 to the Foreign Assistance Act of 1963, which added a new subsection (b) to 231 (a) of the Trade Expansion Act. The effect of this amendment was to permit these two socialist countries, upon presidential determination that it was in the national interest, to continue to receive trade concessions. Congress passed the Foreign Assistance Act in December 1963, after Kennedy's assassination. In March 1964 the new president, Lyndon B. Johnson, made the necessary determination and thereby continued Kennedy's policy of manipulating the export control system to encourage the forces of pluralism within the Soviet bloc.[78]

As in 1961 with the Berlin confrontation, the Kennedy administration's efforts to utilize East–West trade policy in the quest for détente were, unfortunately, out of synchronization with the drift of American–Soviet relations. Three days after Kennedy signed the Trade Expansion Act, the Cuban missile crisis broke. The White House was stunned when, on 14 October 1962, high-reconnaissance U-2 photos revealed the construction of missile launching sites in Cuba, being built and guarded by several thousand Russians. From the beginning the administration was determined that they had to go; in a series of secret meetings the Executive Committee of NSC decided in favor of a blockade of Cuba, which for legal reasons was termed a "quarantine." On 24 October five Russian vessels, probably transporting missiles, stopped short of the quarantine line. Two days later an agent of the Soviet embassy privately approached an American television newscaster with a proposal to remove the missiles in return for a public pledge by the United States not to invade Cuba. After some further high-level diplomatic maneuvering, President Kennedy agreed. On Sunday, 28 October, Khrushchev announced that the missiles would be withdrawn. His statement also included a conciliatory invitation to discuss a broad range of Soviet–American differences. The crisis, which had come perilously close to a nuclear confrontation between the two superpowers, was over.[79]

If the Cuban missile crisis accomplished nothing else, it brought the two great powers to the brink of the precipice. Having peered into the abyss, they now were eager to seek accommodation.[80] And, as Kennedy began the third year of his presidency, his own purpose in world affairs seemed to crystallize. Despite his critics in Congress, he was more than ever determined to effect a détente with the Soviet Union and talked more openly about what he called "the world of diversity"—"a world where, within a framework of international cooperation, every country can solve its own problems according to its own traditions and ideals." As part of the process of lowering the level of tension between the two nations, he renewed his quest for a nuclear test ban treaty, installed a "hot line" between Washington and Moscow to provide instant contact between the heads of government, and removed obsolete missiles from Turkey, Italy, and Britain. On 10 June 1963, he announced in a speech at American University that the United States would soon begin discussions with the Soviet Union, and he called upon the nation to reexamine its attitude toward peace, Russia, and the Cold War.[81]

Even in advance of the American University address, which Khrushchev described later as "the greatest speech by any American president since Roosevelt," Kennedy had turned to East–West trade policy as another instrument for advancing détente. On 16 May he requested ECRB, comprising the secretaries of commerce, state, and defense, to reexamine the system of export controls to determine whether the current restrictions on the export of high-technology equipment and machinery adequately protected the national security interest and, more importantly for détente, whether the United States should reconsider "the whole of our trade with the Soviet Union in the light of trade between Western Europe and the Soviet Union and its European satellites."[82]

In requesting ECRB to initiate a comprehensive review of the existing highly restrictive policy, and by casting his inquiry in the context of the

Western European allies' own commerce with Russia and the bloc countries, Kennedy was transparently searching for a rationale to modify the present policy in the interest of détente and good business. Trade expansion kept American businessmen, workers, and exporters happy, helped to alleviate the nation's imbalance of payments, and strengthened the dollar overseas. After three months of intensive investigation, during which President Kennedy's envoy to Russia, W. Averell Harriman, had been trying to get the stalled negotiations on track, ECRB completed its report.[83]

The resulting document, of 9 August 1963, showed great sensitivity to domestic and foreign political pressures on the desirability of easing trade restrictions and was somewhat tentative—probably reflecting interagency compromise—in its overall tone. It advanced seven recommendations for President Kennedy to consider, a majority of which called for further contingency studies of the probable effects of liberalizing current East–West trade policy—upon the U.S. domestic economy, upon the United States' European allies (who were perceived as enjoying the fruits of a "protected" market in Eastern Europe), and upon the Soviet Union and its satellites.[84] Like the president, ECRB had assumed in its deliberations that an easing of trade restrictions with the Soviet Union and the bloc countries was long overdue. But the three cabinet officers were also concerned about the political fallout from a sudden, dramatic shift in policy. Hence they prefaced their findings with the notation that any redirection "should be negotiated and undertaken only in the context of an easing of East–West tensions over a broad front." This was the sine qua non for selling the policy change to Congress, right-wing groups, and a public that had been conditioned for more than a decade to view *any* trade with communist countries as treasonous.[85]

The dilemma the president's advisers wrestled with came through clearly in their report. On the one hand, the United States, virtually in isolation, had maintained a trade posture of limited economic warfare. This stance had evolved into the symbol of the nation's resolve to resist Soviet military, political, and psychological pressures. The United States had also attempted to induce other noncommunist states to follow its example in order to impede Soviet efforts to build up military and economic strength and to make the West dependent on trade with the East. To relax or abandon export controls, except in the context of a constructive change in Soviet policy, would be difficult to explain at home. On the other hand, the Russians were eager to have the United States lift its restrictions; a signal for détente on their part would materially assist the president in justifying such a course of action. In what may have been an oblique reference to the test ban treaty, ECRB wrote to the president that "since the political and psychological significance of the control[s] system is attested by the Soviet desire to have them removed, it provides us the opportunity to obtain from the bloc some constructive change that will enable us to explain the dismantling of the controls to Congress and the public."[86]

To the administration's relief, the potential criticism anticipated from easing the trade restrictions was to a considerable extent defused when the Kremlin agreed, on 5 August 1963, to a limited test ban treaty. Some legislators, like Democratic Senator Stephen M. Young of Ohio, hoped the president would capitalize on this breakthrough to broaden trade with Eastern Europe.[87] That view closely paralleled the administration's policy of encouraging polycentrism within the communist sphere. Three days after the signing of the treaty in Moscow, David Klein, a member of the NSC staff, wrote to national security adviser Bundy that Hungary, Rumania, and Bulgaria had indicated an interest in improving political and economic relations with the United States. All three had talked about trade. Despite the obstacles, Klein was eager to pursue these overtures and asserted that the United States had the necessary leverage to resolve some of its outstanding issues with these satellites. "On the economic side," he wrote, "we are in a position to serve as an alternative source of supply which would make them less dependent on the Soviet Bloc; on the political side, we have the means for bestowing greater political respectability."[88]

It was all a matter of timing and how the case was managed. The test ban treaty, which the Senate had yet to ratify, and the administration's use of the new foreign aid bill to persuade Congress to allow the president to restore most-favored-nation status to the bloc countries made it imperative to proceed carefully and discreetly. "This does not mean that everything must come to a grinding halt until both measures clear Capitol Hill," Klein wrote. "It does mean, however, that we must avoid giving the impression that our anti-Communist guard has been completely dropped."[89]

As suggested earlier, ECRB's final recommendations were more conservative than either Klein or even the State Department had anticipated. They certainly were less definitive than President Kennedy had hoped for, as it later developed. This is the conclusion to be drawn when comparing ECRB's report to a similar document drafted on 8 July 1963 by the Policy Planning Council of the State Department. Guided by Walt W. Rostow, the State Department's working paper had soft-pedaled both the strategic and the economic importance of trade controls, observing that they had mainly political and psychological significance: "they serve as a symbol of U.S. unwillingness to grant the USSR full respectability as an equal in the post-war world order, a symbol that the U.S. dares to *discriminate* against the USSR under contemporary conditions." Rostow's task force also argued that "no convincing grounds" existed to believe that the United States was a unique source of technology "ardently pursued" by the Soviets.[90]

By the same token, State Department planners interpreted the Cold War of the 1960s as one of movement rather than one of stasis, as in the 1950s. This led them to draw a different set of conclusions from their predecessors'.[91] The United States, they decided, could ease export restrictions without adversely affecting the military balance, and even negotiate an agreement to protect copyrights, patents, and international commodity markets from Soviet disruption. These actions would incidentally help to solidify the Western alliance; they also might lead to discussions with the Soviets on other, more profound differences. As State Department officials observed, "The principal advantage that the U.S. would gain from a change in its trade policy would be the one-shot impetus that would be given to a movement of the USSR toward policies and conduct more compatible with U.S. interests." The lifting of controls, unlike other concessions, was revocable at will and thus had utility for hard political bargaining.[92]

Klein had also read Rostow's paper with a critical eye. Though he agreed with much of its substance, he thought it was flawed because it neglected the domestic political problems inherent in easing trade restrictions and also because it implied that the administration should wait for the Soviets to take the initiative. On 14 August he wrote to Bundy: "No one can seriously assert that our present relationship with Moscow can properly be characterized as 'détente' or 'rapprochement.' Whether either of these is in the cards remains to be seen. But the indisputable fact is that there is an obligation on our part to attempt to ascertain its course and assess its significance." He listed the familiar obstacles to normalizing trade, but concluded nonetheless that trade could advance the political dialogue if the Kennedy administration approached the subject realistically. The president retained substantial discretionary authority, even within the restrictive parameters laid down by Congress, to expand trade with the Soviet bloc, "provided such trade makes political sense." Instead of waiting passively the United States should let the Soviet leadership know that "we would be prepared to meet them part way if they met us in equal measure on significant ground." Again, timing was a critical factor. The United States ought not to move ahead precipitately, Klein advised, but "it is equally important that we remain alert to political developments and aware of the importance of not holding back so long that an opportunity for significant East–West movement might be missed."[93]

Klein continued to press this viewpoint even after ECRB had presented its report to NSC. In a memorandum to Bundy, dated 7 September 1963, he critiqued the report in the light of the president's policy of détente. He noted that the recommendations generally endorsed increased trade with Russia and the bloc countries and flexibility in the application of controls, and said that the next step was "to transfer the further responsibility in this exercise to the operators to put these recommendations into a meaningful political context." In his judgment, "this should result in giving Averell Harriman the mandate to come up with proposals for using trade as a lever for developing our relations with the Soviet Union and the Soviet satellites."[94]

As for the specifics of the ECRB report, Klein declared that the key recommendations called upon Commerce "to tidy up its licensing practices to insure that these do not weaken the future negotiating posture of the U.S., and also recognize possible advantages in liberalizing existing practices to permit better exploitation of the changing situation in the Communist world." By contrast, he was dubious about certain other recommendations. Planning for a potential bilateral trade agreement with the USSR was premature. "It could not be kept under wraps long— and would only get in the way of domestic politics"; appearing too eager for a commercial agreement could also impede rather than advance future negotiations with the Soviets. He also had reservations about seeking congressional action to eliminate legislative restrictions on East–West trade and about asking the Western European allies to review the COCOM restrictions once again. He preferred to follow the advice of experts who argued that the administration already possessed the legislative leeway to act. "If there is progress in East–West trade, these things will have to be dealt with in a more comprehensive fashion," he wrote. "But at this point our emphasis should be on utilizing the discretionary authority the executive branch already has and the credit arrangements which already exist and which, in fact, have been liberalized by the Justice Department's rulings."[95]

Klein advised Bundy to shelve these last recommendations of ECRB but to transmit the first two to the president for his endorsement. Again he reiterated his opinion that trade with the Soviet bloc countries was "a problem of [a] different order and magnitude than trade with the Soviet Union." They were not tied together, and the one should not wait upon the other. "As far as the Soviet side of the picture is concerned," he said in reference to détente, "there is an important place for the trade item in moving along the dialogue—which already includes such items as security (nonaggression pacts, observation posts, etc.), Germany and Berlin."[96]

Despite Klein's advice Bundy forwarded ECRB's entire report to the president. Kennedy accepted the document and asked ECRB to proceed through the appropriate agencies with the studies suggested, but he also indicated that they should remain at the staff level as contingency papers. On 19 September he wrote to Commerce Secretary Hodges, chairman of ECRB, that "in giving this approval I should like to have it understood that I am strongly in favor of pressing forward more energetically than this report and its recommendations imply, in our trade with the Soviet and Eastern Bloc." Kennedy's determination to forge ahead on the trade front was the result of the events of the past two months, especially the test ban agreement, but also of evidence that the United States' European allies were increasing their commerce with Russia and Eastern Europe. Sensitive to America's own balance of payments deficit, which might be reduced somewhat by an increase in exports to Eastern Europe, he told Hodges that "we must not be left behind."[97]

The president then informed Hodges that he intended to designate one official within the government to have the primary responsibility for promoting trade with the European socialist states. A month later, on 21 October 1963, national security adviser Bundy told ECRB that Kennedy was designating Under Secretary of State for Economic Affairs George W. Ball to oversee East–West trade matters, with due regard to the statutory obligations of the Departments of Commerce and the Treasury. The president was acting upon the advice of Secretary of State Rusk, who also recommended that Ambassador Thompson, "under appropriate guidance," conduct the initial trade talks with the Soviet government. In closing, Bundy reminded the members of ECRB of the president's desire for "prompt and energetic action in this field."[98]

Meanwhile, on 24 September, the Senate ratified the test ban agreement. This gave the Kennedy administration a raison d'être for moving détente along and also a golden opportunity to reverse the long-standing restrictive trade policy of cold war. The president garnered support for his actions at a White House conference on trade expansion on 19 September, attended by nearly two hundred businessmen, where he listened receptively to the strong voices for a "reappraisal" of U.S. export policy toward Russia and Eastern Europe. The subsequent announcement, on 9 October, that the United States would sell large quantities of surplus American wheat to the Soviet Union was the initial step along the road to normalizing trade relations.[99] From the perspective of the White House there were advantages to the United States. Wheat was a nonstrategic commodity and, as presidential counsel Theodore C. Sorensen had written, the sale would "bring added income and employment to American agriculture and business, benefit our balance of payments, and reduce federal storage costs." Kennedy also "welcomed the opportunity to demonstrate to the Soviet leaders that the improved climate of agreement could serve the interests of both nations . . . and hoped that more trade in nonstrategic goods would follow."[100]

To the surprise of no one, the White House's announcement touched off a nationwide discussion of why the United States should or should not trade with some or all of the communist countries. The springboard for the debate was the realization that the United States' allies were already trading rather vigorously with the Soviet bloc, and virtually nothing could be done about it.[101] On 16 September, in a television interview, Commerce Secretary Hodges urged taking advantage of the cold war thaw to expand trade with Eastern Europe. Three days later the State Department released its own report endorsing peaceful trade. On 9 October the Research Institute of America reported that sixty-seven percent of one thousand businessmen polled favored expanding exports of nonstrategic goods. The Senate Foreign Relations Committee, more sympathetic to the administration than Congress as a whole, simultaneously announced that it would review U.S. policy with a view toward increasing exports. Its chairman, Democratic Senator J. William Fulbright of Arkansas, noted the Senate's dissatisfaction with current restrictions that penalized American exporters while benefiting America's allies and foreign aid recipients. Two days after the announcement of the wheat deal, the president of the United States Chamber of Commerce called for further study of the easing of trade restrictions, and Senator George Aiken urged his fellow Republicans not to make trade expansion a campaign issue. On 27 October Minnesota Democratic Senator Hubert Humphrey asked for a "bold review" of policy and a relaxation of controls on nonstrategic, "pro-people" goods.[102]

Official U.S. sources moved quickly to correct any misimpression that the administration was not taking seriously either the Cold War or the Soviet menace, as congressional critics of the wheat sale charged. They warned against expecting a quick change of policy—citing practical as well as political and legal obstacles to trade expansion. Even President Kennedy felt constrained to minimize the policy shift. In his press conference that disclosed the wheat agreement, he stated that it did not signal a new Soviet–American trade policy and cited as one of the justifications for the transaction that the Soviet Union would have to use its limited supply of gold, dollars, and foreign exchange, which could not then be used to purchase military equipment. However, in his press conference of

31 October, he observed, somewhat ambiguously, that the wheat deal might be "the bellwether" of further trade agreements.[103]

That President Kennedy was cultivating the ground for a fundamental shift in U.S. trade policy toward the communist countries did not go unnoticed on Capitol Hill. Some legislators, notably Democratic Congressman George Mahon of Texas, a member of the House Appropriations Committee, urged the president to proceed carefully. Mahon had always been a staunch proponent of restriction, but on 8 November he wrote to Kennedy that "we are now confronted with some very hard decisions in the area of East–West trade." He had read a recent speech made by Secretary Hodges in Houston, which had suggested that the issue should be reexamined; though Mahon himself did not have all the facts in hand, he did think it was "highly important" for the country to give it "high priority consideration." The ramifications were considerable, he wrote, "and I believe Congress and the country need to have the best possible understanding of the problem."[104]

Other legislators, such as Republican Senator Jacob Javits of New York, who read the wheat agreement as both a symbolic and a tangible sign of détente, endorsed the president's action but wanted the administration to develop new enabling legislation in cooperation with Congress.[105] Even liberal legislators jealously guarded Congress's prerogatives in shaping foreign economic policy. Still others, notably conservative Republican Senators Karl Mundt of South Dakota and John Tower of Texas and Democrat A. Willis Robertson of Virginia, criticized as foolish and immoral any liberalization of the existing policy. In the congressional debate that followed Kennedy's announcement of the wheat deal, Mundt especially was successful in persuading his colleagues to restrict credits to the USSR and in forcing the administration to say that it was only a one-shot opportunity to get rid of the surpluses, and not the beginning of a new approach to trade with communist countries.[106]

While the debate over the wheat agreement and trade policy was shaping up, Under Secretary Ball asked the U.S. ambassador to Great Britain, David K. Bruce, to transmit a personal communiqué to Edward Heath, the president of the Board of Trade. Ball's telegram of 24 October asked Bruce to inform Heath that the United States was reviewing its policy on East–West trade, "including the Soviet interest in more liberal credits for industrial financing." Because any decision would affect the Western alliance, Ball wanted to consult with the North Atlantic Council when it met on 18 November, immediately prior to the ministerial meeting of the OECD in Paris.[107]

Earlier Secretary Rusk had cabled American diplomatic personnel around the globe to provide them with guidance on the current state of

East–West trade policy. His remarks reflected the Kennedy administration's polycentric view of the communist world, but they also were intended to put détente into perspective. "Any changes made would be to use trade potentialities as means taking advantage current trends among Eastern European states and enhancing range of communication with USSR," he wired. Washington would ease trade restrictions only within the context of the United States' overall relationship with the Eastern bloc countries. Rusk cautioned that "signature nuclear test ban treaty and discussion other disarmament problems does not end cold war, Soviet leaders still hold uncompromising positions on such matters as Berlin, continue to make clear ultimate goal of world communism and advocate what they term QUOTE national liberation of oppressed peoples UNQUOTE."[108]

In closing, Rusk reiterated that the United States would continue to adhere to its ban on exporting strategic items, pending a decision on whether to bring the American list into conformity with COCOM's. The administration would not object to "normal" allied trade with Soviet bloc countries but would discourage a Western credits-race and overdependence on Soviet markets. Washington would continue to utilize trade policy to foster polycentric tendencies among the socialist states of Eastern Europe and would retain its prohibition on all commerce with China, North Korea, and Cuba.[109]

While Ball was carrying the message to the European allies and Rusk was updating U.S. embassy personnel, Kennedy was trying to shore up and advance détente at home, over the opposition of congressional conservatives.[110] A year had elapsed since the passage of the Trade Expansion Act of 1962, and he still had not implemented the section of that law that required the executive, "as soon as was practicable," to withdraw most-favored-nation status from Yugoslavia and Poland. His justification was that subsection 231 (a) closed a major "window to the West" and forced these nations into greater dependence on the Soviet Union. He now asked Congress to use the foreign aid authorization bill currently before it to rectify the earlier mistake. On 15 November 1963, the week before his death, Kennedy wrote to the Democratic Senate whip, Mike Mansfield of Montana, "to urge in the strongest terms that the Senate should not approve any amendment to the Foreign Aid Bill which would prohibit the use of credit guarantees for trade with any Communist country."[111] This was a reference to Senator Mundt's proposed amendment. Kennedy told Mansfield that it would jeopardize not only the sale of wheat but possible sales of tobacco, corn, and cotton. American producers and exporters, not the communists, would suffer.

Four days after Kennedy was shot and killed in Dallas, Texas, the Senate tabled and in effect killed by a vote of 57 to 35 the Mundt bill, which would have barred federal agencies from underwriting private sales to communist nations. The vote was seen as the first victory for the new president, Lyndon B. Johnson, and a personal tribute to President Kennedy, whose letter to Senator Mansfield urging the bill's rejection had been read by the Democratic whip just before the vote.[112]

W I T H the election of John F. Kennedy as president in 1960, the executive branch sought to enhance its discretionary authority to negotiate trade agreements with Russia and the European Soviet bloc countries. Kennedy was motivated by a desire to encourage centrifugal tendencies within the Soviet bloc that had developed following the death of Stalin and, to a lesser extent, by his growing concern for America's trade deficit and the decline of the dollar in international markets. The latter problems were becoming chronic in the 1960s, signaling the end of America's global hegemony and very skewed balance of power that had characterized the fifteen years since the end of World War II.

In 1962 the conflict between presidential discretion and congressional restrictiveness broke into the open. Kennedy had requested legislation that would continue the executive's discretionary authority to confer most-favored-nation status on communist nations, in this instance Yugoslavia and Poland. What really was at issue was whether Congress or the executive branch should control international economic policy for political ends. Congress responded by passing a substitute bill, the Trade Expansion Act of 1962, which, apart from its liberal features, removed the executive's discretionary authority in the case of communist states. Poland and Yugoslavia later received exemptions under the provisions of the Foreign Assistance Act of 1963, but the issue of continuing and extending tariff preference to a communist country remained a sore point between the executive and legislative branches.

In the last year of Kennedy's administration several other factors coalesced that led to new initiatives in the liberalization of trade. Perhaps the most important was the president himself. Kennedy was advocating political détente with the Soviet Union, a limited test ban treaty, and arms limitation. He also was personally receptive to modifying U.S. trade policy, as the sale of wheat to the Soviet Union in 1963 demonstrated. To bring this policy change to fruition Kennedy had to overcome not only congressional opposition but also a federal export-regulating bureaucracy that was cumbersome, initially divided, and incapable of resolving policy differences without appeal to the highest levels of authority.

Supported by key White House and State Department aides, such as McGeorge Bundy, Francis Bator, and Philip Trezise, he established a cabinet-level Export Control Review Board (ECRB) to serve as the final arbiter of disputes and to recommend new trade initiatives. Shortly before his death the president made the State Department the primary coordinator of East–West trade policy, shunting aside the Department of Commerce and ECRB. Trade relations with the USSR and Eastern Europe, however, remained static, and it was left to Kennedy's successor, Lyndon B. Johnson, to accelerate new trade initiatives at a time when executive–legislative relationships experienced unusual stress.

CHAPTER SEVEN

Building Bridges:
Johnson and the Miller Committee

POLICYMAKERS of the Kennedy administration had flirted with the idea of moderating Soviet international behavior by dangling before Moscow the carrot of greater American–Soviet trade. It was not unreasonable to believe, as Anthony Solomon, assistant secretary of state for economic affairs, had observed, that "small steps toward more normal intercourse might over the long term have a cumulative beneficial effect in reducing the aggressive thrust of Soviet policy." When Lyndon B. Johnson entered the Oval Office, he too shared this view and disparaged the notion that trade would give strategic benefits to the Russians. The lines of communication that were opened toward the Soviet Union during the Kennedy years, as symbolized in the wheat sale agreement, were to be sustained by the late president's successor despite a growing American involvement in the war in Vietnam.[1]

This decision was particularly significant because the pressures to liberalize American–Soviet trade policy, which had been mounting since 1959, peaked in the first two years of Johnson's presidency. The timing was opportune for the new president to encourage a thorough reassessment of the United States' trade policy. This was the argument of Harold J. Berman of Harvard University, in a speech delivered on 12 March 1964 at the University of Rochester. "It should be borne in mind," he concluded, "that the more resources which the Soviets allocate to production of goods for export, the fewer, relatively, they can allocate to production of military goods."[2]

Calls for a reappraisal of the United States' position coincided with deep dissatisfaction with the existing policy. In February 1965 James G. Patton, a businessman, wrote to President Johnson criticizing the lack of coordination within the federal bureaucracy and arguing that easing export controls and expanding the sale of agricultural products to the Iron Curtain countries could help rectify the nation's imbalance of payments, a problem that was occupying more and more of the administration's attention.[3] In March and April 1964 and carrying over into February 1965, the Senate Committee on Foreign Relations (often referred to as the Fulbright Committee, from its chairman) conducted hearings on East–West trade. The principal arguments for expanding trade with Russia and the European Soviet bloc countries that came out of these hearings were the ineffectiveness of existing controls to deny strategic materials to the USSR, loss of business to European competitors, the likelihood that trade might promote centrifugal tendencies within the Soviet bloc, and the possibility that trade could improve the cold war political climate and contribute to "the evolution of Soviet society away from political and economic totalitarianism."[4]

Johnson quickly recognized that he was riding a tiger: either he had to take control of the forces that were seeking to liberalize East–West trade and channel their energies in the path he wished, or he could stand aside and risk being left behind while others took the initiative. The latter course was unacceptable to the master of the political midstream. Thus, while the Fulbright Committee hearings were in progress, Johnson accepted an invitation to go to Lexington, Virginia, to speak at the dedication of the George C. Marshall Library at Virginia Military Institute.[5] The heart of his message was that the United States would work to "build bridges"—bridges of trade, travel, and humanitarian assistance—across the gulf that divided that country from Soviet Eastern Europe.[6] The cornerstones of Johnson's policy were a belief that trade would improve the Soviet standard of living and thus promote peaceful relations between the two superpowers, demonstrate the superiority of American productivity and the capitalistic system, and create jobs for American workers and profits for American companies. The last would benefit the balance of payments deficit.[7]

The administration's move in this direction received encouragement from an unexpected source. In April the United States Chamber of Commerce called for increased trade between America and the Soviet bloc nations of Europe, noting that U.S. trade restrictions had not deprived Russia and her satellites of goods but had only increased the sales of Western European producers. Representing the leadership of American industry and business, the Chamber silenced some of the "thunder on the right" that boomed out whenever a government official mentioned increasing trade with Russia and Eastern Europe.[8]

Moreover, the existing restrictive policy, which Kennedy and now Johnson had inherited from earlier administrations when the Cold War was at its fiercest, was becoming a source of contention and confusion within government. Secretary of Commerce Luther Hodges had several times in the past year referred to the "schizophrenic situation" that required him, on the one hand, to promote exports and, on the other hand, to restrict them.[9] On 14 April 1965 national security adviser McGeorge

Bundy called the president's attention to "the tough problem of decisions on export licenses for the Soviet Union" that was scheduled to come before the National Security Council (NSC).[10] The specific case was whether the Department of Commerce should issue an export license to permit the sale of a highly advanced six-row beet harvester to the USSR. Bundy noted that the crux of the problem was the divided responsibility of the executive departments, each of which had a sharply different viewpoint.[11] These divisions and the idiosyncratic nature of each case meant that "in the last three years no one short of the President has had authority to make clear-cut decisions."[12]

The difficulty of establishing broad guidelines had been compounded by the fact that the decision about each sale involved balancing its strategic value to the Soviet Union against its commercial worth to the United States. Each of these estimates was affected by whether one thought that peaceful trade with the Russians was, per se, a desirable policy. In any given case, Bundy informed the president, one could always predict the reaction of an agency's head (or a legislator) more from his basic philosophy than from the evidence presented. Ideally, Bundy wanted Johnson to initiate a general review of export control policy in order to put it on a more rational and solid footing, but he was also a realist: 1964 was an election year and not the time to commence such a review.[13]

Until the election was safely behind, the real question was how best to handle controversial cases, like the beet harvester, that might arise. Bundy advised the president to listen to all of the arguments of the agency heads at the 16 April NSC meeting, state his own attitude, and follow up with a memo to each agency indicating the procedure he wished it to follow in compliance with his views. In a postscript he told Johnson that in his judgment the correct way to deal with cases of nonstrategic trade was to approve export licenses much more broadly than the Commerce Department had been doing, but without trying to obtain political concessions from the Soviets. Apart from strategic military items, there was nearly always an alternative supplier somewhere in the free world; hence too-tight restrictions hurt the United States more, through loss of jobs and profits, without causing equal damage to the Soviet Union.[14]

Bundy's advice was persuasive because it accorded with President Johnson's own basic instincts on East–West trade. Wherever possible, the administration expanded the list of products to be sold to communist nations. Johnson quickly recognized that existing legislative authority did not permit the United States to go as far as the administration desired, and turned his attention to Congress, where there were signs of support for changing the existing policy.[15] From 21 November through

13 December 1964 seven members of the House Committee on Foreign Affairs had toured Russia and Eastern Europe. In Moscow, Walter J. Stoessel, Jr., the acting chief of mission of the U.S. Embassy there, had briefed them on Soviet domestic political and economic problems. Upon their return they recommended to the full House, in February 1965, that the United States thoroughly review its East–West trade policy, observing that an expansion of trade in nonstrategic items "should serve the interests of our foreign policy."[16]

In his State of the Union Message on 4 January 1965 President Johnson signaled the administration's move toward a more liberal trade policy when he said that "your government, assisted by leaders in labor and business, is now exploring ways to increase peaceful trade with the countries of Eastern Europe and the Soviet Union."[17] Two days later he received a summary of the observations of the Business International Roundtable, an organization of nearly one hundred executives representing sixty-five large corporations, who had met with the top Soviet political and economic leadership in Moscow from 15 to 20 November 1964 to discuss the feasibility of broadening peaceful trade between the two countries. The delegation had been genuinely impressed by the Soviets' desire to develop their agricultural and consumer goods industries but had also reminded them of the obstacles to expanded trade, such as the lend-lease quarrel. They had told the Soviet leadership that "trade reflects trust and confidence." On the other hand, they advised the president, if he were seriously interested in pursuing trade and reducing tensions, the United States would have to cut export controls drastically and grant most-favored-nation status, with all that that implied. In the end, the businessmen urged Johnson to broaden trade relations for economic reasons and because of the possibility of influencing "the evolution of Soviet society toward goals that are more acceptable to the West and better for the Soviet people than world communism dominated by the Kremlin."[18] In his reply Johnson, referring to his State of the Union address, indicated that he was already thinking along the lines suggested in their remarks.[19]

Meanwhile, between 4 January and 1 March 1965 eighteen bills and resolutions pertaining to East–West trade were introduced into the Senate and the House, covering a broad spectrum of congressional intent— from establishing a government-sponsored trading corporation to conduct all business transactions with Russia and the Soviet bloc, to prohibiting any trade with communist countries, to South Carolina Senator Strom Thurmond's resolution declaring it the will of the American people and government "to achieve complete victory over the forces of the world Communist movement." On 1 February Democratic Senator Warren G. Magnuson of Washington introduced into the first session of the Eighty-ninth Congress Joint Resolution 36, which would establish a high-level advisory council to develop proposals for increasing trade between the United States and Soviet Eastern Europe.[20]

This flurry of legislative activity, whose course no one could predict with certainty, plus pressures from Mayor Willy Brandt of West Berlin, the European Economic Community Parliament, Japanese organizations, and United Nations agencies, all calling upon the United States and Europe to develop a common policy to expand trade with the communist countries, made it all the more imperative for the Johnson administration to take the initiative or risk either being left behind or having to accept unsatisfactory legislation.[21] To avert both of these possibilities the president disclosed on 18 February that he was establishing a Special Committee on United States Trade Relations with Eastern European Countries and the Soviet Union.[22] The Miller Committee, as it came to be known (from its chairman, J. Irwin Miller), would be the Johnson administration's instrument to sustain the lines of trade and communication opened toward the Soviet Union during the Kennedy years.

Shortly thereafter the administration began to search around for possible candidates to chair the committee. One name prominently mentioned in the early stages was David Rockefeller's, of Chase Manhattan Bank, another was Charles Mortimer's, the chairman of General Foods. Mortimer had support within the administration, but others outside government were less enthusiastic. John McCloy of Chase Manhattan Bank described Mortimer as "a good practical man" but one who was "not too familiar with the flows of international trade." In McCloy's estimation the most important potential commodity the Soviet Union had to sell to the United States was oil, which "has great strategic implications both for our own security and that of Europe." McCloy touted the names of former Treasury Secretary Robert Anderson, because of his experience with the balance of payments problem and "his awareness of the sensitive attitudes of Texas to foreign oil imports" and his keen political instincts, and Jack Rathbone, the retiring head of Standard Oil of New Jersey, "the most moderate and objective minded executive among the big oil companies on this whole question."[23]

While the quest for a chairman continued, national security adviser McGeorge Bundy was developing a preliminary agenda of issues that the administration wanted the committee to explore, "but without prejudging the committee's terms of reference." These issues included export licensing, trade and technology, export credits, Soviet access to the American market, and whether the United States should seek some quid pro quo (and if so, what type).[24]

On 18 February President Johnson announced the selection of J. Irwin Miller, an Indiana businessman with broad interests in industry, finance, academe, and international affairs, to chair the committee.[25] A graduate of Yale and Oxford, Miller was chairman of the board of Cumins Engine Company of Columbus, Indiana, a director of AT&T and Chemical Bank New York Trust Company, a fellow of the Yale Corporation, and trustee of both the Ford Foundation and the Committee for Economic Development. Of great significance to the administration, Miller was acceptable to the leadership of organized labor. Miller did not accept the appointment without first ascertaining for himself that the administration was genuinely interested in liberalizing East–West trade.[26]

Though warmly applauded, Miller's selection also touched off speculation about the other members of the committee, whose names, for political or technical reasons, had not yet been disclosed. The administration, for example, had been anxious to appoint a labor representative, to demonstrate that this was not simply a businessman's committee to promote the interests of business in East–West trade. George Meany, president of AFL-CIO, was of course the logical choice. But, as McGeorge Bundy noted, Meany had "painted himself into a very tight corner on this issue," a reference to the labor leader's die-hard opposition to trade with the Soviets.[27]

On 3 March the president met with Meany to discuss the trade issue as well as his appointment to the committee. Bundy suggested that Johnson emphasize to Meany the number of new jobs that would be created by an expansion of trade.[28] Whatever Johnson told Meany is unrecorded. In any event, Meany refused the appointment but suggested instead the name of Nathaniel Goldfinger, a close associate and the AFL-CIO's director of research. The rest of the committee was a Who's Who of business and academe: Eugene R. Black of Chase Manhattan Bank, William Blackie of the Caterpillar Tractor Company, George R. Brown of Brown and Root, Incorporated, Charles W. Englehard, Jr., of Englehard Industries, James B. Fisk of Bell Laboratories, Crawford H. Greenewalt of DuPont, William A. Hewitt of John Deere and Company, Charles G. Mortimer of General Foods, Professor Max Millikan of MIT, and Chancellor Herman B. Wells of Indiana University.[29]

On 1 April Bundy asked the president whether the timing was appropriate to have press secretary George Reedy release the names of the other members of the Miller Committee. "This Committee is a small but clear signal of your interest in the peaceful side of the road, and the riots at the Moscow Embassy are safely in the past," he wrote. He added that the committee was a "genuinely impressive and well rounded one, and I think its existence would give encouragement to some of our worried liberal friends."[30] Johnson agreed, and three days later he made the announcement, which was lauded by the liberal press and business publications. However, as *Business Week* pointed out, the committee was heavily weighted with international traders, which virtually ensured that it would urge a significant liberalization of East–West trade policy. At the very least, *Business Week* anticipated, the Miller Committee would probably recommend restoration of most-favored-nation status to other communist countries besides Poland and Yugoslavia and liberalization of the licensing provisions of the Export Control Act.[31]

Shortly after the presidential announcement American Ambassador Foy Kohler wired from Moscow his enthusiastic support of the Miller Committee and made several observations about the role of trade in American–Soviet relations. The Soviets' chief economic objective in expanding trade with the United States, he said, continued to be the procurement of technologically advanced equipment and know-how to accelerate their own industrial progress. Politically, the Soviets hoped to remove the stigma of American discrimination, which "galls them" and "hamstrings attainment [of] their economic objectives." Normalization of trade would contribute only modestly to the American balance of payments problem; but, more importantly, it could have a salutary effect by removing one contentious issue between the two superpowers and establishing another area of agreement. Yet even on this last point Kohler was realistic, warning that "we should not harbor illusions . . . either as to importance [of] trade questions in overall political relations or extent to which trade will facilitate effective contact with Soviet society."[32]

Meanwhile the administration prodded the committee to begin its work immediately, in the expectation of receiving an early and favorable report. In fact the committee's deliberations did have a choreographed quality about them; the timetable was tightly managed by the White House, and the agenda for discussion, despite Bundy's earlier disclaimer, was probably drafted by Bundy himself. That document asserted that the policy of containment had defined the narrow parameters of the United States' commerce with the Soviet Union. It then raised a series of questions that had broad political and policy implications.[33]

To expedite the committee's discussion the agenda did target the specific issues that Bundy had raised. With respect to export licensing, the question was whether present policy imposed a serious handicap on American business, in favor of European and Japanese competitors. If so, what changes in administrative practice and legislation would facilitate U.S. exports without impairing security? On technology transfer, could there be a meaningful and politically useful expansion of trade with the Soviet bloc without a corresponding willingness on the United

States' part to license the sale of technology? Subject to the president's determination that trade with a particular communist country was in the national interest, did the United States need greater statutory flexibility to offer credits than the Johnson Act permitted? Should the United States grant preferential tariff treatment to the USSR or any of its satellites? Should it conduct trade with the Soviets on a bilateral basis, or work toward multilateral agreements? What were the losses and gains to the United States, the USSR, and the European Soviet bloc countries from a less restrictive trade policy?[34] In one memorandum to the committee Bundy discouraged the need for additional studies of East–West trade, stating that what the president needed now was "a hard judgment about what practical steps the government might prudently take to move matters forward."[35]

On 4 March 1965 the committee members assembled in Washington's Mayflower Hotel to receive briefings from government experts. State Department official Philip H. Trezise provided an overview of the United States' East–West trade policy that emphasized its flexibility.[36] He concluded that a shift in the focus of the United States' national interest had occurred since 1948. In the early years of maximum East–West tension American policy had primarily been concerned with denying any trade that augmented the Soviet Union's aggressive military posture. As the conflict had shifted to areas increasingly removed from the direct military confrontation inherent in the Berlin airlift, and with the onset of centrifugal tendencies within the Soviet sphere, "the shift in United States policy has been toward the use of trade encouragement rather than trade denial as a tool of policy." Still, serious disagreement persisted between the United States and its NATO allies over the definition of "strategic" goods.[37]

Against this background William Morrell of the CIA assessed the strategic importance of Western trade to the Soviet bloc. By most indices of measurement this trade had been and was likely to remain small because of the limited capabilities of the communist countries to export to the industrial West and because of their earlier decision to structure trade in order to promote autarchy within the bloc. Of more immediate interest to the committee members were Morrell's responses to two questions that would condition the future course of U.S.–Soviet trade: What might have been the effect on Russian military programs if in the past there had been absolutely no imports of Western technology? And, assuming a continuation of the strategic embargo, what effect would a denial of nonmilitary items have on Soviet defense capabilities?[38]

As to the first question, the CIA judged that the effect would have been relatively small. Between 1950 and 1957, when the West had achieved substantial unity in export control policy, the USSR had nevertheless been able, through military and industrial espionage, to build a military establishment second only to the United States'. Between 1958 and 1963, when rigid controls on military items remained, the Soviets had made tremendous strides in missile and space programs. The effect that denying nonmilitary items would have on Russian defense capabilities was more difficult to assess except on a case-by-case basis. However, Morrell insisted, this was not the real issue. The important fact was that over the past decade the Soviet Union had demonstrated its capability to develop and manufacture advanced weapons and space systems, irrespective of Western know-how and technology.[39] Freer trade with the West might have reduced the lag time and costs and perhaps improved the effectiveness of some of these systems, "but the fact remains that the U.S.S.R. now has an established, effective base for the development and production of such systems—*a base relatively independent of the type of Western technology which could have been acquired through trade with the West.*"[40]

The second round of briefings occurred two weeks later, on 18 and 19 March. The agenda focused on the foreign policy implications of broadening nonstrategic trade with Russia and the bloc countries. Llewellyn E. Thompson, the government's leading Soviet expert, presented the State Department's position, which affirmed the political desirability of promoting trade. The department estimated that by 1970 American exports to the USSR could total $300 million to $400 million, not counting another $600 million to the smaller communist bloc countries. From a foreign policy perspective the important consideration was that the volume of trade should become substantial enough to make it an instrument for advancing the United States' interests toward the communist countries. Realistically, Thompson did not envision that expanded trade would induce a fundamental alteration in the communist system, but it did represent "one of the few important means available to us for further significant exploitation."[41]

Assuming that there would continue to be flashpoints of conflict between the United States and Russia, the task was to weave a seamless web of nonpolitical strands that might withstand the trauma of political crises. The United States had been moving in that direction over the past several years, explained Thompson, citing the nuclear test ban agreement and agreements on outer space, desalination, and civil aviation. The development of commercial ties was a logical next step: "The larger and more vital our trade with the U.S.S.R., and the more flexible and sure our controls over that trade, the more effective trade will be as a tool in working toward our foreign policy goals." These goals were, broadly speaking, to check Soviet imperialism and the expansion of Russian territory; to reduce tensions and the risk of war by removing obstacles to better relations and broadening contact between Americans and Russians; and to encourage trends in the Soviet Union toward a more consumer-oriented society, with a greater voice for the average citizen.[42]

Thompson told the Miller Committee that Soviet leaders during the past few years had given indications of wanting to purchase more from the United States and to have freer access to the American market. "The United States embargo over the years has represented a symbolic issue to the Russians—one more important psychologically than as a significant restraint on Soviet economic and military development," he observed. Kremlin leaders unquestionably would attach great importance to being put on an equal footing with other countries in their commercial relations with the United States, he added, and disclosed that both he and Secretary Rusk had received overtures from Moscow that had led them to believe that serious negotiations might be forthcoming.[43]

The United States, Thompson concluded, was prepared to negotiate seriously with the Russians about trade matters as long as they were willing to discuss a realistic settlement of the wartime lend-lease debt.[44] He thought the United States should make clear that it wanted to establish a pattern of regular trade talks, as it had with Rumania, on items it would permit the Soviets to purchase in America. This would enable the United States to exercise authority to monitor trade with the USSR "on a flexible basis rather than primarily as a strategic embargo." This required a significant change of emphasis that would have tough sledding because of domestic American attitudes toward the Russians. Nonetheless, Thompson declared, "the report which this Committee makes will have an important bearing on our success in this delicate and complex enterprise."[45]

However much they were willing to talk trade expansion with the Soviets, State and Commerce Department officials opposed granting long-term credits (in excess of five years) to the USSR. This was the government's position despite long-standing opposition from NATO countries, led by Great Britain. Simply put, the British and the Americans viewed credit from entirely different perspectives. In the British view long-term credit was a commercial matter, and Britain would not discriminate for political reasons. The United States opposed extending long-term credits to the Soviets on the grounds that they constituted a form of economic assistance that had political and military implications, both domestically and abroad. The administration would therefore continue to seek an agreement with its allies to limit credit and "to avoid a credit race which would permit the U.S.S.R. to play off one country against another."[46]

By the close of this second session the committee members had under their belts the relevant background for assessing the diplomatic, economic, and political importance of U.S. trade with Russia and the European Soviet bloc. A third session, scheduled for 25 and 26 March, was reserved for the committee to meet with the various secretaries and heads of executive agencies—the Departments of State, Commerce, and Defense and the Export-Import Bank—to listen to their recommendations for modifying the present policies in order to render trade a more effective instrument of foreign policy. But because of scheduling difficulties and the press of time the committee decided to forgo a formal session and authorized Miller to meet with the cabinet officers and report back their opinions and recommendations. In fact Miller had already been soliciting their views on his own initiative.[47]

On 16 February Miller had conferred with Secretary of State Dean Rusk, who viewed East–West trade as part of a long-term effort to reduce tensions and put relations with the Eastern bloc on a normal basis. Rusk thought that the opportunities for expanding the volume of commerce would be limited by the inability of the Soviets to export items (except minerals and oil) that American businesses would want to purchase, by the United States' refusal to grant preferred tariff treatment, and by Russia's unwillingness to settle lend-lease claims. There were obstacles on the United States' side also: whether an open, capitalistic society could trade effectively with a state-organized monopoly; the Senate's greater interest in encouraging trade than the House's; the attitudes of ethnic groups within the nation on the desirability of trade with communist countries. Rusk did not think the United States could obtain political concessions for specific trade deals, because to the Soviets trade was "clearly subordinate to politics."[48]

Rusk's expectation that the committee's recommendations could improve American–Soviet relations was tempered by his acceptance of political realities. On the one hand, the climate of public opinion (except for organized labor) had become more conducive to East–West trade since the signing of the nuclear test ban treaty; on the other hand, "the present tense situation in Southeast Asia may tend to reverse this overall trend." Rusk also thought that the timing of the committee report's release could be a crucial factor in its success.[49]

Overall, Rusk did not perceive the committee's inquiry as leading to any drastic change in American policy; rather, it might bring the United States in line with what other Western countries had been doing for some time "in a fairly uninhibited manner." By contrast, Miller's interview with Under Secretary of State for Economic Affairs Thomas Mann was definitely downbeat. Whether the United States should increase trade with the European Soviet bloc nations depended upon a delicate combination of issues: the effect that trade would have on the U.S. balance of payments; the United States' desire to separate Eastern Europe from the USSR; and the need to minimize the political impact of that trade on the less-developed countries. In Mann's judgment the United States should place priority on trade with Eastern Europe rather than the Soviet Union, to be conducted "on a strictly cold-blooded, arms'-length basis," and on avoiding a credits race with Western Europe that "could ultimately have the effect of subsidizing the economies of the European communist states." Above all else, however, Mann worried about the effect such trade would have on the developing countries of Africa and Asia. "These nations are not sophisticated in regard to the dangers of Communism," he pointed out. "Our trade tends to enhance Bloc respectability among the developing nations and thus may increase Bloc subversive capabilities."[50]

In contrast to Mann's reservations, especially about the problems that might arise with third world nations, Secretary of Agriculture Orville H. Freeman had no qualms about expanded trade. He agreed with the remark of former Commerce Secretary Luther Hodges that the United States should sell to the communist countries anything they could "eat, drink, or smoke." Freeman's reasoning was that if trade improved the position of the consumer in the Soviet Union, "the Russians will find it harder to push their people around and get them to fight." This was a rather naive view that exhibited little understanding of either the Russian people or the communist system. More valid was Freeman's observation that increased trade could help the United States' balance of payments problem, provided that the committee clarified the definition of "strategic" trade and the United States' position on selling technological know-how to the Soviet Union.[51]

These last two observations also had concerned Secretary of Defense Robert McNamara. He told Miller that past restrictions on East–West trade had been unrealistic and that the United States should not deny to Iron Curtain countries anything not clearly related to military usage, because they could get a good equivalent elsewhere. In fact he doubted that "the denial of *strategic materials* can significantly influence military potential in today's world." The only restrictions he preferred to retain were limited to a very small list of esoteric technology of the most advanced type, and even on these he believed that the United States tended "to exaggerate the extent of our lead and the permanency of a particular advantage." Generally speaking, however, McNamara thought that East–West trade was a political question rather than a military or economic matter; he said he would take his lead from the secretary of state.[52]

McNamara's remarks on East–West trade diverged substantially from the Defense Department's previous position, and in the absence of available documentation it is probably fair to conclude that the Pentagon's military chieftains did not share his view. How, then, may we account for the difference? McNamara's experience before becoming secretary of defense was rooted in the international business community; he had served as chief executive of the Ford Motor Company, a leader in high technology. His civilian background and his stated belief that the United States' international political and military problems were indivisible rendered him more sensitive to the politico-economic dimension of trade and export controls than were most military leaders. Also, he embraced an "active management" philosophy, in which the chief of a corporation or executive department provided aggressive leadership—questioning, suggesting alternatives, proposing objectives, and stimulating progress. This managerial style necessarily reduced the role of the Joint Chiefs of Staff as policymakers from what it had been previously. The military could still discuss the issues and offer advice, but McNamara, as secretary of defense, was invested with the decision-making power under the law. Thus his convictions, his experience, and no doubt his political instincts led him to support the liberalization of trade inherent in President Johnson's bridge-building policy.[53]

The belief that U.S. trade with Russia and the European Soviet bloc was primarily a political question ran through virtually all of Miller's interviews with high-ranking government officials. Under Secretary of State George W. Ball, for example, observed that the committee would not be able to separate the political and economic considerations and recommended that it address the political ramifications of increasing trade at an early point in its investigations. The principal advantages to the United States from increased trade with the communist bloc, he suggested, "may lie in the establishment of easier relations, a less tense situation, the opening of more windows from the East to the West, and the removal of resentment which now exists because of the refusal to trade." Diminishing the Soviets' sense of economic inferiority might be helpful politically in eroding the Iron Curtain: "Among other things, it enables the Russians to identify more closely with the Western 'industrial club' in contrast to an industrially backward Communist China."[54]

Treasury Secretary Douglas Dillon likewise agreed that East–West trade was chiefly a political issue, but unlike George Ball he viewed it first of all as a domestic political problem, and international and commercial considerations as being of secondary importance.[55] The American public needed to be persuaded that trade with communist countries was not treasonous and did not benefit only the Soviet Union. He believed that the United States should use trade to open up Eastern Europe but cautioned Miller to steer the committee away from the China trade issue, saying that it "should not get into this subject lest it endanger its main recommendations on the trade with European Communist countries."[56]

Harold Linder, president of the Export-Import Bank, also believed it was worthwhile to increase U.S. trade with Russia and Eastern Europe, "in line with the President's political objectives." But he tended to emphasize the kinds of impediments that Rusk first had alluded to in his talk with Miller. One matter that concerned Linder, as a banker, however, was whether the government should assume the risk of underwriting a significant expansion of East–West trade. Even if the administration were favorably disposed, it would be very difficult to obtain the required financial data to justify extending credit to these countries. They did not publish all their commercial data and refused to provide information on invisible items, debt-servicing, and gold and foreign exchange reserves. "Without full disclosure of financial information," Linder advised, "the extension of credit on a large scale to these countries would not be justified."[57]

Miller's canvass of the opinions of the highest-ranking government officials had disclosed a decided bias in favor of liberalizing East–West trade. In their collective judgment, a helpful report from the committee would conclude that the United States should encourage East–West trade when it was commercially and financially desirable; the public should be educated to the importance of such trade to achieving the United States' political and foreign policy objectives; this trade should be reviewed regularly in terms of U.S. political relations with Russia and the European Soviet bloc countries; the president should be given discretionary authority to encourage or discourage this trade as U.S. political interests required; and the United States put too much weight on its vaunted technology, disregarding the fact that the Soviets were able to obtain suitable alternatives in other countries.[58]

Meanwhile Edward R. Fried, the committee's executive secretary, who was on loan from the State Department's Policy Planning Staff, sent out letters soliciting the views of private organizations and individuals on whether increased trade with Russia and the bloc countries was in the United States' national interest and, if so, under what conditions.[59] The letters brought responses that were typical of the debate, already widespread and growing in volume, around the nation. At one end of the spectrum were those who rigidly maintained that any commercial contact with the Soviets was an act that undermined the cause of freedom. Typical of this attitude was the letter from George Meany and the AFL-CIO Executive Council, drafted on 1 March 1965. Organized labor deemed it "utterly unrealistic" for American industrialists to believe they could do "business as usual" with the Russians, and pointed to the disastrous experience of the democratic nations with the Nazis and Fascists. The AFL-CIO rejected the suggestion that American industry could or should bail out the Soviet economy or that expansion of trade might lead to an unraveling of Soviet influence in Eastern Europe. The labor organization asserted that above all, there should be no trade without political concessions, specifically concerning Vietnam, Berlin, and "Soviet subversion of the Congo."[60]

The Miller Committee had pretty much expected the AFL-CIO's hostility to East–West trade. A more thoughtful critique came from John J. McCloy of Chase Manhattan Bank, in a lengthy letter to Eugene R. Black, a member of the committee. Dated 29 March 1965, McCloy's letter specifically criticized the findings of the Fulbright hearings on East–West trade, upon which he believed the Miller Committee would base its recommendations. He argued that no historical precedent existed to support the contention that increased trade with the Soviets would lead to peace and friendship, or that Russia's clash with China would promote détente with the West. Pressures for expanding trade, he asserted, came from "certain elements of American industry" who felt that they were being deprived of the economic gain they might enjoy if they were free to compete with the United States' Western European allies. He was unconvinced that the Soviets wanted to purchase American goods on a continuing basis, as opposed to prototypes of plants and technology that could be adapted or duplicated in Russia and the bloc.[61]

By itself, McCloy conceded, a trade embargo would not guarantee U.S. security. However, the national interest was not simply to keep the Soviets from attaining military superiority; it was also "to prevent the economic strength of the Communist World to the point where Communism is in a position to displace United States prestige and influence throughout the rest of the Free World"—a reference to Cuba. Hence McCloy did not believe that export controls had been a failure and should be discarded. They had denied to the Soviets a wide range of technologies and commodities that they either did not possess or could not manufacture economically. In any industrial or military competition, lead time was a vital factor that often could not be surmounted. "Why help a competitor accelerate?" he asked.[62]

These observations would lead one to believe that McCloy saw no basis whatever for trade with the communist world. But however pessimistic his analysis, he shrank from drawing the logical conclusion. Instead he wrote that with appropriate changes in the current political situation (left undefined), there could be latitude for trade between the two wartime partners, even though it would not be conducted on an extensive basis.[63]

At the other end of the spectrum was the view that except for a very small number of militarily strategic items the United States should substantially expand its trade with the communist countries. Echoing the theme of "world peace through world trade," the promoters of this argument, such as the industrialist Cyrus S. Eaton, asserted that the ability of East and West to coexist in an atomic age would be greatly enhanced by increased trade, and that the United States should alter its current policy vigorously and promptly.[64]

Lastly there was a middle group—George F. Kennan, some government officials, and even a handful of labor leaders, with growing support from businessmen and academicians—who asserted that the present trade policy of the United States, which had come into being when the Cold War was at its height, was outmoded in the warmer political climate. "The United States, which has been enveloped in a cold war fog, has not yet fully grasped the significance of the change in the international climate brought about by the political and economic developments of the past ten years," wrote James A. Ramsey, the head of a Washington-based research firm. "Trade is an important part of this shifting scenario, and should be considered as an opening of which one can take calculating and careful advantage."[65]

Ramsey's view was a commonly held one, but even within the middle group there existed some who drew a distinction between encouraging expansion of trade with the satellite countries and promoting commerce with the Soviet Union. Ramsey was not one of these, for he believed that American businessmen and government officials tended to underestimate the Soviet market and the ability of Russia to sell products that the West would want to buy.[66] A. L. Nickerson, chairman of the board of Socony Mobil, George F. Kennan of Princeton University, and the economist George Grossman of the University of California at Berkeley were less sanguine. They advocated a more relaxed trade and credit policy toward Eastern European nations that showed signs of independence of Moscow, and a less permissive, but by no means rigid, policy toward trade with the USSR.[67]

Differences of emphasis aside, they all believed that the existing policy was counterproductive and needed to be reconsidered. This also was the judgment of such diverse figures as Jacob S. Potofsky, head of the Amalgamated Clothing Workers Union, W. H. Page, senior vice-president of the Morgan Guaranty Trust Company, and Charles W. Stewart, president of the Machinery and Allied Products Institute. In letters to Miller and in testimony before congressional committees, they affirmed the need to reexamine the United States' commercial relations with the communist countries, especially in light of the attitudes and actions of the Western allies, who had cast aside their ideological inhibitions and were engaged in a much more extensive trade with Russia and Eastern Europe.[68] William Blackie reiterated to his colleagues on the Miller Committee the point he had made to Senator Fulbright's Committee on Foreign Relations: "A policy which is not effective is not realistic and should be reexamined in the light of its ineffectiveness to accomplish the objectives sought."[69]

Having canvassed a broad range of opinion both within and outside of government, the members of the committee pushed headlong to draft their report. On 26 April 1965 national security adviser McGeorge Bundy forwarded a copy of the preliminary document to President Johnson. It had already been read and endorsed by Rusk, McNamara, and Secretary of Commerce Jack Connor, who had succeeded Luther Hodges. "The report is a very unusual document," wrote Bundy, "in that it recommends a bold policy in language which is carefully designed to protect both you and the committee from charges of softness of any sort." The six pages of introduction built a solid case for the committee's recommendations and affirmed unequivocally that peaceful trade was beneficial both for the United States and for international peace. The report presented incisive and, in Bundy's judgment, persuasive arguments against the basic position of the Commerce Department over the years on export licensing and the sale of technology. It ended with a set of specific, commonsense recommendations that Bundy thought might be of use in negotiating with the Russians on Vietnam.[70]

Only two problems remained: George Meany, and whether to publish the final report. On 27 April Bundy decided to telephone the labor leader personally and "try to keep him from having his agent Goldfinger file a strong dissent or from making other attacks, public or private, on the report." As for the report, Bundy advised the president to publish and publicize it. Ever sensitive to the political winds, he wrote to Johnson: "You do not have to endorse it at this stage, and I think it will win general public approval from those who believe in peace, while attracting only very limited criticism from the other side. This makes it a useful gesture, in the context of Vietnam, whatever you may eventually decide, and I do not see how it could do anything but enlarge your freedom of choice over it."[71]

On 28 April Bundy wrote another memorandum to the president, urging him to follow through on the liberalization of trade. He told Johnson that he understood his feelings: "The problem of Vietnam is obvious, and so is the problem of George Meany." But he was equally determined that Meany not be allowed the opportunity to sink the committee's recommendations in any private meeting with the president.[72]

Bundy's argument and informal appraisal of the report's contents were persuasive; on the next day, 29 April, Miller and the committee members came to the White House to deliver the final document and receive the president's thanks for their work.[73] The only member who had expressed the slightest reservation about either the underlying premises or the recommendations contained in the report had been Nathaniel Goldfinger, organized labor's representative. Goldfinger believed that the committee had not given as much consideration to national security and foreign policy objectives as it had to temporary or marginal commercial advantages in reassessing trade with Russia and the Soviet bloc countries. His reservations, interestingly, did not assume the form of a loud, public protest but rather appeared as a muted "Statement of Comment" appended to the main text. This suggested that the Johnson administration had reached an accommodation beforehand with George Meany and the AFL-CIO, whereby organized labor would not strongly attack the Miller Committee's recommendations.[74]

After the 29 April meeting with President Johnson the committee members reconvened to consider how they might best implement the president's desire to liberalize East–West trade. There was unanimous agreement that the major recommendations of the report would win substantial backing from the leaders of American business; the real task was to sell the report to Congress and to the American people, who had been conditioned, for more than fifteen years, to believe that trade with communists was treasonous. The administration had anticipated this problem and already had taken steps to apprise influential legislators of its new attitude toward trade with the European Soviet bloc. The president, for example, had arranged in advance for Miller to discuss the report with Senators Mansfield and Fulbright, and also with Republican Senator Bourke Hickenlooper of Iowa, a possible foe. Secretary of Commerce Connor was scheduled to confer with Democratic Congressman Wright Patman of Texas about scheduled hearings to extend the Export Control Act, in order to impress upon Patman "the need to establish the principle of flexibility, discretionary authority, and the primacy of foreign politics in administering the Act." Miller would also review the document with Congressman Wilbur Mills of the powerful Appropriations Committee, in particular to discuss the need for executive discretion and most-favored-nation status.[75]

The White House, then, was carefully orchestrating the selling of the report. Johnson knew who in Congress were "the whales and the minnows"—the ones who could move bills or stop them, and the ones who would follow along. On 3 May Miller apprised the president of the committee's activities and progress in enlisting the support of influential legislators. Two principal themes ran through Miller's letter to President Johnson: the necessity for the administration to follow through on the report's recommendations, and the urgency of publicizing the report without delay. In justifying his position, Miller emphasized that "a reasonable reader" of the document would have to conclude that it was *not* soft on communism, that trade was a matter of politics, and not profit. He asked Johnson to make the report public so that its tough-minded conclusions would stand out in any public debate—and warned that if the recommendations leaked out piecemeal, "we are afraid that the tough central theme of the Report will be lost."[76]

Miller hoped to persuade Johnson by noting that both the State Department and the Defense Department had endorsed the recommendations and public release of the report, as had Senators Mansfield and Fulbright, although the latter had expressed his doubts about how much could be accomplished "in this field while the Vietnam crisis deepens." Congressman Patman wanted the report to be made public immediately after a scheduled hearing of the Banking and Currency Committee on extending the Export Control Act. Miller wrote to the president that Patman felt that releasing the report would be "extremely helpful in the Congressional debate which would follow."[77]

Miller's strategy was endorsed by the Committee for Economic Development (CED), an international body of reputable businessmen, which was on the verge of publishing a thoughtful appraisal of the advantages and hazards inherent in encouraging greater trade with the communist nations. CED was about to come down firmly, albeit with reservations, on the side of liberalizing U.S. export control policy. Significantly, the Miller Committee had been provided with the background studies to support CED's conclusion, and its members had been very much concerned that the CED publication might "steal the thunder" of their own recommendations.[78]

Miller's arguments were persuasive, and on 6 May President Johnson released the report to the press. In it, the committee called for "the coordinated use of trade as a flexible instrument" to guide the United States' relations with Russia and the European Soviet bloc countries. In an oblique reference to the containment doctrine, the report asserted that American trade policy had to be an integral "part of our overall strategy toward European Communist countries and must be designed and applied as part of that strategy." This reasoning ran as a leitmotif throughout the report. In another section the committee had written that it was not the volume of trade—indeed they acknowledged that this was very small and would grow only modestly over time—"but the politics of offering trade and of withholding trade that is important to the United States." Political rather than commercial or economic considerations had to be the bedrock upon which the United States formulated and executed its trade policy toward the Soviets. This meant that the United States had to modify its long-standing hostility to trade with the Soviet bloc countries and be prepared to negotiate with each communist state on the basis of hard bargaining, receiving from each satisfactory assurances that commercial obstacles would be removed and outstanding financial claims settled. The last was a reference to lend-lease.[79]

To achieve the broader objective of building commercial bridges to the East, the committee offered a series of specific recommendations that it hoped Congress would find politically palatable. The essence of these lay in a two-tiered approach to East–West trade: the continued application of rigorous export controls on strategic military items, and the adoption of a selective policy on the sale of peaceful goods, applied country by country, to advance foreign policy objectives and the national interest. In each instance the purpose was to render trade an asset that could be employed many times over "to gain improvements in, and build a better foundation for, our relations with individual Communist countries."[80]

The report declared unequivocally that the success of this new approach depended on Congress's giving the president greater flexibility than existed under current statutes, to remove or, if need be, impose restrictions on trade with individual European communist countries.[81] It asserted that if trade with communist countries was going to be utilized to further foreign policy goals and the national interest, the administration would have to educate the American public, Congress, and even the executive branch to a thorough understanding of the problem, the opportunities that trade afforded, and the national interest in this particular arena. "Trade is one of the few channels available to us for constructive contacts with nations with whom we find frequent hostility," the report concluded. Selective trade intelligently negotiated and widely administered might "turn out to be one of our most powerful tools of national policy."[82]

The report was much publicized and received a mixed response. Some of the president's advisers urged that the administration move quickly

for an East–West trade bill that would allow European Soviet bloc countries to sell goods on the American market at the same tariff rates as
other nations. On 7 May President Johnson announced in a speech televised to Western Europe that he would urge Congress to enact legislation
to spur trade with Russia and Eastern Europe. However, a careful check
showed that there would be strong opposition on Capitol Hill to such a
move. Resistance came from several sources. Some members of Congress, as well as others outside government, flatly opposed anything that
looked like a "deal" with a communist nation. A number of legislators
had to consider the sentiments of constituents of Eastern European an-
cestry, who were fiercely critical of any move that appeared to strengthen
the Russian economy. Others demanded political concessions in return
for trade concessions. Still others opposed relaxation of trade barriers
with any country that was giving assistance to North Vietnam.[83]

As Johnson later recalled, congressmen, friends who came to the Oval
Office, and ordinary citizens writing to their president asked how the
United States could be fighting communists in Southeast Asia while negotiating and trading with them in Europe.[84] He explained that these
were two aspects of the same policy: the United States was fighting in
Vietnam to demonstrate that "aggression should not, must not, succeed." But it also had to show that there was an alternative to confrontation: to work, as opportunities arose, to erase the worst features of the
Cold War. By patiently chipping away at the Iron Curtain, by building
bridges to the governments and peoples of Eastern Europe, and by establishing agreements that served both East and West, Johnson believed, the
United States could achieve a foundation for rational international
behavior.[85]

Nonetheless resistance on the Hill—strong enough to spell certain defeat—prompted Johnson to postpone for the moment introducing an
East–West trade bill. Congressional "hawks" held the Soviet Union primarily responsible for the continuing war in Vietnam and would brook
no major policy change on trade with Russia and the European Soviet
bloc.[86] By the end of the year, however, the president decided to press
ahead, hoping that through open hearings and debates the requirements
of the national interest would override legislative and public opposition.
He announced his intention in his State of the Union message in January
1966. In May he asked Congress for authority to "remove the special
tariff restrictions which are a barrier to increasing trade between the East
and the West."[87] Secretary of State Rusk submitted to the Eighty-ninth
Congress the proposed East–West Trade Relations Act of 1966. The bill's
key provision would have authorized the president to negotiate bilateral
commercial agreements with Russia and the European Soviet bloc coun-

tries and to extend highly conditioned most-favored-nation tariff treatment as part of such agreements.

The president's political acumen deserted him this time, for in spite of intensive efforts to educate members of Congress and the public on the advantages of the bill, Congress refused to act. Resentment against nations that were politically and materially supporting Hanoi was too great to overcome.[88] Still, Johnson did not give up easily. To pursue his "bridge-building" policy he fell back on the executive's discretionary authority under existing legislation. In a major foreign policy address on 7 October 1966 he told the National Conference of Editorial Writers that "our task is to achieve a reconciliation with the East—a shift from the narrow concept of coexistence to the broader vision of peaceful engagement" and announced that "we will reduce export controls on East–West trade with respect to hundreds of nonstrategic items."[89] Five days later the Department of Commerce revised its regulations such that nearly four hundred nonstrategic items would no longer require export licenses for shipment to Russia and Eastern Europe. On 20 October the department announced that it was prepared to give "favorable consideration" to Soviet applications for the export of machine tools to manufacture automobiles, thus reversing an earlier (1962) decision.[90]

In December Johnson accepted the strategy of an interagency task force, headed by Francis M. Bator, the White House's liaison with the Miller Committee, to resubmit the proposed East–West Trade Relations Act to the new Ninetieth Congress.[91] According to the White House's plan, once the bill was sent to the Hill, Congressman Wilbur Mills was to hold hearings on it immediately, before the opposition could organize. The major tactical change was that the administration should be prepared, if necessary, to accept certain amendments wanted by Mills. Even so, there was cause for apprehension. Bill Roth, one of the authors of the new strategy, reported on 14 December that Mills believed it would be difficult to pass the trade bill "at this time." State Department officials, however, were pushing for early action. Roth wrote, "We intend to discuss with Mills the possibility of asking the Joint Economic Committee to hold hearings early in February or March, largely to bring the political and economic issues before the public and the Congress."[92]

All of this strategy was of no avail. By the spring of 1967 President Johnson's effort to enlist trade in building a bridge of peace to Russia and Eastern Europe had become, like so many of the Great Society's domestic programs, a casualty of the Vietnam War and partisan politics. Secretary of Commerce Alexander S. Trowbridge reported on 8 May that House Republicans were seeking to force the issue of East–West trade by linking it to a pending authorization bill for the Export-Import Bank.

The bill had been favorably endorsed by the Banking and Currency Committee on a straight party vote, rejecting by 18 to 15 the amendment of Paul A. Fino of New York that would have prohibited the bank from financing trade with any communist nation. "Although Fino and his followers seek an outright ban on East–West trade," Trowbridge informed the president, "it appears that the most serious opposition from the Republicans will be based on an effort to delay or otherwise restrict any East–West trade legislation until there are further developments in the Vietnam War."[93]

Republican hostility to any expansion of trade with the "enemy," while the war dragged on, persisted into 1968. Lawrence A. Fox, deputy assistant secretary for international trade policy, believed that the administration had lobbied adequately for the East–West Trade Relations Act, but the bill never reached the hearing stage.[94]

The coup de grace to the president's "bridge-building" occurred in August 1968, when Russian troops suddenly invaded Czechoslovakia to stamp out the liberalization movement there. Former Assistant Secretary of Commerce Lawrence McQuade later recalled that the Soviet aggression, coming on the heels of the Vietnam controversy, further poisoned the political atmosphere, both domestic and international, for increasing peaceful trade between the United States and communist Eastern Europe. The brutal suppression of "The Prague Spring," the symbol of the liberalization movement, and forceful occupation of the country killed any chances of getting the East–West Trade Relations Act through Congress. It did more than that: it caused the administration to cut its trade with both Czechoslovakia and the Soviet Union and, ironically, revitalized COCOM, which had been on the verge of collapse because of the British and French attitudes toward trade with Russia and Eastern Europe.[95]

U.S. foreign trade policy was a political instrument of the Cold War, only occasionally masquerading as an economic issue. Like his immediate predecessor, President Johnson repeatedly sought opportunities to reduce East–West political tensions and enlisted trade policy as one instrument within his larger political strategy. His efforts to write new and less restrictive trade legislation were not isolated incidents, but one of many activities that came to be called "bridge-building." Between 1964 and 1966 Johnson showed an active interest in effecting trade liberalization by speaking out on the subject and centralizing decisions on East–West trade within the White House and the State Department. However, his major effort to surmount bureaucratic inertia and conflict was to appoint a high-level committee of distinguished businessmen and others to articulate and give credibility to his trade initiatives. The Miller Committee was Johnson's vehicle for persuading Congress and the public of the benefits of East–West trade.

Johnson had intended to use the Miller Committee's recommendations as a springboard to legislation that would give him discretion to negotiate most-favored-nation agreements with communist nations. Although the committee did propose such authority for the president, it also concluded that trade with Russia and Soviet bloc countries should neither be subsidized nor receive artificial encouragement. Nor did the committee propose any basic alterations to the system of export controls, except to suggest that the Department of Defense replace the Department of Commerce as the primary agency responsible for identifying strategic commodities. Its recommendations were less than what Johnson was seeking, although his inclination was to emphasize the more liberal features of the report. What the president failed to acknowledge was that expanding East–West trade through legislation had only a fair chance of passage under the best of circumstances. Conservative groups, organized blue-collar labor, and numerous senators and congressmen opposed liberalization of trade, particularly while U.S. troops were fighting communists in Vietnam. Rather than risk other elements in his legislative program, including Great Society initiatives, Johnson abandoned the effort to dismantle the system of trade controls.

CHAPTER EIGHT

From Détente to Confrontation

WHEN Richard M. Nixon was elected to the presidency in 1968, U.S. foreign policy was in deep trouble.[1] The war in Vietnam was tearing the nation apart, and only a resolution of that conflict could bring it back together. The former "hawks" of the Kennedy–Johnson era now were arguing that the United States should not repeat the error of Vietnam, that American interests should be defined more narrowly, defense budgets reduced, and executive action more closely scrutinized by Congress. Neither President Nixon nor his special assistant for national security affairs, Henry A. Kissinger, shared this view. They perceived the crisis of American foreign policy as psychological: a collapse of confidence at home and abroad. The United States, they believed, had to act purposefully in international affairs and to resist being controlled by other nations.[2]

As to the Soviet Union, Nixon, as president, sloughed off the ideological obsessions of the Dulles Cold War years and displayed a flexibility that irritated conservatives who had hoped for an uncompromising anticommunist posture. He no longer insisted that communist regimes were necessarily identical, that they were bound by a common ideology, or that they were all committed to the destruction of the United States. One of the central assumptions of American cold war thinking had been wrong, as the rift between the Soviet Union and Communist China demonstrated. Security no longer demanded the rollback of communism; the need now was for a reestablishment of the classical balance of power. In tandem with Kissinger, who became secretary of state in 1973, Nixon spoke of moving from an era of confrontation to an era of negotiation.[3]

The shift from polarity to détente was intended to compensate for the erosion of American military superiority.[4] The split between Russia and China offered the United States an opportunity for old-fashioned balance-of-power diplomacy; détente was in large part the response to Russia's domestic economic weakness. Détente would give the Soviets a stake in the international equilibrium by offering the Kremlin a deal it could not refuse: entry into American (and global) markets of trade, investments, and credits; and "legitimacy" in a consultative, coequal superpower relationship with the United States.[5] Through a network of relationships—political, economic, and commercial—joined together and made interdependent by the concept of "linkage," President Nixon and Secretary Kissinger hoped to increase the Soviet Union's stake in peace, increase its incentive to maintain good relations with the West, and open it to "the force of Western example."[6]

The timing of the Nixon administration's shift in policy occurred just when the strategy of economic warfare was coming under a new and more serious round of criticism from businessmen, academics, and legislators. The economic leverage upon which the Battle Act relied had been greatly diminished by the rapid reconstruction of the European and Japanese economies. Revision of the Export Control Act, which was due to expire on 30 June 1969, became a convenient instrument by which the administration could compensate for the inadequacy of military containment, influence Soviet political behavior, and redirect East–West trade policy away from a restrictive, strategic embargo toward a careful expansion of exports.[7]

Kissinger has recounted the circumstances that led to the cautious tilt toward more normal economic relations with Russia and the communist world. On 21 May 1969 the National Security Council (NSC) agreed to ask Congress to extend the Export Control Act; it also decided a number of pending licensing requests: materials for a foundry at a new Soviet truck plant, an oil extraction plant, and a $15 million sale of corn to the USSR. In advance of the meeting Kissinger had forwarded to Nixon the recommendations of the various agencies, his own advice being that the president should acquiesce in a new law that would grant the executive discretionary authority to expand trade only in return for a quid pro quo from the Soviets. Kissinger also recommended that the American control list be tailored to COCOM's, so as not to injure U.S. businessmen. He supported the license for the oil plant, because of the leverage that the long lead time for construction would give the United States. For precisely the opposite reason, he recommended against the foundry and the corn sale.[8]

This early effort at linkage coincided with Nixon's intense—and ultimately futile—attempt to get Moscow to persuade the North Vietnamese to come to the negotiating table. Stung by the Soviets' refusal to help on the Vietnam problem, he rejected Kissinger's recommendations for liberalizing trade; but he agreed to abide by the COCOM list, except for computers and other items over which the United States had a monopoly. Whether the president's decision was made in a fit of pique or was calculated to show that he was not soft on communism is unclear from Kissinger's account. But on 28 May 1969 the president issued a directive, phrased positively, to keep open the possibility of increased trade with Russia if the political atmosphere changed.[9]

No sooner were these instructions issued than the departments began to nibble away at them. In July the Commerce Department, under increased pressure from businessmen, was about to announce administrative decontrol of thirty items for export to Russia and Eastern Europe. It reasoned that the president had ruled only against a wholesale liberalization of trade, not against a selective easing of trade restrictions. The Commerce Department, Kissinger wrote, evidently considered itself free to undertake a substantive liberalization of East–West trade within the existing law. Alarmed, he intervened to prevent this, as well as the requests of the Departments of State and Commerce, in October, to export computers to the Soviet Union and to decontrol 135 other items without political reciprocity. By contrast, he was willing to make trade concessions to Eastern European countries like Rumania, if they pursued policies relatively independent of the USSR.[10]

Meanwhile Congress began to respond to pressures to relax trade controls. In the House the extension of the 1949 law came under the jurisdiction of the Committee on Banking and Currency, which originally reported out a bill with only minor changes that were consistent with the Nixon administration's recommendations at the time. But a liberal dissent to the majority report argued for a fundamental change in the law, declaring that the basic premises that underlay the original Battle Act were no longer valid. The Sino-Soviet bloc was not monolithic, goods withheld from Russia by the United States could be obtained elsewhere, and attempts to impose unilateral controls more severe than the allies' were divisive. These minority views in the House were consistent with the majority view in the Senate Banking Committee, whose opinion ultimately prevailed. "Export control" was replaced by "export administration" when Congress passed the new law.

The Export Administration Act of 1969 significantly modified the 1949 law. It incorporated a policy of selective controls on items that had only a military potential (instead of a "military or economic potential") within a policy framework that encouraged peaceful trade with Russia and Eastern Europe.[11] Various considerations had motivated Congress to modify its attitude from the original policy of military and economic denial to the more narrowly strategic embargo. A majority of legislators also hoped to involve the Soviet Union in a "web of interdependence" with the United States and its allies by liberalizing trade, and thereby to promote détente. Maintenance of a broad trade embargo clearly had not retarded Soviet economic growth, nor had it inhibited Soviet foreign policy. Further, Western Europe and Japan had refused to follow the United States' lead in imposing a broad, ironclad embargo. They sold the Soviets goods and technology that the United States was unwilling to sell, which deprived American companies of the business and the profits.[12]

The Export Administration Act of 1969 was an amalgam of the "bridge-building" philosophy of former president Lyndon B. Johnson, grassroots business and economic pressure for liberalizing trade with the Soviet bloc, and the Nixon administration's increasingly polycentric view of the communist world. Equally important for the strategy of linkage, much of the new law's implementation (excluding most-favored-nation status, which President Nixon had not asked for) was left to executive discretion.[13]

Perhaps the most dramatic liberalization of the export control laws and application of the balance-of-power strategy was the administration's move to open trade relations with China. On 21 July 1969 the State Department announced an easing of restrictions on trade and travel to the People's Republic of China. This was followed by Kissinger's mission to Beijing in July 1971 and Nixon's own trip there early in 1972. These were signals to the Chinese that the United States wished to end twenty-two years of mutual hostility and move toward more normal political and economic relations. The administration was playing the China card: that is, inviting the alliance of China with the United States in a drive to curb Moscow's geopolitical ambitions and render Russia more flexible on East–West political issues. The Shanghai communiqué, issued at the close of Nixon's talks with Chinese leaders in 1972, was a thinly veiled warning to the Soviet Union.[14]

The China opening made it possible to utilize trade with the Soviet Union as an integral part of American foreign policy. The opportunity materialized as early as the fall of 1971, when Soviet Foreign Minister Andrei Gromyko formally raised the issue in a private conversation with President Nixon. Ambassador Anatoli Dobrynin followed this initiative by proposing an exchange of visits of cabinet officers responsible for trade. Late in November 1971 Commerce Secretary Maurice Stans went to Moscow and returned with great expectations of a boom in Soviet trade.[15] Three obstacles, however, remained in the path of a commercial bonanza for American businessmen: most-favored-nation status, lend-lease, and linkage. The United States had withdrawn tariff preference at the time of the Korean War, an action that became symbolic of the division between the two superpowers. Restoration of most-favored-nation status required congressional consent, which Congress would not grant until the Russians repaid their lend-lease debt. The United States had set the debt figure at $800 million; the Soviets were offering $300 million and indicated that they also would be willing to purchase grain from American farmers.[16]

Nixon decided that trade should follow political progress, not precede it, despite protests from Secretary Stans, who wanted to exploit the trade opening to the fullest. Hence he made settlement of the lend-lease claim the prerequisite for asking Congress to grant preferential tariff treatment and also postponed response to a Soviet proposal for joint exploration of Siberian natural gas until the end of the Vietnam War, which was then in the relatively indefinite future. The Russians interpreted Stans's protest and the administration's foot-dragging as part of an elaborate White House scenario to pressure them. In this they were only partially correct: Stans's protest was genuine, but Nixon had made progress toward a settlement in Vietnam a precondition for enhanced economic relations. National security adviser Kissinger conveyed the president's view to Soviet Premier Leonid Brezhnev before their summit meeting.[17]

There were other manifestations of the linkage strategy before the 1972 summit conference in Moscow. Kissinger, for example, sat for nearly three years on the proposal of an American company to sell gear-cutting machinery for a Soviet civilian truck plan on the Kama River, until the Soviets agreed to the compromise on strategic arms limitations (SALT I). Then the plant was quickly approved. Peter G. Peterson, the president's assistant for international economic affairs and later secretary of commerce, worked effectively with Kissinger to coordinate these kinds of economic decisions with the new foreign policy strategy.[18]

The first indication American firms received that the administration was reconsidering East–West trade policy in the light of détente and linkage also occurred in the fall of 1971, when suddenly they began to experience success in obtaining hitherto denied licenses to export their products to the Soviet Union. Thus the Soviets, pitifully short of wheat for the coming winter, received the administration's consent to purchase $1 billion of American surplus food grains. The State Department followed this initiative by signaling its willingness to reduce various discriminatory shipping regulations on Soviet vessels visiting American ports. Secretary of Commerce Stans was forecasting $5 billion in U.S.–Soviet trade annually by the middle of the decade and spoke about cooperative efforts to develop the oil, gas, and minerals of Siberia. By the spring of 1972 progress on numerous bilateral commercial negotiations had advanced sufficiently for the subject of a general U.S.–Soviet commercial agreement to be included as a major item on the agenda for the Moscow summit.[19]

The coincidence of liberalization of export licenses, a grain sale, and a maritime agreement with progress toward a summit conference was hardly accidental. At the Moscow meeting in May 1972 Nixon moved swiftly to spell out the linkage between trade and credits and progress toward arms reduction. He suggested to Premier Brezhnev that a SALT agreement would help him win backing in Congress for expanded trade relations. When the meeting concluded on 29 May, the two leaders signed a document putting U.S.–Soviet political relations on a basis of mutual respect, friendship, and noninterference. The document high-lighted commerce and economic ties as "an important and necessary element in the strengthening of . . . bilateral relations." Both nations promised to foster such ties by facilitating intergovernmental coopera-tion and entering into commercial contracts and trade agreements.[20]

Nixon and Kissinger had shrewdly perceived that their acknowledg-ment of the Soviet Union as a unique state determined to follow its own destiny might well produce meaningful agreements congenial to a new international order.[21] This realism, combined with Moscow's eagerness to achieve economic modernization and to thwart a full-scale Sino-American rapprochement, induced the Russians to enter into a web of attractive—but interrelated—agreements with the United States on spe-cific issues, such as economic and technological cooperation. The pre-sumption in Washington was that if each agreement was linked to all the others in a seamless web, the Soviets would have a strong incentive not to unravel the whole package.

By the end of 1972 these agreements included a Soviet pledge to pay back $722 million on the lend-lease debt by the year 2001; President Nixon's promise to authorize the Export-Import Bank to extend credits and guarantees to the USSR; an agreement to seek congressional exten-sion of most-favored-nation status to the Soviet Union; approval for the delivery of 440 million bushels of wheat to Russia; a maritime agreement opening forty ports in each nation to the other's shipping; and a decision to establish a joint Commercial Commission to encourage, develop, and guide American–Soviet trade.

The new policy rested on a number of publicly stated premises, as well as some that were not articulated for fear of embarrassing the Soviets.[22] The openly articulated premises underlying the expansion of American–Soviet commerce were that progress on SALT and Berlin had made it possible to discuss bilateral cooperation in nonpolitical fields. As coop-eration in nonpolitical fields widened, it would reinforce the trend to-ward more constructive political relations. Bilateral economic agree-ments, initially involving trade, could later be broadened to include more extended cooperative ventures that, as President Nixon told Congress, would "establish an interdependence between our economies which provides a continued incentive to maintain a constructive relationship." As nonpolitical relationships continued to expand, there would be created on each side "a vested interest in restraint and the preservation of peace."[23]

The fullest statement of the basic concept that a growing web of economic agreements could reduce political hostility was contained in a report to the president by Secretary of Commerce Peter G. Peterson, released to the public in August 1972 and widely disseminated.[24] In it Peterson had written that "closer economic ties bear both cause and effect relationships to relaxation of political tension. Improvement in political relationships is a prerequisite for improved economic relationships, but, once in place, economic ties create a community of interest which in turn improves the environment for further progress on the political side."[25]

Unstated but never far below the surface of the Nixon-Kissinger diplomacy was a far tougher set of assumptions: a recognition that continued modernization of the Soviet economy would demand a major diversion of resources from the military sector to the high-technology, largely civilian sectors. To close the modernization gap and maintain military parity with the United States, Russia would have to import sophisticated information technology and electronics systems from this country; these purchases would require large credits from the United States and enhancement of the Soviet Union's export capability. Easing restrictions on credit, liberalizing the strategic lists, and removing political barriers to East–West trade would not occur unless the Soviet Union pursued a credible policy of peaceful coexistence. If the United States shrewdly bargained from this position of economic strength, the Kremlin leadership might be willing to pay a political price for an expansion of U.S.–Soviet commerce.[26]

These were the bedrock assumptions beneath Kissinger's rhetoric that "we have approached the question of economic relations with deliberation and circumspection and as an act of policy not primarily of commercial opportunity." The political price the Nixon administration wanted was that the Soviet Union should cease aiding North Vietnam and pressure Hanoi to negotiate seriously with the United States.[27]

Within six months after the Moscow summit Soviet–American intercourse had broadened to such an extraordinary extent that *U.S. News* reported: "The cold war that has kept the United States and the Soviet Union hostile and at arm's length for 25 years officially ended on October 18, 1972."[28] The reference was to the comprehensive trade agreement signed in Washington upon satisfactory resolution of the lend-lease debt controversy. The new agreement laid down the ground rules for private American firms to participate in U.S.–Soviet trade, banned the "dumping" of products at less than cost, extended Export-Import Bank credit to Russian buyers, and offered (subject to Congress's approval) most-favored-nation status to the Soviet Union. This was followed by a series of pacts encompassing everything from combined efforts by medical experts to combat disease, to partnership in a space-flight project, to nuclear weapons discussions, to environmental pollution control.[29] Assistant Secretary of State for Economic and Business Affairs Willis C. Armstrong made clear the linkage between these agreements and political détente when he told the World Trade Institute of New York, on 28 November 1972: "These programs constitute a framework of interlocking agreements to build a vested interest on both sides in reducing tensions and freeing us from confrontation."[30]

If these agreements were the high point of détente, the downside also occurred in the months just after the Moscow meeting. In 1972 the Soviet Union confronted a catastrophic grain failure, a fact that was unknown to American officials. In April, while Secretary of Agriculture Earl D. Butz was visiting Moscow, the Soviets had told him they might consider a three-year grain agreement, provided that adequate credits were available. Late in June a deputy minister from the Soviet Agriculture Ministry slipped into Washington and, in talks with Commerce Secretary Peterson and Butz, worked out a three-year, $750 million credit, which was announced on 8 July. At that time Kissinger put the grain deal in the context of linkage and détente.[31] Unknown to the Nixon administration, the Soviets proceeded quietly to take advantage of the competitiveness of U.S. grain companies. In a series of separate agreements they purchased nearly $1 billion worth of grain in one year, which represented nearly the entire stored surplus and ultimately drove up prices to the American consumer and cost nearly ten thousand people their jobs, as independent bakeries closed down in response to the high price of flour. In effect the United States had subsidized the Soviets at a time when the USSR had no choice but to buy grain at market prices or face near starvation.

The United States had clearly been outmaneuvered before linkage could be invoked. The problem, Kissinger explained later, was that the sale of grain was considered outside the normal purview of foreign policy.[32] It was not until 1975, when a new grain agreement was signed under President Gerald Ford, that precaution was taken to guard against disruption of the American market. But by then the political, economic, and psychological damage of the 1972 "great grain robbery" had been done, and political conservatives used it to denounce détente and linkage.

The critics' opportunity came not long after the Moscow summit of 1972. Democratic presidential aspirant Senator Henry "Scoop" Jackson of Washington successfully linked the Nixon administration's request for tariff preference for the USSR with the distinctly separate issue of the plight of Soviet Jewry. A hard-liner on national security issues and an outspoken critic of the summit agreements on trade and strategic arms, Jackson advocated, for humanitarian and political reasons, legislation that would make liberalization of Jewish emigration a precondition for granting most-favored-nation status to the Soviet Union. He was not the first to do so, but was simply the most prominent and successful legislator to make the connection. On 22 September 1972 Congressman Charles Vanik of Ohio had proposed an amendment to the Foreign Assistance Bill (H.R. 16705) that would deny Export-Import Bank credits and loans to any nation that charged more than $50 for an exit visa. The amended bill passed the House of Representatives on a voice vote, but Vanik's amendment was later dropped in conference.[33]

Meanwhile other legislators picked up the issue. Richard Perle of Jackson's staff and Morris Amitay of Senator Abraham Ribicoff's staff worked together on a new amendment that would require relaxation of Soviet emigration laws as a precondition for granting tariff preference. A rival proposal drafted by the staffs of Senators Hubert Humphrey and Jacob Javits was less offensive, urging the Soviet Union to repeal its emigration tax and hinting strongly that a better trade relationship might result. In September Jackson vigorously denounced the Humphrey-Javits proposal at a rally sponsored by the National Council of Soviet Jewry, an umbrella lobby of thirty-two American-Jewish organizations; on 4 October he introduced his own legislation in the form of an amendment to the East–West Trade Act of 1971.[34] Seventy-two members of the Senate acted as co-sponsors, including Javits. Despite a show of opposition, on 18 October the Nixon administration signed the comprehensive trade agreement, whereupon Soviet officials began to allow some Jews to leave without paying the obligatory emigration tax. This concession was widely interpreted as a Soviet gesture to assist President Nixon in his reelection campaign, especially among Jewish voters. By chance, Congress also adjourned on 18 October, the day the trade agreement was signed, so that Senate action on the amendment was postponed.[35]

The Nixon administration had not at first taken Vanik's amendment seriously, nor Jackson's. But when Congress reconvened in January 1973, the administration once more faced the prospect of sending the comprehensive trade agreement to the House for ratification. Because the extension of most-favored-nation status to the Soviet Union theoretically affected tariff revenues, the pact fell within the jurisdiction of the

Committee on Ways and Means, one of whose members was Charles Vanik. Vanik, whose district in Cleveland was eleven percent Jewish and composed of many constituents with relatives behind the Iron Curtain, had earlier introduced the House version of the Jackson amendment. By February 1973 the American-Israel Public Affairs Committee, a registered lobby, had mobilized a letter-writing campaign that pushed many congressmen into Vanik's camp, including Arkansas Democrat Wilbur Mills, the powerful chairman of the Ways and Means Committee.[36]

President Nixon played into the hands of both the liberal and conservative critics of détente when he decided not to separate the request for most-favored-nation status from the rest of the trade bill. This decision drew the AFL-CIO and its president, George L. Meany, a longtime foe of trade with communists, into a tight alliance with the Jackson-Vanik forces. When the administration finally recognized the gravity of the threat, it lobbied hard and furiously to carve out a compromise with Congressman Mills. In a gesture of support for the administration and to defuse congressional hostility, Soviet officials announced in March 1973 that they were suspending the emigration tax. This concession failed; on 10 April Senator Jackson, along with seventy-six co-sponsors, again attached his amendment to the Comprehensive Trade Reform Act. American-Jewish leaders who had begun to waver after suspension of the emigration tax were made to toe the mark by Jackson's staff, a chore made easier when the Soviet government then invoked repressive measures against two well-known dissidents, the physicist Andrei Sakharov and the writer Aleksandr Solzhenitsyn. This action swung liberal organizations, like Americans for Democratic Action and the American Psychiatric Association, into a temporary alliance with conservatives and other supporters of the Jackson amendment.[37]

By the time the House Ways and Means Committee officially reported out the Trade Reform Bill (H.R. 1070) on 10 October 1973, Vanik and his allies had successfully added the restrictions on most-favored-nation status. The crucial vote occurred when the committee's chairman, Mills, who had turned against the Jackson amendment, was absent. Vanik then attached to the legislation restrictions on Export-Import Bank credits. The outbreak of the Yom Kippur War in the Middle East in October delayed a final vote on the bill until 11 December. In the interval, Secretary of State Kissinger lobbied vigorously to persuade legislators and Jewish leaders that the Jackson-Vanik amendment was a threat to his efforts to bring peace to the region, but to no avail. The House voted, 319 to 80, to include both portions of the amendment in the bill, which then passed on a vote of 272 to 140.[38]

In March Kissinger was called to testify before the Senate Finance

Committee, which was conducting hearings on the trade bill. Democratic Senator Gaylord Nelson of Wisconsin took advantage of this opportunity to offer a compromise: Congress would give the president the authority to extend most-favored-nation status and credits to the Soviet Union, provided that the arrangement was subject to regular review. If Soviet officials continued to use harsh methods to discourage Jewish emigration, the privileges would be withdrawn. Nelson had no way of knowing that Jackson had already rejected a similar proposal. Ironically, just such a compromise would find its way into the final form of the bill, in the shape of the "freedom of emigration waiver."[39]

By the summer of 1974 the administration was ready to negotiate with Jackson and his supporters in the Senate, Abraham Ribicoff and Jacob Javits. Kissinger served as go-between in the trilateral talks with Jackson, President Nixon, and Soviet Ambassador Dobrynin participating. The negotiations made very little progress, however, as the shadow of Watergate and the impeachment hearings dogged the administration.

After Nixon's resignation on 9 August 1974, President Gerald Ford took up the trade bill. Although he had never been a co-sponsor of the amendment as a congressman, he took a personal interest in it and even suggested that the Jackson-Kissinger negotiations take place in the Oval Office. On 9 September, after the Soviet Union had agreed informally to allow the emigration of sixty thousand Jews annually and to end harassment of those who applied for exit visas, Jackson and the administration reached an agreement. The administration would send Jackson a letter stating that Moscow's "assurances" on emigration were consistent with the purposes of his amendment. Jackson's written response would be construed as formal acceptance of these "assurances." A third letter, sealing the bargain between the executive and legislative branches, eventually was scrapped, because Kissinger was unwilling to commit himself concerning the exact number of Jews that should be allowed to leave the Soviet Union.[40]

On 18 October Senators Jackson and Javits and Congressman Vanik arrived at the White House for a public ceremony to mark the signing of the agreement. Neither Ford nor Kissinger had anything substantive to say about the two letters, but Jackson used the televised press conference that followed the signing to inform the world of his accomplishment. He claimed that the Soviet Union had acceded to American demands only because of constant congressional pressure.

On 13 December the trade bill, with Jackson's original amendment as well as a freedom-of-emigration waiver attached, went before the full Senate for a vote. It passed, 77 to 4. On 18 December the Soviet government released the text of a letter that had been sent to Secretary of State

Kissinger two months earlier, on 26 October. This letter, which Kissinger had kept secret, criticized Senator Jackson's behavior during the televised press conference of 18 October. Soviet officials had never made specific promises about the number of Jews that would be permitted to emigrate, and they viewed the publication of the "sixty thousand" figure as an unwarranted interference in their internal affairs. Nevertheless, on 18 December a House–Senate conference committee approved the Trade Reform Bill as amended, and Ford signed it into law on 3 January 1975.[41]

A second and, in some respects, equally devastating blow to détente took the form of the Stevenson amendment (offered by Democratic Senator Adlai E. Stevenson III of Illinois) to the Export-Import Bank authorization bill. Congress initially had wanted to assert its oversight functions on the bank. Increasingly, however, legislative debate on the amendment came to center on the Soviet Union and the potential threat of a "credit war" among the advanced industrial countries that were seeking to do business with Moscow and the Soviet bloc countries. Since October 1972, when President Nixon had issued an executive order approving the Export-Import Bank's participating in trade with the USSR, the bank had made available $469 million in credits. The Stevenson amendment, as finally worked out at the end of 1974, established a $300 million ceiling on further credits over the next four years, allowing up to $40 million for equipment and services to be used in energy exploration in the USSR but prohibiting the bank from financing any American energy developments in Russia.[42]

Unlike Jackson's, the Stevenson amendment did not engender a lengthy debate in Congress over its implications. The Ford administration did not pay any attention to the shape the amendment was taking, and legislators voted on the basis of very little knowledge and information. In the opinion of one critic this amendment was the decisive reason that the Soviet Union, on 10 January 1975, repudiated the 1972 trade agreement—even more so than their objection to the Jackson amendment, which Ford had signed into law the previous week.[43] From the Soviet perspective the decision to repudiate was a rational one: if trade was to expand substantially, credits were required. But the Stevenson amendment said, in effect, that after having made an important concession on emigration, the Soviets would be eligible for fewer credits over the period 1975–80 than had already been received over past two years, before they had made any concessions at all! It appeared to Moscow as though Congress were putting a ceiling on trade rather than a floor under it.[44]

The bloom was off détente by 1975–76. The Nixon-Kissinger policy had failed to live up to unrealistic expectations and was now the target of conservative and even liberal criticism. The process of disillusionment had begun with the erosion of Nixon's political base in the second half of 1973, after the "great grain robbery"; it continued with the Soviets' crackdown on dissidents, was complicated by Andrei Sakharov's appeal in August 1973 endorsing the Jackson amendment, was deepened by the Yom Kippur War in October 1973, and solidified with the eruption of the Watergate scandal. All along, some critics had questioned whether détente and linkage had reality in and of themselves, or simply affirmed the status quo—as in Europe, where an equilibrium of power already was stable. In the Middle East, Africa, and Asia the Soviets were continuing to pursue a cold war of movement by siding with wars of national liberation.

Moscow's repudiation of the 1972 trade agreement early in 1975 provided critics a reason for questioning the entire direction of the Nixon-Kissinger strategy for foreign policy. Or, as the *Wall Street Journal* observed: "Should the United States continue to try to trade economic concessions for political concessions from the Soviet Union or should it drop the idea of such 'linkage' as a bad show?" The answer was quick in coming. The Reagan wing of the Republican Party attacked Kissinger for giving the Soviet Union more than the United States got in return: in SALT I, in East–West trade, in the discredited grain deal, and in the Helsinki accords. Liberals were disturbed, in addition, by what they regarded as Kissinger's penchant for intervening in countries outside the realm of direct American security interests. So virulent was the criticism, especially from conservatives who feared the loss of military superiority over the Soviet Union, that President Ford—who, ironically, had retained Kissinger as secretary of state to insure continuity in foreign policy—had to exorcise the word "détente" from his administration's vocabulary.[45]

The erosion of détente caused American–Soviet trade to stagnate and ultimately decline in the late 1970s, although at first glance this did not appear to be the case. On paper, the total volume of American exports to the USSR continued to rise: a peak of $1,195 million in 1973 was followed by a drop to $607 million in 1974, and then by further increases, to $1,833 million in 1975 and $2,300 million in 1976. These statistics were misleading. They were distorted by very large agricultural purchases—more than sixty percent of the total in both 1975 and 1976—the result of a second poor harvest within five years. Setting aside this erratic agricultural situation, American–Soviet trade actually was in the doldrums, because many of the transactions officially attributed to 1975 and 1976 were the residue of deals negotiated three and four years earlier.[46] At the time of Secretary Kissinger's resignation in January 1977

East–West trade, perhaps the most important nonmilitary lever on Soviet behavior, no longer performed the linkage function deemed central to détente.

From the outset in 1978, the administration under President Jimmy Carter was deeply divided over the merits of East–West trade. State and Commerce Department officials preferred to maintain the commercial contacts with Russia from the Nixon–Ford years, whereas national security adviser Zbigniew Brzezinski and Energy Secretary James Schlesinger expressed doubt that trade with the West would moderate Soviet behavior. They shared the opinion of Senator Jackson and a significant number of legislators that more, rather than less, stringent restrictions on American exports would cause Kremlin leaders to ameliorate their harsh repression of dissidents and ease their emigration restrictions.[47]

Reminding President Carter of the human-rights theme of his foreign policy, Jackson urged the new chief executive to rescind, cancel, or turn down licenses that enabled the Russians "to purchase our high technology." This was consistent with the recommendations of the Bucy Report of 4 February 1976, from the Defense Department's Task Force on Export of U.S. Technology. In the final days of the Ninety-fifth Congress sixty-seven legislators endorsed this sentiment in a letter to the president, which asserted that the transfer of American technology was contributing to a massive buildup of Soviet strategic and conventional forces.[48]

The immediate focus of the bureaucratic infighting over whether trade actually strengthened the Russians militarily was the decision of 9 August 1978 that approved the sale to the Soviet Union of a computerized electronic welding machine by Dresser Industries of Dallas, Texas, for a multimillion-dollar plant to manufacture oil drill bits. Initially Carter had resisted the hardliners' argument that Washington should utilize trade controls to pressure Moscow to behave, until the Soviets' announcement of the trial of the dissident Anatoli Scharansky put pressure on the president to give substance to his human rights credo. He then intervened to deny a license to Sperry Univac to sell a computer to Tass, the Russian news agency, and to extend licensing requirements to all oil field equipment.[49]

The controversy between the administration's hawks and doves also was implicit in the message carried to Moscow by Treasury Secretary Michael Blumenthal, who—with Commerce Secretary Juanita Kreps, another proponent of trade expansion—led an American business invasion of the Soviet capitol in December 1978. Blumenthal told Russian leaders and trade officials that President Carter "wants to see trade with the U.S.S.R. grow." But, he added: "At the same time President Carter is well aware that trade with the U.S.S.R. must be considered in the light of our overall friendship." Carter evidently had not completely forsaken the strategy of linkage, because beneath those words was a warning: as far as the White House was concerned, trade between the superpowers—and above all the delivery of American technology to Russia—would depend in part on Soviet behavior in terms of human rights at home and military adventures abroad.[50]

Soviet President Brezhnev responded quickly by blaming American rather than Russian behavior for obstacles to trade expansion—a reference to the Jackson and Stevenson amendments. Given the bluntness of his reply, the prospects for modifying U.S. policy in a direction more favorable to Moscow were remote. Indeed U.S.–Soviet relations grew extremely tense in 1979, despite progress toward a second SALT agreement, as Carter lectured the Soviets on human rights violations. Cuban troops, financed by Moscow, roamed across Angola and Ethiopia and, as communist rebels in Yemen, threatened the rear flanks of Saudi Arabia. The hostage crisis in Iran, which began in November 1979, put still another strain on American–Soviet political relations.[51]

In this tense political atmosphere Congress passed the Export Administration Act of December 1979, to replace the 1969 law. The new legislation, the product of a compromise between congressional hawks and doves, emphasized two major themes of U.S. policy: the threat to national security posed by the sale of dual-use technologies to the communist world; and the importance to the U.S. national interest of a positive trade balance and therefore of a healthy export sector. The first theme stemmed from the perception that other foreign-policy instruments had either been insufficiently forceful (diplomatic demarches, cancellation of academic and scientific exchanges) or unsuitable (military response) and the belief that withholding American exports could inflict real economic damage on the USSR. In this context Congress enhanced the role of the Department of Defense in protecting technological lead time by broadening its authority to evaluate the military and strategic potential of critical technologies destined for export. (In 1971 Congress had mandated closer cooperation among the various export control agencies.) The second theme, whose major proponent was Congressman Jonathan Bingham of New York, embodied a policy of encouraging trade with the communist world, particularly where similar items were available from foreign nations. That these aims might not always be entirely consistent was obvious to many at the time.[52]

The first test of the new law occurred almost immediately. Brezhnev evidently calculated that the hostage crisis in Iran would divert attention from still another daring Russian adventure in an area of the Middle East in which the Soviet Union had a direct strategic interest. In December 1979, despite Brezhnev's personal pledges to President Carter, the Soviet army invaded neighboring Afghanistan to rescue the faltering communist government, which was being challenged by Muslim rebels. Outraged, Carter told the American people on 4 January 1980 that "neither the United States nor any other nation which is committed to world peace and stability can continue to do business as usual with the Soviet Union."[53] With that, he significantly tightened national security controls on exports to the Soviet Union and resorted to a number of controversial actions: he shelved SALT II, suspended shipments of grain for feed cattle, interdicted the licensing of high-technology exports, curtailed Russia's fishing privileges in U.S. territorial waters (off Alaska), and campaigned for an international boycott of the 1980 Olympics, which were to be held in Moscow.[54]

Carter's swift invocation of national security export controls, despite contrary advice from Secretary of State Cyrus Vance, who did not believe that economic sanctions would force the Soviets to withdraw from Afghanistan, indicated that Zbigniew Brzezinski, the president's hard-line national security adviser, had prevailed in the bureaucratic infighting for influence. Brzezinski had persuaded Carter, who was in the midst of a hard-fought campaign for reelection, that the Afghan invasion was the first step in a Russian scheme to dominate the oil-rich Persian Gulf.[55] Because military intervention was never a viable option, the grain embargo, like the Olympic boycott, became the most visible—albeit controversial—gesture to Russia and the rest of the world that the United States would not accept this type of behavior. Carter expressed confidence, mistakenly as it happened, that America's allies—notably Argentina, Canada, and Australia—would join in the grain embargo.[56]

American policymakers understood that withholding grain from the Soviet Union would not force Moscow to remove its troops from Afghanistan. Economic sanctions were instead placed to punish the Soviets and to let them suffer, now and in the future, from this unwarranted invasion of a sovereign nation. The decision was not without its political hazards for Carter, who was risking the support of the farmer during a crucial election year. To minimize the adverse effects of a grain embargo on the American farmer, he ordered officials in the Department of Agriculture to remove from the market, through storage and price-support programs, the 25 million metric tons of feed grain that had been destined for the Soviet Union. He further ordered the purchase of the grain at prevailing market prices for distribution to less-developed countries and for boosting the production of gasohol. The taxpayer, not the farmer, would bear the burden of the embargo, a pledge that earned Carter the support of the American Farm Bureau Federation.[57]

Despite Carter's assurances the American farmer in reality bore the brunt of the sanctions. Critics complained that the embargo aggravated an already negative balance of payments and resulted in a major stockpiling of grain. Before the embargo the United States had anticipated doing nearly $4.8 billion in trade with the Soviet Union; the embargo cut this to $1.5 billion. No wonder Senator Edward Zorinski of Nebraska commented: "With the embargo, this country pointed a gun at Russia and shot the U.S. farmer in the foot."[58]

The administration's hard-liners, however, continued to predict that the embargo would achieve its purpose. They noted that the Soviets would have to import large quantities of grain because of an earlier decision to increase the production and consumption of meat and dairy products without slaughtering livestock in years of harvest failure. But as the months slipped past, it was apparent that the embargo was having little effect on either Soviet behavior or the Russian economy. Because the United States was able to restrict only 11 million of the planned export of 25 million metric tons of grain, the Soviet Union experienced a brief and relatively mild economic setback. Swiss bankers reported that the Russians had spent about $500 million in gold to purchase grain from other countries. By September 1980 the Soviets were only 6 million metric tons shy of their yearly expected imports.[59]

Where had the policy gone astray? Why had Carter's grain embargo failed to make the Soviets pay for their aggressive behavior? The reasons were manifold. Contrary to Carter's expectations, Argentina had helped alleviate the Soviets' shortfall by agreeing to sell 22.5 million metric tons of corn, sorghum, and soybeans over a five-year period. As grain prices advanced, Canadian and Australian producers had also moved in quickly to fill the void created by the American embargo—despite the official policy of their governments to support the United States' position. The Soviets further blunted the embargo by cutting back on their own grain exports to Eastern Europe, while permitting the satellites to enter the free-world market to secure their own grain requirements. The U.S. Department of Agriculture had negotiated grain contracts with most of the satellites—which, ironically, helped let the Russians off the hook. Carter himself rendered the grain embargo less than ironclad by deciding to honor contracts signed in 1975 that allowed the Soviets to purchase 16 million metric tons of U.S. grain.[60]

In assessing the effect of the grain embargo at the time, Paul W. MacAvoy, who had been a member of President Ford's Council of Economic Advisers, wrote: "The lesson to be learned from theory versus facts is that selective embargoes of specific countries in world commodity trade do not work." This was no surprise to shrewd Soviet traders, or to economic analysts familiar with the history of embargoes of foodstuffs, raw materials, or sophisticated technology. "The Russians have this ability to suffer and endure, particularly when it's made to look as though all the problems come from the outside," observed one Soviet specialist in the *New York Times*.[61]

The failure of the grain embargo was a bitter lesson in politico-economic affairs for President Carter. Along with his other woes—inflation, the crisis in Iran—the embargo alienated the Democratic vote in the Farm Belt and contributed to his resounding defeat in the 1980 presidential election. The lesson in diplomatic affairs was possibly even more serious: it was difficult to trade an economic for a diplomatic initiative, and it was impossible to do so when the economic initiative was ineffective.

In light of Ronald Reagan's opposition to the grain embargo during his candidacy for president, most observers expected him to lift controls on grain soon after taking office in 1981. The issue, however, proved to be difficult and controversial within the Reagan administration. Agriculture Secretary John R. Block urged an end to the embargo, but Secretary of State Alexander Haig, for tactical reasons, favored its retention. Critics of the embargo argued that it was ineffective and that it harmed the American farmer more than the Soviet Union. Their opponents rejoined that the sanctions *were* having an adverse effect on the Soviet Union's recently instituted Five Year Plan and that the hardship on the United States had been overestimated. Most importantly—and this was the point Haig emphasized—the timing was bad. Soviet troops remained in Afghanistan and were poised on the Polish border. Lifting the embargo would send Moscow the wrong signal.[62]

For the moment Reagan, who had come to the presidency with the reputation of being tough with the Soviets, sided with Haig. On 28 March 1981 he expressed a grim view of U.S.–Soviet relations because of the Polish crisis and, despite his preelection promises, refused to lift the grain embargo.[63] Three weeks later a senior administration official revealed that the president was expected to end the embargo, now in its fifteenth month, despite the State Department's reservations.

On 24 April 1981, after meetings of the cabinet and NSC, the president terminated the embargo, coupling his action with the admonition that Moscow should not interpret the move as a sign of tolerance for its "aggressive acts around the world." The ostensible reason was that the Soviets had eased the military pressure on Poland. The Soviet newspaper *Tass* correctly attributed Reagan's decision to the serious economic losses suffered by American farmers and to the embargo's having presented the United States unfavorably to the world "as an unreliable trading partner." Lifting the embargo *was* an act of domestic expediency. In overruling Secretary of State Haig, the president had capitulated to pressure from farmers and legislators from the grain-producing states, to Agriculture Secretary Block, and to White House political advisers.[64]

Haig attempted, not too successfully, to put the best possible face on his own defeat and the administration's reversal of course, telling reporters that the president not only would reimpose the grain embargo but also would ban all trade with the Soviet Union if it invaded Poland. This empty threat did not sit well with many congressmen. Republican and Democratic members of a House appropriations subcommittee on foreign operations—liberals and conservatives alike—criticized the president's action when Haig appeared before them. Chairman Clarence D. Long, a Democrat from Maryland, said it was inconsistent to risk American lives in El Salvador while selling food to the Russians. Texas Democrat Charles D. Wilson said his constituents, many of whom were farmers, were disgusted by the administration's capitulation. They had expected Reagan to extract some concessions from the Soviet Union.[65]

The conflict over whether and when to lift the grain embargo was symptomatic of the deeper division within the administration on the issue of East–West trade. Secretary of Defense Caspar Weinberger, a hard-liner, wanted economic relations between the two superpowers to be treated as an extension of their military competition. This meant applying national security export controls more rigorously to the sale of strategic equipment and sophisticated technology (such as computers, lasers, fiber optics) to the USSR. Weinberger's position was supported by CIA Director William J. Casey and United Nations Ambassador Jeanne J. Kirkpatrick, a conservative Democrat. On the other side, and virtually in isolation, was Secretary Haig, who argued against a total confrontation with the Soviets that might pressure Moscow into unpredictable behavior. As a matter of tactics, Haig did not believe that the United States should adopt economic policies against Moscow that did not have the support of U.S. allies. Unfortunately for him, he did not have solid support within his own department for this position.[66]

This bureaucratic infighting carried through to the preparations for the forthcoming economic summit conference in Ottawa, in July 1981. As early as May, Haig began a thorough policy review of East–West trade by an interagency group composed of representatives from the Department of Defense, members of NSC and the Office of the Special Trade Representative, and officials from the CIA and the Departments of Commerce, Energy, and the Treasury. This body mirrored the split that had permeated NSC meetings. At the NSC meeting of 7 July, for example, at which President Reagan presided, the representative of each department was asked to state his agency's position on East–West trade. A consensus emerged that Western equipment was important to Soviet economic development and also that the sale of critically strategic material should be curtailed. Beyond this, the State and Defense Departments disagreed, each submitting separate papers to the President.[67]

At the meeting of 9 July national security export controls policy appeared on the NSC agenda, in conjunction with the natural gas pipeline deal between Western Europe and the Soviet Union and the Caterpillar Company's contract to sell $40 million worth of pipe-laying tractors to the Russians.[68] Weinberger, with CIA backing, again advocated a more comprehensive embargo, whereas Haig proposed to add only specific items, such as silicon chips, to the controls list, because COCOM would not support a more general embargo. On the pipeline, Weinberger and Casey again were at odds with Haig, who did not believe that Western Europe would scrap the agreement. Haig declared that the real issue was how to erect a "safety net" that would reduce European dependence on Russian gas—and hence vulnerability to political blackmail. As for the Caterpillar deal, he observed that Japan was prepared to supply the Soviets with all the pipe-laying tractors they required.[69]

After listening to both sides, President Reagan indicated that he would make the final decision, which he did immediately before the Ottawa summit meeting. Rather than confront the allies with the tougher stance advocated by Weinberger, the military, and the CIA, the president asked the Western industrialized nations and Japan to adhere to a more cautious approach to East–West trade. Specifically, he wanted them to exercise prudence in importing Soviet energy and building the natural gas pipeline, but he would not oppose it. This compromise seemed to settle the dispute between Haig and Weinberger that had flared up within NSC.[70]

Haig's modest victory turned out to be only temporary. After the summit in Ottawa from 19 to 26 July, the Reagan administration disclosed that it would continue to press its allies to be more cooperative in stopping the eastbound flow of advanced technology that helped to underwrite the Soviet Union's military capability. To soften the blow it added that it supported peaceful trade, "if the Soviets act responsibly." The message was delivered to the Senate Foreign Relations Committee by three leading officials from the Departments of State, Defense, and Commerce, who voiced the United States' strong concern over the economic and political effects of the multibillion-dollar plan to ship Soviet natural gas to NATO allies. "One of our major goals has been to eliminate the transfer of Western equipment and technology which contributes significantly to Soviet military capabilities," said Under Secretary of State

Meyer Rashish. "Our economic policies must support our key objectives of deterring Soviet adventurism, redressing the military balance between the West and the Warsaw Pact, and strengthening the Western alliance." He conceded that the United States' allies did not necessarily agree with this, preferring to believe that stronger economic ties encouraged by détente would moderate communist attitudes.[71]

In fact the Reagan administration was increasingly troubled by mounting evidence of the transfer of sophisticated dual-use technology to the USSR.[72] In the late fall of 1981 the press brought to light the clandestine activities in 1977 of two former CIA agents and a British businessman to divert to the Soviet Union a computer program used in electronic intelligence-gathering and reconnaissance. A year later, in October 1978, U.S. representatives reported to COCOM that through legitimate purchases and espionage the Soviets had narrowed a ten- to fifteen-year gap in military technology to just one to two years. The problem was a long-standing one and difficult to cope with because of the lack of bureaucratic coordination and a shortage of manpower and agents with technical training. In 1979 the General Accounting Office had described the problem of illegal exports as "a major difficulty."[73]

While the administration focused upon the hemorrhage of Western technology to the Soviet Union, the Polish crisis deteriorated. On 20 December 1981 the United States said it would hold the Russians, as well as the Polish military government, responsible for any "excesses" that accompanied the imposition of martial law. Senior administration officials added, however, that President Reagan would delay imposing sanctions in the hope that the situation would improve. Among the sanctions contemplated, said Secretaries Haig and Weinberger in separate television interviews, was a ban on the sale of any sophisticated dual-use technology—as agreed upon by the allies. The president's options were severely limited: military action might provoke a war; a new grain embargo would upset American farmers and cause Moscow to buy elsewhere. Short of a Russian invasion of Polish territory, the Western Europeans deemed economic sanctions counterproductive. The only recourse for the administration was to try to secure multilateral action when the next crisis arose.[74]

Given the narrowness of his options, President Reagan rhetorically denounced the Soviet Union and, like other chief executives before him, turned to trade policy to pressure the Soviets. Heeding the advice of the Special Situation Group headed by Vice-President George Bush, he ordered a sharp curtailment of trade and scientific exchanges. Specifically, he suspended issuance or renewal of export licenses for electronic equipment, computers, and other high-technology items; postponed negotiations on a new long-term grain agreement to replace the accord that would expire on 30 September 1982; barred new licenses for oil and gas equipment, including that destined for the trans-Siberian natural gas pipeline; closed the Soviet Purchasing Commission in New York; and warned of further measures if the Polish crackdown was not eased.[75] A State Department official added that the United States was hopeful that its allies would take parallel steps and at the very least that they "will not take actions to undermine these steps." This was part of the administration's strategy to persuade the other members of COCOM to follow the United States' lead. *Tass* denounced the president for attempting "to hurl the world back to the dark times of the cold war."[76]

American business leaders reacted very cautiously to the president's economic sanctions. Some urged the administration to seek the support of the allies so that Moscow would be less able to substitute foreign suppliers for American companies. Others argued privately that the trade sanctions were more words than substance. James H. Giffen, president of Armco International, noted that in 1979 Armco and the Nippon Steel Corporation had won a $353 million contract to build a specialty steel mill in the USSR, only to lose it to a French competitor after President Carter suspended export licenses following the Afghanistan invasion. "We applaud the President for making it clear to the world that the United States is sympathetic to the Polish people and their cause," Giffen said. "But if action is to be taken, we believe it must not be taken unilaterally." In Peoria, Illinois, a spokesman for Caterpillar Tractor Company, which appeared to have lost a $90 million contract to sell pipe-laying equipment, said that unilateral action "does not deny pipe-layers to the Soviet Union but only diverts potential sales to suppliers in other countries." The president of the Minnesota Farmers Union declared: "There must be something we can do that doesn't hurt people at home worse than it hurts our enemies abroad."[77]

Once the decision was made, the administration's highest priority was to persuade the industrial countries of Europe and Japan to take parallel action. This was a highly delicate matter, because these nations were quite angry with the Reagan administration for having invoked sanctions without prior consultation. This was done even though Secretary of State Haig had said repeatedly that the president did not want to repeat the mistake of his predecessor.[78]

Like Carter, Reagan ran afoul of an "iron triangle" of powerful interests in Western Europe that were skeptical that trade sanctions could achieve political objectives toward the Soviet Union and that actually favored stronger economic relations with the Soviet bloc countries. This "triangle" consisted of governments that were desperate to continue the benefits of détente and maintain domestic employment levels in a time of severe world recession; industries crying for foreign contracts in order to stay profitable and competitive in global markets; and financial institutions eager to see their large industrial and Eastern European clients remain solvent.[79] The West German government, for example, officially maintained that the situation in Poland was too fragmented and uncertain to allow anyone to draw appropriate conclusions. Actually, Bonn feared that sanctions would upset a decade-long policy of seeking détente and closer business ties with Moscow and the Soviet bloc.

Despite the administration's urgings the COCOM countries, including Great Britain, dragged their heels in imposing economic sanctions.[80] More and more, the Reagan administration was isolated diplomatically from its allies. With great reluctance it announced on 6 January 1982 that it would not press for a concerted program of sanctions against Russia at the forthcoming NATO meeting, but would be content with a vigorous condemnation of her complicity in the Polish crisis. After hurried talks with German Chancellor Helmut Schmidt in Washington, Secretary Haig explained that the United States was sympathetic to the domestic problems that allied leaders faced in following President Reagan's lead. Behind this face-saving announcement the two men had reached a tacit understanding: the United States would not ask its allies to adopt parallel economic sanctions against the Soviet Union, but they, particularly West Germany, would join the United States in placing responsibility for Polish martial law on Moscow. This maintained the facade that the NATO ministers were speaking with a uniform voice.[81]

Nonetheless the administration continued its efforts to persuade COCOM to tighten the curbs it was already applying to the sale of strategic items to Russia and Eastern Europe. The American delegation to the Paris meeting, composed of James L. Buckley, under secretary of state for security assistance, Fred C. Iklé, under secretary of defense, and Lionel H. Olmer, under secretary of commerce for international trade, sought to modify the existing embargo list to effect a much stricter ban on exports of "critical technologies" to the Soviet Union, including advanced computers, fiber optics, and semiconductors; to require that all contracts in excess of $100 million have the approval of COCOM; and to abolish the "exceptions" procedure whereby a NATO country could export goods on the embargo list if other COCOM members agreed to a waiver. This was the first major attempt to tighten NATO's strategic embargo list since COCOM was established in 1949, and reversed thirty years of almost continual liberalization.[82]

By the time the meeting ended, the participants had agreed to reexamine and redefine the guidelines for high-technology exports to the Soviet

Union. A senior official from the U.S. Department of Defense, who had taken part in the negotiations, admitted, however, that many differences still remained. The negotiations also revealed that the United States *could*, if it so chose, delay the Western European plan to import natural gas from Siberia "for many years" by unilaterally banning export of the equipment and technology required to build the pipeline. This was the first hint of possible future action, although the Reagan administration decided for the moment to refrain from taking this drastic step.[83]

The administration's efforts to enlist COCOM to punish the Soviet Union collapsed on 23 January 1982, when France announced the signing of a major natural gas contract with the USSR, despite objections from the United States. The Reagan administration had been particularly worried that Moscow might use the pipeline for political blackmail against Western Europe and to increase its foreign exchange earnings to purchase militarily strategic items from the West.[84] The administration was clearly frustrated at its inability to persuade the NATO allies to scale down their investment in the pipeline. On 9 February Under Secretary of Commerce Olmer told a House subcommittee on science and technology that the administration "remains convinced that it is not in the West's long-term interests to increase dependence on Soviet energy supplies."[85] In Madrid, where he was speaking to the Conference on European Security and Cooperation, Secretary of State Haig expressed "great concern" about the Western European nations' participation in the pipeline and voiced the hope that they would reduce or cancel their plans.[86]

Further complicating an already difficult situation was the fact that the Reagan administration was itself sharply divided over just how far it should—and could—press its allies to adopt economic sanctions against the Soviet Union. What steps should Washington take to slow construction of the $10 billion Soviet gas pipeline? And, having banned U.S. companies from taking part in the gigantic project, should the administration try to prevent foreign subsidiaries of American firms from participating and using American-developed technologies, even if their governments approved of their taking part?

In NSC meetings Secretary Haig fought to maintain the facade of Western unity. On the pipeline controversy, he insisted that since the Europeans were determined to go ahead with the project, which would provide jobs and industrial exports to their hard-pressed economies, it made no sense to try to pressure them into halting the project or to seek to stop American subsidiaries and licensees from taking part. Assistant Secretary of State for Economic and Business Affairs Robert D. Hormats affirmed Haig's position and warned against rupturing the alliance. The

State Department preferred instead to obtain an agreement that would limit future Western credits to the USSR.[87]

Weinberger and the military countered that even at the risk of alienating the allies, the United States must be willing to order the subsidiaries and licensees of American companies to abide by the curbs on sales of equipment and technology that President Reagan had announced in December. In a statement released by the Joint Economic Committee of Congress on 20 February 1982 as part of a report on the pipeline project, the secretary of defense had declared that the Polish crisis "is one of those times when, in order to assert leadership and strengthen security, unilateral initiatives to implement sanctions become necessary."[88] So deep was the division between the Departments of State and Defense on this issue of sanctions that both sides agreed that only the president could resolve it.

Meanwhile the Common Market countries, with Greece abstaining, had agreed, on 22 February, to impose restrictions on Soviet imports in response to the imposition of martial law in Poland. The action was limited in scope, covered only a small percentage of Soviet–European trade, and did not apply to the natural gas deal. Among the items designated for lower import quotas were luxury goods deemed nonessential: diamonds, furs, caviar, and vodka. These curbs on imports satisfied a self-imposed requirement by the Common Market to take sanctions that hurt the Soviet Union without creating economic hardship in Europe. Member countries rejected a ban on high-technology exports, on the ground that it would injure European industry more than the Soviets. "This is a signal to the Soviet Union," declared British Foreign Secretary Lord Carrington.[89]

If the Reagan administration may have wondered just what sort of signal its allies were sending to Moscow, it continued to reassure Congress and the farm bloc that it was not contemplating another grain embargo unless the Soviets provoked it to do so. In March 1982 Agriculture Secretary Block, Trade Representative William Brock, and State Department official Robert Hormats told the House Agriculture Committee that an embargo had been ruled out under present conditions and that the United States intended to honor its current grain contracts with the USSR. Nonetheless the administration remained under intense pressure from agricultural lobbyists not to impose a new grain embargo. In April President Reagan agreed to permit new discussions of grain sales with Soviet officials in Paris on 21–22 May, the first since imposition of martial law in Poland.[90]

This suggested that the president still had not been won over entirely by the military's arguments and remained willing to entertain Haig's position of forgoing opposition to the pipeline if the allies agreed to restrict future credits to the Soviets. For the moment the strategy was to keep pressure on the Soviet economy, which was experiencing financial and hard-currency problems because of the declining volume and world price of oil, its major export, and increased costs of importing food. Secretary Haig told a Senate foreign appropriations subcommittee on 10 March that the United States could not prevent Western Europe from purchasing Soviet natural gas and that efforts to do so would simply damage the alliance. Simultaneously a senior White House official indicated that the administration was ready to drop its opposition to the pipeline if the Western European governments formed an economic bloc with the United States to limit export credits to the USSR. If not, the administration would have to take "another look at the whole series of questions having to do with the pipeline."[91]

This was the message that Under Secretary of State Buckley, whose mission had been delayed once because of the Haig-Weinberger dispute, also was supposed to deliver to the allies. Buckley spent 13–20 March visiting the European capitals. Upon returning to Washington he conveyed to NSC his optimism that the Western Europeans would agree to limit credits to the Soviet Union. However, he did not come back with any firm agreement, as his testimony before the Senate foreign appropriations subcommittee makes clear. In fact, by the end of April the United States and its allies had struck the ultimate diplomatic impasse; each was so locked into its own position that negotiations had become pointless. When Secretary Haig met with the representatives of Britain, France, and West Germany at the United Nations, each reported that the disagreement was so profound that there was no use discussing a compromise. Nor would the Europeans suggest alternative strategies for maintaining economic pressure on Moscow. It was not their responsibility to resolve a problem created by Washington.[92]

The pipeline issue thus became a major concern of the economic summit meeting at Versailles in early June 1982. On 5 June, when President Reagan, "with great intensity," broached the subject of sharply curtailing credits on Moscow, he found himself isolated from the other six Western leaders. Only after intensive negotiations did he obtain a very reluctant agreement to establish guidelines for future commercial credits to Soviet bloc countries. In a post-Versailles communiqué the president put the best possible interpretation on it, stating that it was important to have the principle agreed upon, with the details to be worked out later.[93]

Two weeks later President Reagan not only abruptly refused to ease the ban on American suppliers' selling oil and gas to the Soviet Union but also extended the prohibition to foreign subsidiaries and licensees. In a statement after an NSC meeting, during which the new national security adviser, William Clark, had made the case for extending the ban, the president said he had seen "no movement" by Moscow to persuade him to act otherwise. The press interpreted this action as part of Reagan's "get tough" policy with the Soviets. The prevailing view in the White House and the Pentagon seemed to be that Russia was nearing an economic collapse and that withholding Western support would compel the Kremlin leaders to reduce military expenditures and moderate their behavior toward Poland and Afghanistan.[94]

Predictably, the president's decision sparked an international furor. European, Japanese, and even American State Department experts disagreed with its logic, citing the fact that only one percent of Russia's gross national product was tied to trade with the West and pointing out the Kremlin leaders' prior record of being able to weather internal economic difficulties. Some speculated that President Brezhnev's illness had created a power vacuum at the top, rendering the Soviet Union less of a threat to the West. In any event, the experts predicted, Reagan's decision either would compel the USSR to become self-sufficient in energy technology or would cause American firms to channel more research and development abroad, thereby diffusing technology and making it easier for the Soviets to acquire. British Prime Minister Margaret Thatcher summed up a broad-based feeling when she asserted that the decision appeared to be a dictate from Washington to wage war with the Soviet Union or risk an economic confrontation with the United States. In the midst of this controversy Alexander Haig, who had not been in Washington for the critical meeting of NSC or the president's decision, resigned as secretary of state on 25 June. He protested that U.S. foreign policy was straying off course.[95]

Taken off guard by the intensity of the protests, the administration again shifted course and began to search for a way to ease the sanctions, including scaling back the ban on the pipeline equipment. The *New York Times* reported that reconsideration of the American position came after an "explosive" meeting of cabinet-level officers in the White House on 27 June. According to the *Times*, Brock, the U.S. trade representative, and others commented that the decision had been a disaster for relations with Western Europe and had benefited only the Soviets. The exchanges had become so heated that national security adviser Clark asked two staff members to leave the meeting. In the opinion of some officials the White House was trying to use American businessmen to persuade European leaders to press Polish and Soviet authorities for a face-saving out. This would allow the administration to point to the success of its sanctions while the Europeans and the Soviets went forward with the pipeline. Reagan and Weinberger promptly denied the *Times*'s account.[96]

Whatever truth there was to this soon became irrelevant, as the rug was pulled out from under the American effort altogether. On 13 July 1982 West German bankers signed an agreement with the Soviet Union to finance most of the multibillion-dollar pipeline. A few days later the Reagan administration was stunned to learn of the existence of a secret protocol with the Soviet Union signed by former French President Giscard d'Estaing to grant credits to Moscow. Then, on 21 July, in a political and legal rebuke of the United States the government of President François Mitterand ordered a French company—Alston Atlantic, a subsidiary of the nationalized French electrical and electronics giant CCE— to fulfill its $59 million contract to supply Moscow with giant pipeline rotors developed by General Electric. Three days later Italy decided to honor all signed contracts to supply equipment for a Soviet pipeline. In a legal protest delivered to the Commerce Department on 13 August, the European Economic Community (EEC) blasted the Reagan administration's ban as "an unacceptable interference" in the commercial affairs of the Community, a violation of international law, and contrary to the criteria of the Export Administration Act. It called upon the United States to lift the sanctions.[97]

Clearly the administration had been unable to form a solid front to limit future credits to the Soviet Union or even to persuade its European allies and Japan to adopt parallel sanctions. The issue had become political, and was no longer legal or economic. As the Supreme Court subsequently affirmed, President Reagan had the legal right to insist that European companies not transfer U.S. technology for the pipeline, because the licensees in question had agreed in writing to this caveat. The *real* question was whether the president was wise to reduce a philosophy of peace to an argument over a gas pipeline, and to insist on a legal right that was bound to divide the West without really injuring the Soviets, particularly when the United States was continuing to ship millions of tons of grain to the USSR.[98]

The president seemed to be following no coherent policy but rather reacting ad hoc to Soviet words or actions of the moment. This appeared all the more so as Reagan continued to draw a distinction between American grain sales to Russia and the embargo. At a news conference on 28 July, in which he referred to Europe's protests as "a family fight," he explained that the pipeline technology was mainly available from the United States, whereas Moscow could purchase grain from other countries. Grain sales forced the Soviets to pay out scarce specie, whereas the pipeline would enable them to acquire foreign exchange for the Russian military machine. The distinction was dubious to the administration's critics, who wrung their hands even more tightly when, in August, the president extended the grain agreement. They argued that the president had permitted the issues of Western security, Poland, and grain sales to become confused. The critical reason for opposing the pipeline was that it would substantially improve the Soviet Union's prospects for earning hard currency; in turn these improved prospects would facilitate the Soviets' arms effort, which would bring renewed pressure on Western Europe and the alliance. Why, asked Robert W. Tucker of Johns Hopkins University, obscure "this clear and vital interest by invoking considerations of dubious merit or of secondary importance?"[99]

Undeterred, Reagan threatened to impose sanctions against the French subsidiary of Dresser Industries of Dallas, Texas, if it shipped compressors to the Soviet Union. The John Brown Company of Great Britain and various Italian firms were also put on notice. On 26 August the Commerce Department transferred both Dresser France and Creusot-Loire to its "blacklist" and prohibited them from obtaining pipeline technology either from the parent company or any other American firm. Under Secretary of Commerce Olmer termed the order "a measured response": an effort to show the administration's resolve while keeping relations with Western Europe from becoming more strained than they already were. Washington's quarrel, Olmer insisted, was with the French government and not private companies.[100]

Despite the administration's outward appearance of intransigence, senior officials were working overtime to heal the breach in the Western alliance. On 31 August chief trade negotiator Brock told reporters that sanctions had left America's economic and political relations with its European partners in disarray, which could only be mended by forging a common commercial strategy toward Moscow. He affirmed the necessity of prior consultation with the NATO allies on measures to curb the export of strategic materials and technology to the USSR. On the other side of the Atlantic, British Foreign Secretary Francis Pym was quietly proposing a compromise: the Europeans would impose tougher conditions on future credits to the Soviet Union in return for the United States' rescinding economic sanctions. Neither side wanted to be the first to agree to the compromise, for fear of exhibiting weakness. But on 1 September Secretary of the Treasury Donald T. Regan, head of the senior policy-making group of presidential advisers, announced that the administration had intended to prevent foreign firms from receiving exports of U.S. oil and gas equipment and technology, not all American products. This statement was a signal that the president now wanted to scale back the sanctions and reestablish harmonious ties with the Western allies.[101]

Fresh evidence of brutality by Polish officials forced the administration momentarily to backpedal. George P. Shultz, the new secretary of state, Defense Secretary Weinberger, and even Brock felt constrained to call for even stiffer penalties in order to demonstrate to the allies, the Polish government, and the Soviets that the United States was serious. The administration's tough stance won the reluctant endorsement of the House of Representatives, which voted narrowly (209 to 197) on 29 September to let the sanctions stand for the next ninety days. The closeness of the vote was a clear indication that the sanctions had become increasingly unpopular, especially in those parts of the nation where they had cost jobs. Indeed the vote occurred only after House members had watered down and modified the original bill, which had called for lifting the sanctions immediately and without conditions.[102]

Despite a renewal of harsh rhetoric the administration, succumbing to pressure from farm lobbyists, forged ahead on 15 October with a new grain deal with the Soviet Union, an inconsistency duly noted by its domestic and overseas critics. Immediately thereafter Secretary of State Shultz presented the allies with a proposal that might serve as the basis for rescinding the sanctions. The draft committed them to a fundamental review of Western strategy for dealing with Moscow and obligated them to identify specific pressure points, such as credit and transfer of technology, that could be used as leverage to link trade with Soviet behavior. The intent was to circumvent the pipeline issue, which was divisive, by focusing on the broader questions of East–West trade.[103]

Shultz's proposal was derailed by the French government during three very intense negotiating sessions in Washington, in which it insisted that it had to extend credits to Moscow if its exports were to be competitive. Nonetheless the pendulum was swinging toward the moderates within the administration—toward Shultz and Commerce Secretary Malcolm Baldridge, who vigorously argued for restraint and consistency in the United States' dealings with its allies and the Soviets—and away from the hard-liners, such as Weinberger, Clark, and Lawrence J. Brady, the assistant secretary of commerce for trade administration. The negotiations continued into November. Italian President Giovanni Spadolini, while visiting the White House, predicted that an agreement was near.[104]

On 13 November 1982 President Reagan announced that he was rescinding the sanctions against U.S. and foreign companies' participating in the pipeline project. He gave as the reason for this that the United States and its allies had reached "substantial agreement" on a broad economic strategy toward the Soviet bloc, and he termed the accord "a victory for the allies." As for the terms of the accord, both sides had consented not to enter into trade agreements, especially involving gas and oil technology, that enhanced the military and strategic advantage of the USSR; not to give preferential assistance to the heavily militarized Soviet economy; not to sign any new natural gas contracts with Moscow, pending a study of Western energy alternatives; to standardize and monitor credit policies toward the USSR; and to strengthen COCOM controls. Reagan observed that if the new Soviet leadership acted responsibly, it would meet "a ready and positive response in the West."[105]

The impetus for the agreement had come chiefly from Secretary of State Shultz. He had persuaded the president that this compromise was more desirable in the long run than perpetuating the rift in the alliance. Even though Reagan continued to insist that the sanctions had functioned effectively and thus had served their intended purpose, a more realistic assessment came from Martin S. Feldstein, the chairman of the Council of Economic Advisors: "I think we have inflicted some pain, but we are also creating some side effects for our allies and ourselves so it was an inefficient way to penalize the Russians. We were hurting the allies and ourselves."[106]

European reaction, while favorable, was also qualified. Because of their belief that the sanctions had been illegal to begin with, the French were not party to the agreement; therefore they did not wish to be identified with a quid pro quo arrangement. One West German official asserted that the president's justification of his action was designed to let him abandon the sanctions without loss of face. Moreover, a glut of oil on the market had rendered new contracts for Soviet natural gas unlikely.[107]

At home too there was a feeling that the sanctions had fallen short. Republican Senator Richard Lugar of Indiana told CBS's "Face the Nation" that they had not achieved President Reagan's objectives, a conclusion supported by a study from the congressional Office of Technology Assessment that was released to the public on 8 May 1983. Lingering illwill in Western Europe over the sanctions made it doubtful that the United States' allies would adopt a tougher stance on East–West trade in the future. Their response would be shaped more by "domestic imperatives" and worldwide economic forces than by American concerns over leaks of sensitive technology. The aftermath of the administration's efforts dramatically demonstrated that the United States' power to influence foreign affairs by the leverage of trade was limited. "U.S. sanctions may well have hurt the U.S.S.R.," the report concluded, "but it is unlikely that they have made a real difference."[108]

The Reagan administration's reaching for economic sanctions had symbolized not strength and determination but rather earlier failures to shape effective national security and foreign policies by other means.

Regulating economic relations did have its proper place, but only in the context of broader policies and in concert with other affected countries, so that the United States' purposes could be understood in advance and economic hardship and the various modes of manipulation could be shared fairly. Whether the Reagan administration clearly understood this was uncertain. The president's announcement of 13 November 1982 that rescinded the sanctions was as much a truce within the administration as with the European allies. Secretary of State Shultz may well have persuaded the president that the sanctions policy was damaging the unity of NATO more than the Soviet economy, but he probably had not swayed Reagan from his conviction that the Soviet Union was economically vulnerable. Moreover, Shultz had not moved other key officials of the administration from positions that both mirrored and bolstered Reagan's. At NSC, in the Department of Defense, and even in some corners of the Departments of Commerce and State, important officials continued to advocate economic sanctions as weapons in the United States' competition with the Soviet Union.[109]

IN 1969 President Richard M. Nixon entered the Oval Office reluctant to expand American–Soviet trade. Prodded by substantial congressional support for the liberalization of trade, Nixon and Secretary of State Henry Kissinger soon began to assess the question of economic relations with the USSR as an act of foreign policy rather than primarily a commercial opportunity. Above all, they viewed trade as a bargaining chip for attaining certain foreign policy objectives. The diplomatic goals overshadowed whatever economic, technological, or scientific benefits that might have accrued to the United States. And though the administration advocated a strategy of "linkage" to moderate the Soviet Union's external policies, it criticized attempts to invoke trade as a lever to alter Soviet domestic policies. Unfortunately for Nixon and Kissinger, the policy of détente unraveled over the human rights and Jewish emigration issues, and the fears of conservatives that the Soviets were using détente to disguise a military buildup.

During the Carter administration U.S. policy became one of deliberate flexibility, equally prepared to use promises or threats to elicit more favorable Soviet domestic and foreign policies and to punish the Russians for their invasion of Afghanistan. The result of this policy was an abrupt plunge in American–Soviet trade between 1979 and 1980. Exports to the USSR fell from $3.6 billion to $1.5 billion, and imports of Soviet goods declined from $873 million to $430 million.

Under the Reagan administration the policy tended almost exclusively toward negative linkages. Influential officials of the administration believed that the Soviet Union and its European satellites were on the brink of economic collapse and that because of its economic problems the USSR required an economic lifeline from the West. The conclusion derived from this analysis was that the Soviet Union was vulnerable to the political leverage of economic sanctions. The administration therefore tried to pressure the Soviets economically while holding out the possibility of future trade, credits, and technology in order to force the Soviet leaders to reduce military spending and moderate their international behavior, especially in Afghanistan and Poland. More so than previous occupants of the White House, President Reagan was extremely wary about the political effects of trade and transfer of technology, believing they would provide great economic and military benefits for the USSR and prop up a bankrupt regime.[110] Apparently neither he nor his advisers accepted the possibility that trade with the Soviet Union might become a matter of reciprocal interest.

Past history has been a notoriously poor guide to present policy. The evidence is increasingly clear that unilateral U.S. sanctions on trade are futile as instruments for changing Soviet policy, and that they are levied at considerable cost to the nation's economy in the loss of hard-earned business by American exporters, in undercutting the United States' credibility as a reliable business partner, and in squandering the possibility of useful influence. Nonetheless both President Carter and President Reagan were overly zealous in invoking sanctions to meet foreign policy objectives. They transformed what had been an area of growing cooperation and mutual benefit during the Nixon and Ford administrations into a zone of economic warfare. In doing so they isolated the United States within the Western alliance and became targets of vigorous recriminations from foe and friend alike.[111]

Epilogue

IN 1933, when the United States and the Soviet Union established diplomatic relations, both governments envisioned the possibility of a great expansion of American–Soviet trade.[1] Their optimism did not come to fruition in the ensuing decade. Because of ideological and political differences between Washington and Moscow, which had grown out of the Bolshevik Revolution and the World War I debt claims, the United States' Export-Import Bank refused to extend credits and loans to finance this trade. American entrepreneurs and business firms, unlike their European counterparts, were left to their own devices without official encouragement. The trade that occurred was mostly in raw materials and heavy machinery, but it did not nearly approach in volume and dollar value the peak years of 1930 and 1931, before recognition of the Soviet Union.

The exigencies of World War II required that the United States mute its anti-Bolshevik feelings (as Stalin toned down criticism of the capitalistic West) and to forge a grand alliance with the Soviet Union, despite the totalitarian nature of its government, against the common enemy. Lend-lease was the mortar that cemented two very different political and economic systems.

In the analysis of a controversial historical occurrence like the Cold War, where there is an absence of reasonably complete data from one side, it is difficult to ascertain who provoked whom. The Cold War developed naturally out of the way in which World War II had destroyed the old balance of power in Europe. The need to rearrange that balance inevitably led to some rivalry for territory and influence, but it might have been managed with less disastrous results if the United States and the Soviet Union had possessed some common outlook that could have served as a basis for trust. Instead, within the parameters defined by an abiding belief in democratic capitalism and a dislike of Marxian socialism as a politico-economic system, probably a majority of Americans in 1945–46 had an ambivalent attitude toward the Soviet Union. They respected and admired a courageous and gallant wartime ally, but they also were critical of a system that eschewed individualism, of a society whose innermost workings were alien, secretive, and riddled with suspicion.[2]

This ambiguity manifested itself at war's end in Washington's economic policy toward Moscow. Pursuing a Wilsonian quest for peace and greater understanding among all countries and fearing a postwar economic depression at home, the United States planned for expanded mutual trade.[3] Soviet intransigence over the future shape of the postwar world as envisioned by American policymakers, and the extension of the Soviet system to neighboring states, replete with secret police, the extinction of free speech, and nonelections, led the Truman administration to utilize economic coercion to persuade the Soviets to accept the United States' political objectives.

In pursuing this course of action American policymakers appeared to be guided by the advice of former Ambassador to the Soviet Union W. Averell Harriman. Like almost every American diplomat who was posted to Moscow during the war years, some of whom later played key roles in formulating the containment policy, or who had some contact with the Soviets in an official capacity, as in the administration of lend-lease, Harriman had been profoundly disillusioned by the oppressive nature of Soviet society and alarmed because the defeat of the Axis nations would place Soviet political and military might outside its normal confines.[4]

Different interest groups at the end of the war—some better positioned and more highly leveraged than others—were vying with one another to influence the Truman administration to adopt certain politico-economic policies that accorded with their own perceptions of the Soviet Union. Government officials like Harriman and James F. Byrnes and some business executives were not sanguine about the prospects of an enduring peace or enhanced commercial ties with the USSR. Their outlook had been conditioned by a lingering anti-Bolshevism, by antagonistic wartime encounters with a difficult ally, and by the prewar record of American–Soviet trade. With the Soviet armies encamped in Central and Eastern Europe, they viewed the USSR as a menace to democratic capitalism and feared that the Soviets would deny the United States access to the markets of Eastern Europe. The specter of a resurgent Bolshevism overshadowed the other reality: that the USSR had lost 20 million of its citizens and that much of its economic infrastructure had been reduced to rubble.

Other government officials and businessmen in 1945–46, however, were willing to eschew past ideological and political differences. They viewed postwar Russia almost exclusively in economic terms: as an enormous potential market for American industrial and agricultural products. The head of the Russian desk in the Commerce Department, Ernest C. Ropes, the industrialist Henry J. Kaiser, and the publisher James H. McGraw, Jr., were typical. The Russian market attracted them because it might help to keep the United States (and thus Europe) from sliding into an economic depression, as had occurred in the wake of World War I and again in the 1930s.

Still other businessmen and bureaucrats, like Henry Wallace, thought in politico-economic terms, cautiously optimistic that postwar trade and aid for Soviet reconstruction might become the basis for a political rapprochement. In 1945–46 they advanced the argument that international peace depended upon worldwide economic well-being, and the latter rested upon a healthy foreign trade and prosperity for the United States. According to their analysis, political stability and democratic politics would thrive only in a vigorous, interdependent global economy, free of artificial barriers to trade, in which people's material needs were satisfied. In that setting non-Americans would freely choose democratic capitalism over Marxian socialism, and this would be the best guarantee of the national security of the United States.

Without resorting to a conspiratorial view of the world, and despite the appearance of a consistent pattern of economic coercion, the thrust of U.S. foreign economic policy in 1945–46 was still very fluid, although that would no longer be the case in 1947. By then, the Marshall Plan was put forward in such a way as to preclude Moscow's participation.[5]

The United States and Russia clashed repeatedly throughout 1945–46, rendering hollow the slogan "World Peace through World Trade." Political conflict substituted for political détente. The sources of friction encompassed the disposition of Germany and Eastern Europe, the Bretton Woods Agreement and the future of international finance and trade, and the control of atomic energy. Fully conscious of America's superior economic strength and under congressional and public pressure to get tough with the Soviets, the Truman administration attempted unsuccessfully to moderate Soviet international behavior by abruptly, if legally, terminating lend-lease, by rejecting a Soviet request for a reconstruction loan, and by gradually curtailing loans and trade to countries within the Soviet sphere.[6]

Rather than displaying the minimum of subtlety and flexibility that could have achieved many of his objectives without so sharp and open a break with the West, Stalin actually made these issues irrelevant by engaging in a diplomacy that by its uncompromising objectives and truculent style seemed almost calculated to outrage the American public and policymakers. He also revived his prewar determination to attain national economic self-sufficiency for the USSR, a decision that ran counter to the United States' goal of an open, multilateral trading system in which the United States itself stood at the center.[7]

The result was that the United States and the Soviet Union slipped into a cold war so quickly that some businessmen and a few government officials were slow to recognize the new political reality: confrontation had replaced trade and aid. The proponents of international peace and prosperity through trade found that the ground had been cut from under their feet. With a few notable exceptions, such as the entrepreneurs Cyrus L. Eaton and Armand Hammer, American businessmen enlisted in the Cold War.

Since 1947 the United States has predicated its foreign policy toward the Soviet Union on the concept of containment, that is, halting communist expansion and creating preconditions for the eventual dissolution of the Soviet system. Prodded by a Congress eager to take firm action against the Bolshevik meance, the Truman administration enlisted economic foreign policy in support of its diplomatic objectives. The economic equivalent of political containment was to minimize U.S. and Western trade contacts with the Soviet Union and Soviet bloc countries in order to deny them the benefits of an international division of labor and comparative advantage. Congress, more so than the White House, believed that exports of superior U.S. commodities and technology would contribute to Soviet military and economic might, thereby stabilizing the Soviet political system but imperiling the United States' national security. Unwilling and unable to use military force, the United States saw in export controls an opportunity to enhance its national security, and the security of the free world, at relatively little cost.

To effect this goal American policymakers had at hand the comprehensive system of export controls enacted in the early 1940s to deprive the Axis nations of vital commodities. Congress had perpetuated the control system into the postwar period chiefly for "short supply" and domestic policy purposes: to avert severe shortages and inflationary pressures at home. As political relations between the United States and the Soviet Union grew increasingly acrimonious, national security displaced short-supply considerations.

A first step was taken in connection with legislation authorizing Marshall Plan aid to Europe early in 1948. Section 117 (d) of the Foreign Assistance Act utilized this aid to pressure the Western European allies into complying with the United States' export control policy. Congress gave that policy a firmer legislative underpinning when it enacted the Export Control Act of 1949. This law conferred upon the president discretionary authority to restrict or prohibit the export of any commodity, including technical data, whenever such exportation threatened the national security of the United States.

Despite qualms about the efficacy of this policy the Truman administration instituted a two-tiered licensing system for transfer of technology: most American manufactured goods could be shipped to non-communist nations without specific approval, requiring only a general license from the Department of Commerce for an entire class of transactions; however, certain strategic goods could not be exported without a "validated license," to be granted on a case-by-case basis. The provisions of this law were subsequently extended to cover China, after the communist ascendancy to power in that country.

To render the Export Control Act more effective the United States, also in 1949, joined with the Western European allies to form the Consultative Group (CG) and institute what all hoped would be a parallel system of controls over the shipment of strategic commodities to the USSR and Soviet bloc countries. The Consultative Group implemented the system through the Coordinating Committee (COCOM), a voluntary body not governed by any formal agreement. Under this arrangement each participating nation was supposed to enforce on its own nationals the decisions made by the committee. In 1951 Congress moved to strengthen the United States' position in international negotiations with COCOM and non-COCOM countries by legislating the Mutual Defense Assistance Control Act (the Battle Act). Intended chiefly to put teeth into the Western trade embargo, the law denied U.S. foreign aid to any country that permitted the export of strategic and even nonmilitary goods to communist nations.

The basic economic apparatus for creating the kinds of pressures that would negate Soviet military might and bring down the political system was in place by the end of Truman's presidency. It consisted of the Foreign Assistance Act of 1948, the Export Control Act of 1949, the Cannon amendment of 27 September 1950, and the Mutual Defense Assistance Act (the Battle Act) of 1951. Besides denying military and basic industrial goods, the United States also curtailed export of many consumer items, the rationale being that the availability of such goods might erode the will to revolt. At the height of the Korean War, in 1951, an angry Congress passed legislation abrogating most-favored-nation treatment for Soviet products. This was as much a psychological symbol of the absence of goodwill and friendship as it was an economic slap at the Soviets. Congress also prohibited importation from the USSR of seven kinds of furs. Three years later it enacted laws prohibiting the export of arms, munitions, implements of war, and related technology to the Soviet Union, and also forbade the sale of agricultural commodities to the USSR for local currency or long-term credits.

These measures, coupled with the U.S.-sponsored multilateral system of export trade controls, marked the apex of American and Western allied efforts at an embargo. They allowed both the executive and the legislative branch to demonstrate American leadership in world affairs, to express their moral outrage at Soviet misbehavior, and seemingly to react forcefully to hostile Soviet initiatives without the shedding of blood. This was especially important in the McCarthy era, when the cost of inaction was seen as greater than the cost of sanctions, a recurrent phenomenon whenever American–Soviet relations have been most tense. Further, economic sanctions also were a tangible demonstration of U.S. and Western European unity and determination to resist Soviet aggression.

Underpinning the restrictions was the "bottleneck theory." Simply expressed, it held that in any economic or military structure there were certain specialized components (such as ball bearings) that were essential to the structure. If these components could be identified, isolated, denied, and/or destroyed, the structure must wither and finally collapse. The bottleneck theory fit smoothly with the policy of containment. Trade restrictions and the fear of a majority of businessmen that the American public would regard trade with the Soviet Union as unpatriotic caused American exports to the USSR to drop precipitously from 1946 to the end of Eisenhower's first administration. This also coincided with the most intense period of Western economic warfare against the Soviet Union.[8]

Contrary to the predictions of the bottleneck theory and its most vociferous congressional and military promoters, the Soviet Union neither withered nor collapsed. National Security Council and Central Intelligence Agency reports of the period confirm that the theory and the accompanying embargo amounted to an exercise in futility: a satisfactory definition of "strategic goods" was difficult for policymakers to agree upon; the embargo complicated the United States' relations with its allies and created dissension within NATO; the policy may actually have facilitated Stalin's aim to achieve greater centralization of power behind the Iron Curtain, by providing a scapegoat for many economic difficulties. The Soviet Union was not then, and never has been, dependent enough on U.S. economic aid or trade to make substantial diplomatic concessions to obtain them.[9]

Economic sanctions are a halfway measure between traditional diplomatic forms, such as formal protests and war. When used in conjunction with psychological, political, and military pressures and with full cooperation from allies, they might be useful in influencing the foreign policy of a smaller and weaker nation, though even that might not prove the case.[10] One thing is certain: economic sanctions, especially against a powerful adversary, did not bring about the desired international behavior. The lesson that emerged from the embargo restrictions of 1947–55 was that a large industrial nation with a store of natural resources and manpower, given time, could adjust to denials of the bottleneck type, whether they were imposed by aerial bombardment, as was the case of Nazi Germany in World War II, or by export trade controls. Washington's reaching for economic sanctions symbolized not strength and determination but a failure to shape an effective policy toward the Soviet Union that was both coherent and worked out with the United States' Western European partners.[11]

Economic sanctions neither brought down the Soviet government—contrary to the containment doctrine—nor appreciably retarded its military capability. The embargo of the early Cold War years (and since) was never as ironclad or as comprehensive as its congressional and military proponents had demanded. Instead the questions of whether to resort to export controls, what they could really accomplish, and how to define precisely a "strategic" commodity in the transfer of technology constituted points of friction within the executive branch and between the executive and legislative branches of the federal government.

Each president—and to a greater or lesser degree the entire machinery of the executive branch—though clearly having to be responsive and responsible to the electorate, also had to be sensitive to the wishes and national-interest requirements of the nation's allies abroad. Western Europeans and the Japanese did not invariably perceive the Soviet threat in the same way as did the United States, and often ignored or violated the sanctions policy. Forced international "cooperation," whether brought about by the threat to withhold U.S. economic assistance or by the heavy hand of extraterritorial controls, produced undesirable results for Western unity.

Each president since Truman, often prodded by the State Department, has had to calculate the long-term effects of export controls on foreign policy as well as their domestic political implications. Some were more successful than others in doing so, but each one invariably interpreted the discretionary powers vested in him by the various legislative enactments in a manner that would soften the blow of trade restrictions upon the political economy of friendly nations. On the other hand, presidential initiatives to liberalize American–Soviet trade, though individually successful, were not cumulative in their political effect. In Congress and among parts of the public, notably blue-collar labor unions and conservative groups, opposition to the liberalization of trade with communist nations remained strong.

Legislators, by contrast, tended to react to the popular pressures of the moment, as in the early Cold War era, or to the will of influential minorities and interest groups in matters concerning communism and the Soviet Union. This was probably inevitable in the highly pluralistic society of the United States. But even Congress was less than unified or consistent in its attitude regarding trade and transfer of technology to the USSR. Three distinct attitudes prevailed and essentially continue to do so. The first held that commercial intercourse, including transfer of technology, is integral to a policy of expanded contacts with the communist world; from a policy of détente should arise a series of international and interpersonal relationships that might, over time, contribute to a lasting structure of peace. The second viewed the basic nature of East–West confrontation in Manichean terms, arguing that the adversary relationship between capitalism (the United States) and communism (the Soviet Union) is unlikely to be changed through any gradual relaxation of tension brought about by trade; trade is not an opportunity for strengthening peace, but an instrument for slowly bleeding the United States of its most important assets, by a nation it has every reason to distrust. The third and middle ground was occupied by those who felt that no judgments are necessary about the prospects for détente, and that trade in consumer items is legitimate if the United States can maintain and increase the efficiency and reliability of the export control system.[12]

The consistency of these views over the course of the years was remarkable. But because they were the most vocal and readily identifiable, the rhetoric and opinions of the second group—predominantly conservative legislators—have often been highlighted in this study. More than any others except perhaps the military, these reflected the intensity of feeling of the most anticommunist policymakers in the government. Under the best of circumstances, to effect a better understanding and greater consistency with respect to export control policy, the executive and Congress must have a continuous and harmonious working relationship. This cooperation often was lacking because conservative legislators, seeking to assert congressional authority in foreign policy making, wanted to transform export controls into a total embargo, something the executive branch refused to sanction.

After reading the documents and following the congressional testimony, one is left with the impression that the U.S. government, regardless of party, imposed and has persisted in trade controls and economic sanctions more for domestic political purposes and to give a visible, if meaningless, demonstration to the rest of the world that the United States disapproves of Moscow's aggressive international behavior, than either to bring down the Soviet Union or cause it to modify its actions. Most emphatically, after a decade of practicing economic coercion, no occupant of the White House seriously believed that embargoes or sanctions would in themselves cause the Soviet system to collapse. However, because the fervor of anticommunism persisted in Congress and the populace for a much longer time than in the Oval Office, few presidents were willing to incur the political risks that dismantling the export control system entailed.

Besides divisions within the federal government, uniform compliance within COCOM was never easily obtained—contrary to the view of some scholars[13]—not even in the early years of the Cold War, when American economic and military power was greatest. Within COCOM disagreements about embargo policy originated primarily, but not exclusively, from differing perceptions of the significance of the Soviet threat to the West. America's allies, whose historic trading markets were located in Eastern Europe and Russia, always interpreted COCOM's recommendations narrowly, taking every opportunity to delay, weaken, reduce, and then evade the American program of economic blockade. Only the combination of postwar industrial paralysis in Europe with the United States' aid-giving capacity had elicited allied support for the U.S.-imposed trade embargoes. Once economic recovery was completed, Western Europe (and Japan) depended far more on trade for economic well-being than did the United States, and sought to recapture traditional markets in the East. Exports between Western Europe and the European Soviet bloc expanded considerably between 1954 and 1963, from $750 million to $2 billion.[14] There was no comparable growth in American–Soviet trade.

With economic recovery, the Western allies also became less dependent on American aid, and the threat of the Battle Act receded. This further eroded the ability of the United States to influence allied embargo policies. In 1954 the Eisenhower administration acquiesced in allied insistence to reduce COCOM's embargo list drastically, thereby initiating a trend toward increasing liberalization of East–West trade that culminated in the Export Administration Act of 1979. By the 1960s the United States' technological superiority in several areas had declined, and foreign competitors had fewer reservations about exporting goods and sophisticated technologies to the Soviet Union. Since then they have looked upon American efforts to maintain an embargo or to invoke trade sanctions as discriminatory and hypocritical, especially while the United States is continuing to sell grain to the USSR. The Western allies also have noted that Soviet economic and technological development has proceeded with or without the benefit of American commerce. All things considered, the trade-dependent Western Europeans (and Japan) have seen little justification for persisting in a policy they have long believed has failed.

The natural gas pipeline dispute of 1982 was a dramatic escalation of the long-standing controversy over the propriety and effectiveness of export controls, and also called into question COCOM's usefulness. President Reagan, more rhetorically and overtly outspoken in his condemnation of the Soviet Union than previous recent occupants of the White House, applied controls extraterritorially in an attempt to obtain the participation of Western European firms in actions to which their governments did not acquiesce. Critics viewed the president's action as an infringement upon sovereignty, the outcome of which has still to be finally assessed. In the short term the United States' relations with its allies were badly damaged, but the Soviet Union was little affected. The pipeline controversy further demonstrated the need for achieving a unified Western policy on trade with the Soviet Union, something difficult to achieve as long as Western Europe and Japan persist in holding ideas about the role, importance, and acceptable parameters of Soviet trade that are fundamentally different from those prevailing in the United States.

The failure of economic, political, and psychological pressure to topple the Soviet system, which, after all, was the ultimate aim of containment, forced American policymakers to rethink the rationale for continuing the policy of export controls. The stated goal, after 1955, was no longer to bring down the Soviet system but to keep the Soviets in a position of relative military and economic inferiority, thereby reducing Moscow's opportunities for aggressive behavior in international affairs. This required depriving the Soviets of military and strategic industrial goods, sophisticated technology, and agricultural products so that they would not be able to use Western imports to free up equivalent resources for military use.

Although this objective was not abandoned, pressure from Europe, from some parts of the American business community, and from academics in the late 1950s and the 1960s led to a major reevaluation of the shape and future of export policy. Discussion in the United States increasingly focused upon finding a proper balance between the economic benefits of trade with Russia and the Soviet bloc and the threat posed by this trade to the national security. The history of export controls in this period was a gradual movement from an exclusive emphasis on the security aspects of trade toward relaxation of controls. This resulted in only a modest increase in trade.[15] Except for irregularly exported commodities like grain, U.S. exports to the Soviet Union assumed basically their pre–World War II character, although chemicals (such as fertilizers) and crude materials also became important.

Despite Eisenhower's belated interest in promoting more peaceful trade with the Soviets and a growing awareness that communism was not a monolith, no major change in policy occurred between 1956 and the 1960s. The attempts of the Kennedy and Johnson administrations to dismantle trade restrictions and to use trade to "build bridges" to the East were largely unsuccessful. The chief impediment continued to be legislative (and, increasingly, military) opposition, growing out of the Cuban missile crisis and later the war in Vietnam. Congress refused to reverse the commitment to economic containment as an instrument of cold war foreign policy, fearing that such action would signal tolerance for the Soviet Union's bellicose international behavior. Indeed in 1962 Congress reaffirmed cold war policies by enacting amendments to the Export Control Act of 1949. These required the president to deny an export license for any item that made a significant contribution to the military or economic potential of any nation that threatened the national security of the United States.

The spirit of the 1962 amendments implied the declaration of outright economic warfare on the communist world. Congressional opposition and the escalating American involvement in the Vietnam War made it politically difficult for Presidents Kennedy and Johnson to affect a fundamental change in policy via the legislative route. Presidential direction simply was not strong enough to overcome bureaucratic inertia, congressional opposition, and the hostility of influential segments of the American public, to achieve a major redirection of policy. This coalition threatened any White House move to liberalize East–West trade.

By contrast, the Export Administration Act of 1969, enacted in a different political atmosphere and during a new, Republican administration, constituted a dramatic alteration of long-standing U.S. policy toward East–West trade. Several considerations coalesced to the advantage of the Nixon administration, which prompted Congress to shift from restriction to cautious encouragement of American–Soviet trade: the desire of American firms to compete with foreign businesses in hitherto inaccessible markets; the prospect of increased domestic employment; the hope of ameliorating the nation's balance of payments problem; the "foreign availability" argument, that is, the awareness that restricting U.S. exports of goods and technologies available to the Soviet Union from other nations failed to serve national security needs; and the desire of legislators, such as Senators Walter Mondale and Edmund Muskie, to resolve Soviet–American differences through negotiation and increased mutual economic dependence, rather than through isolation and conflict.[16]

The 1969 law made a serious effort to balance the tension between the older view of the national security interest and the more recent recognition of the potential benefits of East–West trade. In June 1971 President Nixon signaled his willingness to expand trade with the Soviet Union. This departure from previous policy accorded with some of the objectives that Congress had tried to achieve in passing the 1969 act. Nixon too was eager to strengthen the domestic economy and to improve the foreign balance of payments. But he and Secretary of State Kissinger also wanted to accelerate progress in negotiations that would lead to an American withdrawal from Vietnam and to begin a dialogue with the Soviet Union on political questions, including strategic arms limitations. In pursuit of détente the Nixon administration took several steps to promote American–Soviet trade, such as progressively relaxing the licensing of exports and establishing an East–West Trade Bureau in the Department of Commerce. Most of the new steps were linked to corresponding action by the Soviet Union.

Congress continued to respond to pressure from domestic firms, and contributed—albeit more reluctantly—to détente in 1972 by passing the Equal Export Opportunity Act. This law formally took notice of the "foreign availability" argument of the critics of trade restrictions. Perhaps more typical of congressional attitudes, however, was the Jackson-Vanik amendment to the 1972 American–Soviet Trade Agreement. The handiwork of highly influential and well-placed minorities, the amendment linked trade to Soviet emigration and human rights issues and played a crucial role in bringing together liberal and conservative critics of détente. Its passage caused the Soviet Union to annul the trade agreement in 1975, which contributed to the end of détente.

The controversy surrounding the Jackson-Vanik amendment held several important lessons for American policymakers. First, the conscious manipulation of economic ties might well not have been the most effective vehicle through which to secure political objectives. No matter how compelling their economic interests, the political interests of both the Soviet Union and the United States have always taken precedence in determining their mutual trade. Second, any expectation that trade would promote liberalization of the Soviet system was about as realistic as hoping that trade would foster the growth of communism in the United States. Third, whatever might have been perceived as legitimate goals by influential interest groups or political figures—whether Senator Jackson, the military, American-Jewish organizations, or organized labor—was not necessarily desirable for the nation as a whole, or even in the national interest. Fourth, linkages between political goals and economic actions are complicated when dealing with the USSR, particularly when legislative and executive policymakers cannot agree on what the objectives of policy are, what might effectively be linked with commercial concessions, and to what extent and how.[17]

The matter of human rights was, and is, a valid concern. But it probably was unreasonable to link this problem to the United States' trade policy. The United States could not attempt to legislate what was basically the internal affair of another country; nor could it interfere in an uneven manner with regard to different nations, depending upon whether they were classified as adversaries or allies. At best, the United States could—and should—have made human rights a top-priority private objective in negotiations with the Soviet Union, but not a public issue.

Unburdened by the Jackson-Vanik amendment, détente might in time have established a chain of agreements that led to, in Kissinger's words, "a broad understanding about international conduct appropriate to the dangers of the nuclear age."[18] Instead it became the chief casualty in the fight over the Jackson-Vanik amendment. Conservatives and liberals alike questioned the fundamental premises upon which détente had rested and, in the process, reduced the Nixon-Kissinger foreign policy and the administration of export policy to a shambles. In the wake of the amendment there seemed to be no coherent rationale for banning specific exports to particular communist nations; the system was full of leaks and on the verge of collapse. By the mid-1970s U.S. export control policy had become, in the opinion of one expert, "a collage with little rhyme or reason."[19]

When Jimmy Carter became president, the international political milieu surrounding American-Soviet trade had become increasingly complex. Détente was discredited as the Soviets strove for nuclear parity with the United States. Experience with the Export Administration Act of 1969 had revealed two potentially competing goals: on the one hand, it encouraged trade with all nations except those that the president determined to be against the national interest; on the other hand, it restricted the transfer of technology that contributed to the military potential of any nation that posed a threat to the United States. Like Nixon and Ford before him, Carter found that one of his tasks was to define and identify the latter in order to avoid the confusion and inconsistent trade determinations that dogged implementation of the act.

On 22 June 1977 President Carter signed the Export Administration Amendments (formalized subsequently in the Export Administration Act of 1979) to the 1969 legislation that had attempted to address this problem. Responding to pressure from the international business sectors, Congress indicated that U.S. policy toward any given country should reflect that nation's relationship with the United States and should not be dictated solely by its characterization as communist or noncommunist. The amendments also accorded increased weight to the "foreign availability" argument that the Department of Commerce was to consider in scrutinizing applications for export licenses. Carter accepted the changes, despite growing concern in the military and intelligence communities over the transfer of highly sophisticated technologies to the Soviets.

This attempt at liberalization of export policy almost immediately ran afoul of the Soviet threat to Poland, the military invasion of Afghanistan, and the president's own reemphasis on moralism in the conduct of foreign policy. Unwilling to exercise a military option to force the Russians to behave, President Carter resorted to economic coercion to achieve a political objective, with predictably disappointing results. Unlike Kennedy and Nixon, who had utilized grain sales to entice the Soviets toward political détente and, not incidentally, to rid their administrations of domestic pressure from farm lobbyists anxious to dispose of surplus grain abroad, Carter withheld grain sales and resorted to other highly publicized but essentially symbolic actions in order to punish the Soviet Union.

These actions not only were ineffective in achieving their political objective, but they brought down upon the Carter administration the wrath of the nation's grain farmers and their political allies, who saw a guaranteed long-term market being taken over by foreign competitors. The costs borne by the American economy were probably at least as great as those that devolved on the USSR, especially since other countries had replaced the United States as its principal agricultural supplier. When a beleaguered Carter left the presidency in 1980, American–Soviet trade relations, from grain sales to technology transfers, were at a very low ebb, which reflected the state of political relations as well.[20]

The Republican administration of Ronald Reagan, which took control of the White House in 1980, adopted an unabashedly hard-line approach to communism and to Soviet influence in the world. President Reagan restored the policy of containment and confrontation backed by a gigantic military buildup and a return to cold war operations. He made no serious attempt in his first term to restore political dialogue, instead referring to the Soviet Union as an "evil empire." His representatives assumed a similarly tough posture at the nuclear arms control talks in Geneva. Both as candidate and as president, Reagan was a vigorous proponent of using economic leverage to extract political concessions from the Soviets. This was reflected in the renewed focus on the enforcement of export controls, in improving compliance at home through the Department of Commerce and the Customs Service, and in enhancing the position of the Department of Defense in identifying strategic items to be put on the list of prohibited exports. He stopped short of giving the military sole jurisdiction over export control policy, as many right-wing conservatives advocated.[21]

Reagan also continued the policy of economic sanctions against the Soviet Union, but he shrewdly avoided the quagmire of agricultural-interest politics that had gotten his predecessor into domestic difficulty. He simply excluded grain sales from his ban on American trade with the USSR and focused on the more serious problems of curtailing economic credits and technology transfers. This approach did not lack strong critics both at home and abroad, especially when Reagan imposed extraterritorial and retroactive controls on exports of oil and gas technology. This action, made in response to the declaration of martial law in Poland and the Afghan conflict and later upheld by the U.S. judiciary, came like a bolt of lightning that nearly disrupted the Western alliance. Its members were startled by the character and the extent of the American interference in their national sovereignty. Reagan survived the ensuing political storm, but how badly his actions injured the unity of the alliance remains to be determined. At the very least, Europeans viewed his sanctions policy as insincere and based on a double standard, as it insisted that they curb the sale of industrial products and economic credits while the United States continued to sell grain to Russia.

Reagan's reelection in 1984 appeared to signal a new beginning in American–Soviet relations. Some of the harsh rhetoric of cold war that had characterized his first administration was now toned down, and he seemed prepared to engage in normal business diplomacy. At least that was the clear indication that Lionel H. Olmer, the Commerce Department's under secretary for international trade, conveyed to his Soviet counterpart when they met in Moscow in January 1985.[22] Olmer was the highest-ranking U.S. trade official to visit the Soviet Union since the Carter administration, and the visit was linked to a resumption of negotiations between the two superpowers on other fronts, most notably strategic weapons. Olmer's trip might have marginally improved American–Soviet trade prospects, but its more important objective was to lay the diplomatic foundation for a future meeting of the Joint U.S.–Soviet Commercial Commission, a body that had last met in December 1978, when détente was on the way out.

Whether the meeting of the Joint Commission would be a prelude to expanded trade was, of course, open to question. Whether the negotiators could insulate trade from superpower political and military rivalries was doubtful if the past historical record was any guide. One thing was certain: the two nations did have a great deal to discuss if they were to surmount the impediments to normal trade. These included restrictive export control policies, denial of Export-Import Bank financing, the granting of most-favored-nation status to the USSR, protection for patents, copyrights, and royalties, and the removal of discriminatory practices that excluded both nations' companies from bidding on the others' government contracts—in other words, the kinds of politico-economic questions that have stultified American–Soviet trade since the start of the Cold War. One additional roadblock needed to be cleared on the American side: whether U.S. firms would be willing to engage in trade, or hold back for fear of another reversal in policy. As one observer noted: "Some United States firms will never get over the commercial losses they suffered as a result of past American embargoes."[23]

Notes

ABBREVIATIONS

CED	Committee for Economic Development
CFEP Records	Commission [and Council] on Foreign Economic Policy, Records, Dwight D. Eisenhower Library
CG	Consultative Group
CHINCOM	China Committee
CIA	Central Intelligence Agency
COCOM	Coordinating Committee
Cong. Rec.	*Congressional Record*
DCR(NA)	Records of the Department of Commerce, National Archives
DCR(W)	Records of the Department of Commerce, Department of Commerce, Washington, D.C.
DDEL	Dwight D. Eisenhower Library
DDEP	Dwight D. Eisenhower Papers, Dwight D. Eisenhower Library
ECA	Economic Cooperation Administration
ERP	European Recovery Plan
Ex-Im Bank	Export-Import Bank
FOA	Foreign Operations Administration
FRUS	*Foreign Relations of the United States*
HICOG	High Commission, Germany
HSTL	Harry S. Truman Library
HSTP	Harry S. Truman Papers, Harry S. Truman Library
ICA	International Cooperation Administration (Foreign Operations Administration)
JCS	Joint Chiefs of Staff
JFKL	John F. Kennedy Library
JFKP	John F. Kennedy Papers, John F. Kennedy Library
LBJL	Lyndon B. Johnson Library
LBJP	Lyndon B. Johnson Papers, Lyndon B. Johnson Library
MDAC	Mutual Defense Advisory Committee
NIE	National Intelligence Estimates (Central Intelligence Agency)
NSC	National Security Council
NSF	National Security File
OEEC	Organization for European Economic Cooperation
OF	Office File
OHC	Oral History Collection
OIR	Office of Intelligence Research (Department of State)
OIT	Office of International Trade (Department of Commerce)

OSANSA   Office of the Special Assistant for National Security Affairs
PSF   President's Secretary's File
RG   [National Archives] Record Group
WHCF   White House Central File

CHAPTER ONE

1. The incident is recounted in Robert P. Browder, *The Origins of Soviet–American Diplomacy* (Princeton, 1953), 3.

2. The failure of Wilson's policy toward Russia is detailed in Linda Killen, *The Russian Bureau: A Case Study in Wilsonian Diplomacy* (Lexington, Ky., 1983).

3. Joan Hoff Wilson, "American Business and the Recognition of the Soviet Union," *Social Science Quarterly* 52 (June 1971): 349.

4. Ibid., 367. See also Mikhail V. Condoide, *American–Russian Trade: A Study of the Soviet Foreign Trade Monopoly* (Columbus, Oh., 1946), esp. chaps. 5–6; and Ernest C. Ropes, "American–Soviet Trade: 1917–1947," *Soviet Russia Today* 16 (November 1947): 14–15, 45–47.

5. See Edward J. Epstein, "The Riddle of Armand Hammer," *New York Times Magazine*, 29 November 1981, 112, 116, 118; and James K. Libbey, *Alexander Gumberg and Soviet–American Relations 1917–1933* (Lexington, Ky., 1977), passim.

6. U.S. Department of Commerce, Bureau of Foreign and Domestic Commerce, *Foreign Commerce and Navigation of the United States 1931* (Washington, D.C., 1932), table IV, p. 53.

7. The definitive studies of American–Soviet economic contacts prior to recognition are Floyd James Fithian, "Soviet–American Economic Relations, 1918–1933: American Business in Russia during the Period of Nonrecognition" (Ph.D. dissertation, University of Nebraska, 1964); and Antony C. Sutton, *Western Technology and Soviet Economic Development 1917 to 1930* (Stanford, Calif., 1968), esp. chaps. 17–18.

8. Robert Lansing, *War Memoirs* (Indianapolis, 1935), 343–44; Browder, *Origins of Soviet–American Diplomacy*, 16.

9. Philip S. Gillette, "American–Soviet Trade in Perspective," *Current History* 66 (October 1973): 159.

10. Wilson, "American Business and the Recognition of the Soviet Union," 366–67.

11. Ibid.

12. *FRUS, 1933*, 4 vols. (Washington, D.C., 1949–50), 2:805–14.

13. Ibid., 2:804. See also Wilson, "American Business and the Recognition of the Soviet Union," 365.

14. The bank's role is well delineated in Frederick C. Adams, *Economic Diplomacy: The Export-Import Bank and American Foreign Policy, 1934–1939* (Columbia, Mo., 1976), 98–128, 256.

15. *FRUS, The Soviet Union 1933–1939* (Washington, D.C., 1952), 66–67, 71–75, 79–81; Thomas R. Maddux, *Years of Estrangement: American Relations with the Soviet Union, 1933–1941* (Tallahassee, Fla., 1980), esp. chaps. 3–5.

16. Philip S. Gillette, "Recent Trends in Soviet Trade," *Current History* 67 (October 1974): 169; Roy Douglas, *From War to Cold War, 1942–1948* (New York, 1981), 179–86.

17. Edward M. Bennett, *Franklin D. Roosevelt and the Search for Security: American–Soviet Relations, 1933–1939* (Wilmington, Del., 1985), chaps. 6–7; Gillette, "American–Soviet Trade in Perspective," 159.

18. Maddux, *Years of Estrangement*, 94.

19. Ibid., 159–61.

20. Raymond H. Dawson, *The Decision to Aid Russia, 1941: Foreign Policy and Domestic Politics* (Chapel Hill, 1959), esp. chaps. 2–6.

21. Roosevelt, for example, unfroze $40 million of Soviet funds in the United States, and by failing to invoke the neutrality law against the Soviet Union, he insured that Vladivostock would remain open for U.S. shipping. See ibid., 122.

22. *New York Times*, 24 October, 8 November 1941; Warren F. Kimball, *The Most Unsordid Act: Lend-Lease, 1939–1941* (Baltimore, 1969), esp. chaps. 5–7.

23. Maddux, *Years of Estrangement*, 152; Robert Dallek, *Franklin D. Roosevelt and American Foreign Policy, 1932–1945* (New York, 1979), 292–96.

24. George C. Herring, Jr., *Aid to Russia, 1941–1946: Strategy, Diplomacy, the Origins of the Cold War* (New York, 1973), esp. chaps. 3–6; James M. Burns, *Roosevelt: The Soldier of Freedom 1940–1945* (New York, 1970), 110–15, 233–34, 248–49.

25. Some of the difficulties are recounted in John R. Deane, *The Strange Alliance: The Story of Our Efforts at Wartime Cooperation with Russia* (New York, 1947), and Robert H. Jones, *The Roads to Russia: United States Lend-Lease to the Soviet Union* (Norman, Okla., 1969).

26. U.S. Department of Commerce, Bureau of Foreign and Domestic Commerce, "United States Trade with Russia (U.S.S.R.) during the War Years," *International Reference Service Series* 2 (December 1945): 1–10; Leon Martel, *Lend-Lease, Loans, and the Coming of the Cold War: A Study of the Implementation of Foreign Policy* (Boulder, Colo., 1979), 51–52.

27. See, for example, Roosevelt's letter to Director Leo Crowley of the Foreign Economic Administration, 29 September 1944, in *Export Trade and Shipper*, 9 October 1944, 11–12; and John Abbink, "American Prosperity and Foreign Trade," radio transcript reprinted in *Beyond Victory: Program No. 138* (New York, 1946), unpaginated.

28. See, for example, William Diebold, Jr., "East–West Trade and the Marshall Plan," *Foreign Affairs* 26 (July 1948): 709–22; L. C. Boochaver, Jr., "The Significance and Development of East–West Trade," n.d., and Boochaver to Leon Herman, 24 February 1950, DCR(NA), RG 151, Bureau of Foreign and Domestic Commerce, Economic Files of the Soviet Bloc, Foreign Trade Policy, 13.123–28.

29. Diebold, "East–West Trade and the Marshall Plan," 709–22.

30. Thomas G. Paterson, "The Quest for Peace and Prosperity: International Trade, Communism, and the Marshall Plan," in *Politics and Policies of the Truman Administration,* ed. Barton J. Bernstein (Chicago, 1970), 78–79, 82, 85. See also Paterson, *Soviet–American Confrontation: Postwar Reconstruction and the Origins of the Cold War* (Baltimore, 1973).

31. See the printed proceedings of the Congress of American–Soviet Friendship, *American Industry Commemorates the Tenth Anniversary of American–Soviet Diplomatic Relations 1933–1943* (New York, 1943).

32. Ibid., from the Foreword.

33. Ibid. Similarly effusive declarations of amity and support came from RCA, Westinghouse, International Harvester, United Fruit Company, Grace Shipping Lines, Yale & Towne Manufacturing Company, Michigan Tool, General Machine Corporation, Atlas Electric Devices Company, and Hygrade Food Products Corporation, among others.

34. Ibid.

35. Ibid.

36. Ibid., from the Introduction.

37. The chairman of the institute was Wesley Clair Mitchell of Columbia University. "New Interest in the Soviet Union," *Economic Bulletin on the Soviet Union* 1 (December 1944): 1–3. See also William H. Mandel, "Russia—Our Biggest Postwar Market?" *Advertising and Selling,* May 1944, 29, 73–76; and William L. Batt, "Can We Do Business with Russia?" *Sales Management,* 15 October 1945, 202.

38. Eric Johnston, "A Business View of Russia," *Nation's Business* 32 (October 1944): 21–22.

39. Henry J. Kaiser, *American–Soviet Post-War Relations* (New York, 1944), 2–4.

40. "What Business with Russia?" *Fortune,* January 1945, 204. See also Donald Nelson's support for trade in consumer goods in *Business Week,* 22 January 1944, copy in DCR(NA), RG 151, Bureau of Foreign and Domestic Commerce, Economic Files (U.S.S.R.), File 14.80 (Credit: U.S.–Russia).

41. Ernest C. Ropes, "The Union of Soviet Socialist Republics as a Factor in World Trade," *World Economics* 3 (October–December 1944): 76–79, 81.

42. Ibid., 84–88.

43. Ernest C. Ropes, "Future Trade with Russia," *Clevelander,* November 1944, 9, 22. See also Ropes's remarks in "Prospects of Russian Trade with the West Coast," *Pacific Northwest Industry* 4 (June 1945): 134–38, and in the *New York Times,* 15 and 22 February 1945.

44. Ropes, "U.S.S.R. as a Factor in World Trade," 86.

45. S. Beryl Lusk, "Doing Business with Russia," *Soviet Russia Today* 16 (January 1948): 10–11.

46. Dean Acheson, "A Program for Restoring and Enlarging Our International Commerce," *Export Trade and Shipper,* 11 December 1944, 5–6.

47. National Council of American–Soviet Friendship, *U.S.A.–U.S.S.R.: Allies for Peace* (New York, 1945), 13, 20.

48. Ibid.

49. Henry A. Wallace, "Reconversion and Foreign Trade," *Foreign Commerce Weekly*, 2 June 1945, 4; Paterson, "The Quest for Peace and Prosperity," 88–89.

50. Amos E. Taylor, "Foreign Trade and the National Interest," *Foreign Commerce Weekly*, 27 January 1945, 38; Wallace Clark, "World Markets for American Goods," *Credit and Financial Management* 45 (August 1945): 6–8. See also United States Chamber of Commerce, *Postwar Trends in Foreign Trade of the United States* (Washington, D.C., 1947), 16–17.

51. See the *Chicago Herald American* article reprinted in the *Cong. Rec.*, 79 Cong., 1 sess., 91, pt. 12:A3517, and "What Business with Russia?" (n. 40 above), 152–56.

52. "What Business with Russia?" 156.

53. Ibid., 196; "Credits for Russia: I," *The Statist*, 3 February 1945, 99.

54. See *New York Times*, 18 July 1944, clipping in DCR(NA), RG 151, Bureau of Foreign and Domestic Commerce, Economic Files (U.S.S.R.), File 14.80 (Credit: U.S.–Russia).

55. "What Business with Russia?" 201; William L. White, *We Can and Must Trade with Russia* (New York, 1945), 7. See also "U.S. Trade with U.S.S.R. during Calendar Year '45," *Foreign Commerce Weekly*, 29 June 1946, 10, for support of the view that the United States could raise its imports above prewar levels.

56. "What Business with Russia?" 198.

57. V. P. Timoshenko, *Economic Background for the Postwar International Trade of the U.S.S.R.*, Pamphlet Series no. 5 (New York, 1945), 26.

58. Henry A. Wallace, "Expanding World Trade Key to Peace," *Commerce Magazine* 43 (March 1946): 28, 95–96.

59. *Wall Street Journal*, 10 April 1944; Ernest C. Ropes, "What the Russians Would Want Avoided in Credit Terms" (1945?), in DCR(NA), RG 151, Bureau of Foreign and Domestic Commerce, Economic Files, File 13.123 (U.S.S.R. Foreign Trade Policy).

60. Ernest C. Ropes, "Credits to Soviet Agencies in the United States: A Historical Review," reprinted in *Cong. Rec.*, 79 Cong., 1 sess., 91, pt. 11:2689–90; Ropes, "USSR—A Vast Postwar Market," *Soviet Russia Today* 14 (June 1945), 11.

61. As cited in Charles Prince, "The USSR's Role in International Finance," *Harvard Business Review* 25 (Autumn 1946): 124–25. Prince concluded that the fundamental objective of Soviet foreign trade was not imports or exports per se, "but only the monetary exchange needed to achieve the speedy technological, economic and industrial development of the USSR, preferably within the next Five Year Plan period, 1946–1950." Ibid., 125.

62. "Russia's Post-War Trade," *The Statist*, 14 July 1945, 614–16. Soviet interest in expanded trade with the West was expressed in 1944 in the semiofficial Moscow newspaper, *War and the Working Class*. See "Credits for Russia: I" (n. 53 above), 99, and "Russia as a Postwar Market," *U.S. News*, 30 March 1945, 19.

63. "What Business with Russia?" 202.

64. Ibid., 204.

65. Quoted in White, *We Can and Must Trade with Russia*, 3–4. See also New York University's Institute of Economic Affairs, "Living with Russia: II," *Economic Affairs* 4 (November 1946): 4, 8; and "The Prospects of Soviet–American Trade Relations," in the *Bulletin* of the Institute of International Finance, 27 August 1945, 1–2, for similar sentiments.

66. "Postwar Trade between the United States and the U.S.S.R.," *After the War* 3 (March 1945): 2.

67. Arthur Paul, "Problems in International Trade Relations," *Commercial and Financial Chronicle*, 18 July 1946, 357 (emphasis in original).

68. *Cong. Rec.*, 79 Cong., 1 sess., 91, pt. 13:A5736–37.

69. Ibid., 2 sess., 92, pt. 11:A3666–69.

70. Alexander Gerschenkron, *Economic Relations with the U.S.S.R.* (New York, 1945), 6, 14.

71. Herbert Feis, *American Trade Policy and Position* (New York, 1945), 8–9, 18, 23, 26.

72. For a representative sampling of the orthodox and the revisionist arguments on the origins of the Cold War, see John L. Gaddis, *The United States and the Origins of the Cold War, 1941–1947* (New York, 1972), and Walter La Feber, *America, Russia, and the Cold War, 1945–1966* (New York, 1967).

73. "What Business with Russia?" 204. See also Edwin W. Hullinger, "The Russians Are Tough," *Nation's Business* 34 (February 1946): 42–43, 104.

74. See W. Averell Harriman, *America and Russia in a Changing World* (New York, 1971), 42–43.

75. *FRUS, Diplomatic Papers, 1944*, 4 vols. (Washington, D.C., 1966), 4:951.

76. Harriman, *America and Russia in a Changing World*, 42.

77. Ibid., viii–ix.

78. Harry S. Truman, *Memoirs*, 2 vols. (Garden City, N.Y., 1955–56), 1:82.

79. Martel, *Lend-Lease, Loans, and the Coming of the Cold War*, chaps. 6–7.

80. On Potsdam and the reparations issue see *FRUS, The Conference of Berlin, 1945*, 2 vols. (Washington, D.C., 1960), passim; and Charles L. Mee, Jr., *Meeting at Potsdam* (New York, 1975), 244–45, 256–59, 272–73.

81. Cf. George F. Kennan, *Memoirs, 1929–1950* (Boston, 1967), 260.

82. Paterson, *Soviet–American Confrontation*, chap. 2, is definitive on the abortive loan.

83. Ibid.

84. Cf. A. W. De Porte, *Europe between the Superpowers* (New Haven, 1979), 106.

85. Telegram, George F. Kennan to State Department, 29 January 1945, HSTP, PSF, Subject File, Foreign Affairs: Russia.

86. J. Stalin, *Economic Problems of Socialism in the U.S.S.R.* (Moscow, 1952), 30, 35. For the continuity of Stalin's thinking on this point throughout the early Cold War years see CIA, Intelligence Memorandum no. 189, "Popular Reactions to Soviet Propaganda on the Current Economic Recession in the United States," 11 July 1949, HSTP, PSF, Subject File, Foreign Affairs: Russia;

telegram, Walter B. Smith to secretary of state, 5 August 1947, and Floyd Kohler to secretary of state, 10 February 1949, DCR(NA), RG 151, Bureau of Foreign and Domestic Commerce, Economic Files of the Soviet Bloc, File 13.123 (U.S.S.R. Foreign Trade Policy).

87. De Porte, *Europe between the Superpowers*, 106.

88. Gaddis, *U.S. and Origins of the Cold War*, pp. 282–352; La Feber, *America, Russia, and the Cold War*, 21–36.

89. Ben Hill Brown, 24 May 1975, HSTP, OHC.

90. "Russia as a Postwar Market" (n. 62 above), 19; "What Russia Is Seeking: Economic Clues to Actions," *U.S. News*, 9 November 1945, 20–21. See also "Russia's Trade Policy," *The Statist*, 8 June 1946, 532–34.

91. *New York Times*, 7 September 1946.

92. For Roosevelt's problems with Congress from 1937 through the war years see especially James T. Patterson, *Congressional Conservatism and the New Deal: The Growth of the Conservative Coalition in Congress, 1933–1939* (Lexington, Ky., 1967); Roland Young, *Congressional Politics in the Second World War* (New York, 1956); and Margaret Hinchey, "The Frustration of the New Deal Revival" (Ph.D. dissertation, University of Missouri, 1965).

93. This is the model used by James MacGregor Burns, *The Deadlock of Democracy* (Englewood Cliffs, N.J., 1963), which is a schematic convenience for describing a complex and often contradictory institution.

94. Even Vandenberg, a pre–Pearl Harbor isolationist who had been moved by the force of events to accept an internationalist foreign policy, separated that support from the strong presidential power that usually accompanied a strong foreign policy. See *The Private Papers of Senator Vandenberg*, ed. Arthur H. Vandenberg, Jr. (Boston, 1956), 67, 80, 527, 530, 535.

95. This list is meant to be illustrative rather than exhaustive.

96. See the revealing study by David R. Mayhew, *Party Loyalty among Congressmen: The Difference between Democrats and Republicans, 1947–1962* (Cambridge, Mass., 1966). His analysis of roll call votes demonstrates the influence of the conservative coalition, especially on domestic legislation. Besides Mayhew my profile is based on a close reading of David W. Reinhard, *The Republican Right since 1945* (Lexington, Ky., 1983); Robert A. Pastor, *Congress and the Politics of U.S. Foreign Economic Policy, 1929–1976* (Berkeley, Calif., 1980); and Gary W. Reichard, *The Reaffirmation of Republicanism* (Knoxville, 1975).

97. Mayhew, *Party Loyalty*.

98. See, for example, Hadley Arkes, *Bureaucracy, the Marshall Plan, and the National Interest* (Princeton, 1972), esp. chap. 5.

99. *Cong. Rec.*, 79 Cong., 1 sess., 91, pt. 12:A3459, A3517; pt. 11:A1524; 2 sess., 92, pt. 12:A4029, A4678.

100. Henry A. Wallace, "In Memorial of Franklin D. Roosevelt," Churchman Award Dinner Address, New York City, 4 June 1945, copy in Alfred Schindler Papers (HSTL).

101. Henry A. Wallace to Truman, 14 March 1946, DCR(W), OIT, Russia: Public Relations; Wallace to Truman, 15 March 1946, HSTP, PSF, Subject File:

Russia; Truman, *Memoirs*, 1:556; Henry A. Wallace, *Diary* (microfilm, Glen Rock, N.J., 1977), 561–63. Concerning the loan request, see Wallace to Truman, 23 July 1946, reprinted in "The Path to Peace," *New Republic*, 30 September 1946, 404.

102. Truman to Henry A. Wallace, 20 March; Wallace to Truman, 21 March; Truman to Walter B. Smith, 23 March 1946, all in HSTP, PSF, Subject File: Russia; Wallace to Leo H. O'Hare, 29 March 1946, DCR(NA), RG 40, File 82220.1. See also Willard Thorpe OHC (HSTL).

103. Richard M. Hippelheuser to Philip M. Hauser, 17 July 1946, Henry Wallace Papers (microfilm); Wallace to Truman, 23 July 1946, Schindler Papers (HSTL).

104. See Ernest C. Ropes, "Trade Prospects with Russia," *Commercial and Financial Chronicle*, 26 December 1946, 3355, 3373; *Cong. Rec.*, 79 Cong., 2 sess., 92, pt. 12:A4029; Truman, *Memoirs*, 2:552.

105. The Clifford memorandum, considered so explosive that Truman gathered all copies and kept them locked away, advised the United States to prepare for atomic and biological warfare because of Soviet aggressions encouraged by fear of capitalist encirclement. These Soviet aggressions would stop, he wrote, only if met by American counterpressure, both military and economic. See Clark Clifford, "American Relations with the Soviet Union," memorandum, 24 September 1946, HSTP, PSF, Subject File, Foreign Affairs: Russia.

106. George F. Kennan, "Comments on the document entitled 'American Relations with the Soviet Union,' " 16 September 1946, ibid.

107. Ibid.

108. Copy of Wallace's speech of 12 September 1946 in Wallace Papers (microfilm). Also, Henry Wallace, "The Way to Peace," *Vital Speeches*, 1 October 1946, 738–41; *New York Times*, 13 September 1946.

109. Margaret Truman, *Harry S. Truman* (New York, 1973), 317–18.

CHAPTER TWO

1. See *FRUS 1946*, 11 vols. (Washington, D.C., 1969–72), 1:1165–66; John L. Gaddis, *Strategies of Containment* (New York, 1982), 22–24.

2. *Cong. Rec.*, 80 Cong., 1 sess., 93, pt. 12:A2948–50.

3. Ernest C. Ropes, "American–Soviet Trade: 1917–1947," *Soviet Russia Today* 15–16 (November 1947): 14–15. See also Ropes, "Opportunities for Russian–American Trade Expansion," *Dun's Review* 55 (May 1947): 11–14, 52–58.

4. Stella K. Margold, *Let's Do Business with Russia* (New York, 1948), 208.

5. See "Soviets' Urgent Needs: Fuel, Food, and Production," *World Report*, 16 December 1947, 8–9.

6. See the reviews of Margold's book by Alexander Gerschenkron, *Annals of the American Academy of Political and Social Science* 262 (March 1949): 262, and Harry Schwartz, *New York Times*, 28 November 1948, 6.

7. J. Anthony Marcus, *The Real Russian Challenge* (New York, 1947), 1, 6–7, 11–12, 15, 17, 20.

8. Ibid., 27.

9. Ibid., 23–26.

10. *Cong. Rec.*, 80 Cong., 1 sess., 93, pt. 2:1647–48, 2054.

11. This was Senate J. Res. 87. See also for similar expressions House J. Res. 145, House Res. 379, and Senate J. Res. 72, in ibid., pt. 2:1673; pt. 9:10996; and pt. 8:10573.

12. Ibid., pt. 6:7493–97, 9289–90; pt. 12:A3267. The Pearl Harbor analogy is in ibid., 80 Cong., 2 sess., 94, pt. 10:A2169, and pt. 13:A4672–73.

13. See, for example, H.R. 4042 and S. 1653, in ibid., 80 Cong., 1 sess., 93, pt. 8:9921.

14. See memorandum of Under Secretary William L. Clayton, 28 May 1947, in *FRUS 1947*, 7 vols. (Washington, D.C., 1972–73), 3:235; Gaddis, *Strategies of Containment*, 66.

15. *Cong. Rec.*, 80 Cong., 1 sess, 93, pt. 9:10834–38, 10678–79, 11183; pt. 2:1024–25; pt. 3:3234; Thomas G. Paterson, *On Every Front: The Making of the Cold War* (New York, 1979), 59–62.

16. *Cong. Rec.*, 80 Cong., 1 sess., 93, pt. 9:11075–76, 11183.

17. Ibid., pt. 9:10678–79, 10826; 80 Cong., 2 sess., 94, pt. 3:3414; 94, pt. 6:7777; pt. 12:A4568–70.

18. Department of Commerce, OIT, "Secretary Harriman's Views on Trade with the U.S.S.R. and Her Satellites: Excerpts . . . on Interim Aid to Europe before the House Foreign Affairs Committee, Nov. 13, 1947," Dean Acheson Papers (HSTL), Political and Government File, Russia: 1947. See also Files of Under Secretary William C. Foster, 1946–48, "Russian Trade Folder," in DCR(NA), RG 40.

19. "Secretary Harriman's Views on Trade with the U.S.S.R.," Acheson Papers (HSTL).

20. "Statement of Under Secretary of Commerce William C. Foster before the House Interstate and Foreign Commerce Committee Relating to the Mundt Resolution on Exports to Russia," 1 December 1947, DCR(NA), RG 40, Files of Under Secretary William C. Foster.

21. See the remarks of Edward S. Mason in Mason OHC (HSTL), 17 July 1943, 32–33.

22. "Statement of Under Secretary Foster," 1 December 1947, DCR(NA), RG 40.

23. Act of 2 July 1940 (54 Stat. 714).

24. Thomas A. Wolf, *U.S. East–West Trade Policy* (Lexington, Mass., 1973), 47.

25. See Benjamin J. Cohen, "American Foreign Economic Policy: Some General Principles of Analysis," in *American Foreign Economic Policy*, ed. Benjamin J. Cohen (New York, 1968), 31–32.

26. "U.S. Prepares to Squeeze Soviet Trade," *U.S. News*, 27 May 1947, 14–15.

27. Geraldine S. De Puy to Charles Brokaw, 10 November 1947, DCR(W), OIT File, Trade Exports 21–2: Licensing, Russia.

28. See "A Report to the National Security Council (NSC) by the Secretary of

State on Undertakings on Export Control in East–West Trade," 3 May 1949, Appendix A ("A Report of the NSC," 17 December 1947), in NSC Meeting no. 46, HSTP, PSF, NSC Meetings File (cited hereafter as NSC Report, 17 December 1947).

29. See *Economics and World Power*, ed. William H. Becker and Samuel F. Wells, Jr. (New York, 1984), 335.

30. NSC Report, 17 December 1947.

31. NSC Report no. 46, 3 May 1949, HSTP, PSF, NSC Meetings File.

32. *Cong. Rec.*, 80 Cong., 2 sess., 94, pt. 2:1824–25; pt.3:3234–37; pt. 9:A249–50; pt. 10:A2169. For evidence of criticism both within and outside Congress see Harold E. Stassen to Truman, 18 March, and Max Sorenson to Truman, 23 March 1948, HSTP, OF 220–Misc.; and I. E. Ewing to Truman, 21 March 1948, OF 275A.

33. "Minutes of the Cabinet Meeting," 26 March 1948, Matthew J. Connelly Papers (HSTL), Cabinet Meetings, Set I.

34. David K. Bruce to Hon. Mary T. Norton, 27 April 1948, DCR(W), OIT File, Trade Exports 21–2: Licensing, Russia.

35. NSC Report no. 46, 3 May 1949, and Appendix B, "Statement of the Cabinet," 26 March 1948, HSTP, PSF, NSC Meetings File.

36. Ibid.

37. Ibid.; Becker and Wells, *Economics and World Power*, 347.

38. See Walker B. Smith to secretary of state, 10 May 1948, HSTP, PSF, Foreign Affairs File, Russia.

39. "Minutes of the Cabinet Meeting," 25 June 1948, Matthew J. Connelly Papers (HSTL), Cabinet Meetings, Set I.

40. Thomas C. Blaisdell, "Export Policy toward Eastern Europe," 12 August 1948, DCR(W), Thomas C. Blaisdell Papers, ECA: 1951.

41. NSC Report no. 46, 3 May 1949, HSTP, PSF, NSC Meetings File.

42. Ibid.

43. Geir Lundestad, *America, Scandinavia, and the Cold War, 1945–1949* (New York, 1980), 32.

44. *Washington Evening Star*, 15 August 1951, reprinted in *Cong. Rec.*, 82 Cong., 1 sess., 97, pt. 8:10568–69.

45. NSC Report no. 46, 3 May 1949, HSTP, PSF, NSC Meetings File.

46. Ibid.

47. Charles W. Sawyer to Adm. Sidney W. Souers, 31 May 1949; "Minutes of the 39th Meeting of the NSC," 5 May 1949, both in ibid.

48. U.S. Congress, Senate, Committee on Foreign Relations, *A Background Study on East–West Trade*, 89 Cong., 1 sess. (Washington, D.C., 1965), 4–5.

49. CIA, "Possibility of Direct Soviet Military Action during 1948–1949," 16 September 1948, HSTP, PSF, Intelligence File.

50. [George F. Kennan] "Mr. X," "The Sources of Soviet Conduct," *Foreign Affairs* 25 (July 1947): 566–82.

51. The transcript of Swingle's remarks of 25 January 1949 is to be found appended to the memorandum of George L. Bell to William S. Swingle, 3 February 1949, DCR(W), OIT File, Export Advisory Committee Folder. See also

Charles A. Frank to George L. Bell, 28 April 1949, ibid., OIT File, R–Procedure Subcommittee.

52. Unidentified naval attaché, "Soviet Dependence on the West, Its Nature and Implications," 21 September 1949, DCR(NA), RG 151, Bureau of International Programs, Regional Economies, Export Control 12,000.

53. Ibid.

54. Ibid.

55. Nathan Ostroff, "A Summary and Explanation of the New Export Control Law," *Export Trader and Shipper*, 21 March 1949, 19–20, 45–46.

56. U.S. Congress, House, Committee on Banking and Currency, *Export Control Act of 1949*, Hearings . . . on H.R. 1661, 81 Cong., 1 sess. (Washington, D.C., 31 January–2 February 1949), 1.

57. Ibid., 6–7. In 1962 Congress expanded the scope of the Export Control Act to include items of economic significance to the Soviet Union and its satellites. See Senate Committee on Foreign Relations, *Background Study on East–West Trade*, 38.

58. Ibid., 38–39.

59. CIA Intelligence Memorandum no. 174, 31 May 1949, HSTP, PSF, Intelligence Files, CIA Memos: 1949. See also "Russia's Secret Source of Dollars," *U.S. News*, 4 February 1949, 24–25.

60. See, for example, "Examples of Illegal Export from Western Germany to the East," HICOG, Frankfurt 1553, to Department of State, 15 November 1950; and the use of Soviet pressure on Austria, in telegram, Charles Yost to secretary of state, 1 September 1948, DCR(NA), RG 151, Bureau of International Programs, Economic Files, Soviet Bloc: 83.111 and 5–13104.

61. In 1950 the CIA concluded: "In view of Sweden's attitude on neutrality and the importance it attaches to its trade with Eastern Europe, there is only a remote possibility that Sweden will join with other Western countries in parallel action controlling the export of strategic materials." CIA, "Current International Positions of Sweden," 28 August 1950, HSTP, PSF, Intelligence File, CIA Reports.

62. Dean Acheson, "Memorandum of Conversation of NSC Meeting," 1 September 1950, Dean Acheson Papers (HSTL), Memorandum of Conversations File: 1950.

63. Department of State, OIR Report no. 4998, "Soviet Internal Situation: An Analysis of the Thesis That Soviet Internal Weaknesses Constitute the Determining Factors in Current Soviet Foreign Policy," 1 July 1949, Matthew J. Connelly Papers (HSTL), PSF, Subject File: Russia.

64. Charles Sawyer to James S. Lay, Jr., 25 April 1950; "Report to the NSC on Export Controls and Security Policy," 26 April 1950, HSTP, PSF, NSC Files.

65. Ibid.

66. "Report . . . on Export Controls and Security Policy," 26 April 1950; "Minutes of the 56th Meeting of the NSC," 4 May 1950, both in ibid.

67. CIA, Intelligence Memorandum no. 318, "Importance of Strategic Exports in East–West Trade," 8 August 1950, HSTP, PSF, Intelligence Files, CIA Memos.

68. Ibid.

69. Nicholas Spulber, "Effects of the Embargo on Soviet Trade," *Harvard Business Review* 30 (November 1952): 122–25.

CHAPTER THREE

1. *Cong. Rec.*, 81 Cong., 2 sess., 96, pt. 8:11293–95; pt. 17:A6815–16. For similar sentiments see pt. 1:818–26; pt. 17:A6760; pt. 18:A6911–12.

2. Ibid., pt. 18:A7733–34; pt. 9:13763–65. See also pt. 17:A6234–35.

3. *New York Times*, 19 September 1950.

4. Frank L. Howley, "How Big Is Russia's Bluff?" *Nation's Business* 38 (December 1950): 29–30, 72–74; Alf M. Landon, "Our Confused Foreign Policy," *Commercial and Financial Chronicle*, 25 May 1950, 2160, 2185–86; Melchior Polyi, "Fool's Paradise in Liquidation," ibid., 31 August 1950, 801, 818–19. See also Harold E. Stassen, "Our Policy toward Russia," ibid., 17 August 1950, 626, 650–51.

5. Herbert Hoover, "Reorganize United Nations without Russia," *Commercial and Financial Chronicle*, 4 May 1950, 1849, 1864 (emphasis in original); Lucius D. Clay, "Foreign Trade and National Preparedness," ibid., 9 November 1950, 178, 185. See also A. W. Zelomek, "International Trade in a Defense Economy," ibid., 19 October 1950, 1494, 1504–5; and J. Anthony Marcus to Dr. John R. Steelman, 15 February 1950, HSTP, OF 220, Misc.: 1950.

6. See Republican Charles A. Wolverton's House Res. no. 831, dated 29 August 1950, in *Cong. Rec.*, 81 Cong., 2 sess., 96, pt. 17:A6234–35.

7. The Wherry Amendment was initially attached to the 1950 McCarran Internal Security Bill, but later was withdrawn. See ibid., pt. 11:1610–11.

8. "Minutes of the Cabinet Meeting," 15 September 1950, Matthew J. Connelly Papers (HSTL), Set I.

9. Truman to Clarence Cannon, 20 September 1950, HSTP, OF 426 (1949–50).

10. Ibid.

11. See U.S. Congress, House, Committee on Foreign Affairs, *Control of Exports by U.S. and Cooperating Nations to Nations Threatening Our Security, Including U.S.S.R.*, Report no. 703, 82 Cong., 1 sess. (Washington, D.C., 16 July 1951), 6.

12. U.S. Congress, Senate, Committee on Foreign Relations, *A Background Study on East–West Trade*, 89 Cong., 1 sess. (Washington, D.C., 1965), 40.

13. See Dean Acheson to Truman, 10 July; J. Howard McGrath to Truman, 30 July; James W. Webb to Truman, 20 November; and Truman to John Snyder, 20 November 1951, HSTP, OF 275A.

14. See "Draft Statement by President," 14 June; and George Elsey to Charles Murphy, 15 June 1951, both in ibid.

15. "Report to the NSC by the Executive Secretary on Export Controls and Security Policy," 21 August 1950, HSTP, PSF, NSC Meeting no. 66.

16. Ibid.

17. Ibid.

18. Ibid.

19. Ibid.

20. Ibid.

21. Ibid.

22. Ibid.

23. Thomas C. Blaisdell, "Reorientation of Our International Trade Policy," 22 August 1950, Thomas C. Blaisdell Papers, DCR(W), Commercial Policy, 1948–50.

24. "Report to the NSC ... on Export Controls and Security Policy," 21 August 1950, HSTP, PSF, NSC Meeting no. 66.

25. U.S. Department of State, "Memorandum of Conversation," 30 October 1950, Dean Acheson Papers (HSTL), Political and Governmental File.

26. Ibid.

27. Exports to Finland and Yugoslavia continued to be administered separately from those destined for the Soviet bloc countries.

28. "Memorandum for the NSC: Revised Draft Statement of Policy on East–West Trade," 24 November 1950, HSTP, PSF, NSC Meeting no. 72.

29. Charles A. Frank to George L. Bell, 28 April 1949, DCR(W), OIT File, R–Procedure Subcommittee. Also, Blaisdell, "Reorientation of Our International Trade Policy," 22 August 1950, Blaisdell Papers, Commercial Policy, 1948–50.

30. U.S.–Yugoslav relations in this period are discussed in John C. Campbell, *Tito's Separate Road* (New York, 1967), 15–16, 18, 20–21; and *East-Central Europe under the Communists: Yugoslavia*, ed. Robert F. Byrnes (New York, 1957), 23–26.

31. Wayne S. Vucinich, *Contemporary Yugoslavia* (Berkeley, Calif., 1969), 169–70.

32. *New York Times*, 10 July, 28 November, 9–10 December 1948; 26 March, 30 August, 9, 14 September, 11 October, 4 November 1949; 10, 12, 18, 25, 30 November, 14 December 1950.

33. *Cong. Rec.*, 81 Cong., 1 sess., 95, pt. 9:11750, 11762, 11781, 11883, 12164; Robert S. Allen and William V. Shannon, "Why Johnson Was Fired," *New Republic*, 25 September 1950, 11–12.

34. Ibid.

35. The text of the president's letter is in U.S. Department of State, *Bulletin*, 11 December 1950, 937–40. In December 1949 George V. Allen, the new ambassador to Yugoslavia, told the press that the president had included Yugoslavia within the American security sphere. *New York Times*, 24 December 1949.

36. *Cong. Rec.*, 81 Cong, 2 sess., 96, pt. 1:1280; pt. 2:1795; pt. 6:7416; pt. 12:16430, 16542.

37. These were the votes on the bills initially before the two houses. Because of amendments the bills were not identical and were sent to conference. The bill from the conference was accepted without a recorded vote. See ibid., pt. 12:16402–3, 16547, 16738–42, 16763, 17076.

38. Despite the president's action periodic attempts were made in Congress to cut down or cut off the flow of aid to Tito's regime. Congresswoman Edna Kelly of Brooklyn, who had voted for the original food relief bill in 1950, thereafter

led in such attempts year after year as the House considered the annual foreign aid legislation. Military aid to Yugoslavia was terminated in 1957. See U.S. Congress, House, Committee on Foreign Affairs, *The Mutual Security Program*, 82 Cong., 1 sess. (Washington, D.C., 2 July 1951), 109–11, and U.S. Congress, Senate, Committee on Foreign Relations, *Mutual Security Act of 1952*, 82 Cong., 2 sess. (Washington, D.C., 1952), 384–87.

39. Philip C. Jessup to James S. Lay, Jr., 16 February 1951, HSTP, PSF, NSC Meetings File, NSC Meeting no. 84.

40. CIA, "Vulnerability of the Soviet Bloc to Economic Warfare," 19 February 1951, NIE–22, in ibid.

41. ECA, "Trade of the Free World with the Soviet Bloc," 21 February 1951, in ibid.

42. Ibid. See also "A Report to the NSC by the Secretary of State on U.S. Policies and Programs in the Economic Field Which May Affect the War Potential of the Soviet Bloc," 12 February 1951, NSC Memorandum no. 104; and JCS, "Memorandum for the Secretary of Defense," 20 February 1951, both in ibid.

43. CIA, "Vulnerability of the Soviet Bloc," 19 February 1951.

44. JCS, "Memorandum for the Secretary of Defense," 20 February 1951. See also Willard Thorpe OHC (HSTL), January 1978, 220–22.

45. ECA, "Trade of the Free World," 21 February 1951; "A Report to the NSC by the Secretary of State," 12 February 1951.

46. "A Report to the NSC by the Secretary of State," 12 February 1951; see also A. W. De Porte, *Europe between the Superpowers* (New Haven, 1979), 156–58.

47. ECA, "Trade of the Free World," 21 February 1951; "A Report to the NSC by the Secretary of State," 12 February 1951.

48. "A Report to the NSC by the Secretary of State," 12 February 1951.

49. "Statement of Policy by the NSC on Export Control Policy toward the Soviet Union and Its Eastern European Satellites," 21 February 1951, in HSTP, PSF, NSC Meetings File, Meeting no. 84.

50. *Cong. Rec.*, 82 Cong., 1 sess., 93, pt. 1:417, 424.

51. Dean Acheson, *Present at the Creation* (New York, 1960), 560; Gaddis Smith, *Dean Acheson* (New York, 1972), 380.

52. Smith, *Dean Acheson*. See also "A Report to the National Security Council by the Secretary of State on East–West Trade," 30 October 1950, Matthew J. Connelly Papers (HSTL), PSF, NSC Meetings.

53. See "Staff Study by the Special Committee on East–West Trade on NSC Determinations under PL 843, Sec. 1304," n.d., and "A Report to the NSC by the Executive Secretary on NSC Determinations under PL 843, Sec. 1304," 21 December 1950, both in HSTP, PSF, NSC Meetings.

54. James P. Kem to Truman, 9 March 1951, HSTP, OF 220.

55. Ibid. See also *Washington Star*, 11 March 1951.

56. *Cong. Rec.*, 82 Cong., 2 sess., 98, pt. 1:226–27; Acheson, *Present at the Creation*, 560, 634; Smith, *Acheson*, 380, 382.

57. Loring K. Macy to Thomas C. Blaisdell, 4 June 1951, Blaisdell Papers, DCR(W).

58. NSC, "Draft of Letter to Senator Kem," n.d.; James S. Lay, Jr., to Truman, 19 March 1951, both in HSTP, OF 220.

59. House Committee on Foreign Affairs, *Control of Exports by U.S. and Cooperating Nations*, 7.

60. "Statement by the President," 2 June 1951, HSTP, PSF, Bill File.

61. "A Report to the NSC by the Executive Secretary on NSC Determinations under Section 1302," 8 June 1951; NSC, "Report of the Senior Staff and Special Committee on East–West Trade," 13 June 1951, both in HSTP, PSF, NSC Meetings.

62. *Cong. Rec.*, 82 Cong., 1 sess., 97, pt. 6:8336–40.

63. House Committee on Foreign Affairs, *Control of Exports by U.S. and Cooperating Nations*, 1–2.

64. Ibid., 10–11.

65. Ibid.

66. Statement of Loring K. Macy before the House Committee on Foreign Affairs, "Export Controls for Security Purposes," n.d., copy in Blaisdell Papers, DCR(W), ECA–Dept. of Commerce File.

67. Willard Thorpe OHC (HSTL), 120–22.

68. House Committee on Foreign Affairs, *Control of Exports by U.S. and Cooperating Nations*, 16–17.

69. "A Resolution of the Presidium of the Supreme Soviet of the U.S.S.R.," 6 August 1951, HSTP, Subject File, Truman–Shvernik Exchange; Dean Acheson to Truman, 6 August 1951, both in HSTP, OF 220.

70. Shvernik, "Resolution of the Presidium." See also "Report from the Eastern European Section for the Week Ending Aug. 8, 1951," DCR(NA), RG 151, Bureau of International Programs, Regional Economies, 13, 120F.

71. Jack K. McFall to Frederick J. Lawton, 16 October 1951, HSTP, White House Bill File.

72. *Cong. Rec.*, 82 Cong., 1 sess., 97, pt. 7:9714–15.

73. Ibid., pt. 9:11357–58.

74. "East–West Trade," *Fortune*, August 1951, 68–69.

75. Roger W. Jones to William J. Hopkins, 22 October 1951, HSTP, White House Bill File.

76. Acheson, *Present at the Creation*, 634.

77. *Cong. Rec.*, 82 Cong., 2 sess., 98, pt. 1:226–27; *New York Times*, 13, 14, 17 January 1952.

78. Ralph Parker, "International Economic Conference," *New World Review*, June 1952, 40–46; "The Economic Conference in Moscow," *Newsletter from behind the Iron Curtain*, 9 April 1952, 58–63.

79. *New York Times*, 5, 6 April 1952; "Russia's Latest Twist in 'Cold War,' " *U.S. News*, 18 April 1952, 40, 42–45; "Inside Moscow: An Interview with A. Wilfred May," ibid., 25 April 1952, 19–22, 24. See also Dean Acheson to U.S. Embassy, London, 22 October; U.S. Embassy, London, to secretary of state, 26 October; and U.S. Embassy, Moscow, to secretary of state, 6 November 1951, all in DCR(NA), RG 151, Economic Files (U.S.S.R.), 1910–54, File 13, 123–128, Foreign Trade Policy.

80. *New York Times*, 17 April 1952.

81. Ibid., 30 March, 6 April 1952. See also "Speech by M. V. Nesterov," *New Times*, Supplement, 5 April 1952, 1–8.

82. *Cong. Rec.*, 82 Cong., 2 sess., 98, pt. 9:A2308–9.

83. *New York Times*, 29 May 1952.

84. *Cong. Rec.*, 82 Cong., 2 sess., 98, pt. 5:6146–49, 6821, 6838–39.

85. Ibid., pt. 5:6822–49.

86. Department of State, "Memorandum of Conversation," 16 June 1952, Dean Acheson Papers (HSTL), Political and Governmental File.

CHAPTER FOUR

1. See the verbatim transcript of the meeting in DDEP, Ann Whitman File, Cabinet Series.

2. My thinking on Eisenhower's presidency has been influenced by Robert A. Divine, *Eisenhower and the Cold War* (New York, 1981), 22–23; Phillip G. Henderson, "Advice and Decision: The Eisenhower NSC Reappraised," in *The Presidency and National Security Policy*, ed. R. Gordon Hoxie (New York, 1984), 152–86; and Fred I. Greenstein, *The Hidden-Hand Presidency* (New York, 1984), 106–13. For Eisenhower's abhorrence of nuclear war see *Public Papers of the Presidents: Dwight D. Eisenhower, 1953* (Washington, D.C., 1960), 817.

3. U.S. Congress, Senate, Committee on Foreign Relations, *A Background Study on East–West Trade*, 89 Cong., 1 sess. (Washington, D.C., 1965), 6; Burton I. Kaufman, *Trade and Aid: Eisenhower's Foreign Economic Policy, 1953–1961* (Baltimore, 1982), 59; Herbert S. Parmet, *Eisenhower and the American Crusades* (New York, 1972), 276–77.

4. Cf. Senate Committee on Foreign Relations, *Background Study on East–West Trade*, 6–7; U.S. Department of Commerce, "East–West Trade Trends," in *Fourth Report to Congress on the Battle Act* (Washington, D.C., 1954), 26.

5. *New York Times*, 26 August 1951; Michael L. Hoffman, "Problems of East–West Trade," *International Conciliation* 511 (January 1957): 280–81.

6. "Congressional Battle Axe," *The Economist*, 25 August 1951, 432.

7. Quoted in Hoffman, "Problems of East–West Trade," 281.

8. *New York Times*, 29 March, 5, 12, 17 April 1953.

9. See, for example, the debate between A. Wilfred May and Scott Nearing reprinted in A. Wilfred May, "Can We Do Business with Malenkov?" *Commercial and Financial Chronicle*, 19 March 1953, 1208–9. See also *New York Times*, 1, 7 June, 28 September, 14, 20 December 1953.

10. *New York Times*, 7 May 1953; see also 9 May, 3 August.

11. Ibid., 20 March 1953; see also *Public Papers of the Presidents: Dwight D. Eisenhower, 1953* (Washington, D.C., 1960), 104, 187–88.

12. U.S. Congress, House, Committee on Foreign Affairs, *East–West Trade: Hearings*, 83 Cong., 2 sess. (Washington, D.C., 1954), 21–23.

13. Townsend Hoopes, *The Devil and John Foster Dulles* (Boston, 1973), 162.

14. "U.S. Foreign Economic Policy," *Fortune*, August 1951, 71, 153–54.

15. Kaufman, *Trade and Aid*, esp. chap. 3.

16. Dwight D. Eisenhower, *The White House Years 1953–1956: Mandate for Change* (New York, 1963), 357.

17. Clarence B. Randall, *A Creed for Free Enterprise* (Boston, 1952), 147, 156–57.

18. See "New Edition of the Battle Act," *The Economist*, 24 September 1953, which was forwarded to the Department of Commerce by Frank Taylor, the American attaché in London, in DCR(NA), RG 151, Bureau of International Programs, Regional Economies, 13–123.

19. Clarence B. Randall to CFEP, 6 January 1954, DDEP, Records of the President's Commission on Foreign Economic Policy, 1950–54, Policy Papers Series. (As a result of the recommendations of the commission, Eisenhower issued an executive order in December 1954 establishing a wholly distinct organization, the Council on Foreign Economic Policy, to coordinate and develop international economic policy. Since the records of both the commission and the council are grouped together, they are cited collectively in the notes as CFEP Records for the sake of brevity.)

20. CFEP, *Report to the President and the Congress, January 1954*, copy in DDEP, Ann Whitman File, Administrative Series; *Staff Papers Presented to the U.S. Commission on Foreign Economic Policy* (Washington, D.C., 1954), 450; *New York Times*, 7, 24 January 1954.

21. CFEP, *Minority Report*, 30 January 1954, copy in DDEP, WHCF, OF 116–M.

22. "Preliminary Department of Defense Views on Randall Report," 1954, ibid., WHCF, OF 116–J–10; Department of Defense memorandum, "Decreasing Reliance on Markets in the Soviet Bloc," n.d. [1953?], CFEP Records, Policy Papers Series.

23. "Preliminary Comments by Secretary of Labor," 9 February 1954, DDEP, WHCF, OF 116–J–10.

24. *New York Times*, 31 March 1954.

25. Ibid. For congressional discontent see ibid., 3, 26 January 1954.

26. Ibid., 13 January, 2, 27 February, 6 March 1954.

27. See Department of Commerce, press release, 9 April 1954, DCR(NA), RG 151, Bureau of International Programs, Regional Economies, 13, 120F.

28. "Outline of Principal Points to be Made in Personal Communication from the President to the Prime Minister Churchill Concerning U.K. Proposed Revision of East–West Trade Controls," 10 March 1954, DDEP, WHCF, OSANSA Records, NSC Series, Policy Papers Series. See also *New York Times*, 7 March, 3 April 1954.

29. "United Kingdom's East–West Trade Proposal, with attachments," 9 March 1954; "Outline Re: Revisions of East–West Trade Controls," 10 March 1954, DDEP, OSANSA Records, NSC Series, Policy Papers Subseries.

30. See "Disagreed Items in COCOM Negotiations," 11 June; James S. Lay, Jr., to NSC, 11 June; and "East–West Trade Controls," 30 June 1954, all in ibid.

31. *New York Times*, 23 July 1954.

32. Nathan F. Twining to secretary of defense, 15 June; James S. Lay, Jr., to NSC, 16 June 1954, both in ibid. Emphasis mine. For a similar view by Adm. Arthur Radford see *New York Times*, 12 July 1954.

33. *Washington Post*, 2 April 1954, in DCR(NA), RG 151, Bureau of International Programs, Regional Economies, 13, 120F.

34. "Stassen Announces Revisions in Battle Act Embargo List," FOA *Bulletin*, 26 August 1954, 1–4, in ibid.

35. U.S. Department of Commerce, "Revision of Strategic Trade Controls," *Fifth Report to Congress on Operations of the Mutual Defense Assistance Act of 1951* (Washington, D.C., 1954), 20–23.

36. *New York Times*, 30 August 1954.

37. "U.S.–Soviet Trade: Opening Wedge," *Time*, 30 August 1954, 65; *New York Times*, 20 October 1954.

38. *Izvestia*, for the first time, was cool to the easing of the embargo on strategic goods and did not forecast a huge increase in East–West trade. This prompted one close observer of Soviet economic affairs to conclude that Russia would be satisfied with nothing less than complete abolition of export controls. *New York Times*, 12 September 1954, copy in DCR(NA), RG 151, Bureau of International Programs, Regional Economies, 13, 123.

39. *New York Times*, 28 November 1954, copy in ibid.; CFEP, "Summary and Review of Economic Defense Policy," 20 January 1955, CFEP Records, Policy Papers Series.

40. "Minutes of the 3rd, 4th, and 5th Meetings of the CFEP," 11, 21, 25 January 1955; Paul H. Cullen to CFEP, 23 March 1955, in CFEP Records, Policy Papers Series.

41. *New York Times*, 19, 20 January 1955.

42. Joseph M. Dodge to Robert Amory, Jr., 7 February 1955, CFEP Records, Policy Papers Series.

43. Robert Amory, Jr., to Joseph M. Dodge, 10 February 1955, ibid.

44. "Minutes of the 13th Meeting of the CFEP," 22 March; Steering Committee Task Force on Economic Defense Policy to CFEP, 23 March; Paul H. Cullen to Joseph M. Dodge, 29 March 1955, all in ibid.

45. "Minutes of the 15th Meeting of the CFEP," 5 April; Thorsten V. Kalijarvi to CFEP, with Appendix A, 10 June 1955, both in ibid.

46. Paul H. Cullen to CFEP, 24 March; Thorsten V. Kalijarvi to CFEP, 8 July; Cullen to CFEP, 13 July; Cullen to Joseph M. Dodge, 18 July 1955, all in ibid.

47. "Minutes of the 25th Meeting of the CFEP," 26 July; Paul H. Cullen to CFEP, 29 July 1955, both in ibid.

48. "Draft Report: East–West Trade," 25 September; CFEP, "Recommendation Concerning U.S. Position on Trade," 4 October; Paul H. Cullen to Gabriel Hauge, 10 October 1955, all in ibid.

49. This was contingent upon the attorney general's reversing his opinion of 21 February 1955, that such action was in violation of P.L. 480. Ultimately, upon

the advice of Gerald Morgan, the president's special counsel, CFEP decided not to approach the attorney general, because there seemed to be little likelihood of a favorable decision. Cf. "Minutes of the 29th Meeting of the CFEP," 25 October 1955, ibid. The politics of American–Soviet agricultural trade relations are discussed in Chris Hensley, "East–West Trade: Soviet–American Agricultural Trade Relations during the Eisenhower Administration" (seminar paper, College of William and Mary, 1982).

50. CFEP, "Recommendations Concerning U.S. Position on Trade," 4 October 1955, CFEP Records, Policy Papers Series.

51. Ibid.

52. True D. Morse to Herbert Hoover, Jr., 4 August 1955, ibid.

53. Memorandum to CFEP chairman, 5 October 1955, ibid.

54. "Minutes of the 28th Meeting of the CFEP," 11 October 1955, ibid.

55. Thorsten V. Kalijarvi to CFEP chairman, 17 October; Gabriel Hauge to John Foster Dulles, 17 October; CFEP, "Recommendations Concerning U.S. Position on Trade Aspects of Agenda Item on East–West Contacts for Discussion at Forthcoming Four Power Foreign Ministers' Meeting," 17 October; Paul H. Cullen to CFEP, 20 October 1955, all in ibid.

56. It was generally agreed beforehand that as a precondition of relaxing the strategic trade control system the USSR would have to take steps to reduce political tensions. See CFEP Drafting Group, "East–West Trade Controls in Relation to the Forthcoming Foreign Ministers' Meeting," 22 September 1955, ibid. See also *New York Times*, 4 November 1955, copy in DCR(NA), RG 151, Bureau of International Programs, Regional Economies, 13, 120F.

57. Herbert Hoover, Jr., to Sinclair Weeks, 3 December; Hoover to Joseph M. Dodge, 3 December 1955, both in CFEP Records, Policy Papers Series.

58. For the continuity in Eisenhower's view of the Soviets see Eisenhower to Lewis Douglas, 28 March 1955, DDEP, Diary Series; Eisenhower to Douglas, 20 January 1956, CFEP Records, Office of the Chairman, Dodge Series, Correspondence Subseries. See also Kaufman, *Trade and Aid*, 66.

59. *New York Times*, 20 November 1955, copy in DCR(NA), RG 151, Bureau of International Programs, Regional Economies, 13, 120F.

60. See Department of Commerce, Export Policy Staff, to chairman, Operating Committee, 3 January 1955, and Thorsten V. Kalijarvi to Clarence B. Randall, 23 July 1956, both in CFEP Records, Policy Papers Series.

61. An excellent brief discussion of the Soviet economic offensive in the Third World and the Eisenhower administration's reaction is contained in Kaufman, *Trade and Aid*, 58–68.

62. Ibid.

63. Sinclair Weeks to Herbert Hoover, Jr., 23 November; Hoover to Weeks, 3 December 1955, both in CFEP Records, Policy Papers Series.

64. See Thorsten V. Kalijarvi to Clarence B. Randall, 23 July 1956, ibid.

65. Joseph M. Dodge to Herbert Hoover, Jr., 13 January 1956, ibid. Emphasis mine.

66. Herbert Hoover, Jr., to Joseph M. Dodge, 16 January 1956, ibid. See also Hoopes, *The Devil and John Foster Dulles*, 313–14.

67. Thorsten V. Kalijarvi to Clarence B. Randall, 13, 18 July 1956, CFEP Records, Policy Papers Series. Randall replaced Joseph M. Dodge as CFEP chairman after the latter's return to private life in the spring of 1956.

68. *New York Times*, 1, 4, 6, 8 November 1956.

CHAPTER FIVE

1. Cf. Walter LaFeber, *America, Russia, and the Cold War, 1945–1966* (New York, 1967), 151; David B. Capitanchik, *The Eisenhower Presidency and American Policy* (London, 1969), 59.

2. In fact trade to China by non-bloc countries had increased from 2,357,000 gross tons in 1952 to 4,354,000 gross tons in 1954, or from seventy-six to eighty-two percent of the volume of shipping arriving in China. See the memorandum "Ocean Traffic to Communist China," 22 March; Vice-Adm. A. C. Davis to chairman, CFEP, 23 March; and Allen W. Dulles to chairman, CFEP, 22 March 1955, all in DDEP, CFEP Records, Policy Papers Series.

3. "Briefing Paper for CFEP," 3 April 1956, ibid.

4. Ibid.; also James S. Lay, Jr., to chairman, CFEP, 28 December 1955, ibid. See also Gabriel Hauge to John Foster Dulles, 17 October; CFEP enclosure, "Recommendations Concerning U.S. Position on Trade Aspects of Agenda Item . . . for Discussion at Forthcoming Four Power Foreign Ministers' Meeting"; Paul H. Cullen to Hauge, 18 October; Cullen to Herbert V. Prochnow, 29 December 1955; memorandum for Joseph M. Dodge, n.d. [January 1956?]; and Dodge to Dillon Anderson, 13 January 1956, all in ibid.

5. CFEP established an interdepartmental committee composed of Gordon Gray (Defense), Harold C. McClellan (Commerce), Adm. Walter S. DeLany (ICA), and Herbert V. Prochnow (State), chairman. "Minutes of the 36th Meeting of the CFEP," 12 January 1956, in ibid.

6. Herbert V. Prochnow to Joseph M. Dodge, 11 January 1956, in ibid.

7. Joseph M. Dodge to Paul H. Cullen, 26 January; Cullen to Dodge, 1 February; James S. Lay, Jr., to Dodge, 1 February; and Cullen to Maurice J. Williams, 27 January 1956, all in ibid. See also Dodge to CFEP, 26 January 1956, in ibid.

8. CIA, "Gains in Trade Expressed in Dollars Which Might Follow from Virtual Elimination of All Controls on Trade with the Bloc," n.d. [1956?], DDEP, CFEP Records, Office of the Chairman, Dodge Series, Subject Subseries. For the Commerce Department's concurrence with this analysis see Harold C. McClellan to Joseph M. Dodge, 30 January 1956, in DDEP, CFEP Records, Policy Papers Series.

9. CIA, "Gains in Trade"; and Robert Amory, Jr., to Joseph M. Dodge, 30 January 1956, DDEP, CFEP Records, Policy Papers Series.

10. "Briefing Paper for CFEP," 3 April; Herbert Hoover, Jr., to Joseph M. Dodge, 10 February 1956, both in ibid.

11. "Briefing Paper for CFEP"; "Minutes of the 38th Meeting of the CFEP," 14 February; Paul H. Cullen to CFEP, 2 March; and "Minutes of the 39th

Meeting of the CFEP," 16 March 1956, all in ibid. See also Cullen to Edward W. Galbraith, 13 March 1956, in ibid.

12. Harold C. McClellan to Joseph M. Dodge, 20, 30 March; Paul H. Cullen to CFEP, 24, 30 March; and "Briefing Paper for CFEP," 3 April 1956, all in ibid.

13. Joseph M. Dodge to Herbert V. Prochnow, 27 February 1956, DDEP, CFEP Records, Office of the Chairman, Dodge Series, Correspondence Subseries.

14. Selwyn Lloyd to Eisenhower, n.d.; John Foster Dulles to Lloyd, 19 April 1956, both in DDEP, Ann Whitman File, Dulles-Herter Series.

15. John Foster Dulles to Selwyn Lloyd, 19 April 1956, ibid. For conservative pressures see *New York Times*, 20 January, 16–17 February, 7–8 March, 8 April, 19 July 1956.

16. John Foster Dulles to Selwyn Lloyd, 19 April 1956, DDEP, Ann Whitman File, Dulles-Herter Series.

17. Telegrams, Winthrop Aldrich to John Foster Dulles, 18 April; Douglas Dillon to Dulles, 19 April; Perkins to Dulles, 21 April 1956, all in DDEP, CFEP Records, Policy Papers Series.

18. *New York Times*, 8 March 1956.

19. Ibid., 19 July 1956; William T. Sloane, "Trading with Communists," *Editorial Research Reports*, 25 July 1956, 489, 495.

20. *New York Times*, 19 July 1956.

21. Herbert Hoover, Jr., to John McClellan, 20 February 1956, DDEP, CFEP Records, Policy Papers Series.

22. Ibid.

23. Ibid.

24. Eisenhower to Anthony Eden, 27 April; J. E. Coulson to John Foster Dulles, 12 May 1956, both in DDEP, Ann Whitman File, Dulles-Herter Series.

25. John Foster Dulles to Clarence B. Randall, 7 August 1956, DDEP, CFEP Records, Policy Papers Series.

26. Cf. Memoranda, Working Groups I and II to chairman, Economic Defense Advisory Committee (EDAC), 21, 23, 28 August; chairman, EDAC, to CFEP, 10 August; Paul H. Cullen to CFEP, 10 August; "Minutes of the 46th Meeting of the CFEP," 14 August; Herbert V. Prochnow to Clarence B. Randall, n.d.; Cullen to Randall, 14 August; and Walter S. DeLany to Randall, 13 November 1956, all in ibid.

27. Cf. Clarence B. Randall to James S. Lay, Jr., 16 August; Randall to Dillon Anderson, 17 August; Randall to Eisenhower, 17 August; Gordon Gray to Randall, [October?] 1956, all in ibid. For the Commerce Department's opposition to any relaxation of controls see Paul H. Cullen to Randall, 31 October; Randall to Sinclair Weeks, 31 October, 2 November 1956, all in ibid.

28. Gordon Gray to Clarence B. Randall, [October?]; Paul H. Cullen to Randall, 25 September; Sinclair Weeks to Randall, 26 October; and Cullen to Randall, 31 October 1956, all in ibid.

29. The evolution of the policy may be traced in Walter S. DeLany to Clarence B. Randall, 20, 31 August, 14, 28 September, 2, 8, 12 October; Paul H. Cullen to CFEP, 21 August, 4, 14 September; Randall to Herbert Hoover, Jr., 5 October; Randall to DeLany, 26 September 1956, 4 January 1957; Cullen to

Randall, 25 September 1956, 30 January 1957; Randall to CFEP, 31 January 1957; "Minutes of the 53rd Meeting of the CFEP," 5 February; "Briefing Paper for NSC," 5 February; Randall to Gen. Robert H. Cutler, 7 February; and Cullen to Cutler, 4 February 1957, all in ibid.

30. "Statement by Mr. Douglas Dillon on China Trade Control Negotiations," 11 June 1957, ibid. See also, for background on the U.S. position, Walter S. DeLany to Clarence B. Randall, 13 November; Joseph Dodge to Paul H. Cullen, 23 November; CFEP, Memorandum for the Record, 27 November 1956, all in ibid.

31. Telegram, John Foster Dulles to U.S. Embassy, Bonn, 19 May 1957, ibid. The telegram also contained a list of U.S. concessions.

32. Ibid. Also Paul H. Cullen, "Memorandum for the Record," 28 May; Clarence B. Randall to Mr. [Albert] Toner, 28 May; Randall to Gen. Robert H. Cutler, 5 June; telegram, John Foster Dulles to U.S. Embassy, Paris, 5 June 1957, all in ibid.

33. "Dillon on China Trade Control Negotiations," 11 June 1957, ibid.

34. Ibid.

35. C. Douglas Dillon, "Memorandum on China Trade Control Negotiations," n.d., ibid.

36. Clarence B. Randall to Sinclair Weeks, 6 June 1953, ibid.

37. U.S. Joint Chiefs of Staff, "Future Course of Action with Respect to COCOM/CHINCOM," 13 June; Adm. Arthur Radford to secretary of defense, 13 June 1957, both in ibid.

38. Joint Chiefs of Staff, "Future Course of Action."

39. Ibid.

40. The Joint Chiefs of Staff subsequently withdrew the recommendation that sanctions be invoked against OEEC countries that traded with China. See the undated follow-up memo in ibid.

41. Donald Quarles to executive secretary, NSC, 19 June 1957; Office of Assistant Secretary of Defense, "Memorandum of the Meeting of Jan. 16 1958"; Adm. Arleigh Burke to secretary of defense, 21 January 1958, all in ibid. The possibility of placing export controls under NATO jurisdiction was explicitly rejected by CFEP and EDAC as introducing another divisive issue into that already badly divided organization, a reference to the Suez crisis and Britain's unilateral reduction in forces. See John Knoll to Paul H. Cullen, 14 August 1957, also in ibid.

42. *New York Times*, 4 June 1957.

43. NSC, "Report on U.S. Economic Defense Policy," 16 September 1957, DDEP, WHCF, OSANSA Records, NSC Series, Policy Papers Subseries. See also chairman, EDAC, to CFEP, 7 August 1957, DDEP, CFEP Records, Policy Papers Series.

44. NSC, "Report on U.S. Economic Defense Policy."

45. Ibid.

46. Ibid.

47. See, for example, the memorandum discussing this point, from the Executive Committee to the chairman of EDAC, 17 January 1958, ibid.

48. Clarence B. Randall to Sherman Adams, 31 January; Randall to Gen. Robert Cutler, 31 January 1958, both in ibid.

49. Gen. Robert Cutler to C. Douglas Dillon, 8 February; Paul H. Cullen to CFEP, 13 February 1958, both in ibid.

50. Clarence B. Randall to John Foster Dulles, 5 February; Dulles to Randall, 18 February 1958, both in ibid.

51. Douglas Dillon to CFEP, 13 February; Paul H. Cullen to CFEP, 13 February 1958, both in ibid.

52. Paul H. Cullen to Gen. Robert Cutler, 14 February 1958, ibid.

53. Ibid. See also "Significant Actions in the Field of Foreign Economic Policy by the CFEP," n.d., DDEP, WHCF, Confidential File, Subject Series; Paul H. Cullen to James S. Lay, Jr., 17 February 1958, DDEP, White House Office, OSANSA Records, NSC Series, Policy Papers Subseries; Cullen to Albert Toner, 18 February 1958, DDEL, CFEP Records, Office of the Chairman, Randall Series, Correspondence Subseries.

54. Clarence B. Randall to James S. Lay, Jr., 12 August 1958, DDEP, CFEP Records, Policy Papers Series.

55. *New York Times*, 2 July 1958.

56. Ibid.

57. Quoted in "An Active Week," *East–West Trade News*, 17 July 1958, 3, copy in DCR(NA), RG 151, Bureau of International Programs, Regional Economies—USSR, 13, 119B.

58. Douglas Dillon to Clarence B. Randall, 4 August; Randall to James S. Lay, Jr., 12 August 1958, both in DDEP, CFEP Records, Policy Papers Series. Assistant Secretary of Defense Mansfield D. Sprague wrote: "The Department considers that the new controls do not maintain effective coverage over many items which, in its opinion, have a clear military application and incorporate advanced technology of strategic significance not available to the Sino-Soviet bloc." Sprague to Randall, 11 August 1958, ibid.

59. *New York Times*, 24 August 1958.

60. Sinclair Weeks to Marshall M. Smith, 22 August; Weeks to Clarence B. Randall, 22 August 1958, both in DDEP, CFEP Records, Policy Papers Series.

61. U.S. Congress, Senate, Committee on Foreign Relations, *U.S.–U.S.S.R Trade Relations*, 86 Cong., 1 sess. (Washington, D.C., 1959), 3–6.

62. Ibid.

63. Paul H. Cullen to CFEP, 23 June 1958, DDEP, CFEP Records, Office of the Chairman, Randall Series, Subject Subseries.

64. Department of State, "Notes on Expansion of U.S.–U.S.S.R. Trade," 16 June 1958, ibid.

65. Ibid.

66. Ibid.

67. Ibid.

68. Ibid. Rather than provide governmental credits, the State Department suggested that the administration tell the Soviets it preferred to extend credits to less-developed countries whose need was greater.

69. Senate Committee on Foreign Relations, *U.S.–U.S.S.R. Trade Relations*,

7; copy of the letter appearing in *East–West Trade News*, 17 July 1958, 1–3.

70. Senate Committee on Foreign Relations, *U.S.–U.S.S.R. Trade Relations*, 9.

71. Ibid., 9–11.

72. "Realities of Soviet Foreign Economic Policies," a speech by Under Secretary of State Douglas Dillon, in New Orleans, 27 January 1959, reprinted in ibid., 27–32.

73. Ibid., 21.

74. *New York Times*, 5 March 1959.

75. Ibid., 18 September 1959.

76. Clarence B. Randall, "Suggested Position for the President in His Conferences with Mr. Khrushchev Concerning U.S.–Soviet Union Trade," 3 September 1959, DDEP, CFEP Records, Office of the Chairman, Staff Series.

77. Ibid.

78. The lend-lease debt figure was put at $2.6 billion. The United States initially asked for $1.3 billion, and the Russians offered $170 million. When negotiations broke down in June 1952, the United States had reduced its price to $800 million, and the Soviets had raised their offer to $300 million. The $180 million lent to the Kerensky government was not brought up at Camp David. See *New York Times*, 1 October 1959.

79. When Mikoyan visited Eisenhower in January 1959, he had made governmental credits an absolute precondition to increased trade, following Khrushchev's letter of 6 June 1958. At Camp David, though, Khrushchev made no mention of governmental credits, and the administration was not about to ask Congress to endorse the idea while the lend-lease issue was unresolved. See ibid.

80. See "Setback in Washington," *East–West Trade News*, 28 January 1960, 2–3, copy in DCR(NA), RG 151, Bureau of International Programs, Regional Economies, 13, 119B; *New York Times*, 28 January, 5 February 1960.

81. "Back to America," *East–West Trade News*, 11 February 1960, 5, copy in DCR(NA), RG 151, Bureau of International Programs, Regional Economies, 13, 119B; Edward J. Epstein, "The Riddle of Armand Hammer," *New York Times Magazine*, 21 November 1981, 118.

82. Clarence B. Randall to J. Edgar Hoover, 4 May 1960, Gerald Morgan Papers (DDEL).

CHAPTER SIX

1. A useful discussion of the problem is contained in U.S. Congress, House, *Resolved: That Executive Control of United States Foreign Policy Should Be Significantly Curtailed*, Misc. Doc. no. 298, 90 Cong., 2 sess. (Washington, D.C., 1968).

2. Francis O. Wilcox, *Congress, the Executive, and Foreign Policy* (New York, 1971), 133.

3. Ibid., 125, 133.

4. Cf. Arthur M. Schlesinger, Jr., "Congress and the Making of American Foreign Policy," *Foreign Affairs* 51 (October 1972): 80, 96.

5. *New York Times*, 15 January 1960.

6. *American Foreign Policy: Essays and Comments*, ed. Benjamin J. Cohen (New York, 1968), esp. pts. 2 and 4.

7. An excellent convenient summary, though fairly conservative in its own conclusions, is *East–West Trade: Its Strategic Implications*, ed. Samuel F. Clabaugh and Richard V. Allen (Washington, D.C., 1964), published by the Center for Strategic Studies of Georgetown University.

8. U.S. Congress, House, Select Committee on Export Controls, *Investigation and Study of the Administration, Operation, and Enforcement of the Export Control Act of 1949 and Related Acts*, Report, 1961, 87 Cong., 2 sess. (Washington, D.C., 1962), 3.

9. See, for example, Corporation for Economic and Industrial Research, Inc., "Worldwide and Domestic Economic Problems and Their Impact on the Foreign Policy of the United States," in U.S. Congress, Senate, Committee on Foreign Relations, *United States Foreign Policy: Compilation of Studies*, Study no. 1, Sen. Doc. no. 24, 87 Cong., 1 sess. (Washington, D.C., 15 March 1961), esp. paragraph G.

10. U.S. Congress, Joint Economic Committee, *Foreign Economic Policy for the 1960s: Report to Congress with Minority and Other Views*, 87 Cong., 2 sess. (Washington, D.C., 1962), 17.

11. U.S. Congress, House, Committee on Foreign Affairs, *The Soviet Economic Offensive in Western Europe: Report of the Special Study Mission to Europe*, 88 Cong., 1 sess. (Washington, D.C., 31 January 1963), 1.

12. See, for example, Resolution IV of the Economic Committee, U.S. Congress, House, Delegation to the Conference of Members of Parliament from the NATO Countries, *Report of the United States House Delegation to the Eighth Conference of Members of Parliament from the NATO Countries*, 88 Cong., 1 sess. (Washington, D.C., 1963).

13. For example, Dr. Robert Strausz-Hupé, director of the Foreign Policy Research Institute of the University of Pennsylvania, testified on numerous occasions that the United States should take the initiative in persuading its NATO allies that in an era of economic warfare between two irreconcilable systems, the concept of "strategic goods" must be given a broader interpretation to include all goods that may contribute to the industrial and trading capabilities of the Sino-Soviet bloc. See *Report of the United States House Delegation to the Fourth Conference of Members of Parliament from the NATO Countries*, Study no. 3, 84 Cong., 1 sess. (Washington, D.C., 1959), 199–299. Also his testimony in U.S. Congress, Senate, Subcommittee on Internal Security, *Export of Strategic Materials to the U.S.S.R. and Other Soviet Bloc Countries*, Hearings, pt. 4, 87 Cong., 2 sess. (Washington, D.C., 26 October 1962), 55. See also the report by Samuel Pisar, reprinted in U.S. Congress, Joint Economic Committee, *A New Look at Trade Policy toward the Communist Bloc: The Elements of a Common Strategy for the West*, 87 Cong., 1 sess. (Washington, D.C., 1961), esp. 58–60, 71, 83–84.

14. On this point Dr. Hans Morgenthau's critique was most telling. He testified that the deterioration in the United States' relations with its allies was the result of confusing the principle of sharing information and consultation with the principle of sharing the decision-making process and subordinating its interests to the preferences of its allies. He concluded that U.S. policy was aimless and lacking coordination, and added that the executive branch was deterred from embarking upon new initiatives because it feared Congress, and both feared public opinion. U.S. Congress, Senate, Committee on Foreign Relations, *What Is Wrong with Our Foreign Policy*, Hearings, 86 Cong., 1 sess. (Washington, D.C., 15 April 1959), 3–4.

15. C. Edward Galbraith to Clarence B. Randall, 5 September 1958, DDEP, CFEP Records, Policy Papers Series; Will Clayton to J. William Fulbright, 12 February 1959, in *Selected Papers of Will Clayton*, ed. Frederick J. Dobney (Baltimore, 1971), 283–84; Robert Loving Allen, "An Interpretation of East–West Trade," Study no. 19, and Willard Thorpe, "Soviet Economic Growth and Its Policy," Study no. 20 (esp. the section entitled "U.S.–U.S.S.R. Trade"), both in U.S. Congress, Joint Economic Committee, Subcommittee on Economic Statistics, *Comparisons of the United States and Soviet Economies*, 86 Cong., 1 sess. (Washington, D.C., 1960), pts. 2 and 3.

16. See, for example, "East–West Dilemma: To Trade or Not to Trade," *Business Abroad*, 27 July 1964, 9–13; "The Question of U.S. Trade with the Communist Bloc: Pro and Con," *Congressional Digest* 43 (February 1964): 33–64; "A Rush to Trade with Reds—Will U.S. Join It?" *U.S. News*, 30 September 1963, 51–52; Harold J. Berman, "A Re-appraisal of U.S.–U.S.S.R. Trade Policy," *Harvard Business Review* 42 (July–August 1964): 139–44, 147–51.

17. See William H. Peterson, "Should We Trade with the Communists?" *Harvard Business Review* 40 (March–April 1959): 48–54, and the statements of Sydney H. Scheuer, chairman of the board of Intertex International and former director of the Foreign Economic Administration, and Bradley Fish, assistant secretary of commerce for international affairs, in U.S. Congress, Senate, Committee on Interstate and Foreign Commerce, *Foreign Commerce Study: Trade with the Sino-Soviet Bloc*, Hearings, 86 Cong., 2 sess. (Washington, D.C., 1960), 30–47, 92.

18. Arthur M. Schlesinger, Jr., *A Thousand Days* (Boston, 1965), 252.

19. *New York Times*, 2 October 1960.

20. The other task force members included Max Millikan, Walt W. Rostow, John Kenneth Galbraith, and Lincoln Gordon. Schlesinger, *A Thousand Days*, 104.

21. For excerpts of the Ball Report see "Controversy Rising over Trade with Communist Bloc," *Congressional Quarterly Weekly Review*, 18 October 1962, 845.

22. Ibid.

23. Ibid., 845–46. The report also recommended that trade with Cuba and China be dealt with as "a political rather than a trade matter."

24. *New York Times*, 8 January 1962.

25. *Public Papers of the Presidents of the United States: John F. Kennedy 1961* (Washington, D.C., 1962), 24–26; Kennedy to McGeorge Bundy, 15 February 1961, JFKP, NSF, Meetings and Memos, National Security Action Memoranda nos. 8, 20; Theodore Sorensen, *Kennedy* (New York, 1965), 517.

26. *New York Times*, 6 March 1961; *Public Papers: Kennedy 1961*, 158; *The Kennedy Presidential Press Conferences*, ed. George W. Johnson (New York, 1978), 57.

27. U.S. Congress, Senate, Committee on Internal Security, *Export of Ball-Bearing Machines to Russia*, Hearings, 87 Cong., 1 sess. (Washington, D.C., 1960–61), pt. 1:61; and the committee's final report of 28 February 1961.

28. *New York Times*, 6 March; *Wall Street Journal*, 9 March 1961.

29. *New York Times*, 12 March 1961.

30. Cf. Hopkins to Frank B. Ellis, 25 May 1961, JFKP, WHCF, FG 651.

31. Rowland Burnstan to Luther Hodges, 18 May 1961, JFKP, NSF Subjects: Export Control Policy, 18 May 1961–28 May 1963.

32. "U.S. Economic Relations with the Soviet Bloc," 25 May 1961, JFKP, NSF, Countries File, USSR-General.

33. Ibid.

34. Ibid.

35. Ibid.

36. U.S. Congress, Senate, Committee on Foreign Relations, *Amendments to the Mutual Defense Assistance Act of 1951* [Battle Act], Report no. 199, 87 Cong., 1 sess. (Washington, D.C., 27 April 1961), 1–17; "Controversy Rising over Trade," *Congressional Quarterly*, 18 May 1962, 843–44.

37. Schlesinger, *A Thousand Days*, 358–78, 390–400.

38. *Cong. Rec.*, 87 Cong., 1 sess., 107, pt. 9:11550, 11931; pt. 10:13745, 13757.

39. "Pressures Rise for Changes in East–West Trade Laws," *Congressional Quarterly Weekly Review*, 18 October 1963, 1806; Jack N. Behrman to Luther Hodges, 19 July 1961, JFKP, WHCF, FG 651.

40. Behrman to Hodges, 19 July; and Frederick Dutton to McGeorge Bundy, 21 July 1961, ibid.

41. *Wall Street Journal*, 19 July; *New York Times*, 5, 21, 25, 28 August 1961.

42. *New York Times*, 30 August 1961.

43. *Wall Street Journal*, 18 September 1961.

44. In October 1961 the Senate Internal Security Subcommittee charged that the Battle Act had never been enforced due to political considerations. *New York Times*, 23 October 1961, and 25 October (statement of Deputy Assistant Secretary of State Philip Trezise).

45. Ibid.

46. *Cong. Rec.*, 87 Cong., 2 sess., 108, pt. 2:2268.

47. Ibid., pt. 15:19795; pt. 17:22280, 22284–85.

48. *Washington Post*, 28 February 1962, reprinted in ibid., pt. 3:3179.

49. Ibid., pt. 3:3765; pt. 4:4471, 5059; pt. 5:6416–21; pt. 9:11543.

50. *New York Times*, 10 April 1962.

51. *Cong. Rec.*, 87 Cong., 2 sess., 108, pt. 1:1054; pt. 6:8110; pt. 8:10701; pt. 9:12269.

52. *New York Times*, 30 June; *Wall Street Journal*, 2 July 1962.

53. See "Draft Order," and Luther Hodges to Kennedy, 19 March 1962, JFKP, WHCF, FG 651.

54. Ibid., and Luther Hodges to Myer Feldman, 19 March 1962, also in ibid.

55. Douglas Dillon to Kennedy, 3 April; Dillon to Hodges, 3 April, both in ibid.

56. Ibid.

57. Myer Feldman to Kenneth Hansen, 4, 5 April 1962, ibid.

58. Kenneth Hansen to Myer Feldman, 10 April 1962, ibid.

59. Ibid.

60. Carl Kaysen to Myer Feldman, 17 April; Feldman to Luther Hodges, 30 April 1962, both in ibid.

61. Dean Rusk to NSC, 10 July 1962, ibid.

62. Ibid., and Enclosure no. 1, Department of State, "United States Economic Defense Policy," 10 July 1962, and Enclosure no. 2, "Criteria and Licensing Policy," both in ibid.

63. Ibid.

64. Ibid.

65. Ibid.

66. Enclosure no. 3, Department of State, "Amendments to the Export Control Act," in ibid.

67. Ibid.

68. Luther Hodges to Kennedy, 10 July 1962, JFKP, NSF, Subjects: Export Control Policy, 18 May 1961–28 May 1963.

69. Ibid.

70. Ibid.

71. Ibid.

72. Ibid.

73. Luther Hodges to NSC, 16 July 1962, ibid.

74. Ibid.; Department of Commerce, "Suggested Level of Multilateral Export Controls," attachment no. 2; director, Policy Export Staff, to chairman, Advisory Committee on Export Policy, 11 July 1962, in ibid.

75. Dean Rusk to NSC, 16 July 1962, ibid.

76. *Cong. Rec.*, 87 Cong., 2 sess., 108, pt. 1:83; pt. 2:1628; *Public Papers: Kennedy 1962* (Washington, D.C., 1963), 759–60. See also Sorensen, *Kennedy*, 410–12; and Schlesinger, *A Thousand Days*, 704–7.

77. *Cong. Rec.*, 87 Cong., 2 sess., 108, pt. 14:19570; U.S. Congress, Senate, Committee on Finance, *The Trade Expansion Act of 1962*, Hearings on H.R. 11970, 87 Cong., 2 sess. (Washington, D.C., 1962), ibid., pt. 4:2209–13. See also *Trade Expansion Act of 1962*, sec. 231 (a), 76 *Stat.* 872.

78. U.S. Congress, House, Committee on Foreign Affairs, *Foreign Assistance Act of 1963*, Hearings, 88 Cong., 1 sess. (Washington, D.C., 1963), esp. pts. 1–10 and index; *Foreign Assistance Act of 1963*, sec. 402, 77 *Stat.* 379; "Pressures Rise for Changes in East–West Trade Laws," 1806–7.

79. On the Cuban missile crisis see Herbert S. Dinerstein, *The Making of a Missile Crisis: October, 1962* (Baltimore, 1978).

80. Alonzo L. Hamby, *The Imperial Years* (New York, 1976), 292.

81. *Public Papers: Kennedy 1963* (Washington, D.C., 1964), 459–64.

82. Schlesinger, *A Thousand Days*, 904; Kennedy to Export Control Review Board (ECRB), 16 May 1963, JFKP, NSF, Subjects: Export Control Policy, 18 May 1961–28 May 1963; chairman, ECRB, to Kennedy, 9 August 1963, copy of memo in LBJP, NSF, NSC Meetings, 5 December 1963–27 July 1965.

83. Kennedy to Luther Hodges, 16 May 1963, JFKP, NSF, Subjects: Export Control Policy, 18 May 1961–28 May 1963.

84. The Commerce Department undertook several studies of this matter. See acting secretary of commerce to Kennedy, 3 September 1963, JFKP, NSF, Trade: East–West, August–September 1963; and chairman, ECRB, to Kennedy, 9 August 1963, LBJP, NSF, NSC Meetings, 5 December 1963–27 July 1965.

85. Chairman, ECRB, to Kennedy, 9 August 1963, LBJP, NSF, NSC Meetings, 5 December 1963–27 July 1965.

86. Ibid.

87. *New York Times*, 20 August 1963.

88. David Klein to McGeorge Bundy, 8 August 1963, JFKP, NSF, Trade: East–West, August–September 1963.

89. Ibid.

90. Department of State, Policy Planning Council, "U.S. Policy on Trade with the European Soviet Bloc," 8 July 1963, in ibid.

91. Ibid.

92. This point was reiterated by the State Department's Bureau of Intelligence Research. See Thomas L. Hughes to secretary of state, 16 July 1963, Res. Memo RSB–97, LBJP, Vice-President Security File ("Trade with the Soviet Union").

93. David Klein to McGeorge Bundy, 14 August 1963, JFKP, NSF, Trade: East–West, August–September 1963.

94. David Klein to McGeorge Bundy, 7 September 1963, ibid.

95. Ibid.

96. Ibid.

97. Kennedy to chairman, ECRB, 19 September 1963, LBJP, NSF, NSC Meetings File, vol. 1, tab 18.

98. McGeorge Bundy to ECRB, 21 October 1963, JFKP, NSF, Trade: East–West, October–November 1963.

99. *New York Times*, 20 September, 10 October 1963.

100. Sorensen, *Kennedy*, 835.

101. In a memo to the president before the announcement of the agreement, the attorney general ruled that the 1961 Latta amendment was simply a policy declaration for the executive to consider, but it was not binding. For an able discussion see John Alden Pierce, "The Politics of the United States' Sale of Wheat to the Soviet Union in 1963 and 1964" (Ph.D. dissertation, University of Virginia, 1971), esp. chaps. 3–5.

102. *New York Times*, 17, 20 September, 10, 12, 28 October 1963.

103. Ibid., 31 October 1963; *Public Papers: Kennedy 1963*, 830–31.

104. George Mahon to Kennedy, 8 November 1963, LBJP, EX TAI: 1 July 1968, TAI Trade Agreements, 23 November 1963–25 October 1966.

105. *Cong. Rec.*, 88 Cong., 1 sess., 109, pt. 14:18656–71.

106. Ibid. Mundt's statement also was reported in the *New York Times*, 31 December 1963.

107. George W. Ball to U.S. ambassador, London, 24 October 1963, JFKP, NSF, Trade: East–West, October–November 1963.

108. Telegram, Secretary Rusk to U.S. embassies, 14 October 1963, ibid.

109. Ibid.

110. Ball's efforts to persuade the members of the NATO Council to limit credits to five years' duration to keep Moscow more flexible on disarmament were rejected by Great Britain, Canada, Norway, Denmark, and Iceland, who argued that long-term credits would be *more likely* to moderate Soviet aggressive behavior. *New York Times*, 6 November 1963.

111. Kennedy to Mike Mansfield, 15 November 1963, JFKP, NSF, Trade: East–West, October–November 1963.

112. *New York Times*, 27 November 1963.

CHAPTER SEVEN

1. For the element of continuity see Seyom Brown, *The Crises of Power* (New York, 1979), 42; David P. Calleo, "American Power in a New World Economy," in *Economics and World Power*, ed. William H. Becker and Samuel F. Wells, Jr. (New York, 1984), 407; and "Briefing Memorandum," 12 December 1963, LBJP, White House Diary.

2. Harold J. Berman, "A Re-appraisal of U.S.–U.S.S.R. Trade Policy," *Harvard Business Review* 42 (July–August 1964): 141, 148, 151.

3. James G. Patton to Johnson, February 1965, LBJP, NSF, Committee File.

4. U.S. Congress, Senate, Committee on Foreign Relations, *East–West Trade*, Hearings, 88 Cong., 2 sess., 89 Cong., 1 sess., 2 pts. (Washington, D.C., 1964–65), passim.

5. Lyndon B. Johnson, *The Vantage Point: Perspectives of the Presidency, 1963–1969* (New York, 1971), 471.

6. Ibid.

7. "The Department of Commerce during the Administration of President Lyndon B. Johnson: November 1963–January 1969," unpublished narrative history, vol. 1, pt. 3 ("Export Controls"):4–5, LBJP. Cited hereafter as "Department of Commerce Narrative History."

8. Johnson, *The Vantage Point*, 471.

9. See, for example, *New York Times*, 17, 19, 25 September 1963.

10. McGeorge Bundy to Johnson, 14 April 1964, LBJP, NSF, NSC Meetings File.

11. Citing the relevant portions of the 1962 amendment to the Export Control Act, the Department of Commerce opposed the sale on the ground that it threatened U.S. national security by strengthening the Soviet agricultural

economy. Agriculture Department officials agreed but were willing to make an exception if a quid pro quo could be extracted from the Soviets. The State Department supported the sale without attaching conditions. In the 20 January meeting of the Export Control Review Board, Rusk had argued that "we are not in a posture of economic warfare with the Soviets and . . . denial of such equipment implied that we were." The State Department also was concerned that it would send the Russians the wrong signal about the United States' intentions on trade and "seriously detract from the beneficial atmosphere resulting from the wheat sales." It also believed that concessions from the Soviets had to be part of a comprehensive agreement to be worked out after the upcoming presidential election, and after consultation with Congress. See "Minutes of the Meeting of the Export Control Review Board," 20 January 1964, and [McGeorge Bundy], "Summary Positions of the Departments," n.d., in ibid.

12. McGeorge Bundy to Johnson, 14 April 1964, ibid.

13. Ibid.

14. Ibid.

15. Johnson, *The Vantage Point*, 471.

16. U.S. Congress, House, Committee on Foreign Affairs, *Report of Special Study Mission to Europe, 1964*, 89 Cong., 1 sess. (Washington, D.C., 3 February 1965), 1–3. See also CIA, "Soviet Economic Problems Multiply," 9 January 1964, LBJP, NSF, Committee File.

17. Lyndon B. Johnson, "State of the Union: Address to the Congress, January 4, 1965," *Department of State Bulletin*, 25 January 1965, 96.

18. "Summary of Observations: Business International Moscow Roundtable," 6 January 1965, LBJP, NSF, Committee File.

19. Ibid.

20. "Bills on East–West Trade, Introduced January 4–March 1, 1965," 2 March 1965, ibid.

21. For evidence of continuing foreign pressures see *New York Times*, 16 February, 13 September 1964, 16 April, 7, 11 May 1965.

22. Ibid., 19 February 1965.

23. John J. McCloy to McGeorge Bundy, 18 January; Bundy to McCloy, 25 January 1965, both in LBJP, WHCF, Ex FG761.

24. McGeorge Bundy to Johnson, 17 February 1965, LBJP, NSF, Aides Files, Memos for the President, June 1964–February 1965.

25. Biographical sketch, J. Irwin Miller, n.d., LBJP, NSF, Committee File.

26. See, for example, Miller's discussion with Secretary of State Rusk and Secretary of Commerce Connor on 16 February 1965, as well as with other officials, that he later reported to committee members; LBJP, NSF, Committee File, Miller Conversations.

27. McGeorge Bundy to Johnson, 17 February 1965, LBJP, NSF, Aides File, Memos for the President, June 1964–February 1965.

28. McGeorge Bundy to Johnson, 3 March 1965, ibid.

29. See the names in LBJP, NSF, Committee File.

30. McGeorge Bundy to Johnson, 1 April 1965, LBJP, NSF, Aides File, Memos for the President, March 1965–14 April 1965.

31. *New York Times*, 5 April 1965; "Pressure Rises for Trade with Reds," *Business Week*, 8 May 1965, 96.

32. Telegrams, Foy Kohler to secretary of state, 11, 24 March 1965, LBJP, NSF, Committee File.

33. See "Discussion Agenda," n.d., ibid.

34. Ibid.

35. [McGeorge Bundy?], "List of Specific Issues," n.d., ibid.

36. Philip H. Trezise, "Review of U.S. Policy on East–West Trade," 1 March 1965, ibid.

37. Philip H. Trezise, "Attitudes of Western Europe and Japan towards East–West Trade," 1 March 1965, ibid.

38. William Morrell, "Strategic Importance of Western Trade to the Soviet Bloc," n.d., ibid.

39. Evidence from the electronics industry confirmed this evaluation; see ibid.

40. Ibid., emphasis mine.

41. Llewellyn E. Thompson, "The Political Framework: Opportunities and Obstacles," 17 March 1965, ibid.

42. Llewellyn E. Thompson, "The Soviet Union: The Political Background," 15 March 1965, ibid. For further discussion of political leverage see "How to Trade: Bilateralism vs. Multilateralism," n.d., and Dr. Michka, "The Political Case for Relaxation of Trade Controls," 23 March 1965, both in ibid.

43. Thompson, "The Political Framework," 17 March 1965, ibid.

44. For lend-lease as an obstacle see Department of State, "General Information on the Status of Lend-Lease Relations with the Government of the U.S.S.R.," July 1964, ibid.

45. Thompson, "The Political Framework," 17 March 1965, ibid.

46. "Issues in Trade Expansion: Credit," 15 March 1965, ibid. See also Ambassador Fessenden's telegram from Brussels to Secretary Rusk concerning credit, 23 March 1965, ibid.

47. Edward R. Fried to Francis Bator, n.d., ibid. Bator was the White House's liaison with the Miller Committee; Fried was on loan to the committee from the State Department.

48. "Report: Dean Rusk, Secretary of State," 16 February 1965, ibid. This and subsequent reports are located in the "Miller Conversations" folder.

49. Ibid.

50. "Report: Thomas Mann, Under Secretary for Economic Affairs," 3 March 1965, ibid.

51. "Report: Orville H. Freeman, Secretary of Agriculture," n.d., ibid. See also "Report: The Hon. Stewart Udall, Secretary of the Interior," 3 March 1965, ibid.

52. "Report: Robert McNamara, Secretary of Defense," 18 February 1965, ibid.

53. Cf. *New York Times Magazine*, 26 April 1964, pt. 6:13–15, 108–11.

54. "Report: George W. Ball, Under Secretary of State," 3 March 1965, LBJP, NSF, Committee File. See also the report of W. Averell Harriman, under secretary

for political affairs, 16 February 1965, ibid. Reversing his position of a decade earlier, Harriman now was especially critical of the Commerce Department's policy of discouraging expansion of trade.

55. "Report: The Hon. Douglas Dillon, Secretary of the Treasury," 3 March 1965, ibid.

56. Ibid. Dillon, in fact, believed that in the future the United States also would resume trade with Communist China.

57. "Report: Harold Linder, president, Export-Import Bank," 18 February 1965, ibid.

58. The U.S. ambassador to France, Thomas K. Finletter, believed that the NATO countries would not object to granting most-favored-nation status to the USSR, but cautioned against guaranteeing long-term credits, fearing that it would precipitate a Western credit race "beyond what already existed." Telegram, Finletter to secretary of state, 6 April 1965, ibid.

59. Fried's letter and the responses are in ibid.

60. "Statement by the AFL-CIO Executive Council on East–West Trade," 1 March 1965, ibid.

61. John J. McCloy to Eugene R. Black, 29 March 1965, ibid.

62. Ibid.

63. Ibid.

64. See, for example, Charles W. Stewart to J. Irwin Miller, 12 April 1965, ibid.

65. James A. Ramsey, "The Outlook for East–West Trade," n.d., ibid.

66. Ibid. See also Ramsey's "The United States and East–West Trade," n.d., ibid.

67. See, for example, "U.S. Senate Committee Ends East–West Trade Hearings," *East–West Trade*, 1 March 1965, 1–2; *New York Times*, 25, 27 February 1965.

68. See Jacob S. Potofsky to J. William Fulbright, 5 March, and Charles W. Stewart to J. Irwin Miller, 12 April 1965, LBJP, NSF, Committee File; "U.S. Senate Committee Ends East–West Trade Hearings," 1.

69. Quoted in U.S. Chamber of Commerce, *Testimony on East–West Trade before the Senate Foreign Relations Committee by William Blackie*, 24 February 1965, copy in ibid.

70. McGeorge Bundy to Johnson, 26 April 1965, LBJP, NSF, Aides Files, Memos to the President, 15 April–31 May 1965.

71. Ibid.

72. McGeorge Bundy to Johnson, 28 April 1965, LBJP, WHCF, Ex FG761.

73. J. Irwin Miller to Johnson, 29 April 1965, LBJP, NSF, Committee File.

74. "Statement of Comment by Mr. Goldfinger," 29 April 1965, ibid.

75. J. Irwin Miller to Johnson, 3 May; Edward R. Fried to Francis Bator, 30 April 1965, both in ibid.

76. J. Irwin Miller to Johnson, 3 May 1965, ibid.

77. Ibid.

78. See Council for Economic Development, "Crises in World Communism," report, January 1965, copy in ibid.

79. See "Draft Press Summary," 27 April 1965, ibid.; *New York Times*, 7, 8 May 1965.

80. "Draft Press Summary."

81. Ibid.

82. Ibid.

83. *New York Times*, 8 May 1965; Johnson, *The Vantage Point*, 472.

84. For opposition from conservative groups such as Young Americans for Freedom and the president's condemnation of their efforts to organize boycotts of firms that traded with the communist bloc nations see *New York Times*, 28 August, 14 October 1965; and B. L. Masse, "Commerce with Communists," *America*, 1 May 1965, 639–41.

85. Johnson, *The Vantage Point*, 472–73.

86. *New York Times*, 20 June 1965.

87. Johnson, *The Vantage Point*, 473.

88. "Department of Commerce Narrative History," vol. 1, pt. 3:1–3, 18–19.

89. *New York Times*, 8 October 1966. The Soviets noted Johnson's speech, but Leonid Brezhnev asserted that the United States was merely deluding itself in announcing such changes while waging war in Vietnam.

90. "Department of Commerce Narrative History," vol. 1, pt. 3:18–19; *Seventy-ninth Quarterly Report on Export Control* (Washington, D.C., First Quarter, 1967), 5; *New York Times*, 13, 21 October 1966.

91. "Proposed New Trade Legislation," 13 November; Francis Bator to Joseph Califano, 6 December 1966, both in LBJP, Interagency Task Force on Foreign Trade, Task Force Collection.

92. William Roth, "Proposed Briefing Charts for the President," 14 December 1966, ibid.

93. Alexander S. Trowbridge to Johnson, 8 May 1967, LBJP, WHCF, Confidential File, LE/PQ2–LE/WE6.

94. Transcript, Lawrence A. Fox Oral History Interview, 12 November 1968, 23, copy in LBJL.

95. Transcript, Lawrence McQuade Oral History Interview, 15 January 1969, pt. 2:23, copy in LBJL. See also Edgar Kaiser to Joseph Califano, 28 August 1968, LBJP, WHCF, Confidential File, CO 303.

CHAPTER EIGHT

1. My thinking about the Nixon-Kissinger foreign policy and U.S.–Soviet trade has been influenced by the excellent monograph of Seyom Brown, *The Crises of Power: An Interpretation of United States Foreign Policy during the Kissinger Years* (New York, 1979). See also Gary K. Bertsch, "U.S.–Soviet Trade: A Sector of Mutual Benefit?" in *Sectors of Mutual Benefit in U.S.–Soviet Relations*, ed. Nish Jamgotch, Jr. (Durham, N.C., 1985), chap. 3.

2. Brown, *Crises of Power*, 2–3.

3. Cf. *Public Papers of the Presidents: Richard Nixon 1973* (Washington, D.C., 1973), 348–50.

4. See, for example, Richard M. Nixon, "On Economic Power," Op-Ed in the *New York Times*, 19 August 1982.

5. Cf. remarks of William J. Casey, under secretary for economic affairs, made before an East–West Trade Conference at the University of Georgia Law School, 27 April 1973, reprinted as "Prospects and Policy on East–West Trade," *Department of State Bulletin*, 21 May 1973, 638–43.

6. See Henry A. Kissinger, "The Nature of the National Dialogue on Foreign Policy," in *The Nixon-Kissinger Foreign Policy: Opportunities and Contradictions*, ed. Fred W. Neal and Mary K. Harvey (Santa Barbara, Calif., 1974), 11; and Raymond L. Garthoff, *Détente and Confrontation: American–Soviet Relations from Nixon to Reagan* (Washington, D.C., 1985), 87–92.

7. U.S. Congress, Office of Technology Assessment, *Technology and East–West Trade* (Washington, D.C., 1979), 115.

8. Henry A. Kissinger, *White House Years* (Boston, 1979), 154.

9. Ibid.

10. Ibid., 154–55.

11. Export Administration Act of 1969 (P.L. 91–184), esp. secs. 2, 3, 4 (a, b), 5 (a), 7 (d), 9. See also U.S. Congress, House, Committee on Banking and Currency, *Export Control Act Extension*, Report no. 91–524 (Washington, D.C., 29 September 1969), 9–11, 18–19; and U.S. Congress, Senate, Committee on Banking and Currency, *Export Control Act Extension*, Report no. 91–336 (Washington, D.C., 24 July 1969), 2–3.

12. Jonathan B. Bingham and Victor C. Johnson, "A Rational Approach to Export Controls," *Foreign Affairs* 57 (Spring 1979): 896–97.

13. See, for example, the testimony of Hugh Donaghue, A. R. Frederickson, and Thomas A. Christianson in U.S. Congress, Senate, Committee on Banking and Currency, *Hearings on East–West Trade*, 90 Cong., 2 sess. (Washington, D.C., 1968), passim, and the same committee's *Hearings on the Export Expansion and Regulation Act of 1969*, 91 Cong., 1 sess. (Washington, D.C., 1969).

14. Kissinger, *White House Years*, 179–80.

15. "Doing Business with Russia: Interview with Maurice Stans, Secretary of Commerce," *U.S. News*, 20 December 1971, 56–60, 63.

16. Samuel Pisar, "How We Will Do Business with Russia," *U.S. News*, 31 July 1972, 27–29.

17. Kissinger, *White House Years*, 1133, 1151–52.

18. Ibid., 840.

19. Brown, *Crises of Power*, 42–43. For skepticism that détente would produce an immediate spurt in trade see *Wall Street Journal*, 30 November 1971, and "Expanded Trade with Soviets: The Outlook," *U.S. News*, 12 January 1972, 20.

20. *Public Papers: Nixon 1972* (Washington, D.C., 1974), 633–35. See also Garthoff, *Détente and Confrontation*, 290–98.

21. *Public Papers: Nixon 1972*, 623–24.

22. Brown, *Crises of Power*, 44–45.

23. *Public Papers: Nixon 1973*, 370.

24. U.S. Department of Commerce, *U.S.–Soviet Commercial Relations in a*

New Era: Some Personal Reflections by Peter G. Peterson (Washington, D.C., 1972), 3–4.

25. Ibid. Cf. Peterson, "What America Wants from Russia in Trade Deals," *U.S. News*, 4 September 1972, 40–44.

26. Brown, *Crises of Power*, 45–46.

27. Ibid., 46–47.

28. "Meaning of Big Trade Deal between U.S. and Russia," *U.S. News*, 30 October 1972, 36.

29. "Bridging the U.S.–Soviet Gap: Trade Is Just the Start," *U.S. News*, 27 November 1972, 39–42.

30. Willis C. Armstrong, "A New Era for East–West Trade," *Department of State Bulletin*, 25 December 1972, 721–26. For a cautiously optimistic assessment of linkage and détente see John P. Hardt and George D. Holliday, *U.S.– Soviet Commercial Relations: The Interplay of Economics, Technology Transfer, and Diplomacy*, U.S. Congress, House, Committee on Foreign Affairs, Subcommittee on National Security Policy and Scientific Developments, Committee Print (Washington, D.C., 10 June 1973), esp. 73–75, 78.

31. "Other Deals with Russia: How Officials See Prospects," *U.S. News*, 24 July 1972, 49; "$750 Millions in Food for Russia," ibid., 47; Richard S. Frank, "Pact with Soviets Offers Economic, Political Gains Once U.S. Solves Policy Questions," *National Journal*, 18 November 1972, 1764–65; "Three Year Grain Agreement Signed by the United States and U.S.S.R.," *Department of State Bulletin*, 31 July 1972, 144–45.

32. Kissinger, *White House Years*, 1271–72. There is some evidence that the Australian and Canadian Wheat Boards had advised the U.S. Department of Agriculture, as early as July 1972, to reduce U.S. export subsidies and permit world prices to rise. The reduction occurred in September, after most of the Soviet orders were placed. Cf. remarks of Congressman John Melcher of Montana, *Cong. Rec.*, 93 Cong., 1 sess., 119, pt. 7:8643–45; pt. 9:11409; pt. 10:13163; pt. 18:23185.

33. Paula Stern, *Water's Edge: Domestic Politics and the Making of American Foreign Policy* (Westport, Conn., 1979), 30; Garthoff, *Détente and Confrontation*, 456–63.

34. Stern, *Water's Edge*, 20–21, 31–33.

35. Ibid., 33, 45.

36. Ibid., 54.

37. Ibid., 69, 85–86.

38. Ibid., 94, 100–101.

39. Ibid., 105, 108–9.

40. Ibid., 146, 151.

41. Ibid., 162–63, 179–80; Richard S. Frank, "The Impasse over U.S.–Soviet Trade," *National Journal Reports*, 1 February 1975, 182. The most critical assessment of the Jackson-Vanik amendment is in *Common Sense in U.S.–Soviet Trade*, ed. Margaret Chapman and Carl Marcy (Washington, D.C., 1983), a publication of the liberal American Committee on East–West Accord.

42. Cf. Daniel Yergin, "Politics and Soviet–American Trade: The Three Questions," *Foreign Affairs* 55 (April 1977): 531–32.

43. Ibid., 532.

44. Ibid.

45. Cf. Kissinger, *White House Years*, 1255; "Secretary Kissinger's News Conference of January 14 [1975]," *Department of State Bulletin*, 3 February 1975, 139–43; *Wall Street Journal*, 16 January 1975.

46. Yergin, "Politics and Soviet–American Trade," 517–18.

47. Cyrus Vance, *Hard Choices* (New York, 1983), 96–112, 131.

48. Defense Science Board Task Force on Export of U.S. Technology, *An Analysis of Export Control of U.S. Technology—A DOD Perspective* (Washington, D.C., 4 February 1976), 34–37; "Trading with Russia: A Dangerous Game?" *U.S. News*, 18 December 1978, 22. On Carter and human rights see Zbigniew Brzezinski, *Power and Principle: Memoirs of the National Security Adviser, 1977–1981* (New York, 1983), 124–29, and John M. Howell, "The Carter Human Rights Policy as Applied to the Soviet Union," *Presidential Studies Quarterly* 13 (Spring 1983): 283–95.

49. U.S. Congress, Senate, Permanent Subcommittee on Investigations of the Senate Committee on Governmental Affairs, *Transfer of Technology and the Dresser Industries Export Licensing Actions*, Hearings, 95 Cong., 2 sess. (Washington, D.C., 1978), 1–72; "The Rising Sentiment against Sales to Russia," *Business Week*, 11 September 1978, 57, 60; Herbert E. Meyer, "Why the Outlook Is So Bearish for U.S.–Soviet Trade," *Fortune*, 16 January 1978, 102–4.

50. "Trading with Russia: A Dangerous Game?" 22; *New York Times*, 3, 5, 7, 8, 10 December 1978.

51. *New York Times*, 3, 5, 7, 8, 10 December 1978; Vance, *Hard Choices*, 384–88.

52. The legislative history and implementation of the 1979 Export Administration Act are summarized in Office of Technology Assessment, *Technology and East–West Trade*, 120–44, and idem, *Technology and East–West Trade: An Update* (Washington, D.C., 1983), chaps. 2–3.

53. *Public Papers of the Presidents: Jimmy Carter 1980–1981*, 3 vols. (Washington, D.C., 1981), 1:22–23.

54. Vance, *Hard Choices*, 389–90. It should be noted that the Carter administration did not apply sanctions against the other Warsaw Pact countries, on the ground that they did not participate in the Soviet invasion of Afghanistan. Cf. Office of Technology Assessment, *Technology and East–West Trade: An Update*, 36–37.

55. Cf. Elizabeth Drew, *Portrait of an Election* (New York, 1981), 52, for the influence of the forthcoming election on Carter's actions.

56. *Public Papers: Carter 1980–1981*, 1:41.

57. Ibid., 1:41–42, 187–88; Drew, *Portrait of an Election*, 52.

58. *Wall Street Journal*, 7 February 1980; "Time to End Grain Embargo?" *U.S. News*, 21 January 1980, 25; Richard A. Donnelly, "Those Embargo Blues," *Barron's*, 14 January 1980, 19.

59. *Public Papers: Carter 1980–1981*, 2:1728; *Wall Street Journal*, 22 September 1980; "Right in the Breadbasket," *Time*, 4 May 1981, 18; Padma Desai, "Soviet Grain and Wheat Import Demands in 1981–1985," *American Journal of Agricultural Economics* 64 (May 1982): 312–22.

60. *Wall Street Journal*, 14 July, 22 September 1980; "Time to End Grain Embargo?" 25–26; Robert M. Bleiberg, "The Wrong War," *Barron's*, 14 January 1980, 7; Lawrence H. Shoup, *The Carter Presidency and Beyond* (Palo Alto, 1980), 156.

61. Marshall Goldman, quoted in the *New York Times*, 14 March 1982.

62. The best insights into the controversies surrounding the Reagan administration's policies are contained in U.S. Congress, Joint Economic Committee, *East–West Technology Transfer: A Congressional Dialog with the Reagan Administration*, 98 Cong., 2 sess. (Washington, D.C., 1984), 1–40; U.S. Congress, Senate, Subcommittee on Investigations, *Transfer of Technology*, 98 Cong., 2 sess. (Washington, D.C., 1984), 1–32; and Office of Technology Assessment, *Technology and East–West Trade: An Update*, 28.

63. *Washington Post*, 29 March 1981.

64. Newport News, Va., *Daily Press*, 24–26 April, 21 July, 3 October 1981. Because of its proximity to NATO Atlantic Fleet Headquarters in Norfolk, this local paper has unusually comprehensive coverage of U.S.–Soviet relations, including issues of East–West trade.

65. Ibid., 29 April 1981. See also U.S. Congress, House, Committee on Appropriations, Subcommittee on the Departments of Commerce, Justice and State, *Appropriations for 1982*, 97 Cong., 1 sess. (Washington, D.C., 1981), pt. 4.

66. The State Department's Policy Planning Staff and Bureau of Politico-Military Affairs tilted toward the Pentagon in advocating a complete embargo on broadly defined strategic items. The European desk, the Bureau of Economic and Business Affairs, and Under Secretary for Economic Affairs Meyer Rashish opposed the military's hard line.

67. *New York Times*, 19 July 1981.

68. Ibid.

69. For evidence of the continuing concern over the pipeline deal see the speech of Commerce Department official Lawrence J. Brady to the National Association of Manufacturers, reported in the *Daily Press*, 15 January 1982.

70. *New York Times*, 19 July 1981.

71. Cf. testimony of Meyer Rashish, Fred Iklé, and Lawrence J. Brady in U.S. Congress, Senate, Foreign Relations Committee, Subcommittee on International Economic Policy, *East–West Economic Relations*, 97 Cong., 1 sess. (Washington, D.C., 1981), 2–23, 24–36, 37–53.

72. Cf. letter of Deputy Defense Secretary Frank C. Carlucci in *Science*, 1 January 1982, 139–41.

73. *New York Times*, 11 October 1981, 10 January, 3 May 1982; *Daily Press*, 29 April, 6, 7, 15 October 1982.

74. *Daily Press*, 21 December; *New York Times*, 27 December 1981.

75. *New York Times*, 30 December 1981.

76. *Daily Press*, 30 December; *New York Times*, 31 December 1981.

77. *Daily Press*, 31 December 1981, 4 February 1982; *New York Times*, 30, 31 December 1981.

78. Marc D. Millot, formerly senior researcher at the Institute on Strategic Trade, coined the term. Cf. *New York Times*, 6 June 1982.

79. Western European exports to Russia in 1980 were $10.5 billion, seven times greater than U.S. exports. Loans to Eastern Europe amounted to $50 billion. *Daily Press*, 21 January 1982.

80. *New York Times*, 31 December 1981, 3, 7 January 1982; *Washington Post*, 10 January 1982.

81. Ibid.

82. *Daily Press*, 20 January 1982.

83. *New York Times*, 21 January; *Daily Press*, 21 January 1982.

84. *New York Times*, 24 January 1982.

85. U.S. Congress, House, Committee on Science and Technology, Subcommittee on Investigations and Oversight, *American Technology Transfer and Soviet Energy Planning*, 97 Cong., 2 sess. (Washington, D.C., 1982), 182–204.

86. *Daily Press*, 11 February 1982.

87. *New York Times*, 21 February 1982.

88. Ibid.

89. *Daily Press*, 23 February 1982.

90. Ibid., 10 March, 17 April 1982; U.S. Congress, House, Committee on Agriculture, *General Agricultural Export and Trade Situation*, 97 Cong., 2 sess. (Washington, D.C., 1982), 4–50.

91. *Daily Press*, 19 March, 30 April 1982.

92. Ibid., 18, 26 March, 22 April; *New York Times*, 3 May 1982.

93. *New York Times*, 3 May, 6, 7 June 1982.

94. *Daily Press*, 19, 26 June; *New York Times*, 27 June 1982.

95. Haig's resignation was followed by that of Robert Hormats, who was the Department of State's economic expert. This prompted some observers to conclude that right-wing ideologues were gaining the ascendancy in the administration. Cf. *Daily Press*, 22, 23, 26, 30 June, 2 July; *New York Times*, 2, 4 July 1982. See also George W. Ball, "The Case against Sanctions," *New York Times Magazine*, 12 September 1982, 118–20, 126.

96. *New York Times*, 9 July; *Daily Press*, 9, 12, 22 July 1982.

97. *New York Times*, 25 July; *Daily Press*, 14, 16, 23 July, 13 August 1982.

98. *New York Times*, 25 July, 8, 24, 25 August 1982.

99. *Daily Press*, 29, 31 July, 3 August; *New York Times*, 1, 8 August 1982.

100. *Daily Press*, 26, 27, 30 August, 16 September; *New York Times*, 29 August 1982.

101. *Daily Press*, 1, 2, 3, 10 September 1982.

102. Ibid., 9, 13, 14, 30 September 1982.

103. Ibid., 12 October; *New York Times*, 17 October 1982.

104. *New York Times*, 3 November; *Daily Press*, 4, 5, 11 November 1982.

105. *New York Times*, 14 November 1982.

106. Ibid.

107. Ibid.; *Daily Press*, 15 November 1982.

108. *Daily Press*, 15 November 1982; Office of Technology Assessment, *Technology and East–West Trade: An Update*, esp. 6–8.

109. The *New York Times* reported on 10 May 1983 the contents of a secret memo dated 15 March 1983 by W. Allan Wallis, under secretary of state for economic affairs, and approved in general terms by President Reagan, calling for "exerting greater multilateral control over Soviet acquisition from the West of technologies and products which contribute to Soviet military or strategic capabilities." The Defense Department was likewise seeking a wider role in reviewing and vetoing licenses to American companies for the export of "militarily critical technologies." See also *Daily Press*, 10, 11 May 1983.

110. In fact there has been some doubt as to whether the Soviets were successfully exploiting the political advantages of systematically combining Western high-technology imports and domestic reforms in the management of innovation. See the Rand Corporation's report for the Defense Department's Advanced Research Projects Agency, by Thane Gustafson, *Selling the Russians the Rope? Technology Policy and U.S. Export Control* (Santa Monica, Calif., 1981), vi–vii, 76–77.

111. Bertsch, "U.S.–Soviet Trade: A Sector of Mutual Benefit?" 48–49.

EPILOGUE

1. "Foreign Trade Policy of the U.S.S.R.," *Soviet Union Review* 16 (June 1933): 126.

2. Alonzo L. Hamby, *The Imperial Years* (New York, 1976), 120–23; "U.S. Opinion on Russia," *Fortune*, September 1945, 233–38; *American Views of Soviet Russia 1917–1965*, ed. Peter G. Filene (Homewood, Ill., 1968), 166.

3. See the perceptive article of Edward Mark, "American Policy toward Eastern Europe and the Origins of the Cold War, 1941–1946: An Alternative Interpretation," *Journal of American History* 68 (September 1981): 313–36.

4. Reprinted in U.S. Department of State, *Foreign Relations of the United States, Diplomatic Papers, 1944* (Washington, D.C., 1966), 4:951; see also 4:958–60, 960 n. 51, 1033–55.

5. Paterson also suggests that in 1945–46 government policy had not yet been fixed on any one course of action; see Thomas G. Paterson, *Soviet–American Confrontation: Postwar Reconstruction and the Origins of the Cold War* (Baltimore, 1973), 36.

6. Mark, "American Policy toward Eastern Europe," esp. 322, n. 48; see also Thomas G. Paterson, "The Economic Cold War: American Business and Economic Foreign Policy, 1945–1950" (Ph.D. dissertation, University of California, Berkeley, 1968), and Leon Martel, *Lend-Lease, Loans, and the Coming of the Cold War: A Study of the Implementation of Foreign Policy* (Boulder, Colo., 1979).

7. For two opposing views on Stalin's quest for economic autarchy see Adam B. Ulam, *Expansion and Coexistence: The History of Soviet Foreign*

Policy, 1917–67 (New York, 1968), and Gunnar Adler-Karlson, *Western Economic Warfare, 1949–1967* (Stockholm, 1968).

8. Exports fell from $358 million in 1946 to $1 million annually from 1951 to 1955. Imports from the USSR were similarly affected, dropping from $101 million in 1946 to $17 million annually from 1951 to 1955. See Philip G. Gillette, "American–Soviet Trade in Perspective," *Current History* 66 (October 1973): 159.

9. See Robin Renwick, *Economic Sanctions* (Cambridge, Mass., 1981), 18.

10. See the report on sanctions against Nicaragua reported in the Newport News, Va., *Daily Press*, 28 October 1985, and Gary C. Hufbauer, Jeffrey C. Schott, and Kimberly Ann Elliott, *Economic Sanctions Reconsidered* (Washington, D.C., 1985), 81–91.

11. On this point see also Angela Stent, *From Embargo to Ostpolitik: The Political Economy of West German–Soviet Relations, 1955–1960* (New York, 1982).

12. U.S. Congress, Office of Technology Assessment, *Technology and East–West Trade* (Washington, D.C., 1979), 3–4.

13. See, for example, Andreas F. Lowenfeld, *Trade Controls for Political Ends* (New York, 1983), 13–14, 112, and Jeffrey W. Golan, "U.S. Technology Transfers to the Soviet Union and the Protection of the National Interest," *Law and Policy in International Business* 11 (1979): 1042.

14. U.S. Congress, Senate, Committee on Foreign Relations, *A Background Study on East–West Trade*, 89 Cong., 1 sess. (Washington, D.C., 1965), 7.

15. See the figures in Gillette, "American–Soviet Trade in Perspective," 160.

16. Golan, "U.S. Technology Transfers to the Soviet Union," 1046–47.

17. Cf. The Atlantic Council, *East–West Trade* (Boulder, Colo., 1977), 3–4; and Robert C. Stuart, "United States–Soviet Trade," *Current History* 76 (May–June 1978): 208.

18. See Henry Kissinger's remarks to the Joint Economic Committee, reprinted in *Cong. Rec.*, 93 Cong., 1 sess., 119, pt. 1:24.

19. Robert E. Klitgaard, "Limiting Exports on National Security Grounds," in *Commission on the Organization of the Government for the Conduct of Foreign Policy*, 7 vols. (Washington, D.C., 1975), vol. 4, pt. 7:447.

20. CIA, *Soviet Acquisition of Western Technology* (Washington, D.C., April 1982), 12.

21. Steven R. Weisman, "The Influence of William Clark: Setting a Hard Line in Foreign Policy," *New York Times Magazine*, 14 August 1983, 17.

22. *New York Times*, 10 February 1985.

23. Quoted in ibid.

Bibliographical Essay

IT would be foolhardy—and probably gratuitous—to attempt to list every letter and report, every article, every monograph from which I have drawn raw evidence, valuable leads, and interpretative ideas or organizing principles. The citations in the notes attest to some of the specific kinds of materials I used. I intend here to select and to discuss merely those materials, primary and secondary, that were most useful to me and presumably would be most helpful to the serious reader.

PERSONAL PAPERS

Any discussion of the use of the personal papers of the presidents or other public officials should begin with an acknowledgment that, because of national security considerations or references to friendly foreign governments, certain materials relevant to "American–Soviet trade," "East–West trade," "export control policy," and "technology transfer" are considered sensitive and remain closed to scholarly inquiry. Through the use of the Freedom of Information Act, I was able to have declassified a number of documents from the Truman, Eisenhower, Kennedy, and Johnson presidencies. In other instances, however, the originating agency, frequently the National Security Agency or the Central Intelligence Agency, exempted a requested document wholly or in part. (The Freedom of Information Act cannot be employed without first identifying specific documents for release.) The presidential papers relevant to American–Soviet trade from 1968 onward are, for national security and other reasons, unavailable for scrutiny.

The Harry S. Truman Library, in Independence, Missouri, is the repository for the papers of numerous figures whose activities touched upon the salient aspects of the Cold War: the deterioration of U.S.–Soviet political relations, the concern over Soviet military aggression and political subversion, the development of East–West trade restrictions, the Marshall Plan, and the Korean conflict. The starting point for tracing the evolution of export control policy is the Harry S. Truman Papers. The President's Office File contains relevant correspondence and memoranda on trade and politics; the President's Secretary's File contains memoranda from the CIA, the Commerce Department, and the State Department assessing Soviet intentions and the efficacy of trade as an instrument of foreign policy. The National Security Council Meetings File is indispensable for understanding the considerations that went into the making of policy.

The Truman Papers should be supplemented with the Papers of Matthew J. Connelly, the president's appointments secretary. Connelly's files contain typed summaries of longhand notes on Cabinet meetings. The Cabinet from time to time discussed Soviet activities and American–Soviet trade. The Dean Acheson Papers likewise deal with various aspects of U.S.–Soviet relations, including the Marshall Plan, in both the Political and Governmental File and the Memoranda of Conversations File. Acheson was under secretary of state, 1945–47, and secretary of state, 1949–53. Thomas C. Blaisdell, Jr., assistant secretary of commerce, 1949–51, wrote important memoranda and reports on export policy toward Europe and the Soviet Union; these are found in the Blaisdell Papers. The Alfred Schindler Papers document the growing estrangement of Henry A. Wallace from the Truman administration. Schindler was under secretary of commerce in 1945 and 1946. The Papers of Charles Sawyer, secretary of commerce, 1948–53, have recently become available. They tend to duplicate material found in the Truman Papers and in the Records of the Department of Commerce.

The Papers of Henry A. Wallace, deposited in the University of Iowa Library, are available on microfilm. Consisting of letters, memoranda, diaries, speeches, and similar materials, they are useful for charting deteriorating relations with Russia and Wallace's own declining influence with Truman.

The Dwight D. Eisenhower Library, in Abilene, Kansas, has a substantial amount of material, including reports, policy papers, bills, correspondence, and memoranda, that bears directly on U.S.–Russian commercial relations. It may be found in Eisenhower's Papers as President (Ann Whitman File), Eisenhower's Records as President (White House Central File), the Records of the U.S. Council on Foreign Economic Policy, and the Records of the President's Commission on Foreign Economic Policy (the Randall Commission). The last of these are particularly valuable for tracing the evolution of policy. Also providing some valuable insights into export control policy and the complications it presented for friendly foreign governments are the Records of the Office of the Special Assistant for National Security Affairs, 1952–61, particularly the National Security Council Series. The Gerald Morgan Papers contain some pertinent correspondence between Morgan and Clarence Randall.

Secretary of State John Foster Dulles had little interest in economic matters. The Dulles Papers consequently contain little information bearing directly on trade policy. The same is true of the Clarence Francis Papers and the C. D. Jackson Papers, although both contain references to trade fairs, trade missions, P.L. 480, and Soviet steel.

I invoked the Freedom of Information Act to have declassified a substantial number of documents originating with the Commission on Foreign Economic Policy and other executive agencies concerned with U.S.–Soviet trade relations. Although some material remains classified, enough has been released to reconstruct in detail Eisenhower's East–West trade policy.

The John F. Kennedy Papers, at the Kennedy Library in Boston, Massachusetts, make it possible to trace the Kennedy administration's approach to the domestic and international aspects of U.S.–Soviet trade. The papers indicate that despite continued congressional hostility and cold war crises, the Kennedy administration took the first substantive steps toward détente by trying to expand nonstrategic trade with Russia and the European Soviet bloc. It also was the first to acknowledge and act upon polycentric tendencies within the communist world, utilizing trade to exploit differences between Russia and her European satellites. Documentation relative to altering the export control laws can be found in the White House Central Subject File, the President's Office File, and the National Security File. In the last, the Subject Series: Meetings; Action Memoranda; and Country Series (USSR) records are particularly useful.

The National Security File: Subject Series: Export Control Policy, was declassified in September 1984. Although not very extensive, it contains pertinent memoranda from President Kennedy to the Export Control Review Board, from Secretary of State Dean Rusk, and from Commerce Secretary Luther Hodges. Other records listed in the Kennedy Papers inventory that appear to be relevant remain classified, notably the Carl Kaysen Series in the National Security File. By contrast, the White House Staff Files of Christian Herter, Myer Feldman, and Howard Peterson are of limited usefulness.

The Lyndon B. Johnson Papers, at the Johnson Library in Austin, Texas, are important for continuing the analysis of the use of trade to encourage political détente. The White House Central File, Countries 303, marked "confidential," contains relevant information about the USSR. Useful, though scattered, information on East–West trade also exists in the White House Diary, the Vice-President's Security File (which offers revealing insights into President Kennedy's attitude toward U.S.–Soviet trade), the Records of the Interagency Task Force on Foreign Trade, and the narrative history that the Department of Commerce, like other executive offices, was requested to prepare before Johnson left the presidency in 1968.

Easily the most important source of information for reconstructing Johnson's effort to encourage more peaceful trade with the Soviet Union is the National Security File. This was the working file of McGeorge Bundy and Walt W. Rostow, special assistants for national security affairs. The Committee File Series includes the unusually complete Records of the Special Committee on U.S. Trade Relations with East European Countries and the Soviet Union. The files of the Miller Committee (named after its chairman, J. Irwin Miller) consist of memoranda, minutes of meetings, reports from the CIA and the State Department, correspondence with the White House, and background papers on East–West trade. They also provide useful insight into the Johnson administration's management style. Most of the memoranda from Bundy and Rostow to the president, which cover the period from 1965 to 1967, remain classified.

ARCHIVAL RECORDS

The National Archives, in Washington, D.C., is the repository of the Records of the Department of Commerce for the Truman years. They contain useful information on U.S.–Soviet trade, including statistical data, reports, memoranda, and news clippings. Record Group 151 consists of the holdings of the Bureau of Foreign and Domestic Commerce and the Bureau of International Programs. The Economic File of the latter is relevant to the early Cold War years, but it should be supplemented with Record Group 40, which contains the files of Under Secretary of Commerce William C. Foster. The folder in Record Group 40 marked "Russian Trade" contains material for the years from 1946 to 1948.

The Commerce Department holdings in the Archives are supplemented by the department's own files, also in Washington, D.C. These include the Thomas C. Blaisdell, Jr., Papers, which have information concerning the formulation of export control policy from 1949 to 1951. Blaisdell was under secretary at the time. The Office of International Trade (OIT) File, Russia: Public Relations, also has bits of information on export control policy and the USSR. The ECA–Department of Commerce File sheds light on the relationship between the Marshall Plan and trade with the Soviets. Beyond the Eisenhower administration, the department's records on U.S.–Soviet trade are either unavailable or classified.

ORAL HISTORY COLLECTION

Each of the presidential libraries also maintains an extensive oral history collection. The Willard L. Thorpe and Edward S. Mason interviews deposited in the Truman Library are valuable for analyzing State Department attitudes toward postwar trade, especially the question of multilateral versus bilateral trade agreements, and the prospects of American–Soviet trade specifically. Thorpe was assistant secretary of state for economic affairs, 1946–52, and Mason served as an economic consultant to the department, 1946–47. The Ben Hill Brown interview also is useful for documenting the growing fear of communism in the United States and its impact on the Truman administration. The oral history interviews of Lawrence A. Fox and Lawrence McQuade, two figures of the Johnson administration, deposited in the Johnson Library, document the adverse impact of the Vietnam War on efforts to persuade Congress to relax trade controls. The oral history interviews of President Kennedy's secretary of commerce, Luther Hodges, and former State Department official George F. Kennan, in the Kennedy Library, provide background on attitudes toward the Soviet Union and the wheat deal of 1963–64.

PUBLISHED SOURCES

The number of publications touching upon American–Soviet trade, technology transfer, and export control policy churned out by the Government Printing Office is extensive. These take the form of legislative debates, congressional hearings, agency annual reports, special studies, and statistical data. The *Congressional Record* is useful for analyzing attitudes toward the Soviet Union and East–West trade at various stages in the Cold War. Legislative, academic, and business opinion may also be gauged from the innumerable congressional hearings and resolutions that were held. These are listed by committee hearing and subject in the *Monthly Catalogue of Government Documents* and its successors. (The hearings I found most relevant for this book are cited in the notes.) *East–*

West Trade: Its Strategic Implications, a publication of Georgetown University's Center for Strategic Studies, edited by Samuel F. Clabaugh and Richard V. Allen, is a good introduction to the congressional committee hearings as of 1964.

The *Public Papers of the Presidents* (Washington, D.C., 1961–82) conveniently assembles the addresses, messages, and executive orders pertaining to U.S.–Soviet diplomatic and trade relations that have emanated from the Oval Office. The Department of State's *Papers Relating to the Foreign Relations of the United States* (Washington, D.C., 1861–) is another important source of information about American–Soviet diplomatic relations during and immediately after World War II. It should be supplemented with the State Department's *Bulletin*, which publishes items relevant to trade and export control policy. The Department of Commerce has issued a variety of reports on East–West trade. A good starting point is the quarterly and annual reports to Congress on the operation of the Battle Act and the Bureau of Foreign and Domestic Commerce's annual statistical data published as *Foreign and Domestic Commerce of the United States*. Commerce official Peter G. Peterson's *U.S.–Soviet Commercial Relations in a New Era: Some Personal Reflections* (1972) is useful on détente and trade. Other government agencies have issued reports on matters of trade and transfer of technology. The most valuable for this book were CIA, *Soviet Acquisition of Western Technology* (1968); U.S. Congress, Office of Technology Assessment, *Technology and East–West Trade* (1979); and Department of Defense, *An Analysis of Export Control of U.S. Technology: A DOD Perspective* (1976). The Eisenhower administration's Commission on Foreign Economic Policy published its staff papers separately in 1954, a segment of which deal specifically with East–West trade.

Besides these governmental publications and others cited in the notes, various presidents, White House advisers, and other government officials have published their memoirs and recollections. John R. Deane recounted the military's problems with the Soviets during World War II in *The Strange Alliance: The Story of Our Efforts at Wartime Cooperation with Russia* (New York, 1947). Harry S. Truman's *Memoirs*, 2 vols. (Garden City, N.Y., 1955–56), Dean Acheson's fascinating *Present at the Creation* (New York, 1977), and *Selected Papers of Will Clayton*, edited by Frederick J. Dobney (Baltimore, 1971), provide insights into the deterioration of U.S.–Soviet political relations, the origins of the Cold War, the lend-lease controversy, the Marshall Plan, and other topics that bore directly on trade policy of the time. Stalin's analysis of the capitalistic economic crisis following the war is contained in his *Economic Problems of Socialism in the USSR* (Moscow, 1952). Dwight D. Eisenhower's *White House Years 1953–1956: Mandate for Change* (New York, 1963) discusses relations not only with the Soviets but with the United States' European allies, who frequently chafed under the trade restrictions. Lyndon B. Johnson's *Vantage Point: Perspectives of the Presidency, 1963–1969* (New York, 1971) describes his attempt to ease cold war tensions by building economic bridges to Russia and Eastern Europe and to exploit differences within the Soviet bloc. Former Secretary of State Henry A. Kissinger describes Richard Nixon's use of trade to effect political détente with the Soviet Union and also the adverse impact of the Jackson amendment in his revealing memoir, *White House Years* (Boston, 1979). The crises that enveloped the Carter administration over Iran, Afghanistan, and Poland and the president's use of economic sanctions to modify Soviet actions are delineated in former Secretary of State Cyrus Vance's *Hard Choices* (New York, 1983) and in Zbigniew Brzezinski's *Power and Principle: Memoirs of the National Security Adviser, 1977–1981* (New York, 1983).

Newspapers provide extensive coverage of virtually every facet of U.S.–Soviet politics and trade, from cold war to détente to confrontation. They are valuable sources of information about government attitudes and policies for the period since 1968, the point at which national security and other considerations make it difficult to consult the traditional primary sources and archival records. The *New York Times* offers consistent, in-depth coverage of the political and economic dimensions of East–West trade. The *Washington Post* and the *Wall Street Journal* can be fruitfully consulted for specific aspects of national security and technology transfer. The *Daily Press*, of Newport News, Virginia, serves as a good illustration of how a local newspaper can provide excellent coverage of national issues. Because of its proximity to major military installations and what President Eisenhower referred to as the "military-industrial complex," the *Daily Press* has proved especially sensitive to the policies of the Carter and Reagan administrations as they affected the hostage crisis in Iran, the Soviet invasion of Afghanistan, martial law in Poland, the transfer of militarily sensitive technology, the wheat embargo, and the natural gas pipeline embargo.

SECONDARY WORKS

The literature of U.S.–Soviet relations is enormous and proliferates at a rapid rate. Eldon E. Billings, of the Library of Congress, Economic Division, has compiled a selected bibliography on East–West trade that is a good introduction to the subject as of 1965. It appears as Appendix IX, pp. 131-41, in U.S. Congress, Senate, Committee on Foreign Relations, *A Background Study on East–West Trade*, 89 Cong., 1 sess. (Washington, D.C., 1965). Another useful introduction to the subject is Nathaniel McKitterick, *East–West Trade: The Background of U.S. Policy* (New York, 1966). Marshall I. Goldman's *Détente and Dollars* (New York, 1975) is primarily a guide to doing business with the Soviets but contains a useful brief historical introduction.

For the pre–World War II period Robert P. Browder's *Origins of Soviet–American Diplomacy* (Princeton, 1953), Robert Lansing's *War Memoirs* (Indianapolis, 1935), and Linda Killen's *The Russian Bureau: A Case Study in Wilsonian Diplomacy* (Lexington, Ky., 1983) are especially useful for the official American reaction to the Bolshevik Revolution. Joan Hoff Wilson's "American Business and the Recognition of the Soviet Union," *Social Science Quarterly* 52 (June 1971): 349–68, argues persuasively that business pressure was not as decisive as hitherto believed in bringing about diplomatic recognition in 1933. Soviet–American economic relations in the period of nonrecognition are well described in Mikhail Condoide, *American–Russian Trade: A Study of the Soviet Foreign Trade Mo-*

nopoly (Columbus, Oh., 1946); Floyd James Fithian, "Soviet–American Economic Relations, 1918-1933: American Business in Russia during the Period of Non-recognition" (Ph.D. dissertation, University of Nebraska, 1964); Antony C. Sutton, *Western Technology and Soviet Economic Development 1917 to 1930* (Stanford, 1968); James K. Libbey, *Alexander Gumberg and Soviet–American Relations 1917-1933* (Lexington, Ky., 1977); and Edward J. Epstein, "The Riddle of Armand Hammer," *New York Times Magazine,* 21 November 1981, 68–73, 112–22.

The unfulfilled expectation that diplomatic recognition would lead to a great expansion of American–Soviet trade is well documented in Frederick C. Adams, *Economic Diplomacy: The Export-Import Bank and American Foreign Policy, 1934-1939* (Columbia, Mo., 1976); Robert Dallek, *Franklin D. Roosevelt and American Foreign Policy, 1932–1945* (New York, 1979); Thomas R. Maddux, *Years of Estrangement: American Relations with the Soviet Union, 1933–1941* (Tallahassee, Fla., 1980); and Philip S. Gillette, "American–Soviet Trade in Perspective," *Current History* 66 (October 19739): 158–83. Edward M. Bennett's *Franklin D. Roosevelt and the Search for Security: American–Soviet Relations, 1933–1939* (Wilmington, Del., 1985) is critical of the president and the State Department for failing to deal realistically with Soviet initiatives to deter Axis aggression in the interwar period.

The interplay of politics and aid during the war years is ably discussed in Raymond H. Dawson, *The Decision to Aid Russia, 1941: Foreign Policy and Domestic Politics* (Chapel Hill, 1959); James M. Burns, *Roosevelt: The Soldier of Freedom 1940–1945* (New York, 1970); and Roy Douglas's thought-provoking *From War to Cold War, 1942–1948* (New York, 1981). Aid to Russia is described in Warren F. Kimball, *The Most Unsordid Act: Lend-Lease, 1939–1941* (Baltimore, 1969), for the period prior to American entry into the European conflict; and in George C. Herring, Jr., *Aid to Russia, 1941–1946: Strategy, Diplomacy, the Origins of the Cold War* (New York, 1973), and Robert H. Jones, *The Roads to Russia: United States Lend-Lease to the Soviet Union* (Norman, Okla., 1969). A study of the implementation of foreign policy decision making that bore on the controversy over the origins of the Cold War is the thoughtful assessment of Leon Martel, *Lend-Lease, Loans, and the Coming of the Cold War: A Study of the Implementation of Foreign Policy* (Boulder, Colo., 1979). Martel argues that lower-level bureaucrats exceeded Truman's (and Harriman's) intentions in the manner in which lend-lease was terminated and loans to the Soviet Union denied.

Many of the titles covering World War II also deal with the beginnings of the Cold War, whose origins are shrouded in historical and ideological controversy. John L. Gaddis's *The United States and the Origins of the Cold War, 1941–1947* (New York, 1972) presents the orthodox viewpoint. Revisionist perspectives include Walter La Feber's *America, Russia, and the Cold War, 1945–1966* (New York, 1967) and Thomas G. Paterson's *On Every Front: The Making of the Cold War* (New York, 1970). Adam B. Ulam's *Expansion and Coexistence: The History of Soviet Foreign Policy* (New York, 1968) transcends the issue of causation specifically to delineate long-term patterns of Soviet behavior. A. W. De Porte's

Europe between the Superpowers (New Haven, 1979) is excellent on the role of Western Europe in the postwar international system. Geir Lundestad's *America, Scandinavia, and the Cold War, 1945–1949* (New York, 1980) is a case study that contains some relevant information on how U.S. trade policy affected the Scandinavian countries in the early years of the Cold War. Gaddis Smith's *Dean Acheson* (New York, 1972) describes the career of the secretary of state who was present at virtually every major crisis of the Cold War. It contains an informative account of the Kem Amendment. Margaret Truman's biography, *Harry S. Truman* (New York, 1973) recounts the dispute between the president and Henry A. Wallace.

The most comprehensive and critical treatment of the evolving economic restrictions against Russia and the Soviet bloc in the early Cold War years is Gunnar Adler-Karlson's *Western Economic Warfare, 1949–1967* (Stockholm, 1968). New documents and archival materials that have become available since its publication suggest that there was far less unanimity in Washington toward the use of trade controls than hitherto supposed. The economist Thomas A. Wolf has approached the subject historically and econometrically in *U.S. East–West Trade Policy* (Lexington, Mass., 1973). Thomas G. Paterson also has written extensively on the economic aspects of the Truman administration's Soviet policy, most notably "The Economic Cold War: American Business and Economic Foreign Policy, 1945–1950" (Ph.D. dissertation, University of California, Berkeley, 1968); "The Quest for Peace and Prosperity: International Trade, Communism, and the Marshall Plan," in *Politics and Policies of the Truman Administration*, edited by Barton J. Bernstein (Chicago, 1970), 78–112; and *Soviet–American Confrontation: Postwar Reconstruction and the Origins of the Cold War* (Baltimore, 1973). John L. Gaddis's excellent monograph *Strategies of Containment* (New York, 1982) traces the development of the doctrine of containment, demonstrating also its economic dimension. Hadley Arkes's *Bureaucracy, the Marshall Plan, and the National Interest* (Princeton, 1972) is outstanding on the politics of the European Recovery Program and U.S.–Soviet relations.

A good deal of the contemporary writing on U.S.–Soviet trade, especially in the period of transition from wartime alliance to cold war antagonism, has been polemical. Most relevant for the attitudes they reveal are Congress of American–Soviet Friendship, *American Industry Commemorates the Tenth Anniversary of American–Soviet Diplomatic Relations 1933–1943* (New York, 1943) and *U.S.A.–U.S.S.R.: Allies for Peace* (New York, 1945); Stella K. Margold, *Let's Do Business with Russia* (New York, 1948); J. Anthony Marcus, *The Real Russian Challenge* (New York, 1947); and William L. White, *We Can and Must Trade with Russia* (New York, 1945). More dispassionate assessments of postwar trade include Herbert Feis, *American Trade Policy and Position* (New York, 1945); Alexander Gerschenkron, *Economic Relations with the U.S.S.R.* (New York, 1945); and V. P. Timoshenko, *Economic Background for the Postwar International Trade of the U.S.S.R.* (New York, 1945).

Tito's break with Stalin and its implications for East–West political and economic relations, particularly the congressional debate over whether to grant most-favored-nation status to Yugoslavia, is documented in the *Congressional*

Record. But see also John C. Campbell, *Tito's Separate Road* (New York, 1967); *Contemporary Yugoslavia*, edited by Wayne S. Vucinich (Berkeley, Calif., 1969); and *East-Central Europe under the Communists: Yugoslavia*, edited by Robert F. Byrnes (New York, 1957).

The profile of Congress presented in this book, especially for the early Cold War years, is based on the following accounts: James M. Burns, *The Deadlock of Democracy* (Englewood Cliffs, N.J., 1963); Margaret Hinchey, "The Frustration of the New Deal Revival, 1944–1946" (Ph.D. dissertation, University of Missouri, 1965); David W. Reinhard, *The Republican Right since 1945* (Lexington, Ky., 1983); Robert A. Pastor, *Congress and the Politics of U.S. Foreign Economic Policy, 1929–1976* (Berkeley, Calif., 1980); Gary W. Reichard, *The Reaffirmation of Republicanism: Eisenhower and the Eighty-third Congress* (Knoxville, 1975); Paula Stern, *Water's Edge: Domestic Policy and the Making of American Foreign Policy* (Westport, Conn., 1979); and Hadley Arkes's *Bureaucracy, the Marshall Plan, and the National Interest* (cited above). In addition, various newspaper and periodical items shed light on congressional attitudes.

My thinking about the Eisenhower administration's approach to U.S.–Soviet trade relations was influenced by David B. Capitanchik, *The Eisenhower Presidency and American Foreign Policy* (London, 1969); Robert A. Divine, *Eisenhower and the Cold War* (New York, 1981); Fred I. Greenstein, *The Hidden-Hand Presidency* (New York, 1982); and Herbert S. Parmet, *Eisenhower and the American Crusades* (New York, 1972). *The Presidency and National Security Policy*, edited by R. Gordon Hoxie (New York, 1984) contains useful insights into Eisenhower's management style. Burton I. Kaufman's *Trade and Aid: Eisenhower's Foreign Economic Policy, 1953–1961* (Baltimore, 1982) presents a shrewd assessment of the president's attitudes toward the Soviets and the use of trade as an instrument of foreign policy. Townsend Hoopes's *The Devil and John Foster Dulles* (Boston, 1973) is a provocative study of Dulles's ideas and foreign-policy-making role.

Besides the documents in the Kennedy presidential library, two accounts by White House aides are important for understanding Kennedy's use of trade to promote détente and to exploit differences between Moscow and her satellites: Arthur M. Schlesinger, Jr., *A Thousand Days* (Boston, 1965), and Theodore Sorenson, *Kennedy* (New York, 1965). George W. Johnson has conveniently collected and edited *The Kennedy Presidential Press Conferences* (New York, 1978). The comments regarding the Soviet Union are especially useful. Herbert S. Dinerstein, *The Making of a Missle Crisis: October 1962* (Baltimore, 1978), is informative for showing the obstacles to détente. John Alden Pierce, "The Politics of the United States' Sale of Wheat to the Soviet Union in 1963 and 1964" (Ph.D. dissertation, University of Virginia, 1971), shows how domestic politics and foreign policy requirements merged to justify the wheat agreement, despite trade restrictions.

The fortunes of American–Soviet trade since the mid-1960s have reflected the state of political relations between the two superpowers. An excellent introduction to the recent political history of the period is Raymond L. Garthoff's *Détente and Confrontation: American–Soviet Relations from Nixon to Reagan*

(Washington, D.C., 1985). My thinking about Nixon's use of trade to promote détente has been heavily influenced by Seyom Brown's fine study, *The Crises of Power: An Interpretation of United States Foreign Policy during the Kissinger Years* (New York, 1979). Fred W. Neal and Mary K. Harvey's *The Nixon–Kissinger Foreign Policy* (Santa Barbara, Calif., 1974), an outgrowth of the Pacem in Terris conference held at Santa Barbara, emphasizes the opportunities and contradictions inherent in détente. W. Averell Harriman's *America and Russia in a Changing World* (New York, 1971), given initially as a series of lectures, reflects the growing intrest in détente and also provides a participant's insights into the origins of the Cold War. Revealing on the obstacles to détente from congressional sources is Paula Stern's *The Water's Edge: Domestic Policy and the Making of American Foreign Policy* (cited above), a study of the Jackson Amendment, which formally linked American–Soviet trade to the Jewish emigration–human rights issue.

The unraveling of détente, which continued under Gerald Ford and Jimmy Carter, had as one of its casualties U.S.–Soviet trade. Two accounts that are informative on the link between foreign policy, domestic politics, and East–West trade during that era are Lawrence H. Shoup, *The Carter Presidency and Beyond* (Palo Alto, Calif., 1980), and Elizabeth Drew, *Portrait of an Election* (New York, 1981).

Spurred by the Department of Defense, both Carter and Ronald Reagan became increasingly sensitive to the transfer of highly sophisticated technologies to the Soviet Union, raising anew the question of trade and national security. Useful for understanding this problem are Robert E. Klitgaard, "Limiting Exports on National Security Grounds," vol. 4, part 7 in *Commission on the Organization of Government for the Conduct of Foreign Policy*, 7 vols. (Washington, D.C., 1975); Jeffrey W. Golan, "U.S. Technology Transfers to the Soviet Union and the Protection of the National Interest," *Law and Policy in International Business* 11 (1979): 1037–1107; and Thane Gustafson, *Selling the Russians the Rope? Technology Policy and U.S. Export Control* (Santa Monica, Calif., 1981). Sympathetic to nonstrategic trade and critical of the Jackson Amendment are the publications of the Committee on East–West Accord, especially *Common Sense on U.S.–Soviet Trade*, edited by Margaret Chapman and Carl Marcy (Washington, D.C., 1983), and the perceptive, scholarly assessment by Gary K. Bertsch, "U.S.–Soviet Trade: A Sector of Mutual Benefit?" in *Sectors of Mutual Benefit in U.S.–Soviet Relations*, edited by Nish Jamgotch, Jr. (Durham, N.C., 1985), 22–49.

A broad overview of foreign economic policy appears in a collection of essays edited by William H. Becker and Samuel F. Wells, Jr., *Economics and World Power* (New York, 1984). *American Foreign Economic Policy*, edited by Benjamin J. Cohen (New York, 1968), is another useful introduction to the subject. The efficacy of using trade controls and economic sanctions for foreign policy purposes favorable to the United States and the West has been a matter of debate since the start of the Cold War and may be expected to continue into the foreseeable future. From Truman to Reagan, each administration has had to wrestle with the question whether trade restrictions or the threat of economic sanctions would influence the Soviets to modify aggressive political or military behavior. Four authoritative works examining this issue from varying perspectives that are especially informative are Angela Stent, *From Embargo to Ostpolitik: The Political Economy of West German–Soviet Relations, 1955–1980* (New York, 1982); Gary C. Hufbauer et al., *Economic Sanctions Reconsidered* (Washington, D.C., 1985); Andreas F. Lowenfeld, *Trade Controls for Political Ends* (New York, 1983); and Robin Renwick, *Economic Sanctions* (Cambridge, Mass., 1981).

Finally, contemporary periodicals of both a professional and popular nature have devoted countless articles to foreign economic policy, East–West trade, and U.S.–Soviet political relations. The most obvious starting point from which to begin to examine these topics is the Public Affairs Information Service (P.A.I.S.) *Bulletin*, a weekly bibliography not unlike the *Reader's Guide to Periodical Literature*. The most significant entries for the present research were culled from approximately forty-seven journals, whose citations are given more fully in the notes to each chapter. These journals appear to be reliable barometers of attitudes toward the Soviets, as well as sources of information about export control policy. Business periodicals that report on these topics include *Business Week*, *Commercial and Financial Chronicle*, *Export Trade and Shipper*, *Fortune*, and *Nation's Business*. *East–West Trade News*, a British publication, is particularly useful for its reporting on the Eisenhower administration and U.S.–Soviet trade. Government actions often are reported in the *Congressional Digest*, *Congressional Quarterly Weekly Review*, and the *Bulletin* of the U.S. Department of State (cited above). Academic journals that from time to time contain useful analyses include *Foreign Affairs*, *Harvard Business Review*, *American Journal of Agricultural Economics*, *Law and Policy in International Business*, and *Social Science Quarterly*. *Soviet Russia Today* contains articles on diplomatic recognition and trade expectations as well as postwar trade and reconstruction.

Index